ANCIENT INDIAN TRADITION & MYTHOLOGY

TRANSLATED BY

A BOARD OF SCHOLARS

AND EDITED BY

Dr. G.P. BHATT

VOLUME 41

ANCIENT INDIAN TRADITION AND MYTHOLOGY SERIES

[PURĀṆAS IN TRANSLATION]

VOLUMES

ŚIVA 1-4
LIṄGA 5-6
BHĀGAVATA 7-11
GARUḌA 12-14
NĀRADA 15-19
KŪRMA 20-21
BRAHMĀṆḌA 22-26
AGNI 27-30
VARĀHA 31-32
BRAHMA 33-36
VĀYU 37-38
PADMA, PARTS I-III 39-41

VOLUMES UNDER PREPARATION

BHAVIṢYA
BRAHMAVAIVARTA
DEVĪBHĀGAVATA
KĀLIKĀ
MĀRKAṆḌEYA
MATSYA
PADMA, PARTS IV-X
SKANDA
VĀMANA
VIṢṆU
VIṢṆUDHARMOTTARA

THE PADMA-PURĀṆA

PART III

TRANSLATED AND ANNOTATED BY

Dr. N.A. DESHPANDE

MOTILAL BANARSIDASS PUBLISHERS
PRIVATE LIMITED
Delhi

First Edition : *Delhi, 1990*

ISBN: 81-208-0624-7

Also available at :
MOTILAL BANARSIDASS
Bungalow Road, Jawahar Nagar, Delhi 110 007
Chowk, Varanasi 221 001
Ashok Rajpath, Patna 800 004
24, Race Course Road, Bangalore 560 001
120, Royapettah High Road, Mylapore, Madras 600 004

UNESCO COLLECTION OF REPRESENTATIVE WORKS—Indian Series
This book has been accepted in the Indian Translation Series of the Unesco Collection of Representative Works jointly sponsored by the United Nations Educational, Scientific and Cultural Organization (UNESCO) and the Government of India.

PRINTED IN INDIA
BY JAINENDRA PRAKASH JAIN AT SHRI JAINENDRA PRESS, A-45 NARAINA INDUSTRIAL AREA, PHASE I, NEW DELHI 110028 AND PUBLISHED BY NARENDRA PRAKASH JAIN FOR MOTILAL BANARSIDASS PUBLISHERS PVT. LTD., BUNGALOW ROAD, JAWAHAR NAGAR, DELHI 110007.

PUBLISHER'S NOTE

The purest gems lie hidden in the bottom of the ocean or in the depth of rocks. One has to dive into the ocean or delve into the rocks to find them out. Similarly, truth lies concealed in the language which with the passage of time has become obsolete. Man has to learn that language before he discovers that truth.

But he has neither the means nor the leisure to embark on that course. We have, therefore, planned to help him acquire knowledge by an easier course. We have started the series of Ancient Indian Tradition and Mythology in English Translation. Our goal is to universalize knowledge through the most popular international medium of expression. The publication of the Purāṇas in English Translation is a step towards that goal.

PREFACE

This is the third part of the *Padma Purāṇa* translated into English and the 41st Volume of the *Ancient Indian Tradition and Mythology* series. Herein are included Chapters 1-90 of Bhūmikhaṇḍa or the Section on the Earth which is the second of the seven sections into which the Purāṇa is divided.

The reader would naturally expect, as the name 'Bhūmikhaṇḍa' suggests, a description of the geography and history of the Earth in this section, but will actually find nothing like that. And this is true about all the sections. As a matter of fact, the names of the sections here as well as in the other Purāṇas are just arbitrary, having in the present shape no relevance to the contents. Perhaps in the remote past or originally they had a relevance but in the course of time their logical structure was lost and a lot of interpolation made them all alike dealing with similar topics irrespectively of the names assigned.

As usual, this part contains a number of well-known legends, especially those of Vena, Pṛthu and Yayāti, and also the oft-repeated myths of the slaying of the demons Bala and Vṛtra, Hiraṇyakaśipu and Hiraṇyākṣa, the birth of Maruts, the anecdotes of Ikṣvāku's hunting, Diti's wailing and the like.

The section begins with the story of Śivaśarman and his virtuous sons whose devotion to parents is put to severe test and finally established as constant and firm. The glorification of devotion to parents (*pitṛbhakti*) is again taken up in chapters 63 and 84 and parents are given as high a status as that of a sacred place of pilgrimage in chapter 62. One will find allegorical description of body and soul in chapters 7 and 8. In the story of Suvrata (Ch. 11) four kinds of sons are described followed in the subsequent chapters by the enumeration of the basic virtues and the post-mortem status and suffering of the virtuous and sinners respectively. The virtue of *dāna* (charity) is highly praised and treated of in detail along with a description of those who deserve it and the fruits of making gifts to Brāhmaṇas and other deserving persons (Chs. 38-40). The fruits of *nityadāna* (regular charity) and *naimittikadāna* (occasional charity) are described in detail separately.

Devotion to god Viṣṇu is a recurring theme of this section, though it is also said that all the gods of the Hindu Trinity—Brahmā, Viṣṇu and Śiva, are equal. To propitiate Viṣṇu a number of vows are enjoined and the recitation of a hymn containing a hundred names of the god is recommended as giving salvation in chapter 87. Yayāti is mentioned as the greatest patron of the Vaiṣṇava faith. It was during his reign that Vaiṣṇavism enjoyed the greatest propularity.

Chapter 37 countains (unfortunately) an adverse reference to Jainism. There a heretic, who is none else but a follower of Jina, is described who is dead against the Vedic religion, who by his radical doctrines turns king Vena away from the practice of Dharma and makes him a sinner leading ultimately to his total ruin.

Acknowledgements

It is our pleasant duty to put on record our sincere thanks to Dr. R.N. Dandekar and the UNESCO authorities for their kind encouragement and valuable help which render this work more useful than it would otherwise have been. We are grateful to Dr. N.A. Deshpande for translating the text. We are also thankful to all those who have been helpful in our project.

—*Editor*

CONTENTS

ABBREVIATIONS

Common and self-evident abbreviations such as Ch(s)—Chapter(s), p—page, pp—pages, V—Verse, VV—Verses, Ftn—footnote, Hist. Ind. Philo.—History of Indian Philosophy are not included in this list.

ABORI	*Annals of the Bhandarkar Oriental Research Institute*, Poona
AGP	S. M. Ali's *The Geography of Purāṇas*, PPH, New Delhi, 1973
AIHT	*Ancient Indian Historical Tradition*, F. E. Pargiter, Motilal Banarsidass (MLBD), Delhi
AITM	*Ancient Indian Tradition and Mythology* Series, MLBD, Delhi
AP	*Agni Purāṇa*, Guru Mandal Edition (GM), Calcutta, 1957
Arch.S.Rep.	Archaeological Survey Report
AV	*Atharva Veda*, Svādhyāya Mandal, Aundh
Bd. P.	*Brahmāṇḍa Purāṇa*, MLBD, Delhi 1973
BG	*Bhagavadgītā*
Bh. P.	*Bhāgavata Purāṇa*, Bhagavat Vidyapeeth, Ahmedabad
Br.	*Brāhmaṇa* (preceded by name such as Śatapatha)
BS. P.	*Bhaviṣya Purāṇa*, Vishnu Shastri Bapat, Wai
BV. P.	*Brahma Vaivarta Purāṇa*, GM, 1955-57
CC	*Caturvarga Cintāmaṇi* by Hemādri
CVS	*Caraṇa Vyūha Sūtra* by Śaunaka, Com. by Mahidāsa
DB	*Devī Bhāgavata*, GM, 1960-61
De or GDAMI	*The Geographical Dictionary of Ancient and Mediaeval India*, N. L. De, Oriental Reprint, Delhi, 1971
Dh. S.	*Dharma Sūtra* (preceded by the author's name such as Gautama)
ERE	*Encyclopaedia of Religion and Ethics* by Hastings
GP	*Garuḍa Purāṇa*, ed. R. S. Bhattacharya, Chowkhamba, Varanasi, 1964

GS	*Gṛhya Sūtra* (preceded by the name of the author such as Āpastamba)
HD	*History of Dharma Śāstra*, P. V. Kane, G. O. S.
IA	*The Indian Antiquary*
IHQ	*The Indian Historical Quarterly*
JP	*Purāṇa* (Journal of the Kashiraj Trust), Varanasi
KA	*Kauṭilya Arthaśāstra*
KP	*Kūrma Purāṇa*, Veṅkaṭeśvara Press Edn., Bombay; also Kashiraj Trust Edn., Varanasi, 1971
LP	*Liṅga Purāṇa*, GM, 1960; also MLBD, Delhi, 1981
Manu.	*Manusmṛti*
Mbh.	*Mahābhārata*, Gītā Press, Gorakhpur, VS 2014
MkP	*Mārkaṇḍeya Purāṇa*
MN	*Mahābhārata Nāmānukramaṇī*, Gītā Press, Gorakhpur, VS 2016
MtP	*Matsya Purāṇa*, GM, 1954
MW	Monier Williams' *Sanskrit-English Dictionary*, MLBD, Delhi, 1976
NP	*Nāradīya* or *Nārada Purāṇa*, Veṅkaṭeśvara Press, Bombay
PCK	*Bhāratavarṣiya Prācina Caritrakośa*, Siddheshwar Shastri, Poona, 1968
Pd.P.	*Padma Purāṇa*, GM, 1957-59
PE	*Purāṇic Encyclopaedia*, V. Mani, English version, MLBD, Delhi. 1975
PR or PRHRC	*Puranic Records on Hindu Rites and Customs*, R. C. Hazra, Calcutta, 1948
ṚV	*Ṛg-Veda*, Svādhyāya Mandal, Aundh
Śat.Br.	*Śatapatha Brāhmaṇa*
SC or SMC	*Smṛti Candrikā* by Devanna Bhaṭṭa
SEP	*Studies in Epics and Purāṇas*, A.D. Pusalkar, Bharatiya Vidya Bhavan (BVB), Bombay

II BHŪMIKHAṆḌA
(Section on the Earth)

CHAPTER ONE
The Story of Śivaśarman

Om, salutation to Śrī Gaṇeśa.

The sages said:

1-2. O glorious Sūta, O you who know the significance of the essence of everything, (please) listen to the terrible doubt, destroying understanding, that has occurred to us. Some describe in the Purāṇas that when Prahlāda was five years old he pleased Keśava (i.e. Viṣṇu).

3. How did (the war) between gods and demons come about? How did the demon fight with Viṣṇu? He, killed by Viṣṇu, entered his body.

Sūta said:

4. This was formerly known (i.e. conceived) by Kaśyapa and was composed by the intelligent Vyāsa. It was formerly narrated by Brahmā himself before (i.e. to) the lord Vyāsa.

5. I shall, O brāhmaṇas, describe the same before (i.e. to) you. The cause of the doubt that arose was removed by Brahmā.

Vyāsa said:

6. O Sūta, O glorious one, listen to (the account) of the birth of Prahlāda as told in the Purāṇas and as heard (i.e. learnt) from other (sources).

7. As soon as Prahlāda, the greatest among the devotees of Viṣṇu and honoured by gods, was born, he resorted to the path of Viṣṇu, giving all happiness.

8. With his sons he went to the battle-field to fight with Viṣṇu. Being killed by Viṣṇu, he entered Viṣṇu's body.

9-10a. Listen to the birth of just this magnanimous one. The brave one, going with his sons to fight with Viṣṇu, entered Viṣṇu's lustre, which he obtained through his own lustre.

10b-11a. O glorious one, I shall narrate in brief the account of that hero—how that powerful one was born in the former Kalpa.

11b-12a. At the extreme point in the west of the ocean, there was a city by name Dvārakā. It was full of all magnificence and all prosperity.

12b-13a. There perpetually lived a divine (man) knowing abstract meditation, and the best among those who knew abstract meditation, known as Śivaśarman, who was well-versed in all Vedas and sacred texts.

13b. He had five sons who were well-versed in (all) branches of knowledge.

14. (They were:) Yajñaśarman, Vedaśarman, Dharmaśarman, the glorious Viṣṇuśarman, who knew their own duties.

15a. The fifth one was Somaśarman, who was greatly devoted to his father.

15b. The best brāhmaṇas knew no other duty than devotion to their father.

16a. The magnanimous ones (always) had thoughts about him (only).

16b-17a. Seeing their devotion, the intelligent, best brāhmaṇa Śivaśarman, thought: 'I shall extort (these) learned men.

17b-18a. They do not have that feeling in their mind which is found in the devotees of Viṣṇu. I shall, therefore, find it, and will do so thoughtfully.'

18b. Due to the favour of Viṣṇu, he had all superhuman faculties.

19-20a. O best of Brāhmaṇas, he conceived a fine idea to suggest to them (what their duty was). The best brāhmaṇa, the best among those who knew Brahman, knowing a remedy due to the lustre of his penance, adopted it.

20b-21a. Then Śivaśarman presented before them a trick. He showed their mother to be dead of a great fever.

21b-24a. They saw their dead mother, and said (these) words to their father: "O glorious one, she, who nourished us in her womb, has, casting her body, been dead. Having left (us), she has gone to heaven. O father, what can be said (by us)?" Śivaśarman, the excellent brāhmaṇa, called his eldest, most devoted son, Yajñaśarman and said to him.

Sivaśarman said:

24b-25a. With this very sharp and whetted weapon cut off her limbs and throw them here and there.

25b-27. The son did it as he had heard (i.e. received) his father's order. He came back, and again said (these) words to his father: "O father, I have done everything as I was ordered. Today (i.e. now) entrust to me some other work. O father, I shall do it all, (even though) it (enemy/thing) be difficult to subdue or procure".

28-30. Having ordered the glorious one, devoted to his father, the brāhmaṇa (i.e. Śivaśarman), thinking of the second son, called (him viz.) Vedaśarman (and said to him): "Go by my order; being stupefied by passion of love (i.e. sex) I cannot stand without a woman (by my side)." He presented, by means of his magical power, a woman full of all charm (before Vedaśarman). (He told him:) "O boy, determined for me, bring this woman to me."

31a. Thus told, he said: "I shall do what is very dear to you."

31b-33a. Having saluted his father, and having gone from there, he said to her: "O respectable lady, my father tormented by the arrow of love, seeks you. So be favourable to him who is old. O you beautiful lady, O you one whose all limbs are charming, resort to my father."

33b. Thus (i.e. these words) spoken by Vedaśarman were heard by the woman created by magic. The woman said:

34-35a. "I do not at all long for the company of your father who is afflicted with old age, whose mouth has malady due to phlegm, and who is now afflicted with diseases, who is feeble, who is sick and old.

35b-36. I desire to dally with you, I shall do what is very dear to you. (I desire to dally with you) who are adorned with good fortune like a (handsome) form, and with gems of virtues, who are endowed with divine characteristics, who possess a divine form and great prowess.

37. What will you do with (your) old father? O you who destroy the pride (of others), by enjoying my body you will obtain all things difficult to obtain.

38a. O brāhmaṇa, there is no doubt that I shall give you whatever you desire."

38b-41. Hearing these disagreeable and evil words,

Vedaśarman spoke:

O respectable lady, your words are unjust, improper and mixed with sin. Do not talk like this to me who am devoted to my father and who am innocent. O auspicious one, I have come to you and am soliciting you for my father. Do not talk something else; (please) resort to my father. O you respectable lady, O you beautiful one, there is no doubt that I shall give you everything in the three worlds, with the mobile and the immobile—even more than the kingdom of gods.

The woman said:

42. If, for the sake of your father, you are thus capable of giving me (anything), then show me, today only, the great gods with Indra.

43. Indeed you are able to give me now what is difficult to be obtained. O glorious one, show me what power you possess.

Vedaśarman said:

44. O respectable lady, see the power of my penance. The best gods, Indra and others, being invited by me, have come.

They said to Vedaśarman:

45. O best brāhmaṇa, what should we do?. O brāhmaṇa, we shall give you, whatever you ask for. There is no doubt about it.

Vedaśarman said:

46. If the gods are pleased with me and are inclined to favour me, then they should give (i.e. produce in) me pure devotion to the feet of my father only.

47. (Saying) "Let it be so", the gods left as they had come. (The woman) seeing (the gods had come) like that said to him: "I have seen the power of your penance.

48-49a. I have nothing to do with the gods; if you want to give me (what I want) and if you are taking me for your father, then do that (which is) dear to me; O brāhmaṇa, cutting off your head with your own hand, give it to me."

Vedaśarman said:

49b-50a. Today I have become blessed; I have been free from the three debts.[1] O respectable lady, I shall give my head; O beautiful one, do take it.

50b-51a. Having cut off his own head with a whetted and sharp weapon, the best brāhmaṇa, gave it to her and laughed.

51b. She took it, covered with blood, and went to the sage.

The woman said:

52-53. O brāhmaṇa, your son, Vedaśarman, has sent this head; take it; he had himself cut off his own head. For you, he, devoted to his father, gave me his head. O best brāhmaṇa, enjoy me.

54-56a. The brothers (of Vedaśarman) saw the daring act of Vedaśarman. Their bodies trembled (and they said to) one another: "Our virtuous mother died with real intentness. This glorious, virtuous one died for the sake of (our) father. He is blessed, he has become fortunate (as) he has done an auspicious (deed) for (our) father."

56b-58. Thus the virtuous brothers talked (to one another). The brāhmaṇa heard these words full of devotion, and knowing that his son, Vedaśarman, had cut off his (own) head, said to Dharmaśarman: "Take this head".

1. *Ṛṇatraya*—Everyone that is born has three debts to pay off, viz. Devaṛṇa, Ṛṣiṛṇa, and Pitṛṛṇa. The first is paid off by performing sacrifices, the second by learning the Vedas and the third by begetting a son.

CHAPTER TWO

Life is Restored to Vedaśarman

Sūta said:

1-2a. Then taking it the virtuous one quickly left. By his devotion for his father, his austerities, and the power of his truthfulness and straightforwardness, Dharmaśarman attracted Dharma (i.e. Yama).

2b-3a. Attracted by the penance of that intelligent (Dharmaśarman), Dharma, who had come (there), said these words to Dharmaśarman:

3b-4a. "O Dharmaśarman, why did you invite me? I have come. Then tell me about your work. I (shall) do it. There is no doubt about it."

Dharmaśarman said:

4b-5a. If I have (properly) served the elders, if I have devotion and steady penance, then, O Dharma, let Vedaśarman be alive, due to that (and) due to my truthfulness.

Dharma said:

5b-6. O you of a good vow, as a result of your purity with restraint, truthfulness and penance, and due to your devotion to your father, your great-souled brother Vedaśarman, of mighty arms, will again obtain (i.e. come to) life.

7. O you highly intelligent one, I am pleased with this your penance and devotion to your father. Well-being to you; ask for a boon difficult to be obtained by those who know righteousness.

8. That Dharmaśarman thus heard those good words. He, of a great glory, said to the magnanimous Vaivasvata (i.e. Dharma or Yama):

9. "Give me steady devotion to the worship of my father's feet, and also liking for piousness and salvation, if you are well-pleased with me."

10a. Then Dharma said : "This will take place by my favour."

10b-11a. When these very significant words were uttered, the very wise Vedaśarman got up, as if he had slept; he said to Dharmaśarman:

11b. "O brother, where has that respectable woman gone? Where would be the father?"

12. He told him in brief how the father had appointed him. Knowing that, Dharmaśarman, who was delighted, said to him:

13. "O glorious one, O brother, be favourable to me today only with (my having restored your) head and life. Who else is there like you to me on the earth?"

14. Saying so to his brother he was eager to go to his father. He (i.e Vedaśarman) decided to go, with his brother Dharmaśarman, to their father.

15-17a. Both, delighted in their minds went to their father there (i.e. to the place where he was). Both stood close together. Then Dharmaśarman spoke to his father, the excellent and lustrous Śivaśarman: "O glorious one, due to my penance and life Vedaśarman has been brought (back). (Please) take him—your son."

17b-18a. Then Śivaśarman, knowing his devotion, was delighted; (but) he did not say anything to him, and thought.

18b-23. He (then) spoke to the very intelligent Viṣṇuśarman, who politely remained before him: "Child, do as I say. Today go to Indra's heaven and fetch nectar from there—the nectar that came up from the ocean and that destroys diseases. Now I desire to stay with this wife (of me). With good (intention) she desires me. Do that quickly so that I obtain her; otherwise she may go to other (man). Knowing me to be old this young beautiful woman might think lightly of me. O son, if you are devoted to me, do that by which I shall, in the company of this one dear to me, be faultless and free from disease."

24-25a. Hearing these words of his magnanimous father, Viṣṇuśarman then said to his father of a blazing lustre: "I shall do all this that pleases you most."

25b-27. Speaking thus, that pious, very intelligent Viṣṇuśarman saluted his father and went round him keeping him to his right, and due to great power, penance and restraint, went into the intermediate region between heaven and earth.

When the intelligent one was (thus) going, he went to Indra with the speed of a violent wind.

CHAPTER THREE

The Heroic Deed of Viṣṇuśarman

Sūta said:

1. Proceeding along that path, he entered the heaven. He was seen by the intelligent Indra, the lord of gods.

2-4a. Knowing his exertion, the king of gods put in an obstacle. He said to that (nymph) Menikā: "Go by my order; O you of beautiful waist, going quickly create an obstacle (in) his (way). Well-being to you. Do that to the son of that excellent brāhmaṇa Śivaśarman by which he would not come to my house." Hearing these words of him, Menikā started quickly.

Sūta said:

4b-6. She, who was endowed with beauty, and virtues like generosity, and adorned with all ornaments, sat on a swing in Indra's garden. That clever one with large and charming eyes, singing, in a sweet voice, like the notes of a lute, a song (was seated on the swing).

7-8. Knowing her intention of causing a great obstacle, and realising that, she, being sent by Indra, would not be favourable, the best brāhmaṇa went quickly. She saw him and asked him: "O you highly intelligent one, where are you going?"

9. Then Viṣṇuśarman spoke to that Menikā, who moved according to her will: "I am hurriedly going to Indra's heaven for my father".

10-11a. Menikā again spoke pleasing (words) to Viṣṇuśarman.

11b-12. "Being pierced with Cupid's arrows, I have today sought your shelter. O best brāhmaṇa, if you desire to protect piety, (please) protect me. When I, with my mind affected by passion of love, saw you, then only I was burnt by fire of Cupid.

I am bewildered, I am tormented by love. Please be disposed to favour me."

Viṣṇuśarman said:

13-15. O you of a beautiful face, the character of the lord of gods is known to me. I also know your character. O you auspicious one, I am not like this. O you lovely lady, other men like Viśvāmitra are deluded by your lustre and beauty; O you respectable lady, I am the son of Śivaśarman who has attained divine faculties through abstract meditation and is accomplished in penance. I have avoided the great blemishes like desire for sensual enjoyments right from the beginning.

16a. O you of large eyes, choose someone else; I am going to Indra's world.

16b-17. Saying so, the best brāhmaṇa went hurriedly. Menakā was unsuccessful. Being asked by god Indra she repeatedly scared him in many ways.

18. (All) those scares (put forward by her) were burnt as the heaps of hay are burnt by fire.

19. O excellent brāhmaṇas, all those terrible scares perished due to the lustre of that brāhmaṇa, devoted to his father.

20. That Indra again and again presented obstacles; the brāhmaṇa of great glory destroyed them by his lustre.

21. Thus by means of the lustre of his penance, the intelligent one destroyed all the obstacles created by even that magnanimous Indra.

22-25a. When those great, fearful obstacles disappeared, he, knowing that those obstacles (i.e. scares) which were fierce and of fearful forms, were brought about by Indra, the best brāhmaṇa Viṣṇuśarman of great lustre became angry. The glorious one, with his eyes red due to anger (said) about Indra: "Today I shall cause to fall down from his heaven Indra, who would create an obstacle to me engaged in my own duty. I shall punish him; he, who would strike, is struck.

25b. I shall thus make someone else as the guardian of gods."

26. Thus the best (brāhmaṇa) became ready to destroy Indra. Just then only Indra arrived there (and said:)

27-28. "O brāhmaṇa, O you very wise one, there is none else like you in penance, restraint, self-control, truth and purity. Due to this your devotion to your father, I with (all other) deities have been won over (by you). O best one, (please) forgive all my fault.

29. Well-being to you, ask for a boon, I shall give it (even if) it is difficult." Then Viṣṇuśarman spoke to the king of gods who had come like that:

30. "O great Indra, the lustre of a brāhmaṇa is unbearable for gods and deities. O lord, it is (especially so) in the case of a brāhmaṇa who is devoted to his father.

31-32a. Destruction of the dignity of magnanimous brāhmaṇas should never be done. If the best brāhmaṇas are angered, they destroy Brahmā, Viṣṇu and Hara along with their sons and grandsons. There is no doubt about this.

32b-35. Had you not come today, then, I, with my eyes full of anger, would have given this best kingdom to some other person, magnanimous due to the prowess of his penance. Now that you have come, and desire to grant a boon, (then) O lord of gods, give me nectar and steady devotion to my father. O you killer of (your) enemies, if you are pleased, grant me such a boon." (Indra said:) "So I shall give you a pious boon with nectar."

36-38a. Speaking thus to the brāhmaṇa, Indra himself gave him nectar. He, with his heart pleased, gave it along with the pitcher. (He also said:) "O brāhmaṇa, may you always have unswerving devotion to your father." Speaking in this way, and having dismissed the brāhmaṇa, the thousand-eyed (Indra) became pleased on seeing the brāhmaṇa's lustre, very difficult to endure.

38b-42. Then Viṣṇuśarman, having gone to his father, said to him: "O father, I have brought from Indra, nectar, that destroys all maladies. O glorious one, with (i.e. by taking) it be healthy always. Today be greatly satisfied with (this) nectar." Hearing these great words of his son, Śivaśarman, with his mind full of love, having called all his sons, (said to them): "(My) sons, you are devoted to (me) your father, and you do what I tell you. Be pleased (my) sons, and ask for a boon difficult to be obtained on the earth." All listened to his words with approval.

43-45a. Having pondered, all of them said to their father: "Bring back to life that mother of us, who has gone to the dwelling of Yama. May she, of a good vow, be healthy due to your favour. O father, may you be (our) father, and this one (our) mother, even in existence after existence, and may we be your meritorious sons."

Śivaśarman said:

45b-46a. Even today, your dead mother, affectionate to her sons, will come alive; there is no doubt about it.

46b-47a. When these auspicious words were uttered by the sage Śivaśarman, their mother arrived (there) and being delighted said (these) words:

47b-50a. "A brave son is born from one's womb for this purpose only. Men desire a good son, who would bring glory to his family and race. In the world, glorious, meritorious and pure and affectionate women everywhere desire a son of a pleasing body and bringing about merit. That woman, the very meritorious foetus after having gone into whose womb revolves there, and who would give birth to meritorious sons, is pleased.

50b-56a. How can a woman obtain, without merit, the best son, performing duties peculiar to his family, prop of the family and emancipating the father and the mother? I do not know due to which meritorious deeds (of mine) this very meritorious man, having piety as his power, righteous, and loving piety has become my husband, from whose semen I have obtained you as my sons, superior to him. This is the power of merit. You, my sons, are born as loving virtue and intensely devoted to your father. Oh, in the world even one good son is had by means of religious merit. (But see,) I got five great-hearted sons, who are sacrificers, who are righteous, and who have the prowess due to the lustre of penance." When they were thus repeatedly congratulated by their mother, they, being full of great joy, saluted their mother.

The sons said:

56b-58a. Due to great religious merit (only) a mother—a good mother or a good father is obtained. You are a virtuous mother, who became so due to our good fortune, and having reached whose womb we were nourished as a result of our great virtue. In existence after existence you two should be our mother and father.

The father said:

58b-59a. O my sons, listen to a good boon, causing religious merit. When I am pleased, may my sons enjoy inexhaustible pleasures.

The sons said:

59b-60a. O father, if you are pleased, and desire to give a boon now, then send us to Goloka, the heaven of Viṣṇu, which is free from tormentation.

The father said:

60b-61a. By my favour, your penance, and this your devotion to (me) your father, go, with your sins perished, to Viṣṇu's heaven.

61b-64a. When the sage said good words, then (Viṣṇu) having the conch, disc and mace in his hands and mounted upon Garuḍa, came there; and repeatedly said this to Śivaśarman with his sons: "O brāhmaṇa, today you with your sons, have won me over by your devotion. With your four virtuous sons and this virtuous and very loving wife come (to me)".

Śivaśarman said:

64b-65. May these (four) sons of me go to the excellent heaven of Viṣṇu. I shall pass some time on the earth with my wife and this last, excellent son, Somaśarman.

66-67a. When the sage, who (always) spoke the truth, uttered these auspicious words, the lord of gods said to those good sons of Śivaśarman: "May they go to the world causing salvation and free from tormentation and destruction."

67b-71. When this was said (by the Lord), all the four brāhmaṇas of truthful hearts, in a moment only took up Viṣṇu's form. In complexion they resembled sapphires; they had held conch, disc and mace; were charming on account of all ornaments; had great prowess; were endowed with the beauty of necklaces and bracelets; they looked charming due to jewelled necklaces; they resembled the sun's lustre and were covered with bright flames. They entered Viṣṇu's body when Śivaśarman was looking on (i.e. in Śivaśarman's presence). As lights go to another light, they became absorbed in Viṣṇu's form. The best brāhmaṇas, due to their devotion to their father, went to Viṣṇu's abode. I shall tell accurately the prowess of Somaśarman.

CHAPTER FOUR

Somaśarman's Devotion Put to Severe Test

Sūta said:

1. When they had gone to the Goloka of Viṣṇu, beyond darkness, the very wise Śivaśarman said to his youngest (son):

The brāhmaṇa said :

2-3. O very wise Somaśarman, you are very much devoted to (me) your father. Now protect this pitcher of nectar given by me. With this wife I shall go on a pilgrimage.

"O glorious one, let it be so. I shall protect the auspicious (pitcher)".

4. The intelligent one (i.e. Śivaśarman) having given the pitcher into the hands of the magnanimous one, continuously practised penance for ten years.

5. The righteous one (i.e. Somaśarman) carefully protected the pitcher day and night. Then that Śivaśarman of great fame again came back.

6. Using a trick the very wise one, becoming (i.e. turning himself into one) afflicted with leprosy, (making) his wife also like that, came, with his wife, to his son.

7-12a. The two had become lumps of flesh, as they were made so by his trick. They came near that violent (*ghora*?) brāhmaṇa Somaśarman. Somaśarman, of great glory, seeing them completely afflicted, was full of great compassion. With his neck bent through devotion, he saluted their feet (and said:) "I have never seen (persons) like you. (I have not seen anyone else) endowed with penance, with hosts of virtues and great religious merit. What has happened to you? O best of brāhmaṇas, all deities, attracted by your lustre, getting your order, always behave like your servants. Tell me the cause, O best brāhmaṇa, by which this painful disease has appeared on your wretched body?

12b-15a. This my meritorious mother, who is a loyal wife and has great religions merit, desires (i.e. is capable) to create the three worlds due to her husband's favour. How does she suffer pain? Is there no fruit of penance? How is it that she, who is affectionate to the elders, and who serves her husband as a god, contracts an extremely painful disease like leprosy?"

Śivaśarman said:

15b-16a. O glorious one, do not be sorry; the fruit due to his deeds is enjoyed by a man who has (done) a good or a bad deed.

16b-17a. O glorious one, if you desire religious merit in this world, then clean both of us who are suffering from the disease, and nurse us.

17b-19a. Thus addressed with good words, Somaśarman of great glory (said:) "I shall nurse you both who are meritorious. O best of brāhmaṇas, what has one to do (i.e. what would one get) in this world, if one does not nurse one's elder today (i.e. at the present time) only?"

19b-28a. Speaking thus, he who was grieved due to their malady, cleansed the phlegm, urine and excrement of both of them. He washed their feet and shampooed their bodies. He himself bathed them and helped them to stand. The best and virtuous brāhmaṇa, Somaśarman, of great glory, placing them on his shoulders took them to sacred places. The virtuous (Somaśarman), conversant with the Vedas, bathed them according to sacred precepts with his own hands, and with (the recitation of) auspicious, excellent, sacred hymns, and made both of them offer oblations to the manes and worship to the deities everyday. He himself offered ghee for gods into fire and cooked excellent food. He then called both the respectable elders, well-pleased with him (for food). The brāhmaṇa (i.e. Somaśarman) everyday put them to sleep on a bed. Daily he gave them garments, flowers etc. He offered very fragrant tāmbūla to both of them. The glorious Somaśarman everyday gave them roots, water, good eatables etc. Somaśarman, of great glory, daily gave them whatever they desired.

28b-29a. In this way he always pleased them. The very pious Somaśarman (everyday) worshipped his parents.

29b-34. Calling Somaśarman, his cruel father (Śivaśarman) always abused him with censurable and harsh words; and in the presence of the sages he everyday beat his son who did his duty and did meritorious deeds. (He said to him:) "O you, disgrace to the family, you have not done well to me (i.e. have not served me properly)." He condemned him with many harsh and painful words. That Śivaśarman who was always sick, beat him with the strokes of a stick. Even though Śivaśarman did (i.e. treated him) like this, he (i.e. Somaśarman) who was pious, was never angry with him. Always happy in mind, speech and the three kinds of deeds Somaśarman propitiated his father; similarly he also daily propitiated his mother, knowing which Śivaśarman considered his own behaviour.

35-46. (He thought:) 'Viṣṇuśarman brought nectar for me. That righteous one has religious merit and is always devoted to (me) his father.' When thus many days which can be counted in hundreds, passed, Śivaśarman too, seeing his devotion, thought: 'Formerly I had told by son named Yajña (i.e. Yajñaśarman): O son, throw here and there the pieces (of the dead body) of your mother. He obeyed my words (i.e. order), and did not show compassion for his mother. This grief of one who desires to give strokes on an inanimate body is smaller; but that son Vedaśarman did a bold act; but I think that this one is superior since he does not swerve (from duty) even for a moment. He may also again do a rash act. Again he has the prowess, along with truth, due to penance. Even in everyday attendance he appears excelling (others). So at the right time I have tested his penance. (This my) son will never perish because of his devotion and truthfulness. I showed the disease of leprosy on my body through illusion; (but) he does not have disgust for phlegm, urine or excrement. He, of a great glory, cleanses the sores with his own hand. The very intelligent one shampoos (our) feet and cleanses us (i.e. our bodies). He always puts up with unbearable words (uttered by) me. (Even though I) reproached and beat (him), he always talks pleasing words. Thus my very intelligent son is unhappy. I think that he, who is troubled with many afflictions, is the ocean of maladies. I shall remove his unhappiness by the favour of Viṣṇu.'

47-53a. Thinking (thus) in his mind (i.e. to himself), the very intelligent Śivaśarman, again created the illusion and took away the water (i.e. the nectar) from the pitcher. Then afterwards, having called that Somaśarman, he said to him: "I had given (i.e. placed) in your hand nectar, that removes maladies. Give it to me quickly, so that I shall drink it. By (drinking) that I shall today be free from the disease due to the favour of Viṣṇuśarman." When the sage Śivaśarman uttered these words, Somaśarman hurriedly got up (and rushed to) the pitcher. Seeing it empty (that is) without nectar (he thought:) 'Which sinful person has done this deed? Who has thus harmed me?' Somaśarman was thus worried and very unhappy. 'If I tell this account before (i.e. to) my father, he—my father—tormented by the disease, will be angry.'

53b-55. For a long time the very intelligent Somaśarman thought (to himself): 'If I have truth and have served the elders or have practised penance with a sincre mind, or have observed the proper code of conduct by means of restraint, purity etc. then this pitcher will have nectar in it. There is no doubt about it.'

56. When the glorious one thought (like this) and saw, the pitcher was again full of nectar.

57. Seeing it, Somaśarman of a great glory, became joyful, and going to his father, saluting him, quickly fetching the pitcher (said to him):

58. "O father, please take this pitcher of water (i.e. nectar) that has come (i.e. is brought by me). O magnanimous one, drink it, and quickly be free from the disease."

59-60. Hearing these greatly meritorious and truthful and righteous and sweet words of (i.e. uttered by) his son, Śivaśarman was full of great joy and said these words:

CHAPTER FIVE

The Consecration of Indra

Śivaśarman said:

1. O good son, today I am pleased with your penance, restraint, purity, and with your service to the elders and your devotion and resolution.

2. I (shall) abandon this deformed body; obtain happiness from me.

Saying so to the son, he showed him that (former) body.

3. He saw both the elders (i.e. his parents), who became as they were before, who were bright, who were magnanimous and who resembled the orb of the sun.

4-5. He devoutly saluted the feet of both the noble ones. Then full of great joy, he, the best one, took his leave of his son, and due to Viṣṇu's favour, his own religious merit and the practice of abstract meditation, the pious one went, with his wife, to Viṣṇu.

6-8. That sage entered Viṣṇu's abode, a place difficult to be obtained. This place granting salvation is not obtained by means of other (kinds of) religious merit or penance, or by means of meditating upon Viṣṇu, or renunciation, or contemplation, or knowledge, or hymns of praise. Viṣṇu is not seen by means of gifts or pilgrimages. The highest place is seen (only) by resorting to concentration and knowledge, as the brāhmaṇa entered Viṣṇu's body by means of deep and abstract meditation.

Sūta said:

9-10. Then that very lustrous Somaśarman practised penance there. He also looked upon gold and ornaments like a stone or a clod of clay. The righteous one had controlled his diet, he had given up sleep. Giving up all objects of senses he resorted to solitude.

11-12a. He had taken to the posture suited to profound and abstract meditation, was desireless and had no possessions. Then the time of his death arrived. Demons came to that brāhmaṇa, Somaśarman.

12b-16. When the time of death of him who was living (like that) at the great sacred place, Śāligrāma, adding to the honour of sages arrived, some demons and goblins who knew thus (i.e. knew that his death was imminent), spoke. The great sound (of the words uttered by them) entered the cavity of the ears of Somaśarman, the best brāhmaṇa. Fear of the demons entered him, who had adhered to knowledge and meditation. Due to that meditation and the fear of the demons the life of the noble one quickly departed. Being full of the fear of the demons he died.

17-18. Therefore, he was born in the house of the demon (Hiraṇyakaśipu) as Hiraṇyakaśipu's son. In the war' between gods and demons he was killed by Viṣṇu. The noble Prahlāda, while fighting well saw (the form of) Vāsudeva, endowed with the universal form.

19. Due to his former practice of abstract meditation, the noble one had the knowledge (of his former birth, so) he recollected all the former life of Śivaśarman:

20-22. "Formerly, I whose name was Somaśarman, entered the body of a demon. When shall I, due to my great religious merit, called knowledge, reach, from (i.e. casting) this body, the absolute, pious, excellent, abode granting salvation?" The noble Prahlāda, thought like this when he died formerly; O best of brāhmaṇas, listen. I have thus told you everything that removes (your) doubts.

Sūta said:

23-25a. When Prahlāda was killed in the battle by the disc-holder (i.e. Viṣṇu), the lord of gods, that beautiful woman, Kamalā, whose son was killed, wept. She was the mother of Prahlāda and the beloved (wife) of Hiraṇyakaśipu. Due to the grief caused by Prahlāda's death she, the loyal, glorious wife, (of Hiraṇyakaśipu), who was dear to him, lamented day and night.

25b. Nārada spoke to her, who was weeping day and night:

26-27a. "Do not grieve, O noble and meritorious one, for your son. Your son, the very intelligent one, who is killed by Viṣṇu, will come back endowed with his own (former) characteristics.

27b. He will again have his name as Prahlāda.

28-30a. He will be without the demonish thoughts, and will be endowed with godhead; he will be saluted by all gods and will enjoy the position of Indra, O good lady. O illustrious lady, always be happy with that son. (Please) do not reveal this good news to anyone. You should feign ignorance, and always keep this as a great secret."

30b. Saying so, the brāhmaṇa, the best sage, Nārada, left.

31-33. He (i.e. Prahlāda) got an excellent birth in the womb of Kamalā (i.e. Prahlāda was born as the son of Kamalā). He was named Prahlāda; the account of that illustrous one (will be narrated by me). O brāhmaṇas, when he was a child, he thought of Kṛṣṇa (i.e. Viṣṇu) only. Due to the favour of Narasiṁha (i.e. Viṣṇu) he would be the king of gods in heaven. After having obtained godhead, he would also get the position of Indra; he, the all-wise, will attain salvation—Viṣṇu's abode.

34. There are innumerable glorious individuals, there are many forms of creation. (So) the great-souled, wise ones should not commit errors.

35-36. O best brāhmaṇas, I have told you everything that you have asked. O glorious one (ones) you may ask anything else. I shall remove your doubt: (I shall tell you about) the victory of gods and the destruction of demons brought about by the lord of gods, and (about) how he re-established the three worlds.

The sages said:

37. Who got the position of Indra, which sustained the title of gods? O best of brāhmaṇas, tell (us) in detail, who gave (him) the position of Indra?

Sūta said:

38. I shall tell you in detail for which best merit the best one, the glorious one, obtained the position of Indra.

39-40. When all the demons were killed in the great war, and when the sinners were completely annihilated by the magnanimous Viṣṇu, gods along with gandharvas, nāgas, vidyādharas, spoke, with their palms foldedi n obeisance, to Mādhava (Viṣṇu):

41. "O venerable one, O lord of gods, O Hṛṣīkeśa, our salutations to you. We are going to tell you something respectfully; (please) understand all that.

42-43a. O Keśava (i.e. Viṣṇu), make for (i.e. give) us a ruler, a protector, who is meritorious; (give us) a god, a king, viz. Indra, who is righteous and who would rule the worlds, and resorting to whom the beings in the three worlds would obtain happiness."

Vāsudeva (i.e. *Viṣṇu*) *said*:

43b. O you illustrious ones, the best brāhmaṇa, endowed with the Viṣṇuite lustre, lived in my heaven for a long time.

44-48a. O you best gods, the period of stay in my heaven of that brāhmaṇa, that magnanimous devotee of me, was over. Due to Viṣṇuite lustre in him the pious one will be your guardian; and he loves righteousness; he, the best pious brāhmaṇa, will be your king and supporter for protecting you. The large-hearted son of Aditi will be known as Suvrata. He, the very powerful and very brave one will be Indra.

Sūta said:

48b-49. In this way, the lord of gods, granted best boons to the gods; then all the victorious and best gods went with Viṣṇu to see their father, Kaśyapa, and their mother.

50. The magnanimous ones saluted both (the parents) seated comfortably. Full of great joy, and with the palms of their hands joined, they said:

51. "Due to your favour we have attained to godhead." Full of great joy, he (i.e. Kaśyapa) spoke (these) words to the gods:

Kaśyapa said:

52a-55a. You have always been following the virtuous path. Due to our favour and the power of penance, you have attained to the position of gods which is inexhaustible. To these I (now) give a boon: Full of great love you—gods, nāgas, gandharvas and great deities—will be immortal, will not be subject to old age, will be imperishable, will have all your desires satisfied, and will be endowed with all perfections.

Viṣṇu said:

55b-56a. Well-being to you, O successful mother of gods; ask for a boon. I shall certainly give you whatever is desired by your mind.

Aditi spoke:

56b-59. O Mādhava (i.e. Viṣṇu), due to your favour I had become a mother. I obtained these sons that are immortal, ageless, eternal, and righteous and affectionate, O Madhusūdana (i.e. Viṣṇu), (please) listen: O Govinda, you are one who fully satisfies all desires and gives prosperity. Remaining in my womb (you should be born as) my son, so that with you as my son I shall be delighted. O lord, thus satisfy my desire, leading to prosperity.

Vāsudeva said :

60-65. For the mission of gods, you should go to (i.e. take up) a human form. Then I shall surely remain in your womb. O goddess, when the twelfth yuga comes, I shall, for removing the burden of the earth, and for killing all the kṣatriyas, be (born as) your son, viz. (Paraśu) Rāma, Jamadagni's son, the best of brāhmaṇas and endowed with valour and lustre, and best among all those who wield weapons. Similarly, when the twentyseventh yuga called Tretā arrives, I shall be, O loyal wife, (born as) your son, named Rāma. O you of pious mind, when at the end of Dvāpara, the twentyeighth yuga arrives, I shall be undoubtedly (born as) your son, by name Vāsudeva (i.e. Kṛṣṇa), for the destruction of all demons and for removing the burden of the earth.

66a. O you auspicious one, now please do what I tell you.

66b-70a. O you goddess, who grant everything, having created an omniscient, handsome son, I shall give him the position of Indra, (so that) he too will be Indra.

Having heard thus that due to the favour of the lord of lords the son will be Indra, she was full of great joy. (She said:) "O magnanimous one, let it be so; I shall do as you tell me."

Then all the deities, free from fear and full of joy, went to their own abodes.

Sūta said:

70b-71. Having gone to Kaśyapa after she was in menstruation, the high-minded Aditi (said to him:) "O revered one, give me a son who will enjoy the position of Indra." The brāhmaṇa (i.e. Kaśyapa), having thought for a moment, said to the high-minded lady:

72-82a. "O illustrious one, let it be so. You will have a son, who will be the creator of the three worlds and also enjoyer of the sacrifices." Having put his hand on her head, the lustrous, best brāhmaṇa, who was endowed with truth and piety, practised penance. O best of brāhmaṇas, he (i.e. the son) would always live in the heaven of Viṣṇu. O best of brāhmaṇas, when his religious merit would be exhausted, be would, due to (the fruit of) his acts, fall from there; then he, of a great penance, would go to the womb of Aditi, with the desire to enjoy the position of Indra. Due to her truthful and meritorious deeds, and due to her religious merit and penance, the goddess conceived. Having gone to reside in a forest, she practised penance without laziness. A hundred divine years passed, when the mother of gods was (thus) practising penance. She practised penance difficult to be practised by gods and demons. She, bright with that penance and lustre, resembling the sun's lustre and (looking) like another sun, resorted to meditation and shone brightly. Then due to the lustre of her penance, she looked superior in her beauty (i.e. looked more beautiful). That goddess, Dakṣa's devout daughter, engrossed in penance and meditation, and feeding herself on air, shone more (i.e. looked more beautiful). All siddhas and sages, and gods of great prowess, closely intent (on looking after her), praised and protected the illustrious one.

82b-84. When a full hundred years were over, Viṣṇu came there. He said to that illustrious Aditi, endowed with penance: "O goddess, the foetus has fully developed; the time for delivery has come; the foetus is nourished by your penance and grown by your lustre. O you glorious one, today only you deliver the embryo."

85-89. Speaking thus, the lord of the gods went to his own

abode. When a very prosperous time arrived, the goddess delivered a son, who was lustrous, who was as it were another sun, who was pleasing, who was charming in all limbs, who was endowed with all (good) characteristics, who had four arms, whose body was huge, who was regent of a quarter, who was the lord of gods, who was covered with lustrous blazes, whose hands looked lovely on account of disc and lotus; who, the very intelligent one, shone with a face resembling the orb of the moon, who was very wise, who was adorned with the lustre of Viṣṇu, with other good characteristics and divine disposition, who was full of all (good) characteristics, whose face was like the moon, whose eyes resembled lotuses.

90-92a. The gods, the sages who had mastered the Vedas, gandharvas, nāgas, vidyādharas, the seven sages, of inferior and superior prowess, came there. Other virtuous, magnanimous sages, giving merit and auspiciousness, with their minds full of joy also came there.

92b-94. When that glorious one of great prowess was born, all revered gods, all mountains, ascetics, milky and other oceans, unsullied rivers, all those that were affectionate and other mobile and immobile objects came there. All lords of gods happily celebrated (the occasion) with auspicious rites.

95-102a. The hosts of the celestial nymphs danced and the gandharvas sang songs. Gods and sages who had mastered the Vedas praised the magnanimous son of Kaśyapa with Vedic hymns. When he of great prowess was born, Brahmā, Viṣṇu, Rudra and all the Vedas together with the Vedāṅgas and the Upāṅgas[1] came there. All the beings in the world that were endowed with religious merit came there only, when he of great prowess was born. With auspicious great festivals all of them performed sacred rites. The three gods led by Brahmā, as well as Kaśyapa and Bṛhaspati, of great prowess and full of joy and worshipping him, performed the naming ceremony of that magnanimous one. (They said:) "You will be known as Vasudatta; you are also (named) Vasuda; your names will be Ākhaṇḍala, and also

1. *Sāṅgopāṅgaiḥ*—With Aṅgas and Upāṅgas. The six Vedāṅgas are: (1) Śikṣā (Phonetics); (2) Kalpa (Rituals); (3) Vyākaraṇa (Grammar); (4) Nirukta (Etymology); (5) Chandas (Metrics); and (6) Jyotiṣa (Astronomy). The Upāṅgas are said to be: Purāṇa-nyāya-mīmāṁsā-dharma-śāstrāṇi.

Marutvān; you will also be known as Maghavan, Biḍaujas, and Pākaśāsani." (They said to Aditi:) "This your son will also be known as Śakra and Indra."

102b-105. All the deities, pleased and delighted in mind, gave these names to that magnanimous one only. The great gods took bath and performed the purificatory rites. Having called Viśvakarman, they gave that magnanimous one propitious and divine ornaments. All the gods of great prowess were thus glad when that glorious, magnanimous king of gods was born.

106-108. On an auspicious day, at an auspicious time, the magnanimous gods consecrated him with auspicious rites and established him as Indra. By the favour of the disc-holder (i.e. Viṣṇu) he obtained the position of Indra. That Vasudatta, the lustrous lord of gods, practised penance. He was endowed with brilliant lustre, and had held weapons like the thunderbolt, the noose, and the goads.

Sūta said :

109. Seeing the great, entire power of penance, Śukra uttered a verse : "In the worlds, there will be none else as much handsome as this one.

110. This other great magnanimous one has obtained this divine grandeur by Viṣṇu's favour.

111. None else, of a strong power due to penance will there be in the worlds, who can be compared with this one".

CHAPTER SIX

Diti's Wailing

Sūta said :

1-2. The other miserable wife of Kaśyapa, named Danu, being tormented by the grief due to the son (of Aditi) came to Diti's house. She was weeping, she who was reached by (i.e. was full of) great grief, saluted the two lotus-like feet of Diti. Diti advised her.

Diti said :

3. O glorious one, what is the cause of your weeping? Women are (said to be) 'Putriṇī (i.e. endowed with sons) (even though) they have (only) one son. O beautiful, auspicious one, you are the mother of even a hundred magnanimous sons like Śumbha.

4-7a. Tell me the reason why you are unhappy—(you) who have the two magnanimous and very mighty and valorous sons like king Hiraṇyakaśipu and the very mighty Hiraṇyākṣa. O friend, tell me why you are having this great grief. Tell me fully the reason for which you are weeping now.

7b. Having thus spoken to the queen (i.e. Danu), the high-minded (Diti) ceased speaking.

Danu said :

8-9. See, see, O magnanimous one, the desire of my co-wife (i.e. Aditi) has been fulfilled by the god of gods—the disc-holder (i.e. Viṣṇu). As Viṣṇu had formerly granted a boon to Aditi, even now he has granted a great boon to her son.

10. This son is known to be born from Kaśyapa, and is the guardian of the three worlds. Snatching the position of Indra from your son, he has given it to him (i.e. to Aditi's son).

11-12a. (Now) Aditi, who is full of desires (i.e. whose desires are fulfilled) is exalting with happiness, (since) her younger son, Vasudatta, along with the gods, is enjoying Indra's position which is very difficult to be obtained.

Diti said :

12b-13. O you glorious one, tell me of which position my very intelligent son is deprived; O friend, (tell me) also how other demons and goblins are deprived of lustre. Tell me in detail the cause of this.

14a. Saying (these) words to her (i.e. to Danu), Diti, who was extremely unhappy, stopped speaking.

Danu said :

14b-16a. Gods and demons, being enraged, went to fight (i.e. fought). A great war, causing the destruction of the demons, took place. The gods and Viṣṇu struck down my sons in the war;

so also your sons (were struck down) by the god of gods, viz. the disc-holder (i.e. Viṣṇu).

16b-20. As a lion would frighten with his own lustre (beings) that have gone to the forest, in the same way your sons and my sons were killed by him having the conch in his hand (i.e. by Viṣṇu). He destroyed, crushed, made to flee, and unnerved the army (of the demons) led by Kālanemi and unconquerable even for the gods and demons (together). As, in the forest fire would burn grass with its flames, so Keśava (i.e. Viṣṇu) completely consumed all the hosts of demons. Many of my sons, O respectable lady, and many of your sons also died (in the war). As all the moths perish after reaching (i.e. coming in contact with) fire, similarly all the demons reaching (i.e. coming in contact with) Hari (i.e. Viṣṇu), perished.

21a. Diti thus listened to this fearful account.

Diti said :

21b. O you good one, how do you tell me this, which is like the fall of the thunderbolt?

22-23a. Saying so, that respectable lady fell down in a swoon. She, who was very much oppressed by the grief due to her son, said : "Alas ! a misery has come about; it is very troublesome and tormenting."

23b-32a. Seeing her, the greatest sage said (these) auspicious words: "Well-being to you; do not weep; O you illustrious one, persons like you, who are energetic and free from greed and infatuation, do not grieve like this. O honorable lady, in this mundane existence, to whom do the sons belong? To whom do the good relatives belong? One has nothing to do with anyone (else). O dear one, listen to it all. You are the daughters of Dakṣa and are my beautiful wives. O auspicious one, I am your husband, who fulfils your desires. I bring you together; I am your guardian, and protector, also, O you of a beautiful face. Why did the cruel demons, not controlling themselves, entertain enmity (with the gods)? O you magnanimous one, your sons are destitute of truthfulness. Due to that fault (of them) and due to your morbid affection (for them), O auspicious one, they were killed by Vāsudeva (i.e. Kṛṣṇa, i.e. Viṣṇu) and were thrown down by the gods. Therefore do not entertain grief which destroys real salvation. Grief would destroy (i.e. destroys) religious merit, and one perishes by the loss of religious merit. Therefore, O you of a beautiful face, give up the grief being of the nature of an obstacle. Due to the power of their own faults the demons died. The gods were (just) an apparent cause; they (i.e. the demons) were destroyed by their own deeds. Realising this, O you glorious one, be happy".

32b-33. Having thus spoken to his dear wife who was unhappy, the very intelligent, great contemplative saint, withdrew through dejection and stopped (speaking).

CHAPTER SEVEN

Account of the Body

Diti said :

1-2. O Lord, you have spoken all the truth; there is no doubt about it. Abandoning love for my husband, I entertained rivalry (with my co-wife), O brāhmaṇa. (Now) being tormented by pride, agony, humiliation and great grief, I shall, O best one, give up my life.

Kaśyapa said :

3-5. (Please) listen, I shall tell (i.e. explain) you in such a way that there will be (i.e. you will have) peace (of mind). O auspicious one, nobody is anybody's son, or mother or father. Nobody has a brother or a relative. None has kinsmen and friends. In the mundane existence such is the relation, affected by illusion and infatuation. O respectable lady, one is one's own mother, one's own relatives and kinsmen. One is oneself the eternal moral virtue.

6-8. O you honourable lady, a man becomes happy due to (good) conduct. He surely perishes due to bad conduct and sin. Due to this he even goes to (i.e. is born in) a wicked species; there is no doubt about this. A man, deluded by an untruthful act and a great sin, always remains as an enemy of (other) beings. Here and there (i.e. everywhere) he has enemies; there is no doubt about this.

9. O you dear, auspicious and beautiful lady, when a man lives in a friendly way, he has friends everywhere.

10-11. O respectable lady, when the seed is concealed (underground) and is well-placed, the farmer gets the fruit exactly in accordance with it. Similarly your sons have vied with the good. Enjoy the fruit of that deed that has come to you.

12-13a. O illustrious one, your sons are destitute of penance and peace; due to that sin they have fallen from a great position. Realising this, be tranquil, and give up pain or pleasure.

13b-14a. To whom do the friends belong? To whom do relatives and friends belong? Beings live happily in accordance with their own deeds.

14b-15a. Due to their knowledge of the reality, the wise and the glorious do not think about another's interest. (To do so) is futile; there is no doubt about this.

15b-21a. The body is constituted of the five elements, and is just infirm because of the joints. O respectable lady, with a hope for happiness, it has befriended everything. Ātman (i.e. the soul) is greatly meritorious, omnipresent, and sees everything; he is virtuous, and grants all (kinds of) prosperity. Thus occupying everything, and being untinged, he, O respectable lady, moves all alone. While (thus) moving, he saw, in a secluded place, four meritorious best brāhmaṇas, (as it were) great power embodied. The fifth one was Wind, the friend of the former (four). Then the soul sought the help of Knowledge. The illustrious one, seeing them, said to Jñāna (Knowledge): "O Jñāna, see these five; they are consulting one another. Go to them and talk to them. Ask them: 'Who are you?' "

21b-22. Hearing those very significant words of that glorious one, Jñāna (Knowledge), propitiating him, said to him: "What have you to do with them? Tell me the truth (since) you are always pure."

Ātman (soul) said:

23-24. These five are glorious, handsome and high-minded. I shall go, meet them, and shall speak to them. O Jñāna (Knowledge), listen: I shall speak to these worthy ones, who have come to the fifth one viz. Speed (i.e. Wind). O Knowledge, be (my) messenger; you are skilled in the act of a messenger.

Jñāna (Knowledge) said:

25-26. O soul, listen to my words, I am telling you the truth, and the truth (only). O dear one, O you of pure heart, you, desiring for the good, should never have the company of these five. O you very intelligent one, this Moha (i.e. Infatuation) is longing for your company.

Ātman (the soul) said :

27. Why do you, O Jñāna, avoid the company of these? O wise one, tell me the real reason of this.

Jñāna (Knowledge) said:

28. There will be great grief just due to their company. These five are the root of grief and cause affliction and tormentation.

Ātman said:

29. Let it be so; I shall do as you tell me.

That Ātman, (thus) speaking to Jñāna, associated himself with Dhyāna (Meditation).

Kaśyapa said:

30. Then all the five saw that Ātman. Having called Buddhi (Intellect) they said to her: "Be united with Ātman only.

31-32. O you auspicious one, act as the messenger between Ātman and us. O Buddhi, having gone to him say to him: 'The five elements,[1] the magnanimous ones, the supporters of the world and the auspicious ones desire your friendship.' You have to do this mission of ours. (Please) go from here." (*Buddhi said*:)

33. "Let it be so; O glorious ones, I shall carry out this best mission of you." Having thus spoken to them, she went to that Ātman, and said to him:

---

1. The five elements are: Earth, Water, Fire. Wind and Ether.

34-35. "O blessed one, I am Buddhi, I have approached you as a messenger from (i.e. of) the great (elements). Listen to their words (i.e. message). The five-natured (elements) desire your eternal friendship. Form friendship (with them), O you highly intelligent one, and abandon (i.e. keep) Dhyāna far away."

Dhyāna (*Meditation said*):

36. O Ātman, you should not have their company. Merely by their contact there will be great grief (i.e. great grief will befall you).

37. How would you do your duty, when you are forsaken by Jñāna and me? So, you should not at all associate yourself with them.

38. O mighty one, they will make you live in the womb; there is no other go. Without Jñāna and me, you will certainly go to Ajñāna (i.e. Ignorance).

39. Thus speaking to that highly intelligent Ātman, Dhyāna ceased to speak. Then, Ātman, who was determined (to form friendship with the five elements), spoke to Buddhi, who had come to him:

40. "The illustrious Jñāna and Dhyāna are my virtuous ministers. It is not proper to go to them. So, O Buddhi, what shall I do (now)?"

41. Hearing thus (i.e. these words), the glorious Buddhi told in the vicinity of (i.e. to) them (i.e. the five elements) the full narration of Jñāna and Dhyāna (i.e. told everything that Jñāna and Dhyāna had said).

42-43. Then all the five (elements) went to Ātman (and said to him):) "We constantly desire your friendship only. O you lord of the worlds, since you are pure, we have approached you. Thinking for yourself only (i.e. independently of Jñāna and Dhyāna), please give us a reply."

Ātman said:

44. All you five have come; (and) you seek my friendship. Tell before (i.e. to) me your merit and power.

Bhūmi (*the Earth*) *said*:

45. My firmness rooted in the bones is the basis of all operations, is connected with skin and flesh, and with nails and the hair on the body.

46. O you very wise one, my strength is in the body. That magnanimous odour passing through the nose is my servant.

Ākāśa (*Ether*) *said*:

47-48. I, Ether, have come. Listen; I shall tell you about the lustre, of the nature of the highest Brahman; space is without and within; I live in a vacant place. My ministers are the two ears; they are set up for hearing.

Vāyu (*Wind*) *said*:

49. I remain in five forms,[1] and in this way I perform auspicious and inauspicious things. My minister, remaining on the habitation of the skin, resorts to the quality of touch.

Tejas (*Fire*) *said*:

50-54a. Always remaining in the body, I digest (articles of food). I manifest all matter and non-matter, without and within. I send forth semen, marrow, saliva, and also blood remaining in the skin and joints. I remain in the body. The two eyes are my ministers that cause the perception of matter. Thus before (i.e. to) you I have narrated my function. Everyday I well nourish the body with nectar. Such is my operation in the dear city of the body. Know[2] the tongue to be my minister who very much enjoys the tastes.

Nāsikā (*Nose*) *said*:

54b-56. I give great nourishment to the body with fragrance. Casting off bad odour, I manifest (good) odour over the body. O you illustrious one, united with Buddhi, and displayed by her existence, I remain steady in this body for the mission of my master. Know odour to be my quality which proceeds in two ways.

1. The five forms of Vāyu are: Prāṇa, Apāna, Vyāna, Udāna, Samāna.
2. Before this verse some such words as 'Āpaḥ ūcuḥ' are missing.

The two Ears said :

57-58. Remaining in our body (i.e. the body to which we belong), we hear words telling about what ought or ought not to be done, and also auspicious and inauspicious words, true and false words, pleasant and unpleasant words uttered by people. My (i.e. our) quality is sound, and there is no doubt that I (i.e. we) employ my (i.e. our) operation when the intellect would intensify me (i.e. us).

The Skin said:

59-62a. The five-formed wind is well-settled without and within the body. I feel the movement of these (five forms). I feel cold, hot, sun, rain, and throbbing of the wind. I feel every touch, every contact (with) phlegm etc. of men. My quality is touch alone. I am telling the truth. Thus I have told you about my function.

The two Eyes said :

62b-64a. O best one, when the Intellect urges, and not otherwise, we observe all proper and improper forms that exist in the world. We remain in the body, and form is our quality. Thus is the propriety of our function in the body, O you highly intelligent one.

The Tongue spoke:

64b-66a. O dear one, united with Buddhi, I spread the kinds of taste. I find out every (taste) like saline, sour, insipid or sweet. Always associated with this function, I remain (in the body). This Intellect is the leader of all the sense-organs.

66b-67a. O dear one, listen, thus these five sense-organs have come together; and they again and again narrated their respective functions.

67b-68. Then Intellect approached the very intelligent one and said to him: "When the body is without me, it perishes; not otherwise. Therefore, O you highly intelligent one (i.e. Ātman), carry on, after having resorted to flesh (i.e. body).

69-70a. Then Karma (Fate) came there and said this (i.e. these words) to Ātman: "O you very wise one, I am Karma, and have approached you. I send you along the path by which you go here (i.e. in the world)."

70b-72a. Having heard all that, Ātman said to them: "You are united with the five-natured ones and are indeed common to all. Why do you seek the friendship of the five-natured one? You may (please) tell before (i.e. to) me the entire reason."

The five-natured ones said:

72b-74a. Due to our contact the body is produced; O you of a high intelligence, you who follow a good vow, stay in that body. Due to your favour all of us (also) stay there. For this reason we always desire your friendship.

Ātman said:

74b-75a. O illustrious ones, let that, which is dear to you, be so. There is no doubt that I shall befriend you through affection.

75b-76a. The glorious and high-minded one, though warded off by the noble Jñāna and also by Dhyāna, sought their company.

76b-77a. Then the lord, being deluded by attachment and hatred, and associated with the five elements, became embodied.

77b-80a. When he (i.e. Ātman) goes to the womb (i.e. is conceived), he, fallen into the lubricious eddy, full of excrement and urine, along with them, with his body distressed, said to the five-natured ones. "O you five-natured ones, all of you listen to my words. Due to your contact, I, being deluded by great grief, have fallen into this lubricious, very terrible and fearful (eddy)."

The five-natured ones said :

80b-82a. O lord, remain there till the foetus is full (i.e. mature). Then, there is no doubt that, you will come out of it. You are our lord, settled in the region of the body. Thus you should rule; you will be enjoying pleasures.

82b-83. Hearing those words of (i.e. uttered by) them, Ātman, oppressed by grief, and desiring to go (away), became intent on running (away).

CHAPTER EIGHT

Account of the Soul

Kaśyapa said :

1. He, being afflicted day by day, became bewildered in the womb. The rightenous one, harassed by all kinds of suffering, was overcome with grief.

2. With his face turned down he remained in the womb. He was overcome with mental agonies and physical diseases; he was lamented over; he was senseless.

3a. He was full of great grief. Being (thus) tormented, he said to Jñāna:

Ātman said:

3b-4. O you very wise one, at that time I did not do what you told me (to do). In spite of being prevented by Dhyāna, I fell into the danger caused by delusion. Therefore, O you highly intelligent one, protect me from this very fearful stay in the womb.

Jñāna said :

5. O Ātman, you were prevented by me; but you did not do what I told (you). You were put in this calamity of (remaining in) the womb by the very cruel five-natured ones. Now go to Dhyāna; you will obtain pleasure from him (in it). There is no doubt that you will be free from the residence in the womb.

6-8a. Understanding (i.e. hearing) those words—the fact—from (i.e. spoken by) Jñāna, he, having called Dhyāna, said (to him): "Please listen to my words. O Dhyāna, I have sought your refuge. (Please) protect me always."

8b. "Let it be so, O you very wise one." Thus Dhyāna spoke to that highly intelligent one (i.e. Ātman).

9. Hearing these words, Ātman then approached Dhyāna. With Dhyāna, and free from delusion, he lived in the womb.

10-11. When Ātman went to Dhyāna, he forgot the fear caused by (remaining in) the womb. The Ātman accompanied by the two (i.e. Jñāna and Dhyāna) and dissociated from delusion (remained) thinking about his own happiness only. "As soon as

I go out of this (womb) I shall give up the body formed by the five-natured ones."

12-19. The lord, living in the womb, always thought like this. O you of a beautiful face, at the time of the delivery of the one related to Prajāpati the foetus is shaken by wind, and also by the strong breath of life. The vulva expands (only) twenty-four fingers; the foetus is (of the size of) twentyfive fingers; therefore he is troubled. O dear one, thus being troubled by swoon, he falls, with Jñāna and Dhyāna, on the ground, . He is separated from it by the divine wind related to Prajāpati. Merely by the touch of the ground, Jñāna and Dhyāna are forgotten. Ātman, confounded in the bondage of the worldly existence, remains there through love (for it). Filled with virtues and vices, and connected with great delusion, he everyday desires everything like eatables and drinks. Ātman thus being nourished with the five-natured ones is covered over with the sense-organs and all sinful objects of senses. O respectable lady, enticed by his relatives like his wife and others, day by day he becomes afflicted and agitated.

20-21a. This lord, Ātman, confounded by great delusion, (and thus) caught in the net of delusion, and being bound, as a fish is bound in a net by a fisherman, is unable to move.

21b-23. He is bound with strong bonds of the nets of infatuation. Deprived of Jñāna and Vijñāna, and struck by attachment and hatred, he is thus pervaded by the pervading universe. Being tormented by desire, and also by anger and bound by Prakṛti (i.e. the natural disposition) by means of his deeds, he became (i.e. becomes) greatly confounded.

Sūta said:

24-25. When Ātman was thus deluded and was occupied with all the wicked ones like greed, attachment, he was bound by the delusion of the form of the worldly existence like: 'This is (my) wife; this is (my) son; this is (my) friend; this is (my) house.'

26. He is then distressed by griefs like bereavement of the

son etc., and is also consumed by old age, physical diseases and mental agonies also.

27. Thus Ātman is tormented by very fearful misery and delusion; and is frustrated by pride, humiliation and many miseries.

28. O respectable lady, he is, in the same way, troubled by old age in various ways. Constantly lamented over and senseless he thinks of misery (only).

29. At night he sees dreams, and by day he is without vitality. O respectable lady, similarly, day by day, he is full of the imperfections of the limbs.

30. When he was wandering in the mundane existence, he saw Vairāgya (i.e. detachment), that was fearless, friendless, very tranquil and contented.

31-32. Then Ātman spoke to him, that was free from desire and anger: "Who are you (remaining) with a naked form? How is it that you are not ashamed of your friends? Moving in the place where there are groups (of the elements), women, old persons, young women and mothers, you, who are uncovered, are not afraid (i.e. are not ashamed)."

Vītarāga said :

33-34. Who would be seen naked here? I am never naked. Even though you are well-dressed, you are very much bound. O divine one, I am never naked. You who live under the sway of the objects of senses and are without (i.e. do not care for) any bounds of morality appear to be naked.

Ātman said:

35. O you of a good vow, tell me in detail what the bounds of morality are, if you know them definitely.

36-37a. The very wise, very intelligent Vītarāga said to him: "The mind resorts to great firmness in (times of) happiness and unhappiness. And (when) it is troubled by respective objects, it should be given up to them.

37b-38. I shall now explain to you the sense of shame, which fully enters the mind. I have nothing to do today; I am removed from my position, I am naked—(when thus) one is absorbed in remorse, that is said to be the sense of shame.

39. Of whom should one be ashamed? There is never a second. The divine Puruṣa (Person) is just one. What would he destroy and of whom?

40-42. Now I shall explain to you the groups which you mentioned. As a potter would put a lump of clay on the wheel, and then would cause it to revolve with a string, and would, with a firm mind, manifest (i.e. fashion) them (i.e. the pots) as he desires, in the same way—and in no other way—the creator fashions various forms. Later, for one reason or another, they perish.

43. One should be ashamed of the eternal groups (of the elements) that always remain, for they do not rest (i.e. depend) on the earth.

44. They are: Ether, Wind, Fire, Earth and Water as the fifth. These groups, that are present everywhere, shine.

45. These five well-settled in the regions of the bodies of beings, are present everywhere. (Then) of whom should one be ashamed?

46-47a. O dear one, I shall now explain to you the nature of women. As in thousands of pots with (i.e. containing) water the one (and only) moon shines (i.e. is reflected), similarly you shine everywhere.

47b-54a. You, who are very magnanimous, and who, remain in thousands of beings, and in the mobile and the immobile, are deluded. Through the door (i.e. opening) of the vulva, which is sinful and full of illusion and delusion, and also through the breasts and buttocks and age, you shine. Here also is seen the increase in (the shape of) the heart and flesh. For the fall of the people the form of delusion is manifested. There is no woman that is mentioned by you. The creator ever fashions the creation for his diversion. The soul of the man like that of a woman remains everywhere. Those that are free from breasts (i.e. from sexual desire) are always liberated. Man is called Puruṣa (i.e. the soul) and woman is said to be Prakṛti (i.e. nature, original source of the material world). She sports with him and is never free. You, united with Prakṛti, are seen among Puruṣas (i.e. men). Who causes shame (and) to whom? Knowing thus go happily.

54b-56. O beautiful lady, I shall explain to you the old woman who is always old. The skin on her body, O lady of a beautiful face, is worn out. She is full of white and grey Hair. She is feeble, miserable and is covered over with folds. Such a woman would not be old; but she is called old.

57-58a. I have narrated her characteristics. Now I shall tell (the characteristics of) a young woman. She, living near the soul, always grows richer in knowledge. She is called Sumati (i.e. good intention), and is both old and young. The woman is always settled in puruṣas (i.e. souls). One should be ashamed of her. I shall also tell (you something) else.

58b-62a. I shall explain to you the mother, whom you mentioned. She is Cetanā (i.e. consciousness) always living in the bodies of beings. She gives the highest knowledge, and (therefore) she is called Prajñā (i.e. discernment). Prajñā is called mother as she lives in all the worlds for the protection, nourishment and well-fare of beings. That one who is described as Sumati, is called mātā (i.e. mother).

62b-63. All the forms always leading to the gates of the mundane existence are these mothers. They cause great misery. I have explained to you the nature of the mother. What else should I tell you?"

Ātman said :

64. Who are you, that have come here, and are removing my tormentation? (Please) explain to me in detail your own nature.

Vītarāga said :

65-67a. Well-being to you; I am Vītarāga, from whom all desires, being frustrated, turn away; whom these vile deeds do not see due to their wickedness—this has no alternative; whom hope never approaches; due to whose fear anger, greed and infatuation have perished; and Viveka (i.e. discrimination) is my brother.

Ātman said :

67b-68a. Of what nature is this your brother named Viveka? Tell me his—your brother's characteristics and also of your own.

Vītarāga said :

68b-70a. I shall not narrate before (i.e. to) you his characteristics and form. O glorious one, I shall (just) call that brother (himself). O Viveka, my brother, listen to our speech (i.e. words). O you very glorious one, O you very intelligent one, (please) come out of affection for me.

Kaśyapa said :

70b-76. He, omniscient, omnipresent, pervading, devoted entirely to truth, the enemy of all errors, and lover of knowledge came (there) with his two wives, Śānti (Tranquility) and Kṣamā (Forbearance). Dhāraṇā (Retentive memory) and Dhī (understanding) are the two daughters of the same magnanimous one (Viveka). Yoga (Abstract meditation) in his eldest son, and Mokṣa (salvation) is his great preceptor. That Viveka, who is spotless, ego-less, desire-less, having no possession, with his mind pleased at all times, free from the pairs of opposites (like pleasure and pain) and hihgly intelligent one, came (there) adorned with all jewels. That Viveka, whose ministers were the very glorious and highly intelligent Dharma (Piety) and Satya (Truth) came (there), accompanied by Kṣamā and Śānti. He said to Vītrarāga: "Invited (by you) I have come. So, O brother, tell before (i.e. to) me the full reason resorting to (i.e. for) which you have invited me."

Vītarāga said :

77-79. This man, who is before (us) is restrained by great nooses, is deluded by Moha's arrows, and also by the bonds of the worldly existence. He pervades everything, and is the master of all, and also of me. He is seized by the five elements; and is bereft of Jñāna and Dhyāna. You who know facts should ask this Ātman.

Hearing the words of Vītarāga, Viveka spoke these words:

Viveka said :

80. O lord of the universe, you are carrying on happily, What pleasure did you yourself enjoy after coming to the worldly existence?

Ātman said :

81-86. O you highly intelligent one, I, void of knowledge, always experienced the great, unbearable and terrible grief of the residence in the womb. Being deprived of knowledge while in the body, I was born in many ways. When I was in childhood, O lord, I did undeserving deeds. As a youth I sported, and enjoyed my wife in many ways. When I reached old age I was tormented by the grief of (i.e. the bereavement of my) son etc. Due to the separation from my wife etc. I was burnt day and night. Everyday I was tormented by miseries of many kinds. O you highly intelligent one, I am not at all having any pleasure by day or at night. O you very intelligent one, what do (i.e. should) I, very much tormented by agonies, do (now)? Just tell me the means by which I shall get happiness. (Please) make me free from this great bond—this heap of the noose of the mundane existence.

Viveka said :

87-93. O you lord of the world, you are pure, you are free from the pairs (like pleasure and pain), and are free from sins. Go to this glorious Vītarāga, who gives happiness, whom you have undoubtedly seen naked and without any formality. He shows (the way to) happiness and destroys all distress.

Hearing thus (i.e. these words), the pure soul again went to Vītarāga. The melancholy one, sighing deeply, said to him (i.e. to Vītarāga): "(Please) listen to my words. Show me that way by (i.e. following) which I shall get happiness." "O very intelligent one, let it be so. I shall do as you tell me. Again go to Viveka; you have told me a pleasant news. He (i.e. Viveka) only will tell you the way to happiness." The lord, (thus) sent by virtuous Vītarāga, went (to Viveka); and spoke to the glorious, pure and best Viveka: "(Please), show me (the way to) happiness. Sent by Vītarāga, I have sought your refuge. Protect me from the frightful worldly existence."

Viveka said :

94a. O you very wise one, go to Jñāna; he will explain everything to you.

94b-95. Ātman, thus told, went to the place where Jñāna stayed. (He said to Jñāna): "O Jñāna of great lustre and illumining all objects, I have sought your refuge; show me the way to happiness."

Jñāna said :

96-97. O lord of the worlds, I am your servant. O you of a good vow, you do not know (i.e. you have not recognised) me. Formerly Dhyāna and I had repeatedly warded you off. Due to your contact with the five-natured ones (i.e. the elements), you have met with a calamity. O you highly intelligent one, go to Dhyāna, he will grant you happiness.

98-105. Sent by Jñāna, Ātman remained after having resorted to Dhyāna. (He said to Dhyāna): "O Dhyāna, show me the happiness that is perfectly accomplished. Thus protect me who have sought your shelter." Dhyāna having heard these words spoken to him by Ātman, was delighted, and again said to that Ātman: "O dear one, well-determined in (doing) all deeds, by you and by Vītarāga and Viveka, I am never to be forsaken. Be endowed with Dhyāna, and observe yourself, by being self-possessed, firm, free from fear and doubt. You will go to (i.e. obtain) salvation by burning (i.e. destroying) your blemishes, as a lamp in a place sheltered from wind is firm and emits soot. Always remain in a secluded place; remain without food (or) with limited food. Be without the pairs of opposites (like pleasure and pain), without words, and firmly remaining on your seat. Reflecting, with a firm mind, on your self only you will reach that highest place of Viṣṇu, (which is also) my place."

CHAPTER NINE

Instructions to Diti

Kaśyapa said :

1-2. The intelligent Ātman, thus addressed by Dhyāna and others, desiring to give up the product of the five-natured ones, and finding out motives, abandoning his aimless body, which he did not notice when it fell down, went to them.

3. There is no connection between life and body that were brought up together. For what reason is there a relation with wealth, sons or wife?

4-13a. O you very dear one, realising thus, be calm; do not be weak-minded. He alone is the highest Brahman; he alone is eternal. This Ātman lives in demons and gods in his own nature. He is Brahmā; he is Rudra; he is the eternal Viṣṇu. He creates all things; he protects the beings. This (Ātman) Janārdana (i.e. Viṣṇu), the pious one and of the nature of virtue withdraws (all). O you very dear one, he has created gods and demons. Gods are liberated due to their piety (while) your sons are wanting in piety. This virtue is Viṣṇu's body, preserved by all gods. O respectable lady, one (i.e. a man) should think about proper conduct and follow proper conduct only. The meritorious Viṣṇu always favours him. Gods always lived with piety, truth and penances. Those, with whom Viṣṇu is pleased, have practised virtue here (i.e. in this world). This proper conduct is the body of Viṣṇu and truth is his heart. Viṣṇu is pleased with him who always practises them. He, who would defile truth and piety would always have sin. The very powerful Viṣṇu would be angry with him and would destroy him. Viṣṇu's devotees, abiding by truth and penance practised piety. The virtuous one is pleased with them and protects them thus.

13b-14. Your sons, as well as the sons of Danu and Siṁhikā, who were wicked-hearted, and who lived by (i.e. committed) impiety and sins, were killed in battle by Viṣṇu, having the disc in his hand.

15-17. That Ātman whom I formerly described before (i.e. to) you only, is Viṣṇu (himself); there is no doubt about it. He is meritorious and is the guardian of all. He who lived comfortably in the bodies of the demons, resorted to sin only. He, O respectable lady, the highly intelligent one, became angry, and killed the demons. Being within and without he struck down your sons. O respectable lady, they were struck down by him who had created them.

18-19a. You should not have any infatuation for them. Listen (to my words). He who lives sinfully, dies (i.e. perishes). Therefore, give up infatuation, and always practise piety.

Diti said :

19b-20. Let it be so, O glorious one; I shall do as you have told me.

She, who was afflicted, and who was addressed by the sage, gave up her sorrow, after having said these words.

CHAPTER TEN

The Practice of Penance by Demons

The sages said :

1-2. O you very intelligent one, what effort did all the demons, who were accompanied by Hiraṇyakaśipu and had fled from the battle, do? Tell us in detail their excellent account. O brāhmaṇa, we all now desire to hear it from you.

Sūta said :

3. All the demons who had fled from the battle, who had become powerless, prideless and distressed with grief, went to their father.

4-5a. Having devoutly saluted (their father) Kaśyapa, they then said to him:

The demons said :

O best brāhmaṇa, we demons are born from your semen, so also are gods.

5b-9. All we demons are strong, powerful and brave; we also are knowers of expedients; we are very courageous and full of exertion. We are many, and the gods are few. How is it that they are victorious and we, endowed with power and lustre, have fled from the great battle? What is the reason for that, O father? Each one of the demons has the strength of a thousand intoxicated elephants. The gods do not have (strength) like that; and yet in the great war victory is had by the gods. So (please) tell (the reason for) all this. Please remove (our) doubt.

Kaśyapa said :

10-12a. O all my sons, listen to the reason for the victory (of the gods)—due to which the gods became victorious in the battle. The father is the giver of the semen (i.e. the seed); and the mother is always the soil. She conceives, protects and nourishes (her son). What would a father do in the case of a son whose intentions are fearful?

12b-18. Here (the son's) fate is (i.e. his deeds are) important (i.e. responsible). This is what I think. Association with Karma is due to two things: sin and merit. Proper conduct can be practised by resorting to truth only. Truth endowed with penance and meditation leads to emancipation, O (my) sons. There is no doubt about this that (even) with power, (good) attendants and nobility of birth, sin always leads to a fall, O (my) sons. All that power (etc.) of him who is without religious merit is impaired. O (my) good sons, there are tall and dense trees on the mountains and inaccessible places, (but) by the force of the wind they fall down along with their roots. Similarly those who are without truth and piety go to Yama's abode. O (my) good sons, this is a common rule (applicable) to (all) beings. You have abandoned the truth associated with piety, due to which a being is emancipated here (i.e. in this) and the next world.

19-24. O (my) sons, you, who were destitute of truth, have resorted to impiety. Fallen from truth, piety and penance, you have fallen into the ocean of grief; and (i.e. on the other hand) the gods who are endowed with truth and virtue, and with penance, tranquility and restraint, have a great religious merit and are sinless. Victory is seen there where there are truth, piety, penance, religious merit and Viṣṇu Hṛṣīkeśa. Eternal Vāsudeva i.e. Viṣṇu helps them (only). Therefore, gods endowed with truth and piety become victorious with (Viṣṇu as their) helper and also due to power and valour. O (my) sons, you are destitute of penance and truth. Those who are conversant with (laws of) morality, know that that man who has Viṣṇu as his helper, and who has penance and power is alone seen to get victory.

25. You are without piety and also deprived of penance and truth, and you had also formerly secured Indra's position by force.

26. O (my) very intelligent sons, Indra's position cannot be obtained without penance, piety and glory (and merely) with qualities of power and pride.

27-28. O sons, those getting Indra's position (without penance, piety etc.) fall from it. Therefore, O (my) sons, you (should) together practise penance without quarrel and endowed with knowledge and meditation. You should never entertain enmity with Keśava (i.e. Viṣṇu).

29. O (my) sons, when you will be blessed like this; then (only) you will obtain highest success; there is no doubt about this.

30-31. Thus told by the noble Kaśyapa, the very vigorous demons, having listened to the words of their father, devoutly saluted Kaśyapa and rising hastily, gathered together and held thorough consultation among themselves.

32-34. Then king Hiraṇyakaśipu said to the demons: "We shall (now) practise penance difficult to practise (but) giving everything." At that time Hiraṇyākṣa said : "I shall practise terrible penance. Then with (my) power I shall seize (all) the three worlds. There is no doubt about this. Having vanquished in battle that wicked-hearted Govinda (i.e. Viṣṇu) and having killed all gods, I shall reach Indra's position."

Bali said :

35. O lords—the sons of Diti—it is not proper for you to act like this. That enmity which you have with Viṣṇu, is the cause of destruction.

36. Men obtain happiness by propitiating that Hṛṣīkeśa (i.e. Viṣṇu) with charity, religious merit, penance, and performance of sacrifices.

Hiraṇyakaśipu said :

37-38. Like this (i.e. as advised by Bali) I shall never propitiate Hari (i.e. Viṣṇu). The wise ones take it to be excelling death if one, by giving up one's nature, serves one's enemy. Neither I nor other demons will serve Viṣṇu.

39-43. Then Bali again said to that magnanimous grandfather (of him) : "This is what is observed in the codes of laws by sages knowing truth—an advice full of statesmanship—especially regarding an enemy. Knowing oneself to be inferior, and the enemy to be powerful one should go near the enemy and wait for the time (i.e. opportunity) for victory. Darkness always stays by resorting to the shadow of a lamp. Darkness knowing the oiliness of the wick of the lamp and the very powerful light, goes to it and increases. Similarly remaining screened, and showing love actually, O demons, you should form friendship with gods following piety.

44. O prudent king of kings, formerly sage Kaśyapa has given good advice; do your deeds in accordance with it."

45. Having heard those words of (i.e. uttered by) him, the powerful demon said : "O grandson, I shall not humiliate myself like this."

46-48a. Other kinsmen also said to him who was proficient in statesmanship : "What Bali said is meritorious and dear to the gods; what he said would increase Indra's pride and is fearful to the demons. All of us will just practise excellent penance. Having vanquished the gods with penance, we shall forcibly (regain) our position."

48b-50. Having thus conversed and having repudiated Bali at that time, the great demons entertaining great enmity with Viṣṇu in their heart, practised penance in mountaneous inaccessible places and (mountain-) peaks. Thus the demons had abandoned attachment, were well-determined, were free from desire and anger, remained without food and had overcome fatigue.

CHAPTER ELEVEN

The Story of Suvrata

The sages said :

1. You, the omniscient one, have narrated (to us the account of) the war between (the gods and) the demons. Now we desire to hear (the account) of the noble Suvrata.

2. Of whom was he—the very intelligent one—the son? In whose family was he born? What (kind of) penance did the brāhmaṇa have (i.e. practise)? How did he propitiate Hari (i.e. Viṣṇu)?

Sūta said :

3-4. O brāhmaṇas, I shall tell you the account of the noble Suvrata as I had heard it due to the power of my intelligence. I shall tell you, with Viṣṇu's favour, the divine, purifying account bringing the Viṣṇuite merit (to the narrator and the listener).

5-7. O illustrious ones, in the former Kalpa, the best brāhmaṇa, named Somaśarman was born in Kauśika's family at an excellent sacred place which removed sins and which was very meritorious, named Vāmana, on the bank of Revā. Being sonless and full of great grief, he was always oppressed by painful poverty. Day and night he thought about the means (to have) a son and wealth also.

8-12. Once his dear wife, Sumanā by name, and of a good vow, saw her husband full of worry and with his face hung down. The devout (woman), seeing her husband (like that) said to him: "Your mind is overpowered by innumerable worries. You are confounded by infatuation. O you very intelligent one, give up your worry (i.e. stop worrying). Tell me (about) your worry. Be composed and happy. There is no (other) distress like worry which parches up the body. He who lives by giving up his worries, enjoys happily. O Brāhmaṇa, tell me the cause of your worry." Hearing the words of his beloved (wife) Somaśarman said to her :

Somaśarman said :

13. Thoughts (are) due to desire, O good lady; and thinking is the cause of grief. I shall tell you all that. Having heard it, understand it accurately.

14. O you of a good vow, I do not know due to which sin I am poor and sonless. This is the cause of my grief.

Sumanā said :

15-16. Listen. What I say will remove all doubts; the advice (should be such as) shows the correct knowledge. Greed is the seed of sin, and delusion is its root. Falsehood is its trunk, and deceit is its well-expanded branch.

17-22. Religious hypocrisy and crookedness are its leaves; it is always flowered with wicked intellect. Deception is its fragrance, and ignorance is its fruit. The sinful cruel birds like dishonesty, heresy, theft, envy have resorted to the branch of deceit of the tree of delusion. Its good fruit is ignorance; and the juice of the fruit is unrighteousness. Nourished by the water of thirst (i.e. desire) faithlessness is its exudation, O dear one. The good juice of it viz. impiety is (felt to be) superior and becomes sweet, and the tree of greed has fruits of such a type only. That man who is happy after resorting to its shadow, who everyday eats its very ripe fruits, and who is nourished by the juice of fruits i.e. impiety, becomes pleased and proceeds towards a fall.

23-27. Therefore giving up worrying a man should not have greed. He should not at all worry about wealth, sons and wife. Even if he is a learned person he goes along the path of fools, O dear one (if he worries). Everyday a fool thinks: 'How can I get wealth? How can I get a good wife? How can I have sons?' Being deluded, he thinks like this day and night. (Just) for a moment he (is deluded and) finds great pleasure while worrying; again he comes to his senses and is oppressed by great grief. O brāhmaṇa, give up worry and delusion and act. O you highly intelligent one, nobody has (any) connection with anyone (else) in the worldly existence.

28. Friends, relatives, sons, fathers and mothers with servants, and wives come to have a (chance) relation with a man.

Somaśarman said :

29. In the same way, O good lady, tell (me) in detail what kind of relation is there, by which wealth, sons and other relatives become related.

Sumanā said :

30. Some are relations through debt; some are those who had taken away (other's) wealth; some are helpful; others are indifferent.

31-35. Sons, friends or wives are born (and are) of (these) four kinds. So also wife, father, mother, servants, relatives and friends are born on the earth in accordance with their connection with a person. The person, whose deposit was taken away by another person becomes the latter's virtuous and handsome son on the earth—(is born) in the house of him who has taken away his deposit; there is no doubt about this; because he had left after giving him terrible grief by taking away his deposit. O glorious one, the owner of the deposit becomes the good son of him who had taken away his deposit; he is virtuous, handsome, and is endowed with all good characteristics. Being (born) as his son, he everyday shows devotion to him.

36-38. He speaks sweetly, is attractive and healthy, and shows great love for him; producing excellent love in him by being born as his son and by means of his great qualities, he gives him the same terrible fatal grief by taking away his wealth as he had given him by taking away his deposit in a former existence. So also being short-lived, he dies (a premature death).

39-40a. Thus again and again he is born, gives grief, and dies. When he (i.e. the father) laments, 'Oh my son !' he (i.e. the son) just laughs. So who is whose son and who is the father?

40b-42. (The son says:) "The deposit that was helpful to me was taken away by him. Even by taking away the wealth my life did not formerly depart, even due to great, unbearable grief. Therefore, giving him grief and taking away excellent wealth I shall today go. Whose son am I, who am like this?

43. He is not my father, nor was he the son of anyone. To this wicked one only I have given the state of a goblin."

44-45. Speaking like this, he repeatedly laughs, and goes. Giving him very terrible grief, he goes along this way. O dear one, thus (persons) become the sons of them who had taken away their deposits. Everywhere in the mundane existence, (fathers) full of great grief are seen.

46. I shall later explain to you the son connected (with the father) through debt.

CHAPTER TWELVE

Dialogue between Somaśarman and Sumanā

Sumanā said :

1-3. (Now) hereafter I shall describe to you the son who is related through debt. He, from whom a man takes a loan dies—i.e. the creditor, being (i.e. is born as) the son or the brother or the father, or might be (born as) a friend (and) is always very cruel, O dear one. The cruel one of a rough form, does not notice the virtue (in others), and always utters harsh words among his relatives.

4-7. He always eats sweets and desired articles (of food) and enjoys pleasures. He is ever engaged in gambling and has a desire to steal. He forcibly enjoys the wealth which is in the house (i.e. wealth of the family) and gets angry if prevented (from doing so). Everyday he abuses his father and mother. He is a thief, causes fear and talks too much and harshly. Thus enjoying that wealth (of the family etc.) he lives happily. Being very cruel he makes money by means of birth-rites in childhood, and in many ways through various kinds of marriages.

8-10. Thus wealth is obtained by him and he gives it in this way also. (He thinks:) 'The house, field etc. are mine. There is no doubt about it.' Everyday he hits his father and mother with pestles by giving them many very fearful strokes. When his father or mother is dead, he who is very cruel becomes affectionless and rough. There is no doubt about it.

11. He never performs the Śrāddha-rites and never gives gifts. Sons of this type are born on the earth.

12-16a. O best of brāhmaṇas, I shall explain to you a hostile son. When he reaches childhood, he always behaves like an enemy (with his parents). Even while playing he would beat his father and mother; and after repeatedly beating them he laughs and departs. Again being fearful, he comes to his father and mother; and after repeatedly beating them he laughs and departs. Again being fearful, he comes to his father and mother. He is always angry; and again and again abuses (them). Thus he is always engaged in hostile acts. Having again beaten his father, and also his mother, the wicked one departs as a result of the former enmity.

16b-21. Now hereafter I shall describe the son from whom desired things can be obtained. As soon as he is born he does dear things to (i.e. pleases) his parents, and (delights them) by indulgence and sports in childhood; and immediately after he attains youth he does things liked by his mother and father. With devotion he pleases and delights them by means of affectionate words and conversation dear to them. When he comes to know about the demise of his parent, he weeps through affection (for the parent). Extremely grieved, he performs all rites like Śrāddha and offering piṇḍas. He also offers them maintenance. Conforming to (the repayment of) the three debts, he always feeds them. O you very intelligent one, O my dear husband, being their son he returns in this manner whatever would be (i.e. is) obtained from them.

22-24a. O dear one, now I shall describe to you (the son called) indifferent. He does not give and now receives; he is neither angry, nor pleased. O best of brāhmaṇas, an indifferent (son) does not give by making a sacrifice. I have told you everything—i.e. this mode of existence (of various types) of sons.

24b-35a. Like the son are the wife, the father, the mother and the kinsmen; so also are said to be the others (like) the servants, beasts and horses; so also elephants, buffaloes and attendants. All these are connected through debt. We have for that reason not taken a debt from anyone; so also in the former existence we have not made any deposit with anyone. O dear husband, we are not indebted to anyone. (Please) listen. We have no hostility with anyone which is entertained in a previous existence. O my husband, O best brāhmaṇa, we have not given up anything. Realising this, be calm and give up (your) worry causing unhappiness. Whose are the sons, or whose is the dear wife? Whose are the relatives and friends? You have never snatched (anything) from anyone and have given nothing to anyone. Then how can wealth come to us? O my husband, do not have any doubt. O best brāhmaṇa, whatever wealth is to be obtained, it easily comes to the hand (of a person). A man preserves wealth with great care; but the departing one (i.e. the one that dies) departs (all alone); but the wealth remains just there. Realising this, give up your worry which is useless and be calm. Whose are the sons? Whose is the dear wife? Whose are the relatives and friends? O best brāhmaṇa, in this mundane existence, nobody belongs to none (else), since there is no connection (between the two). Men of wicked hearts and deluded with great infatuation (say:) 'This is my house; this is my son; the women are mine only.' O dear husband, this bond of the mundane existence is seen to be unreal.

35b-36a. Thus advised by his dear wife, the respectable lady, he again spoke to his dear wife Sumanā, who expounded knowledge.

Somaśarman said :

36b-38a. O good lady, you have spoken the truth, which has removed all (my) doubt. Still good men, really wise men become fascinated (with all these). O dear one, as I am anxious to have a son, I am also anxious to have wealth. I shall produce (i.e. have) a son by this or that means.

Sumanā said :

38b-43a. A man conquers the worlds with a son; a son emancipates the family. Due to a good son alone the father and the mother are (i.e. proved to be) living beings. One learned son is most precious. What is the use of having many worthless sons? The first (i.e. the good) one emancipates the family, (while) the others cause tormentation. I have previously only told (you) that others are (just) relations. Due to religious merit (only) a son is obtained; (similarly) due to religious merit (birth in a good) family is obtained. A good embryo is obtained by religious merit; therefore practise religious merit. One that is born gets death (i.e. is sure to die); and one that dies gets birth. Due to meritorious acts a good birth (i.e. birth in a good family) is obtained, so also is obtained (peaceful) death; and O dear husband, he obtains happiness and wealth due to meritorious deeds.

Somaśarman said :

43b-44a. O dear one, tell me about the practice of good deeds, and also about the (various) existences. Of what nature is a man of meritorious deeds? (i.e. What are the characteristics of the man of meritorious deeds?) O good lady, tell (me) the characteristics of religious merit.

Sumanā said :

44b-45. I shall first explain to you (what) merit (is), as I have heard about it; and also (I shall explain to you) how a man or a woman behaves everyday, and how by means of meritorious deeds he or she obtains fame, dear sons and wealth.

46a. O dear husband, I shall tell you all the characteristics of merit.

46b-48. One should practise virtue which has these ten components viz. celibacy, truthfulness, performance of five sacrifices,[1] charity, restraint, forbearance, purity, harmlessness, good prowess and non-stealing, O dear one. Complete merit is produced as satisfaction (is produced) in the belly by mouthfuls (of food after they are swallowed).

49-50a. A righteous person creates Dharma by means of three kinds of acts. Dharma, with his heart pleased leads him to religious merit only. The wise one gets whatever he desires (even though it is) difficult to obtain.

1. Pañcamakha—The five daily sacrifices or acts of piety to be performed by a householder: (1) Brahmayajña i.e. teaching; (2) Pitṛyajña i.e. offering oblations to the manes; (3) Devayajña i.e. performing sacrificial rites; (4) Bhūtayajña i.e. an offering to all created beings; and (5) Nṛyajña i.e. honouring guests.

Somaśarman said :

50b. O you beautiful lady, what kind of form does Dharma have? What are the parts of his (body)? O my dear wife, kindly tell (it) to me; strong desire (to hear it) is produced (in me).

Sumanā said :

51-60. O best brāhmaṇa, in this world none has seen the form of Dharma. He, of a true nature and with his course seen by none, is not seen (even) by gods and demons. The brāhmaṇa Dattātreya, Anasūyā's son and born in Atri's family has always seen that great Dharma. The two noble ones (i.e. Dattātreya and Durvāsas) practising excellent penances, behaving righteously, shining with a more praiseworthy form than that of (even) Indra due to penance and prowess, remained for ten thousand years in a forest; the two of a charming appearance ate (i.e. lived on) wind or went without food. For ten thousand years they practised penance. Merit was observed in them who practised penance. O best brāhmaṇa, they both performed the (vow of) five fires till (i.e. during) that period (of ten thousand years). They practised it for all the three times and (during that period) did not eat food. Dattātreya and the sage (Durvāsas) remained in water during that period. The best sage Durvāsas was tormented by penance. The best sage got angry with Dharma. O noble one, when the best sage was (thus) angry, the intelligent Dharma came there in his own form along with Celibacy etc. and Austerities.

61-68. Truth in the form of a brāhmaṇa, also Celibacy, similarly Penance in the form of an excellent brāhmaṇa, and Restraint as an intelligent excellent brāhmaṇa, so also Control, and Charity in the form of a brāhmaṇa maintaining the sacred fire and offering oblations to it, came to (Durvāsas), the son of Atri. O best brāhmaṇa, all these having female forms, viz. Forbearance, Tranquility, Shame, Harmlessness, and Imagination, arrived there. So also Intellect, Wisdom, Faith, Retentive Faculty, Good Act, Tranquility, all the five Sacrifices, the holy Vedas with their limbs (i.e. the Vedāṅgas), were ready. The Consecration of Fire, the holy Horse-sacrifices and others, endowed with good forms and handsomeness, adorned with all (kinds of) ornaments, wearing divine flowers and garments, besmeared with divine sandal, endowed with crowns and earrings and adorned with divine ornaments, bright and handsome, filled with lustrous flames (came there). Thus Dharma, accompanied by his retinue came there where the angry Durvāsas remained like death.

Dharma said :

69-70. O brāhmaṇa, why are you angry? You are endowed with penance. There is no doubt that anger would destroy virtue and penance. Anger destroys everything; therefore one should avoid anger. O best brāhmaṇa, be at ease; the fruit of penance is excellent.

Durvāsas said :

71-72a. Who are you that have come with these best brāhmaṇas? Seven beautiful and well-adorned women are standing (by you). O you highly intelligent one, tell me in detail (as to who you are etc.).

Dharma said :

72b-73. See, in front of you has come this Brahmacarya (i.e. Celibacy), in the form of a brāhmaṇa, endowed with all lustre, well-pleased, having a staff in his hand and holding a water-pot.

74-76. O best brāhmaṇa, see this other bright one viz. Satya (i.e. Truth), tawny (in complexion) and having reddish-brown eyes. Similarly, O you pious one, see this Tapas (i.e. Penance), lustrous like all gods, the one that you practised and resorting to all gods; it has come into your vicinity.

77-78. Similarly Dama (i.e. Self-restraint), that is lustrous and intent on being kind to all beings, and that always nourishes, has come.

79-80. O best brāhmaṇa, Niyama (i.e. Control) has come to you. He is wearing matted hair, is rough, tawny, very sharp, and a great master. With a sword in his hand, he is the destroyer of sins. He is tranquil, of a great merit, and always endowed with rites. Here in your vicinity (i.e. to you) has come Śauca, the brāhmaṇa, who is free, very bright, resembling crystal, holding a pitcher of water and a twig used as a toothbrush.

81. This Śuśrūṣā (i.e. Service), extremely chaste and very noble, adorned with the ornaments of truth, with her body charming with every ornament, has come.

82-86. O best brāhmaṇa, this Kṣamā (i.e. Forbearance), extremely wise, of a pleasing body, fair (in complexion), of a smiling face, with a lotus in her hand, a foster-mother, lotus-eyed, extremely beautiful, and endowed with divine ornaments has arrived. (This) Śānti (i.e. Tranquility) extremely peaceful, famous, endowed with many auspicious things, looking charming due to many divine jewels, adorned with divine ornaments, engaged in obliging others, full of many truths, of a limited speech, always incomparable, pleased, and with Kṣamā, adorned with all ornaments, having a lotus as her seat, beautiful, of a dark complexion, successful and noble, has come to you, O you highly intelligent one.

87-89a. This noble Ahiṁsā (i.e. Harmlessness) has come to you. Her complexion is like heated (i.e. bright) gold; she is looking graceful with red garments; she is well-pleased; she has a good counsel; and she is not looking here and there.

89b-94. See, O noble one, see, this Śraddhā, full of knowledge, of pious hands, devout, endowed with beauty due to pearls, spotless, and smiling charmingly, has come. O you very wise one, full of much intelligence and much knowledge, with her form strongly attached to good pleasures, well-settled, charming and auspicious, endowed with all desirable meditation, the victorious mother of the worlds, endowed with beauty on account of all ornaments, having plump buttocks and breasts, of a fair complexion, adorned with flowers and garments, is standing by you only. O you noble one, this Prajñā (i.e. Intellect) resembling a swan and the moon, having put on a pearl-necklace, adorned with all ornaments, well-pleased, high-minded, covered with a white garment, having a lotus as her couch, having books in her hands, always shining as she is seated on a lotus, has come to a fortunate person (i.e. to you).

95-98. O best brāhmaṇa, this Dayā (i.e. Pity) with her complexion like lac juice, always well-pleased, wearing a garland made of yellow flowers, having ornaments like necklaces and armlets, endowed with rings and bracelets, adorned with ear-rings has come near you. The respectable lady always shines with a yellow garment. She is (simply) matchless in helping and nourishing the three worlds. She, whose character is always glorified has come.

99. This old, pious one is the wife of Thought, O you highly intelligent one. O best brāhmaṇa, she is my mother. O you of a good vow, I am your Dharma (i.e. Merit).

100a. Realising this, be calm and preserve me.

Durvāsas said :

100b-101a. If now Dharma has approached me, then tell me the reason for this (i.e. your arrival), O Dharma, what do (i.e. can) I do for you?

Dharma said :

101b-102a. O best brāhmaṇa, why are you angry? What wrong have they done? Tell me the reason, O Durvāsas, if you (so) desire.

Durvāsas said :

102b-104. O god, listen to the reason for which I am angry. I have purified my body with restraint, purity and sufferings. I have practised penance for a period of a lakh of years. You see me like this, (and yet) compassion is not produced in you. Therefore, I am angry with you, and today only I shall give you a curse.

105a. Having heard thus (i.e. these words) from (i.e. uttered by) him, the very intelligent (Dharma) said to him.

Dharma said :

105b-108a. O you very intelligent one, when I perish, the world will perish. O dear brāhmaṇa, I very much remove the root of grief. Then afterwards I give pleasure (to the man) if he does not give up truthfulness. One who depends upon (i.e. is after) happiness, is a sinner. Merit is gained with pain. (When) a being thus practising merit casts his life, I give him great happiness in the next world; there is no doubt about it.

Durvāsas said :

108b-110. Great grief is reached by him (in the next world) by whom pleasure is obtained (here); but one mortal gives it up, and somebody else enjoys it. Then who knows (what) happiness (is)? Nobody sees (i.e. knows) it definitely. I am not seeing (any) felicity; you have done an unjust thing. The body which does (certain things) does not enjoy that happiness.

111-113. Suffering is had by one body (while) happiness is enjoyed by another body. So who knows happiness, injustice or righteousness? One suffers, while someone else gets happiness. O Dharma, whatever a man enjoys is accompanied with felicity. By it alone he gets religious merit, and also (good) fruit. The (fruit of) pious rites done by one is enjoyed by another.

114-117a. All that is called happiness, whose characteristics are narrated in scriptures, and it is not otherwise. They suffer unhappiness with the same body with which they perform (bad acts). Therefore by this (behaviour) they do not enjoy in the next world also. Realising this, you who are righteous, should properly observe. How is it that happiness is not enjoyed (by a man) as the very sinful thieves suffer poignant grief with great difficulty with their bodies?

Dharma said :

117b-118. The sinful ones suffer pain with that body only with which they commit sins; for that is the fruit of a sin. The wise have observed in the law-books that Daṇḍa (i.e. punishment) is superior.

119a. You yourself (should) understand it in its essential characteristics according to these rules.

Durvāsas said :

119b-120a. O lord of virtue, listen, what, I think, (conforms to justice): I, being angry, will give you three curses; this cannot be otherwise.

Dharma said :

120b-122. O you highly intelligent one, since you are angry, (please) forgive me. If you are not (prepared) to forgive me, then,

O best brāhmaṇa, make me the son of a maid, also a king, and a Cāṇḍāla also, O great sage. O brāhmaṇa, be favourably disposed to me, who am always bowing to you.

Then the angry Durvāsas cursed Dharma.

Durvāsas said :

123. O Dharma, you today become a king, (then) the son of a maid, not otherwise; go to (i.e. be born in) the family of a Cāṇḍāla; O Dharma, go as you desire.

124. Thus giving three curses, the best brāhmaṇa left. It is said that formerly Dharma was seen in this connection also.

Somaśarman said :

125. How (i.e. in what form) was Dharma born when cursed by that noble (Durvāsas)? O you beautiful lady, if you know, (then) tell me (about) his form.

Sumanā said :

126-128. Being Yudhiṣṭhira, Dharma was born in the family of the Bharatas. He was also born as Vidura, a maid's son. I (shall) also tell you something else. When King Hariścandra was tormented by Viśvāmitra, the very intelligent one became a Cāṇḍāla. Thus even the noble Dharma enjoyed the fruit of his actions due to Durvāsas' curse. I have told the truth to you.

CHAPTER THIRTEEN

Sumanā Explains Ten Basic Virtues

Somaśarman said :

1. O beautiful lady, tell me in detail the characteristics of Celibacy if you know them. Of what nature is Celibacy?

Sumanā said :

2. (He is a true celibate) who is always interested in truth; he the righteous one would (i.e. is) always be satisfied; and

being free from faults would approach (i.e. cohabit with) his own wife when she menstruates.

3-4a. He never gives up the good practices of his family. O best brāhmaṇa, I have told you this (i.e. these characteristics) of a householder. I have indeed explained to you the celibacy of (i.e. as observed by) householders.

4b-6a. Now I shall explain to you the celibacy of (i.e. as observed by) the ascetics. Listen to me who am explaining it. He is always endowed with restraint and truthfulness; and is always afraid of sin. Avoiding (i.e. he avoids) union with his wife, he is settled in meditation and knowledge. I have (thus) told you the celibacy of the ascetics.

6b-9a. (Now) I shall just explain penance. Listen to me who am explaining it. Free from carnal desires and anger he should behave according to the (proper)rules. He remains full of exertion for obliging beings. I have thus explained penance. (Now) I shall speak about truthfulness in the same manner. He is called truthful, whose mind, on seeing other's wealth or wives, would (i.e. does) not have longing for them.

9b-16a. I shall just explain charity by means of which human beings live. He who desires his own happiness in this or in the next world, should make the great gift of food or (i.e.) of eternal happiness. Similarly at least a morsel should be given to one who is oppressed by hunger. There is no misgiving about it. When (food) is given (like this) it leads to great religious merit, and he ever obtains immortality. Everyday a man should give, as is possible according to his wealth, grass, a bed, words, very cool shadow of (i.e. shelter in his) house; so also he should give land, water, food, excellent pleasing words, a seat, words free from crookedness. He, who, for his own existence, daily does this, and honouring deities and manes, thus give gifts, is happy in this world and in the next world also. He, who, even being born as a human being, would make (every) day fruitful by means of giving gifts, study and (other) rites, is (just) a god; there is no doubt about this.

16b-18a. I shall explain to you restraint (*niyama*) —the excellent means of religious merit. (He is a restrained person) who is engaged in worshipping deities and brāhmaṇas, is always full of restraint and is engaged in vows like giving gifts and other meritorious obligations. This is restraint that I have explained.

18b-20. O best of brāhmaṇa, I shall now explain the nature of forgiveness. (Please) listen. Hearing the loud cry of someone being beaten by someone else, he should not get angry, and should not beat (back) even if he is beaten. The pious one should be patient. He has no attachment. He gets great happiness here (i.e. in this world) and in the next world.

21-22a. I have thus explained forgiveness. Now I shall explain purity. He is pure, who is pure externally and internally, and is free from attachment. He lives with such practices as bath and sipping water.

22b-23. I have thus explained purity. Now I shall tell you about non-violence. One who knows should not (i.e. one should not deliberately) pull off even (a blade of) grass. He should be devoted to harmlessness; should look upon others as upon himself.

24-25a. I shall (now) explain tranquility. A man gets happiness through tranquility. He should observe tranquility, and should not at all give it up because of trouble. Giving up enmity with beings, he should thus make up his mind.

25b-26. Thus I have explained tranquility. Now I shall tell about non-stealing. A man should not snatch away other's wealth or should not kidnap other's wife, mentally, by words or physically (i.e. should not think or talk about or do these things). Thus he should make up his mind.

27-28a. O best brāhmaṇa, I shall just explain to you sense-control (dama). Being sensible and controlling himself, he should destroy the insolence of his senses and his mind susceptible to emotions by curbing them.

28b-32a. I shall explain to you service (śuśrūṣā) as is told in religious texts, and shall tell you about it as it is explained by former preceptors. By means of words, mind and body one should accomplish his preceptor's mission. That is said to be service where (i.e. by which) favour is produced. O best brāhmaṇa, I have explained to you Dharma (i.e. righteousness) in all its forms. O my husband, I shall tell you anything more that you desire to hear. A man who always lives in (i.e. practises) Dharma like this is never again born in this mundane existence.

32b. By means of (practising) Dharma he goes to heaven. I am telling you the truth, (and) the truth (only).

33-34a. Knowing thus, O you highly intelligent one, go to (i.e. practise) Dharma. O dear one, everything, that is difficult to be accomplished on earth is obtained by the favour of Dharma. (Please) do only what I tell you.

34b-35. Hearing the words of his wife, the very intelligent Somaśarman, again spoke to his wife, Sumanā, who explained Dharma.

CHAPTER FOURTEEN

Sumanā Describes the Death of the Virtuous

Somaśarman said :

1. O good lady, how do you do such an excellent and highly meritorious exposition of Dharma? From whom did you learn this?

Sumanā said :

2. O you very intelligent one, well-known Cyavana, well-versed in all (branches of) knowledge, and born in the family of the Bhārgavas was my father.

3-4. I was his dear daughter, dearer to him than his own life. Always playing, I used to go with him wherever he went—to sacred places, groves, assemblies of sages and temples of deities, O you of a good vow.

5-6. Very intelligent Vedaśarman, born in the family of Kauśika, a friend of my father, overcome by great grief and repeatedly brooding, while wandering by chance came (to my father).

7. My father said to the noble one who had come (to him): "O you of a good vow, I feel that you are tormented by grief. Tell me the cause by which you are (thus) afflicted."

8-10. Hearing these words of that magnanimous Cyavana, he i.e. Vedaśarman, of a good vow, told my father the cause of his entire grief, O you very wise one: "My very chaste wife, solely devoted to me—her husband—is sonless; I do not have any lineage. I have told you the cause, since I was asked about it by you."

11-12a. In the meantime, there came a divine seer having supernatural faculties. Both my father and that Vedaśarman got up and honoured him with devout offerings, food and sweet words; and both of them asked the secret, as you had asked me before.

12b-14. The pious one told both my father and his friend the means of Dharma, as I had told you before: "By (practising) Dharma (i.e. religious precepts), a son, wealth, corn, and also wives are obtained."

15. Then that Vedaśarman fully practised Dharma. From that (i.e. by practising that) Dharma, there was great happiness, along with a son, for him.

16. In consequence of that meeting (between the Siddha and the two friends) I am convinced as I told you about the very auspicious words, O my dear husband.

17. Always follow the practices laid down for a brāhmaṇa, as were heard from the great Siddha, and which would remove all (your) doubts.

Somaśarman said :

18. O my dear wife, tell me what kind of death or birth (does one have?). Tell me all about the nature of both.

Sumanā said :

19. I shall tell you how death comes to him who has practised Dharma by means of truthfulness, purity, forbearance, tranquility and religious merit (and by visits to) sacred places etc.

20-22. He does not contract any disease, nor is there any suffering in his body. He does not have to toil, he has no fatigue, perspiration, and he does not commit an error. Gandharvas, and brāhmaṇas, taking up divine forms and ready with Vedic texts, and conversant with the knowledge of singing, come to his side (i.e. to him) and sing his matchless praise. He is composed, and seated on a seat is indeed engaged in the worship of deities.

23-30. He, very much devoted to religious practices, and a wise one, obtains a sacred place for bath. If a man remains in a fire-chamber, in a cowpen, in temples of deities, in a grove or a lake, or a place where there is the aśvattha tree, and also if he remains by resorting to (i.e. under) a palāśa or an undumbara tree or a bilva tree[1] also, and by resorting to (i.e. in) a stable of horses, or of elephants, or if he remains by resorting to (i.e. under) an aśoka three or a mango tree, also in the vicinity of brāhmaṇas, or (even) if he has gone to the abode of old age (i.e. even if he has become old), or after he resorts to (i.e. goes to) a battle-field and dies, these places where he dies are holy. The cause for this (i.e. such a death) is Dharma alone. Reaching (i.e. choosing) the sacred place called Gographa or Amarakaṇṭakā,[2] he, loving pious practices and of a pious conduct, also practices Dharma. When the best man resorts to death (i.e. when he dies), he sees his mother and his meritorious father; also, he sees his brother endowed with virtue, his kinsmen and friends. In the same way, he, being praised by bards, would not at all see his most sinful mother or father etc.

31-34. The Gandharvas sing songs and the panegyrists praise him with panegyrics; brāhmaṇas would honour him with the recitations of hymns and his mother would honour him with love; his father, the groups of his relatives would honour the pious and highly intelligent man. O lord, I have thus narrated to you the messengers and the holy places. He actually sees the messengers full of love (for him). That king of Dharma (i.e. Yama) would invite you, not in a dream or through troublesome delusion. O noble one, come (to that place) where that Dharma stands.

35-38. He (i.e. who practises Dharma) has no delusion, not error, no languor, no confusion of memory. There is no doubt that he remains with a pleased mind. Endowed with sacred and worldly knowledge, and remembering god Janārdana (i.e.

1. Brahmavṛkṣa—palāśa or udumbara tree. Śrīvṛkṣa—bilva tree, or aśvattha or the sacred fig-tree.

2. Amarakaṇṭaka—Name of that part of the Vindhya range, which is near the source of the river Narmadā.

Viṣṇu), he, with his mind thus pleased, goes with them. In his case, when he casts his body, unity (with the Supreme Spirit) takes place. Resorting to the tenth aperture[1] his soul goes (out of his body). A palanquin or a beautiful vehicle with swans yoked to it, or an aeroplane or an excellent horse or elephant comes (to carry him).

39-41. Then the pious and meritorious man, with an umbrella held over his head, being fanned with chowries and fans, and endowed with all pleasures, being praised with songs by singers and bards, and eulogised by learned brāhmaṇas—masters of the Vedas, and praised by the good, obtains the fruit in accordance with the efficacy of his charity.

42-43a. Happily he goes to the gardens and orchards. Mixed (i.e. surrounded) with celestial nymphs and endowed with auspicious things, and being praised by gods, he sees the lord of Dharma (i.e. Yama).

43b-47. Gods with Dharma go forward to (greet) him (and say:) "O magnanimous one, come, come (and) enjoy pleasures as you like." In this way he sees the very intelligent Dharma of a pleasing form; and due to the efficacy of his own religious merit he enjoys heaven itself. The pious one, after the exhaustion of his pleasures, is reborn. Due to his own religious merit he goes to (i.e. is born in) the family of a pious brāhmaṇa or a kṣatriya, or of a rich man, or of a very pious vaiśya, O you very intelligent one. There he rejoices with (i.e. due to) his pious acts and he again performs (deeds leading to) religious merit.

---

1. Daśamadvāra=Brahma-randhra.

CHAPTER FIFTEEN

The Death of Sinners

Somaśarman said :

1. O good and beautiful lady, tell me, if you know it, in detail, what characteristics apper at the death of sinners.

Sumanā said :

2-4a. O my dear husband, listen; I shall tell you what I learnt from the Siddha about the death of the sinners and what its marks are. I (shall) also tell you about the place and actions of great sinners. A very wicked man reaches a region which is inauspicious due to its being impure on account of excretion and urine; and has a painful death.

4b-7a. That (wicked man) being afflicted, reaches the land of a cāṇḍāla, or a land roamed over by donkeys or resorts to a prostitute's house, and dies in a painful condition; (or) he dies after having gone to the house of a seller of spirituous liquors which is full of bones, skins and nails, and full of evils and blemishes. Having reached that (place) the wicked one surely dies; (or) having reached some other place with evil practices, he dies.

7b-12a. Now I shall tell you the movements of (Yama's) messengers, desiring (to take) him (to Yama's abode), and frightful, terrible, fearful, very dark and of large bellies, of tawny eyes, yellow and dark-blue, or very white and large-bellied, very tall, very dreadful, resembling dry flesh and marrow, of fearful fangs, fearful, having faces like those of lions and having serpents in their hands. O you very intelligent one, seeing them he trembles and is repeatedly afflicted. All the messengers make loud cries like those of jackals into his ears. Having tied him with nooses round his neck, waist and belly, and overcoming him knock him down. He repeatedly cries—'Ah', 'Ah'.

12b-15a. Now I shall tell the actions of the dying sinners who have taken away another's wealth, molested another's wife, not returned debt or wealth of others taken through greed, enjoyment and infatuation. All the (messengers) seize the neck of the dying man who commits the great sin of accepting a gift from a bad person.

15b-16a. Whatever sins were formerly committed by that great sinner come to his throat; (this) does not (happen) in any other manner.

16b-21a. Due to obstruction caused by excessive phlegm they produce affliction. Due to servere pains his throat snorts. He weeps and trembles very much. He repeatedly remembers his mother, father, brother and wife. Being deluded by great sin he again forgets them. His life, full of many afflictions, does not depart. He falls, trembles and swoons again and again. The deluded one, thus full of suffering, experiences grief. O my dear husband, listen. His life going (out) with great grief and pain, resorts to his anus and pass out (through it).

21b-22. In this way a being, who is greatly deluded and who is full of greed and infatuation, is carried by Yama's messengers. I shall now tell you about the suffering.

CHAPTER SIXTEEN

The Death & Post-mortem State of Sinners

Sumanā said :

1. That wicked man being burnt and struggling again and again is taken along a path full of a heap of charcoals.

2. Being tormented by the sun's rays, he is taken along that path on which the sun's heat is intense and which is heated by twelve suns.

3. The wicked-minded one is taken along the path, on mountains, inaccessible and shadow-less places, while he is very much tormented by hunger and thirst.

4-5. Being hit by the messengers (of Yama) with maces, swords and hatchets, and being beaten with whips and being censured by them, he is then taken along a cold path and is again served (tormented) by wind. Due to that (severe) cold he becomes afflicted. There is no doubt about it.

6-11a. Being dragged by (Yama's) messengers he is taken to many inaccessible places. In this way, the sinner, the wicked-minded man, who reviles gods and brāhmaṇas, and who commits all sins, is taken by Yama's servants. The wicked-hearted man sees Yama, king of Dharma, who resembles a heap of black collyrium, who is fierce, ruthless, fearful and with (i.e. surrounded by) fearful messengers, who is full of (i.e. who has with him) all diseases, who is accompanied by Citragupta, who is mounted upon a buffalo, who is very fierce due to his large teeth and is very fearful, O best brāhmaṇa. His face resembles death. The wicked-minded man sees Yama, who has worn a yellow garment, who has a mace in his hand, who is besmeared with red sandal, who has adorned himself with red flowers, and whose body is huge. He sees Yama like this.

11b-12. Seeing him approaching, Yama observes him who is outcast from all religions, who is wicked, most sinful and an enemy of the customary law. He would punish (i.e. he punishes) him with tortures and with wooden mallets.

13a. Till the end of the period of a thousand yugas he is parched with heat.

13b-14. Again and again he is roasted in hells of various kinds. The sinner goes to (i.e. is born in) a hellish species among crores of insects. Being miserable and senseless he is parched with heat in an impure (place).

15. Thus certainly does the wicked-hearted man die. Thus the wicked-minded man experiences the fruit of his association with sin.

16-19a. I shall (now) explain (to you) rebirth and the species to which he goes. Having obtained a hundred births as dogs he again experiences (the fruit of) sin. The wicked-hearted one becomes (i.e. is born as) a tiger, and goes to the species of (i.e. is born as) a donkey. Then he goes to the species of (i.e. is born as) a cat, pig or a serpent. He is repeatedly born in all the species of various kinds and in (those of) lower animals. He goes to (i.e. is born among) the sinful birds and in other great species. The sinner goes to the species of (i.e. is born as) cāṇḍāla, bhilla or (as a member of the barbarous tribe called) pulinda.

19b. I have (thus) told you everything about the birth of sinners.

20-21. O my dear husband, listen to the very fearful struggle of them (i.e. of the sinners) at the time of their death. I have told before (i.e. to) you (i.e. explained to you) the practice of sin and merit. O you who show respect to others, like this I shall tell you something else, if you ask.

CHAPTER SEVENTEEN

The Story of Somaśarman's Previous Birth

Somaśarman said :

1-2. O respectable lady, you have told (me) the excellent form of Dharma. O you noble one, O you of a good vow, tell me if you know how I would get a son endowed with all virtues. There is no doubt that good acts like charity (are fruitful) in this and the next world.

Sumanā said :

3. Go to Vasiṣṭha who knows (what) virtue (is). Request that great sage. From him you will (learn how to) obtain a son knowing piety and loving it.

Sūta said :

4. When she had said these words, Somaśarman, the best brāhmaṇa (said to her:) "O auspicious lady, I shall follow your words (i.e. advice). There is no doubt about it."

5-6. Speaking thus, the best brāhmaṇa, Somaśarman, quickly went to the omniscient, divine Vasiṣṭha, who was the best among those who practised penance, who lived on the bank of the Ganges in a hermitage, who was the best among the brāhmaṇas, who was full of the flames of lustre and was as it were another sun.

7. He repeatedly, devoutly, saluted the shining, noble, best brāhmaṇa, well-versed in the Vedas, in the manner of a staff (i.e. by prostrating himself before Vasiṣṭha).

8. The very lustrous, sinless son of Brahmā (i.e. Vasiṣṭha), said to him: "O you highly intelligent one, (please) sit comfortably on the auspicious seat."

9-10. Saying so, the best of the yogins again said to him, who was rich in penance: "O noble one, O dear one, is there all well in your house, with your sons, wife, servants, and fires used for sacred rites? Are you alright, and do you always practise virtue?"

11. Speaking thus, the very wise one (i.e. Vasiṣṭha) again said to Suśarman (i.e. Somaśarman): "O best brāhmaṇa, what work dear to you should I do for you ?"

12a. Speaking thus to the brāhmaṇa, Vasiṣṭha ceased (to speak).

12b-13. When that best, noble sage Vasiṣṭha spoke (like that), he (i.e. Somaśarman), spoke to noble Vasiṣṭha, the best among those who practise penance: "O revered sir, (please) listen to my words with a very much pleased mind.

14. O best among the sages, O best brāhmaṇa, if you want to do what I like, (then) remove the doubt expressed by my question.

15-17. O dear one, due to what sin (does) poverty (come to one) and how is it that one does not get happiness? This is my doubt. Tell me due to what sin (this happens). O brāhmaṇa, I am confused with great delusion. I was advised by my dear wife. I, who was eager, was sent to you by her. Then tell me all that which would remove all my doubts. (Please) relieve me from the bondage of the worldly existence."

Vasiṣṭha said :

18. Sons, friends, brother, and kinsmen and relatives are the five kinds of men, according to the difference (depending upon the relation).

19. (About) all of them Sumanā has already told you. O best brāhmaṇa, all those are bad sons, connected on account of debt.

20-24. I shall (now) tell you the auspicious characteristics of a son. That son whose mind is attached to merit, who is always engaged in religious conduct, who is endowed with purity and knowledge, who practises penance, who is best among speakers, who is very steady in all his acts, who is devoted to Vedic studies, who knows (i.e. has studied) all sacred books, who honours gods and brāhmaṇas, who performs all (kinds of) sacrifices, who is a donor, who gives away (in charity without expecting any reward in return), who speaks agreeable words, who is always intent upon meditation on Viṣṇu, is tranquil, restrained and friendly, who is always devoted to his father and mother and affectionate to his kinsmen, who is a saviour of his family, who is learned, who supports his family—a son endowed with such virtues gives happiness.

25-26. Others connected by relation (as a son) cause grief and tormentation. What is the use of such a useless son? All such (sons) come into the worldly existence as sons and go out of it after causing great tormentation, O you best brāhmaṇa.

27. Again listen to all the wonderful account which I shall tell you about the religious merit which you did and (the practices) you maintained in the previous birth.

Vasiṣṭha continued :

28-31. O you very intelligent one, in the former birth you were a Śūdra, and none else. You were a farmer; you were ignorant; you had great greed; you had one wife; you always hated (others). You had many sons; you never gave away (anything in charity); you did not know religious conduct at all; you had never heard (what) truth (is). You had never given a gift; you had never listened to sacred texts; O you highly intelligent one, you had never undertaken a pilgrimage to a sacred place.

32. Thus, O brāhmaṇa, you practised agriculture repeatedly. O best brāhmaṇa, you again and again guarded animals, all cows, buffaloes and also horses. O best of brāhmaṇas, such deed(s) you did formerly (i.e. in your previous birth).

33. Similarly, through greed you collected much wealth; but you never spent it in a good way.

34. You never gave any present to a worthy person, or seeing a weak person you never showed him any compassion and never gave him money.

35. You also collected beasts like cows and buffaloes, and having sold them you hoarded ample wealth.

36a. (And also you hoarded ample wealth) by selling butter-milk, ghee, milk and curd.

36b-38. Being deluded by Viṣṇu's Māyā, O brāhmaṇa, you, thinking of (i.e. taking advantage of) bad times, made food more costly here (only), O best brāhmaṇa. You, who were cruel, never made any present (to anyone). O brāhmaṇa, you never worshipped deities. When the parvan-days arrived, you never gave money to the brāhmaṇas.

39-40a. When the time for Śrāddha came, you never performed it with faith. Your virtuous wife (used to) say: "O you very intelligent one, the day has come. It is time for offering Śrāddha to (my) father-in-law, and to (my) mother-in-law also."

40b-42a. Hearing those words of (i.e. uttered by) her, you (used to) abandon and run away from your house. You never saw (i.e. cared for) the path of righteousness nor did you ever hear about it. Greed (was) your father, your brother. Greed (was) your kinsmen and relatives. Always forsaking religious conduct, you cherished greed alone.

42b. Therefore, being extremely oppressed by poverty, you became unhappy.

43-48. Everyday great greed increased in your mind, whenever in your house wealth increased. Being burnt by the fire of anxiety, you definitely used to think of wealth even when you used to sleep at night. When the day dawned, you were always pervaded by great delusions: 'When will there be a thousand, a lakh, a crore or one hundred millions or one thousand crores or a billion (coins) in my house?' Thus a thousand, a lakh, a crore, a hundred millions, a thousand crores, a billion (coins) were (collected by you); but (your) greed never went away leaving (i.e. from your) body. (On the contrary) it always increased. You never gave (in charity); you never offered oblations to fire, you never enjoyed (wealth); you dug the earth and deposited (the coins in it) without the knowledge of your sons. O brāhmaṇa, you also always adopted other means to get wealth.

49-51. Being intelligent you also asked people about other means of getting wealth. Asking (people) about spades, collyrium[1], explanation (of secret formulae) and minerology, and being fully deluded by greed, you wandered all alone. You always thought of sexual union, and about procedures giving superhuman powers. Always thinking about entering into fissures you asked (people about them).

52-54a. Due to the blazing of fire of greed, you were (reduced to a pitiable plight, always) saying 'Alas, Alas', and had become senseless. O best brāhmaṇa, you were thus infatuated; and had been subdued by destiny. When your wife and sons asked you about that wealth, you never told them (any) account of it, and abandoning life, you went to Yama.

54b-57. Thus I have told you all your former account. O brāhmaṇa, due to this deed (i.e. these deeds) you became indigent and poor. Viṣṇu is pleased with him in whose house, in his worldly existence, the sons are of good character, endowed with knowledge and always interested in truthfulness and in good conduct. He with whom Viṣṇu is pleased, endlessly enjoys in the world of mortals wealth, grains, wife, sons and grandsons. O brāhmaṇa, without Viṣṇu's favour he cannot obtain a wife, sons or a good birth or a good family. That is the highest position of Viṣṇu.

CHAPTER EIGHTEEN

The Account of Somaśarman's Birth in a Brāhmaṇa Family

Somaśarman said :

1-2. O sage, you told me about my sin in the former birth. O best brāhmaṇa, in what way was I forsaken by śūdrahood and did I obtain brāhmaṇahood? O you well-versed in spiritual and worldly knowledge, tell me all about it.

Vasiṣṭha said :

3. If you think (like listening to them) listen; I shall explain to you, O brāhmaṇa, what religious deeds you did in the former birth.

1. Añjana—seems to refer to the practice of putting a particular kind of collyrium into the eyes and then to see where wealth may be found. Vāda—seems to be a reference to the exposition of certain secret spells helping to obtain wealth.

4-6. A certain innocent, well-learned brāhmaṇa of a good conduct, religious-minded, and always solely devoted to Viṣṇu wandered over the earth for pilgrimages to sacred places. He, the very intelligent one, while (thus) wandering, came to your house. O best of brāhmaṇas, he requested you for a place to stay (i.e. for accommodation). You with your wife and sons gave it to him (saying:)

7-9a. "O brāhmaṇa, come, come happily (i.e. you are welcome) to my house." You repeatedly said these words to that brāhmaṇa, the devotee of Viṣṇu: "O you of a good vow, live here comfortably; this is your house. Today I am blessed; today I have visited a sacred place. Today I have obtained the fruit of a visit to a sacred place by seeing your two feet."

9b-12. (Then) you showed him the cowpen for his lodging. Having massaged his body you also shampooed his feet. You also washed them with water. You also bathed with the water with which his feet were washed. You thus forthwith gave ghee, curd, milk, food and buttermilk to that noble brāhmṇa. Thus with your wife and sons you pleased that very learned, noble brāhmaṇa, Viṣṇu's devotee.

13-16. When it was the dawn of the auspicious and blissful day, on which fell (i.e. which was) the Ekādaśī (eleventh day) of the bright fortnight of Āṣāḍha (called) Pāpanaśinī (the destroyer of sins), which destroyed all sins, and on which day god Hṛṣīkeśa (i.e. Viṣṇu) goes to sleep (called) Yoga-nidrā, O brāhmaṇa, when that day came, all wise men having given up all domestic duties, became engrossed in meditating upon Viṣṇu. With songs and (playing upon) musical instruments they celebrated a great festival. All the brāhmaṇas praised (Viṣṇu) with (hymns from) the Vedas, and very auspicious hymns of praise.

17. When the great festival had come, the best brāhmaṇa stayed there on that day. He (also) fasted properly.

18. The brāhmaṇa recited the hymn to Ekādaśī. With your wife and sons you also listened to the excellent (account of) religious virtue.

19. When that very auspicious (account) was heard by your wife and sons they urged you: "Observe this vow in the company of this brāhmaṇa."

20-26a. Hearing those great (i.e. very important) words, giving all merit, you were determined (to observe it and so said:) "I shall observe this vow." Then going to the river with your wife and sons, you bathed in the river. O brāhmaṇa, with a pleased mind you worshipped Viṣṇu with all (kinds of) auspicious presents and with sandal, incense etc. You kept awake by dancing and singing songs during that night. In the company of that brāhmaṇa you again bathed in the river. Saluting Viṣṇu with devotion and bathing him again and again, you worshipped the lord of gods with auspicious (objects like) flowers, incense etc. and similarly gave a present to that noble brāhmaṇa. O brāhmaṇa, having devoutly saluted that brāhmaṇa, you gave him ample presents. Then you broke the fast, O brāhmaṇa, with your sons, wife etc. You sent him (away) with devotion and good feelings.

26b-30a. O best brāhmaṇa, you yourself observed the vow like this, due to the company of that brāhmaṇa, and due to the favour of Viṣṇu. You, endowed with a truthful conduct became (i.e. was born as) a brāhmaṇa. Due to the efficacy of that vow you obtained (i.e. were born in) a great family of brāhmaṇas, wise and of truthful conduct. To that noble brāhmaṇa, devoted to Viṣṇu, you gave well-cooked food with faith and truthfulness. Due to the efficacy of that food sweet food comes to you.

30b-33. O brāhmaṇa, in your previous birth you were deluded through folly, and your mind was pervaded with desire. (So) you collected money only. You did not give it to brāhmaṇas or to helpless persons, or to your wife, as you died through desire for a son (not being satisfied). (So) due to the effect of that sin, poverty, non-fulfilment of your desire, and loss of affection came to you. It is just the result of that sin that you were born sonless.

34-35. O brāhmaṇa, a family with good sons, wealth, grains, excellent wife, good birth or death, excellent enjoyments and happiness, kingdom, heaven and salvation, and all that is difficult to obtain (are obtained) through the favour of that magnanimous Viṣṇu.

36-38. Therefore, by worshipping that Govinda, Nārāyaṇa, Anāmaya, you will obtain that highest position i.e. the highest position of Viṣṇu. O brāhmaṇa, I have fully told you about having good sons, wealth, grains, excellent enjoyments and happiness, and all the deeds that you did in your former birth. O blessed one, knowing thus be solely devoted to Viṣṇu.

39-41. The best brāhmaṇa of great prowess was (thus) advised by Brahmā's son (i.e. Vasiṣṭha). The noble one, being full of joy, having saluted Vasiṣṭha there, and having taken his leave of that brāhmaṇa (i.e. Vasiṣṭha) went home. Joyfully approaching his wife Sumanā, (he said to her:) "O auspicious lady, due to your favour that brāhmaṇa, Vasiṣṭha, told me all my former account and behaviour. Today only my delusion is destroyed. I shall just propitiate Viṣṇu and shall reach that highest position, viz. salvation."

42. Hearing those excellent, great, very auspicious words bringing about happiness, she, full of joy, said to her husband: "You are lucky (that) you are advised by that brāhmaṇa."

CHAPTER NINETEEN

Somaśarman's Eulogy of Viṣṇu

Sūta said :

1-3. The very intelligent, the best (brāhmaṇa) Somaśarman, having bathed, with (his wife) Sumanā, at the auspicious (sacred place called) Kapilāsaṅgama,[1] on the bank of Revā, causing great merit, he, the intelligent one, and of a good vow, having gratified (with oblations) gods and manes, practised penance there, with a very calm mind and with meditation, muttering with the hymn of twelve syllables (the name) of auspicious Viṣṇu—that Vāsudeva, the magnanimous god of gods.

4. Always being steady and without desire and anger he saw Viṣṇu (only) (while sitting) on a seat, or (lying) on a bed or (going) in a vehicle or in a dream.

---

1. Kapilāsaṅgama or Kapilā-tīrtha—Anyone bathing there and performing worship obtains a thousand brown cow. See Mahābhārata (critical edition published by the Bhandarkar Oriental Research Institute, Poona) 3.81.38.

5. That virtuous, glorious Sumanā, devoted to her husband, served only her husband endowed with penance.

6-9. Various obstacles frightened him who was meditating. Great black serpents of strong poison came near that Somaśarman; and also were seen lions and tigers. They simply frightened him. Vampires, demons, imps, spirits of dead persons and also jackals showed him terrible fear, (capable of) destroying life. Very terrible lions of various kinds, with fearful fangs and cruel came there and roared very fiercely.

10-26. The best, virtuous sage, the intelligent (Somaśarman), disturbed by the growing great obstacles was not distracted from his meditation on Viṣṇu. (Though) the best brāhmaṇa Somaśarman was very much harassed by very high winds in the rainy season, cold, or heavy showers, he did not move away from meditation. A very fearful lion roaring (terribly) came there. Seeing him, and being frightened, the brāhmaṇa (Somaśarman) remembered god Viṣṇu, who resembled a sapphire, who had put on a yellow garment, who was having a great prowess, who held a conch and a disc and a mace and a lotus, who was shining with a necklace of big pearls resembling the moon in beauty and also with jewel (called) Kaustubha[1], whose chest shines with the divine mark (called) Śrīvatsa, whose body looked charming due to all ornaments, whose eyes resembled lotuses, whose face had a charming smile on it, and was very much pleased, who looked charming and shone with a jewelled necklace. He verily meditated upon (Viṣṇu:) "O Kṛṣṇa, affectionate to those who seek your shelter; my salutation (to you) the god of gods; what will fear do to me? I have sought the refuge of him, in whose belly remain the three worlds and the seven magnanimous ones. Where then is fear for me? I have sought the refuge of him, the destroyer of all fears, from whom all very powerful fears like Kṛtyā etc. proceed. I have sought the refuge of him, who is a great fear to all sins and demons, and who is the protector of Viṣṇu's (i.e. his) devotees. I have sought the refuge of him who is the refuge of all the eminent, magnanimous demons, the devotees of Kṛṣṇa (i.e. his devotees). I have sought the refuge of him, who being fearless destroys fears, and who

1. Kaustubha—Name of a celebrated gem obtained with 13 other jewels at the churning of the ocean and worn by Viṣṇu on his chest.

possessing knowledge, destroys sins, and who alone remains in the form of Indra. I have sought the refuge of him, who, being of the form of herbs, removes diseases, and who (himself) is pure and entirely full of bliss. I have sought the refuge of him, who, himself being fixed, would move the worlds, and being sinless is knowledge (itself); (then) what will fear do to me? He, Anāmaya (i.e. Viṣṇu) is the guardian of all good people; he, the universal soul, protects the universe. I have sought his refuge. I have sought the refuge of him who, in the form of a lion, shows great fear to me (standing) in front (of me). I salute that (Viṣṇu) in the form of Narasiṁha.

27-28. (In the form of) an intoxicated, huge elephant (he) has come. I have well sought the refuge of him, who has the face of an elephant, who is endowed with knowledge, who holds a noose and a goad, who has a black face like that of an elephant.

29. I have sought the refuge of (that Viṣṇu who in his) Boar[1] (form) killed Hiraṇyākṣa. I have taken shelter with that Vāmana, affectionate to those who seek his shelter.

30. All the short, dwarfish, hump-backed spirits of dead persons and imps etc., holding the form of death, frighten me.

31-38. I have taken shelter with the immortal. What will fear do to me? Viṣṇu is of Brahmā, he is the giver of Brahman (i.e. takes one to the supreme spirit), he is Brahmā, and is full of the knowledge of Brahman; I have taken shelter with him; what (then) will fear do to me? He who is fearless, who removes the fear of the world and himself causes fear, and is of the form of fear—I have taken shelter with him. What will fear do to me? I have sought the shelter of that Janārdana (i.e. Viṣṇu) of the form of Dharma, who is the emancipator of all worlds and the destroyer of all sinners. I shall seek his refuge who takes up a wonderful form, foreign to gods, in a war. He is always my shelter. A terrible storm afflicts my body very much. I have taken shelter with him; he is always my refuge. I have sought the refuge of that god who torments in these forms viz. of very cold, heavy showers and heat. These, of the form of death have come here, and are disturbing me. I have always taken the shelter of these forms of Viṣṇu.

1. Varāha—the Boar-form of Viṣṇu.

39. I take the shelter with that Viṣṇu, the first Siddha and the lord of Siddhas, whom they call all-good, the highest lord, exclusively alone, full of knowledge and brilliant."

40. Thus everyday meditating upon and praising Viṣṇu, the destroyer of afflictions, he brought Hari (i.e. Viṣṇu) into his heart through devotion.

41. Seeing the exertion and courage of that Somaśarman, Viṣṇu, being delighted, manifested himself before him and said:

42. "O very intelligent Somaśarman, listen with your wife. O best brāhmaṇa, I am Viṣṇu; O you of a good vow, ask for a boon."

43-47. (Thus) addressed by him, the best brāhmaṇa (i.e. Somaśarman) having opened both his eyes, saw that god, the lord of the universe, who was dark like a cloud, who was very glorious, whose body was charming due to all ornaments, who was endowed with all weapons, who was endowed with divine characteristics, whose eyes resembled lotuses, who was with (i.e. who was clad in) a yellow garment, who, the lord of gods, was shining, who was mounted upon Garuḍa, who had held a conch, a disc and a mace (in his hands), who was the great saviour of Brahmā and others, and also of this world, who was always beyond this universe, who was above (all) forms, who was the lord of the worlds. The very glorious brāhmaṇa, full of great joy, prostrated himself before him who was accompanied by Śrī (Lakṣmī or grandeur), who was shining, and had the lustre like that of a crore of suns.

48-57. With Sumanā, he joined the palms of his hands (i.e. saluted him) and said: "Victory to you; victory to you, Mādhava, who removes pride. Victory to you, who sleep on the body of the serpent (viz. Śeṣa). Victory to you, O Yajñāṅga, O lord of sacrifices. Victory to you, O eternal and omnipresent one. Victory to you, O lord of all, O eternal one, O you of the form of sacrifice; my salutation to you. Victory to you, O best among those who possess knowledge. Victory to you, O giver of everything; victory to you, O omniscient one, and cause of all. Victory to you, O lord of the original forms of souls; saltuation to you, O great soul. Victory to you, O giver of wisdom, O Prajñāṅga (i.e. having wisdom as one of his parts); victory to you, O giver of life. Victory to you, O destroyer of sins, the lord of merit.

Victory to you, O Viṣṇu, the controller of merit. Victory to you, O you of the form of knowledge; salutation to you, who can be comprehended by knowledge. Victory to you, O you having eyes like lotus-petals. Salutation to you, Padmanābha (from whose navel sprang the lotus). Victory to you, O Govinda, O Gopāla, victory to you, O holder of the disc; salutation to you whose forms are unmanifest and manifest. Victory to you, O you, whose body is charming due to your valour; victory to you, the leader of valour; victory to you, O you, who have Lakṣmī as a part of your sport. Salutation to you, full of the Vedas. Victory to you, O you whose body is charming due to your valour; victory to you, O you who give diligence; victory to (you) who put an end to all exertion, victory to (you, O Viṣṇu who are yourself) exertion. Victory to you who are capable of elevation, victory to you who had the three elevations (i.e. three steps). Salutation to you, who undertake exertion and who are Dharma.

58-59. Salutation to you, having a golden seed. Salutation to you who are lustre. Salutation to you, who are of the form of great brilliance, and who are full of all lustre. Salutation to you, who destroy the prowess of the demons, and who remove evil lustre. Salutation to you who (work) for the well-being of cows and brāhmaṇas, and to you, who are the highest soul.

60-71. Salutation to you, the enjoyer of the offerings and the carrier of the oblations to gods. Salutation to you, the carrier of the oblations to the manes and to you of the form of Svadhā. Repeated salutations to you, of the nature of Svāhā, to you, who are the sacrifice and who are the purifier. Salutation to you who hold the Śārṅga bow in your hand, to Hari (i.e. Viṣṇu) the remover of sins. Salutation to you who direct the good and the bad, and who shine with wisdom. Salutations (to you), of the form of Vedas, and the purifier. Salutation to you of tawny hair, and the remover of all afflictions, to (you) the highest Keśava, and the sustainer of everything. Salutation to you who favours (all) and who are full of joy. My constant salutation to you, the eternal, pure one, the destroyer of suffering. My constant salutation to you, who are joy, who are pure and who are perfect; to you, whose feet are saluted by Rudra and who are saluted by Brahmā. Salutation to you, whose lotus-like feet are saluted by the lords of gods and demons. Repeated salutations to you who are the highest lord, who are unconquered and whose heart is full of nectar. Salutation to you, whose abode is the milky ocean; to you to whom Lakṣmī is dear. Repeated salutations to you, who are Oṁkāra, are pure, and who are stable. Repeated salutations to you who are comprehensive and who pervade (everything), and you who destroy all calamities. Repeated salutations to you of the form of Vāmana, and to you, noble Nṛsiṁha. Salutation to you, divine Paraśurāma, who killed all the kṣatriyas. Salutation to you, who are omniscient, who are Matsya and Rāma. Salutation to you, who are Kṛṣṇa, Buddha and the destroyer of Mlecchas. Salutation to you, the brāhmaṇa (named) Kapila, and Hayagrīva. Salutation to you, of the nature of Vyāsa and to you who have every form."

72-75. Having thus praised Hṛṣīkeśa, he then said to that Janārdana: "O you purifier, Brahmā does not know you, the farthest limit of virtues; neither omniscient Rudra (i.e. Śiva), nor the thousand-eyed (Indra) is able to praise you. Who can describe you? O lord, of what kind (i.e. how limited) is my intellect? O Keśava, I have praised you, who are qualityless and having qualities. O you of a good vow, (please) forgive me for my words—bad words; I am your servant. O you purifier, O you lord of the words, (please) forgive me, birth after birth."

CHAPTER TWENTY

The Birth of Suvrata

Hari said:

1-2. O brāhmaṇa, I am pleased by this meritorious penance of yours, and also by your truthfulness; and I am also pleased by the holy hymn of praise. Choose a boon. O you illustrious one, I shall grant you the boon that you have (i.e. cherish) in your mind. I shall fulfil (i.e. satisfy) whatever desire you entertain.

Somaśarman said:

3. O Kṛṣṇa (i.e. Viṣṇu), first, with a pleased mind, grant

me a boon much desired by me, if you have good (i.e. great) pity for me.

4. Getting birth after birth (i.e. in every existence) I shall be devoted to you. Show me the highest, stable place, giving (me) salvation.

5-8a. O Keśava, (give me) a son, who will emancipate his family, who will be endowed with divine characteristics, who will be always intensely devoted to Viṣṇu, who will sustain (i.e. continue) my family, who will know everything and grant everything, who will be endowed with the lustre of penance, who will always protect and honour gods, brāhmaṇas and (other) people, who will be pious, who will be a donor and will be mature in intellect due to knowledge. Give me such a son, (and) remove my poverty. May it be so certainly (lit. there is no doubt). I choose this boon.

Hari said:

8b-11. O best brāhmaṇa, may it be so. Undoubtedly it will take place. By my favour, may you have a good son, who would emancipate your family. You will enjoy divine and human boons here (i.e. in this world). Perceiving great, virtuous happiness due to your son, you will, O brāhmaṇa, not see (i.e. experience) unhappiness as long as you live. You will be a donor, an enjoyer and will appreciate merits. There is no doubt about this. You will meet with death at a sacred place (and) will obtain the highest position.

12. Thus having granted a boon to that brāhmaṇa dear to him, the lord vanished. He was seen as (though seen) in a dream.

13-21. Then that best brāhmaṇa Somaśarman, (accompanied) with (his wife) Sumanā, gave auspicious gifts at the great and purifying sacred place Amarakaṇṭaka, on the auspicious bank of Revā, giving merit. When a very long time of that Somaśarman passed (i.e. when he thus passed a long time), he bathed at the confluence of Kapilā and Revā and set out. In front of him the brāhmaṇa saw a white elephant, which was very bright, beautiful, divine, of a profuse ichor, and of charming (i.e. auspicious) marks, with his body looking beautiful on account of many ornaments, and endowed with great grace.

Both his temples shone with red lead and saffron. (He saw the elephant) whose ears were having blue lotuses on them, and which was having a banner and a staff. On the elephant was seated a divine, very bright man, who was endowed with divine marks, and who was adorned with all ornaments, who had put on divine flowers and who was besmeared with divine sandal. The best (brāhmaṇa, Samaśarman) saw him to be very pleasing like the moon, and endowed with an umbrella and chowries, and going, after having mounted the elephant (i.e. being carried by the elephant). (He saw the man) who was very auspiciously being praised by Siddhas, bards and Gandharvas. Seeing that beautiful, excellent elephant and the man with divine characteristics, Somaśarman, with his mind full of amazement, reflected :

22-27. 'Who is this, of a divine body and a good vow, going after having reached (i.e. along) the path?' When, thinking like this, Somaśarman came to his house, (he saw) the divine charming form entering (through) the door of his house. Full of great joy, the religious-minded, best brāhmaṇa, Somaśarman, quickly went to his house; but when he went upto the door of his house he did not see him, (but instead) the very intelligent one (saw) charming divine, fragrant flowers fallen in the courtyard (of his house). Seeing this courtyard besmeared with auspicious, fragrant sandal and saffron, and with dūrvā grass and sacred rice grains, he, thus amazed, and reflecting repeatedly, saw Sumanā with divine and auspicious excellence.

Somaśarmana said :

28. Who gave (you) these divine ornaments, (this) fortune in the form an excellent dress, and decoration (in the form) of garments and ornaments?

29. O good one, then, without any apprehension tell me the reason.

Thus speaking to his wife, the best brāhmaṇa ceased (speaking).

Sumanā said :

30-31. O my husband, listen. Someone best among the gods, mounted upon a white elephant, adorned with divine ornaments, with his body smeared with divine sandal, endowed with divine wonders, had come. I do not know which deity he was (who was) served by brāhmaṇas and Gandharvas.

32-38a. He, who was being praised by gods, Gandharvas and bards, had come. With him were ladies who were endowed with auspicious forms, with beauty and excellent dresses, with charm due to all ornaments, and all with their desires satisfied. In front of them the illustrious man filled our quadrangle with gems and is (therefore) endowed with all charm. Then I was placed on an auspicious seat by brāhmaṇas. All of them gave me garments, ornaments and decorations. They all consecrated me with auspicious Vedic hymns and meritorious songs from the sacred texts, and they again disappeared. O best brāhmaṇa, all of them (being) around me, again said : "We shall always dwell in your house. O you auspicious one, always remain undefiled along with your husband." Speaking thus, they all left. Thus only (i.e. this much only is what) I saw.

38b-45a. The very intelligent one, having heard the account told by her, again reflected: 'What is this brought about by the lord?' Thus thinking the very wise Somaśarman engaged himself in the religious duties of a brāhmaṇa. That illustrious Sumanā observing a vow became pregnant from him. That respectable lady then looked more beautiful due to that embryo. She was endowed with the flame of lustre as she was having that bright son (in her womb). She, due to (the efficacy of) her penance, gave birth to a son resembling a god. At that time divine drums resounded in the sky. Great gods blew conches, Gandharvas sang charming songs; and indeed all the celestial nymphs danced at that time. Then the calm, best brāhmaṇa, Brahmā, having come there with gods, named him (i.e. the boy) Suvrata. Having named him, all the gods of great prowess left.

45b-57. When the gods had left, the best brāhmaṇa Somaśarman performed rites like the birth-rite (of the boy). When the illustrious son Suvrata, brought into existence by gods, was born, there was great prosperity in his house mixed with (i.e. full of) wealth and grains; and also (there were) elephants, buffaloes and cows, gold and jewels. The house of that Somaśarman shone as the house of Kubera shone with heaps of wealth.

The best brāhmaṇa performed rites like meditation (and other) auspicious deeds. The brāhmaṇa, full of many merits went on a pilgrimage. The intelligent one, endowed with knowledge and merit, gave there auspicious gifts. With great joy he celebrated the marriage of the son. The son's sons, virtuous and endowed with good signs, were born. They were endowed with truthfulness, righteousness and penance. Somaśarman performed all auspicious rites of (i.e. about) them; and the illustrious one was happy with their grandsons. He enjoyed all pleasures and was without (i.e. free from) old age and diseases. His body was as (if) he was twentyfive years old. That very wise Somaśarman was lustrous like the sun. That noble, respectable lady Sumanā also shone with pious and auspicious (things), with sons and grandsons, and with vows and restraints. With auspicious vows like (being very loyal to) the husband, the large-eyed one shone excellently. She was (so much) endowed with youth that she was as it were sixteen year old.

58-60. The magnanimous, righteous, very prosperous, charming and auspicious couple was delighted and full of joy. O best brāhmaṇas, thus was their behaviour full of auspicious practices. I shall now tell you the observance of the vows by Suvrata (and) how he (obtained bliss) by having propitiated Nārāyaṇa Anāmaya (i.e. Viṣṇu).

CHAPTER TWENTYONE

Suvrata's Devotion to Viṣṇu

Sūta said :

1. Once that resplendent Vyāsa, being extremely amazed, asked Brahmā, the lord of the world, (about) the entire account of Savrata.

Vyāsa said :

2. O soul of the worlds, O you in whom the worlds are deposited, O god of gods, O great lord, I now desire to hear the life-account of Suvrata.

Brahmā said :

3. O you noble Pārāśarya (i.e. son of Parāśara), listen to the meritorious, excellent account, full of practice of penance, of the brāhmaṇa Suvrata.

4-8. The intelligent Suvrata reflected upon Nārāyaṇa (i.e. Viṣṇu), even from his childhood, (since) he had seen (that) god Puruṣottama Nārāyaṇa while (still) in the womb (of his mother). Due to his having performed (good) deeds (in the) former (birth), he always meditated upon Hari (i.e. Viṣṇu). He meditated and reflected upon that god Padmanābha, holding a conch and a disc and giving great merit, in (i.e. while he sang) songs, (did) study and recitations. Thus the best brāhmaṇa, the excellent boy, always reflecting upon Hari (i.e. Viṣṇu) only, always played with children. The intelligent, pious one, loving merit, named the sons of him, the magnanimous one (i.e. his own sons), after Hari. The very intelligent one called his friend by Hari's name:

9-16. 'O Keśava, come, come along; O Mādhava come; O Cakradhṛk (i.e. the disc-holder i.e. Viṣṇu) come; O Puruṣottama, play with me only. O Madhusūdana, we shall go together only.' In this way the brāhmaṇa called (others) by the names of Hari, while playing, reciting, laughing, lying, singing or viewing (something), or in a vehicle, on a seat, while meditating, (reciting) sacred hymns, or comprehending or (doing) good acts. He saw Janārdana (i.e. Viṣṇu) the lord of the world only; he talked to him only. He the very wise one, meditated upon (i.e. saw) that great lord, the ruler of the world viz. Keśava, Govinda, having lotus-like eyes, in grass, in wood, in a dry or wet (object), and also in the sky, on the ground, on mountains, in forests, in water, on dry land, in a stone or in beings. (Thus) Sumanā's son, that brāhmaṇa Suvrata, that religious-minded one, saw Nṛsiṁha (i.e. Viṣṇu) everywhere. Resorting to a child's sports he thus played everyday; and sang about Kṛṣṇa with songs with good musical modes, couched in sweet words, having beating times,[1] or *laya* (i.e. times in music), with charming notes of the gamut and melodies.

1. Rāga, tāla, laya etc. are terms used in music. Laya—Time in music. It is of three kinds: druta, madhya and vilambita. Mūrcchanā—The rising of sounds, an intonation, a duly regulated rise and fall of sounds, conducting the air and the harmony through the keys in a pleasing manner, changing the key or passing from one key to another.

Suvrata said :

17-24a. Those who know the Vedas always meditate upon him, who is the enemy of demons, in whose body (remains) the entire universe, who is the lord of reflective meditation, and who destroys all sins. I shall seek the shelter of (that) Madhusūdana (i.e. Viṣṇu), who occupies all the worlds, and in whom all the worlds abide. I salute that highest lord free from all faults and I always salute his pair of feet. Those whose minds are purified by the (study of) Vedānta everyday recite (the hymns about) Nārāyaṇa, the treasure of virtues, and of unlimited power. I seek his shelter in order to cross the entire ocean of the worldly existence which is endless, fathomless and difficult to cross. O enemy of demons, protect this poor one viz. me (who am devoted to) the pure and large pair of the feet of him who is the royal swan in the Mānasa lake (i.e. the minds) of the best reflecting sages, who is pure and whose entire prowess always (continues). I meditate upon the god, the lord of the entire world, who is the moon (that has come) here only to destroy the darkness in the form of grief, who has led Dharma (i.e. piousness) for the protection of the world, who is endowed with truth, who, the lord of the worlds, is the chief of all the worlds. With charming songs and measuring the beatings of time I constantly medidtate upon Śrīraṅga (i.e. Viṣṇu), the lord of the world, destroyer of ignorance, comparable to the sun only, the root of joy, and full of all prowess. I sing with unique joy (the praise of) him who alone is full treasure of the portion of nectar, who is endowed with his senses of deep meditation and who has the true perspective. He always observes the mobile and immobile universe. The very sinful people do not at all see him to be here.

24b. He (i.e. Suvrata) always sought the shelter of that Keśava.

25. Beating the time with (the clappings of) the hands he sang songs (about) Kṛṣṇa and rejoiced with (other) children.

26. Thus, being a child, Suvrata, Sumanā's son, intent on meditating upon Viṣṇu, was engaged in sports.

27. His mother said to Suvrata of fine characteristics, (and) playing: "O my boy, have your meal; hunger might oppress you."

28. The wise Suvrata again said to his mother: "I am satisfied with the great nectar viz. the delight (derived) from the meditation upon Hari."

29-34a. When he got (i.e. sat) upon the seat (used while taking) meal he saw sweet food. (He reflected:) "This food is Viṣṇu (himself); the soul has resorted to this food. May that Viṣṇu who is (present here) in the form of the soul be gratified with this water in which he dwells due to his remaining in the milky ocean. May Keśava, satisfied with his own form be gratified with tāmbūla, sandal, fragrant substances and these charming flowers." When the religious-minded one went to bed, he would reflect upon Kṛṣṇa: "I have sought the refuge of that Kṛṣṇa who is endowed with the Yoganidrā (i.e. his sleep at the end of a yuga)." The brāhmaṇa (Suvrata) would reflect upon that Vāsudeva, while taking meal, while covering himself, on a seat or bed, and would prepare everything for him.

34b-37. When the religious-minded one attained youth, he gave up enjoyment of pleasures and was engaged in meditating upon Keśava on the excellent Vaidūrya mountain, where there is the symbol of Viṣṇu called Siddheśvara and destroyer of sins. He, reflecting upon the great lord called Maheśvara glorified by Brahmā (and situated) on the right bank of Narmadā, and having resorted to Siddheśvara, thought of (practising) penance.

CHAPTER TWENTYTWO

Dharmāṅgada Born as Suvrata

Vyāsa said :

1-3. O noble one, I shall put one question to you. Now speak (i.e. answer) it; you yourself had formerly said that Suvrata meditated upon lord Nārāyaṇa Anāmaya, due to former practice. In which caste was Suvrata born in his former birth? Now tell that to me (and also) how Hari was propitiated by him. O lord of gods, who is he that is full of merit?

Brahmā said :

4-13. In the auspicious city (called) Vaidiśa, full of all prosperity, (lived) a very lustrous, powerful king, the son of Ṛtadhavaja. His very intelligent son was well-known as Rukmabhūṣaṇa. His loyal wife was the glorious Sandhyāvatī. The king's son (i.e. Rukmabhūṣaṇa) having produced a son on her like himself, named him Dharmāṅgada. This (Dharmāṅgada), the most fortunate son of Rukmāṅgada, was endowed with all auspicious marks and was intensely devoted to his father; and he, for the happiness of his father, even gave his own head to Mohinī. Hṛṣīkeśa (i.e. Viṣṇu) was pleased by his Viṣṇuite way of life and devotion to his father; and took him physically to Viṣṇu's position. He, who knew all codes of conduct, who was a devotee of Viṣṇu, who was best of the Sātvatas, he—Dharmāṅgada, who was very wise, who was well-versed in judgement and knowledge, who was an ornament of piety, living there only gladly enjoyed all divine pleasures according to his desire. When a full thousand yugas were over, he who was piety (himself) and an ornament of piety, dropped from that position, and due to the favour of Viṣṇu, was born as the eldest and most fortunate and intelligent son of Somaśarman, increasing the delight of Sumanā, and named Suvrata. The intelligent one practised penance and was intent upon meditation on Viṣṇu.

14-18a. The best brāhmaṇa, having abandoned blemishes like desire and anger, having controlled the group of senses, continuously practised penance by concentrating his mind and uniting it with Viṣṇu, near Siddheśvara on the best mountain Vaidūrya. The lord of the world, holding a conch, a disc and a mace was well-pleased with the meditation of the noble one, who thus had remained in it for a hundred years. That Keśava, with Lakṣmī, granted him another boon: "O you pious Suvrata, O you best among the wise sages, well-being to you; choose a boon, I am Kṛṣṇa that have come to you."

18b-19. Having heard these excellent words of Viṣṇu, the intelligent one was full of great joy, and seeing god Janārdana (i.e. Viṣṇu), he joining the palms of his hands, saluted him.

Suvrata said :

20. The ocean of mundane existence is full of the waves of

very great (i.e. poignant) griefs, and of the ripples of the heaps of follies. Through my vices and virtues I have reached it. O Janārdana, from it quickly take up me who am helpless.

21-28. When the great cloud of my deeds is thundering, it is raining, lightning is flashing; due to the heaps of my sins and coverings of the darkness of delusion, I do not have (i.e. I have lost my) sight. (So) O Madhusūdana, give your hand to me, who am helpless. This dense forest of the worldly existence is resorted to by (i.e. has) many trees of great grief, and by many lions of the form of follies. It is blazing with the lustre of the great fire of compassion. O Kṛṣṇa, protect me who am constantly being burnt. The tree of the worldly existence is extremely old and also high. It has the bulbous root of illusion and many branches of pity and many afflictions; it has the leaves of union with one's wife etc. It has borne fruit. O lord Murāri, protect me who climbed it and fell from it. O Kṛṣṇa, I am constantly burnt by the fires of griefs, with profuse (columns of) smoke in the form of various delusions, and with distresses like separation resembling death. Give me salvation. Always sprinkle me with water of knowledge, me—who have fallen in the great ditch covered with fearful darkness and called Saṁsāra (i.e. the worldly existence). O Kṛṣṇa, you show a great favour to me who am distressed and suffering from fear. Being disgusted with it, I have sought your refuge. Those, who with controlled minds and full of devotion, meditate upon you with their minds (full of) knowledge, obtain the (highest) position; since saluting the very auspicious pair of your feet the groups of Kinnaras and gods think of you (only). I do not talk to anyone else, I do not worship anyone else, I do not think about anyone else. I (just) continuously salute the pair of your lotus-like feet. O Kṛṣṇa, today satisfy my desire. Let the heap of my sins go far away. I am your slave, I am your servant in existence after existence. I constantly remember the pair of your lotus-like feet.

29-30a. If, O Kṛṣṇa, you are pleased, then grant me a good boon: O great god, with me take (also) my parents physically to your abode. There should be no hesitation about it.

Śrikṛṣṇa said :

30b. There is no doubt that this great affair of you will take place.

31-35. Hṛṣīkeśa was pleased with him and was very much delighted by his devotion. Free from tormentation and destruction the two viz. Sumanā and Somaśarman, went, along with Suvrata to Viṣṇu's heaven. O you very intelligent one, till a couple of yugas came (i.e. was over) the brāhmaṇa Suvrata enjoyed repeatedly divine worlds. And by the words (i.e. order) of that disc-holder (i.e. Viṣṇu) the very intelligent one again came down to (i.e. was born in) the house of Kaśyapa for the mission of gods; and enjoys Indra's position due to Viṣṇu's favour. Well-known as Vasudatta, and saluted by all gods, he enjoys the position of Indra at present.

36. Thus I have told you the entire cause of the propriety of creation. I shall (even), tell (i.e. explain to) you anything else that you ask.

Vyāsa said :

37. The powerful and very intelligent Dharmāṅgada, the son of Rukmāṅgada, was Indra at the time of creation in the first Kṛtayuga.

38-39a. Then, O lord of gods, how is it that there is another Dharmāṅgada on the earth, and also another king (named) Rukmāṅgada, and how is it that this one is also the lord of gods (i.e. Indra)? This doubt has arisen (in my mind); please explain (i.e. remove) it.

Brahmā said :

39b-40a. Oh, I shall tell you that which will remove your doubt. O best brāhmaṇa, the sport of the god is for the creation.

40b-42. As days, fortnights, months, seasons, years and Manus pass (i.e. come and go) in the same way the yugas again and again pass. Then arrives the Kalpa; then, O very intelligent one, I myself go to Janārdana (i.e. Viṣṇu) and the mobile and the immobile go to (i.e. merge into) me. (Then) he, whose nature is contemplation, again creates the universe as before.

43-44a. Again, I, the Vedas, the deities and brāhmaṇas, as well as all kings with their dispositions are born, O noble one. A wise man is not confused by this.

44b-47. As in the former Kalpa the magnanimous king Rukmāṅgada was born, in the same way this well-known brāhmaṇa Dharmāṅgada is born (now). The very intelligent ones like Rāma, Yayāti, Nahuṣa,[1] and also the magnanimous Manu and others are born and die. Kings devoted to piety enjoy the position of Indra, as the hero Dharmāṅgada is now enjoying (that) great position. In the same way Vedas, gods, Purāṇas, preceded by Smṛtis (come and go)

48-49. O best brāhmaṇ, I have thus narrated to you Suvrata's entire account which is meritorious and which leads to good position. O noble one, I shall explain to you the invisible (one).

CHAPTER TWENTYTHREE

The Slaying of the Demon Bala

The sages said :

1-2. O you best among speakers, you have told us this wonderful, meritorious, excellent tale, bringing about glory, and destroying all sins. Please tell us the propriety of the creation.

---

1. Yayāti—Name of a celebrated king of the lunar race. He was the son o Nahuṣa. He married Śukra's daughter Devayānī, who was cursed by Kaca that she would marry a Kṣatriya. Śarmiṣṭhā, daughter of the king of Asuras was told by her father to be Devayānī's servant as a sort of recompense for her formerly having slapped and thus insulted Devayānī. Yayāti fell in love with Śarmiṣṭhā and secretly married her. Devayānī came to know about the marriage, and complained to her father of the conduct of Yayāti. Śukra cursed him that he would be prematurely old. Yayāti propitiated him and obtained from him permission to transfer his infirmity to anyone who would accept it. His youngest son Pūru agreed to take it. Yayāti enjoyed youth for a thousand years. With a strenuous effort he renounced his sensual life and restoring youth to Pūru, and appointing him as his successor, he left for a forest to lead a pious and meditating life.

Nahuṣa—He was Āyus' son, Purūravas' grandson, and Yayāti's father. He was a very wise and powerful king. For some time, he deputed Indra at latter's request. He made the Seven Sages to carry him in a palanquin to Indrāṇī's house, whose love, he thought, he would win. On his way, he insulted the Sages by ordering them to move on (*sarpa, sarpa*). One of the Sages cursed him to be a *sarpa* (serpent). He fell down on the earth and remained as a serpent, till he was freed by Yudhiṣṭhira from that condition.

O son of Sūta, tell us in detail, as to how the creation (took place) formerly.

Sūta said :

3-5. I shall tell in detail the cause of creation and destruction, merely by hearing which a man would become omniscient. Hiraṇyakaśipu occupied the three worlds. Having propitiated Brahmā by penance, he obtained a boon, difficult to obtain, and also immortality from that noble god. He, having pervaded gods and the worlds secured mastery (over all).

6-9. Then gods with Gandharvas, sages who had mastered the Vedas, and Nāgas, Kinnaras, Siddhas, Yakṣas and others, led by Brahmā, went to lord Nārāyaṇa, who was enjoying his sleep at the end of a Yuga in the Milky Ocean. With the palms of their hands joined, the gods awakened him with (i.e. by singing) hymns of praise. When the lord of the gods awoke, O you very wise one(s), they told him the account of that wicked one (i.e. Hiraṇyakaśipu). Having heard it, the lord of the world, resorting to the form of Nṛsiṁha, killed Hiraṇyakaśipu.

10-15. Then with the Boar-form he killed the very powerful Hiraṇyākṣa. He lifted up the auspicious Earth, and killed that demon at that time. He also killed other fierce-looking demons. When thus the great demons had perished, when the others i.e. Diti's sons had (also) perished, when the gods had attained great positions, when sacrifices and other religious rites had proceeded (i.e. were being performed), when all the worlds had well-settled, that Diti who was oppressed by grief, who was tormented by the bereavement of her sons, who cried 'alas, alas,', and had become senseless, devoutly saluted her husband Kaśyapa who resembled the sun, who was endowed with the lustre of penance, who was a donor and was magnanimous, and said to that very intelligent best brāhmaṇa:

16-20. "O revered sir, that god—the holder of the disc—has made me sonless. Gods have struck down all the sons of Diti (i.e. of me) and of Danu. O best sage, I am burnt by the fire of grief (due to the loss) of my sons. O lord, give me a son, who would delight (everyone), who would remove the lustre of all, who would be very powerful and charming in all limbs, who would be lustrous like the king of gods, who would be very intelligent and omniscient, who would be learned and wise, who would be endowed with the lustre of penance, who would be strong and would have auspicious marks, who would be well-versed in the Vedas, who would be knowing (i.e. possessing knowledge), who would honour gods and brāhmaṇas, who would be the conqueror of all worlds, and, who would, O brāhmaṇa, give me joy, and who would, O lord, be endowed with all (good) characteristics."

21-23a. Having heard these excellent words of her, the noble Kaśyapa with his mind full of pity and pleased with her who was grieved, who was helpless and whose mind had become distressed, and having put his hand through great love for her, on her head, said to her: "O glorious one, a son, as desired by you, will be (born to you)."

23b-28. Having said so, he went to Meru, the best mountain. He of a great vow, all alone practised great penance (there). In the meanwhile, she conceived an excellent embryo. That high-minded Diti, knowing all rules of conduct, doing good deeds, remained with a pure heart for a period of hundred years. She gave birth to a son who was endowed with Brāhmaṇic lustre. Then Kaśyapa, full of great joy, came there; (and) the best and intelligent one named him. He called his son 'Bala', who, the great one, was like (i.e. true to) his name. Thus he named him, and performed his thread-ceremony. He said to him : "O (my) glorious son, practise celibacy."

29. (Bala said) : "O best brāhmaṇa, I shall just do as you tell me. O best one, with (i.e. practising) celibacy, I would study the Vedas."

30-31. Thus an entire century of years passed while he was practising penance. He, endowed with the lustre of penance, came to the presence of (i.e. came to) his mother. Diti, full of great joy saw the divine celibacy, full of the power of penance, of her magnanimous son.

32-35. She said to that son (of her) viz. Bala, who was magnanimous, who was possessed of penance, who was intelligent, who was great-souled, who was well-versed in judgement and knowledge : "O intelligent one, as long as you live, my sons like Hiraṇyakaśipu killed by him who holds a disc in his hand (i.e. by Viṣṇu), will live onward. O my boy, conclude the hostility (i.e. take revenge), kill in battle (our) enemies—the gods." That Danu said to that very powerful Bala these words: "Son, first quickly kill Indra, the lord of gods. Then strike down gods, and after that (strike down) him, whose vehicle is Garuḍa (i.e. Viṣṇu)."

36. Having heard (the words) of the two (i.e. Diti and Danu), Aditi, who looked upon her husband as a god, and who was full of great grief, said to her son, Indra :

37-38a. "Diti's son, of a huge body, is increasing with brāhmaṇic lustre. For killing gods, he practised penance in (honour of) Śiva. Understand like this, O lord of gods, if you desire happiness here."

38b-39. Having thus heard those words of his mother, Indra, the lord of gods, was extremely worried due to uneasiness. Being tormented by great grief, he then thought:

40-45. 'How shall I kill this (Bala) who is polluting the piety of gods?' Thus the lord of gods decided to kill Bala. Once that Bala resorted (i.e. went) to the ocean to offer his daily prayers. He shone with a divine skin of an antelop and a piece of stick, and with spotless merit and that (i.e. undescribable) celibacy. Indra saw him seated upon the seat meant for daily prayers, near the ocean, muttering prayers and extremely tranquil. That Diti's son was hit (by Indra) with that divine thunderbolt. Seeing Bala fallen dead on the ground, the king of gods full of great joy was then delighted. The pious Indra, having thus struck down that demon, Diti's son, ruled happily.

CHAPTER TWENTYFOUR

Vṛtra Duped

Sūta said :

1-2. Having heard that her very powerful son Bala was killed, Diti piteously wept saying: "Oh, I am facing a great misery." Having thus very piteously wept for a long time, the miserable, glorious one went to Kaśyapa, her husband, and said to him :

3-4a. "Seeing your son who had gone to the ocean, the very sinful Indra, the lord of the host of gods, with his thunderbolt killed him having the characteristics of a brāhmaṇa and just practising *sandhyā* (i.e. the daily prayer)."

4b-5. Having heard thus, (Kaśyapa) Marīci's son got angry at that time, and was full of great anger, as it were, burnt with fire. The best brāhmaṇa plucked a hair from his matted hair, (and putting it into) pure fire (said:)

6-10a. "I shall create a son just for killing Indra." From that fire-pool, from the mouth of fire was produced a fierce figure, full of black collyrium (i.e. very dark), and tawny-eyed, with the interior of his mouth fearful on account of the fangs, causing fear to the worlds, capable of giving a big blow with the flat of his hand, holding a sword and a shield, bright with lustre of the entire body, resembling a large cloud and strong. He said to the brāhmaṇa viz. Kaśyapa: "Give me an order. O brāhmaṇa, tell me the purpose for which I was produced; I shall accomplish it through your favour, O you of a good vow."

Kaśyapa said :

10b-11. O you highly intelligent one, fulfil the desire of this Aditi (Diti?) and of me also. Kill the wicked Indra; and when that king of gods (i.e. Indra) is killed, enjoy Indra's position.

12-14. Thus ordered by that noble Kaśyapa, Vṛtra exerted to kill Indra. Endowed with valour, he practised archery. The thousand-eyed one (i.e. Indra), seeing the demon's strength, power and his lustre with courage befitting a kṣatriya, was afflicted by fear. He thought of a means to kill that wicked Vṛtra.

15-16. Having called the Seven Great Sages, the god of gods sent them to Vṛtra, the lord of demons: "O best sages, you may please go (to the place) where Vṛtra is staying, and bring about a treaty between them (i.e. the demons and me)."

17. Thus ordered and urged by that thousand-eyed (Indra) the Seven Sages then said to that demon Vṛtra:

18-21a. "Indra offers to make friendship (with you), O best demon; make that friendship." The Seven Sages, knowing the fact, said to the very powerful Vṛtra: "O best one, the very wise Indra desires your friendship. Then how is it that you do not do it (i.e. do not accept his offer)? O hero, enjoy happily half the position (i.e. kingdom) of Indra; let Indra have the (remaining) half. Giving up their enmity, let all demons and gods live happily."

Vṛtra said :

21b-23a. If the best lord of the gods really desires friendship, I (too) shall do (the same) by resorting to truth (i.e. truthfully); there is no doubt about this. O brāhmaṇas, if, by putting forward (i.e. by resorting to) dishonesty, Indra plays mischief, then what is the surety in this matter?

23b-24a. The sages said to Indra : "Give certainty about this. Tell us the truth if you desire friendship here (with Vṛtra)."

Indra said :

24b-25a. If I behave with you falsely and dishonestly, then I shall be stained with the sins of killing brāhmaṇas etc. There is no doubt about it.

25b-27a. The very powerful (brāhmaṇas) again spoke to Vṛtra, the lord of demons: "'I shall be stained with the sins of killing brāhmaṇas etc. There is no doubt about it.' Thus, O very wise one, Indra has said to you. O you very intelligent one, form friendship (with Indra), with this (i.e. taking those words to be the) surety."

Vṛtra said :

27b-28a. O best brāhmaṇas, on account of your respectable manner and this truthfulness of him, I shall likewise form friendship with him.

28b-33. The chief brāhmaṇas took Vṛtra into the vicinity of Indra. Seeing Vṛtra, ready for friendship, having arrived, the pious Indra got up from his seat, and taking the material of worship quickly, offered (the same) to Vṛtra: "O very wise one, enjoy half of this great position of Indra. O best of demons, we two should stay happily." O best brāhmaṇa, having thus produced confidence through friendship of Vṛtra, the wicked-minded one always saw his weak point. Vṛtra too was always cautious. Indra also would think day and night (to find out his weak point). He did not find out the weak point of the noble Vṛtra.

34-43a. He thought of a stratagem to kill him. He sent Rambhā (after telling her:) "With this or that trick, delude the great demon. O auspicious one, do that to delude the great demon, so that by killing him I shall get happiness." (Rambhā resorted to Nandanavana—Indra's garden,) the garden which was auspicious, very divine, resorted to by pious trees, full of many trees with fruits, full of beasts and birds, looking beautiful all around with divine heavenly cars, always full of divine music of the Gandharvas and bees, full of auspicious, sweet and prolonged cooings of cuckoos everywhere, full of the notes of peacocks and the sounds of antelopes at every place, everywhere adorned with divine sandal trees and also with charming wells, pools and lakes full of water and lotuses in bloom; it looked beautiful with gods, Gandharvas, Siddhas and Kinnaras as well; also with divine sages and with an excellent garden. It was crowded with hosts of celestial nymphs; and with various curious and auspicious objects. It was thronged with golden palaces, and was everywhere adorned with staffs, umbrellas and chowries, and with pitchers and banners. It was full of the sounds (of the recitation) of the Vedas and with the sounds of songs.

43b-44a. Reaching the Nandana like this, that sportive Rambhā, smiling charmingly sported there with celestial nymphs.

Sūta said :

44b-51. Once that Vṛtra, dragged by death, went very joyfully with some demons, to that forest. The lord of gods and brāhmaṇas, looking for his weak point, moved unnoticed by the side of that noble one. That very wise Vṛtra, confiding (in Indra) in all matters, and knowing Indra to be a great friend, was not afraid of him. Moving (i.e. he moved) in the great auspicious forest. The forest was very charming and (full of) curious objects and crowded with bevies of women. That glorious and noble Rambhā, of large eyes, who had resorted to the cool and very auspicious shade of a sandal-tree, was seated on a swing and was playing dice with her friends. She (also) sang a melodious song, infatuating the entire universe. Vṛtra, having come there, saw that Rambhā, with charming, large eyes with his mind full of sexual desire.

CHAPTER TWENTYFIVE

The Killing of Demon Vṛtra

Sūta said :

1. (Vṛtra thought:) 'Who is this woman with charming eyes, singing in graceful modes? This attractive woman shines all round. She would delude people with full emotions.'

2-3. Seeing that Rambhā, of large eyes like lotuses, of plump breasts, with her body smeared with sandal, with her face resembling a lotus, (he thought) 'Is she the abode of my sexual desire or is she charming and attractive Rati ? Sent here only by Cupid, I shall certainly approach her, who is full of emotion, endowed with good form, disposed to sex, and of an extremely good disposition.'

4. Thus the demon, very much distressed, full of great anxiety, deluded by sexual desire, prompted (like this) for a long time, went there quickly, and with his mind afflicted said to her, whose eyes were charming:

5. "O beautiful lady, whom do you belong to? By whom are you sent (here)? Tell me what your most auspicious name is. By your extremely lustrous beauty I am infatuated. O you young lady, come under my influence."

6-7. Thus addressed (by Vṛtra), the large-eyed one (said to him:) "O noble one, I am Rambhā; I have come to this excellent forest, Nandana, with my friends, to sport. But who are you? Why have you come to me?".

Vṛtra said :

8-10. Listen, I shall tell you who I am that have come here, O young lady. O you auspicious one, I am Kaśyapa's son, born from fire. O you of a beautiful face, I am also the friend of Indra, the lord of gods. I am enjoying half the portion (i.e. the kingdom) of Indra. I am Vṛtra, O you respectable lady; how do you not recognise me, under whose control have come all the three worlds, O you of an excellent complexion?

11. O you beautiful lady, I have sought your shelter. Protect me from the (disturbance caused by)sexual desire. O you of large eyes, resort to me, who am, O dear one, distressed by sexual desire.

Rambhā said :

12. There is no doubt that today I shall submit myself to you; O hero, you should do whatever I tell you to do.

(He said:)

13a. "O you noble one, let it be so; I shall do all that (you will tell me to do)."

13b-14a. Having thus established a relation with her, the very powerful best demon enjoyed in that very meritorious forest.

14b-15. The great demon was very much stupefied by her singing, dancing, charming smile and sexual intercourse (with her). She said to that noble and best demon:

16a. "(Please) drink wine; (please) drink madhu-mādhavī (a kind of intoxicating drink)."

16b. He said to that Rambhā of large eyes and of a moon-like face:

17. "O good lady, I am a brāhmaṇa's son, who has mastered the Vedas and the Vedāṅgas. How shall I drink wine (an act) that is condemned?"

18-20. But that respectable lady Rambhā lovingly gave wine to him against his will. Due to civility for her he drank wine at that time. When he was extremely stupefied by the wine, and lost his senses, just then Indra struck him with his thunderbolt. Then that killer of Vṛtra (i.e. Indra) was tainted with such sins as killing a brāhmaṇa. Then the brāhmaṇas said: "O Indra, you have committed a sin.

21. That very powerful Vṛtra relied on (you) due to our words (i.e. because we told him). You have killed him through (falsifying that) reliance on you."

Indra said :

22-24. An enemy should always be killed by this or that means. You are angry because the wicked demon, the lord of even the three worlds, the killer of gods and brāhmaṇas, the enemy of sacrifices and righteousness is killed. Is it a sign of justice? O best brāhmaṇas, first think (properly), then you may be angry if you think my injustice (i.e. if you think I have done injustice).

25-26. The brāhmaṇas were thus addressed by Indra. The best ones were also admonished by all gods like Brahmā. When that demon, the enemy of righteousness was killed, they went to their respective abodes.

CHAPTER TWENTYSIX

The Origin of Maruts

Sūta said :

1-3. O best brāhmaṇas, that Diti, hearing that her son was killed, was afflicted with pain and tormented with grief due to (the death of) her son. She again said to that noble, best sage Kaśyapa: "O best brāhmaṇa, to kill that very wicked Indra, give me, O lord, a son having Brāhmaṇic lustre, strong and unbearable to all deities, if I am very dear to you, O my beloved husband."

Kaśyapa said :

4-5. Wicked god Indra, resorting to sinful ways, killed my very strong sons, Bala and Vṛtra. To kill him only, I shall give (you) one son. O you glorious one, be pure for one hundred years.

6-12. Speaking like this, that best meditating sage, put his hand on her head and he, with her only, went to a penance-grove (on) Meru. Always remaining pure, that respectable lady, living in the penance grove, practised penance for a son, O best brāhmaṇa. Then knowing about the assiduous effort of Diti, that thousand-eyed god, O noble one, saw her weakness. The god of gods becoming (i.e. turning himself into a youth) twentyfive years old, and resembling a deity went, in the form of a brāhmaṇa, near her. The thousand-eyed righteous one saluted the mother, endowed with penance, and was (thus) addressed by her: "O best brāhmaṇa, who are you?" The thousand-eyed one (i.e. Indra) said to her: "O you beautiful, auspicious lady, I am your son, a brāhmaṇa, knowing the Vedas. I (also) know Dharma. I shall help (you) in your penance. There is no doubt about it." He served that respectable mother, endowed with penance.

13. She did not know him to be Indra, of wicked deeds, that had come there. She looked upon him as her lawful son, serving her everyday.

14-15. He would (first) shampoo the body of that respectable lady, and would then wash her feet. The virtuous one always gave Diti leaves, roots, bark-garments and the skin of an antelope. Pleased with his devotion, she, being delighted, said to him:

16. "O you blessed one, when a very meritorious son will be born (to me), and when Indra will be killed, you rule over the divine kingdom along with my son."

17-20. (Indra said:) "O you fortunate one, let it be so; it will be like that due to your favour." Indra desired to find her weak point only. For ninetynine years he kept on looking for her weak point. (Once) without washing her feet, Diti entered into (i.e. slept on) her bed. She put her head on the border of the bed. She, with her hair loose and being very much perturbed, (tried) to get sleep. Indra entered her side, and with his thunderbolt of a sharp edge, cut the embryo lying in the womb, into seven pieces; it wept.

21-25. O best brāhmaṇas, the very lustrous Indra again and again said to that large embryo, weeping due to being in Indra's hands, "Do not weep". Again Indra cut that embryo born of (i.e. conceived by) Diti into seven parts. That king of gods cut each (portion of the embryo) that was weeping. In this way the Maruts of great prowess were born. Since they were (thus) addressed by Indra (*mā rodiḥ*) they got this name. The Maruts, of great vigour and huge bodies, of sharp lustre and valour, were fortynine (in number). They were known as Maruts and attended on Indra only.

26-28.* They illumine the great host of all beings. Hari, the lord of beings, successively gave in (various) habitations, kingdoms (to kings) preceded by Pṛthu. That supreme spirit Kṛṣṇa (i.e. Viṣṇu), who pervades everything, who is the lord of the world, who is triumphant with penance, who has great lustre is all alone the lord of the beings.

29-32. O best brāhmaṇa, to him who knows correctly, belongs merit, and this immobile and mobile world, this creation of beings. He has no fear of again being born here (i.e. in this world); then wherefrom can he have fear in the next world? That man, who devoutly listens to this meritorious, auspicious (account of) the creation that removes all sins, is free from all sins. He is blessed, he is meritorious and is endowed with truth. He, who listens to (this account of) creation, gets the highest position. With his heart cleared of all sins, he goes to Viṣṇu's world.

CHAPTER TWENTYSEVEN

Coronation of the Kings

Sūta said:

1-3a. That lord, Brahmā, the master of all worlds, having then consecrated on the entire kingdom (i.e. as the king of all the kingdom) that great lord, king Pṛthu, Vena's son, of large arms and a huge body, and resembling Indra, the lord of gods, and taking into account (other) kingdoms one by one, proceeded to give each one that kingdom, which he deserved.

3b-4. The highly intelligent one consecrated Soma (i.e. the Moon) as the king of the trees, brāhmaṇas, of planets and stars, of all pious acts, of religiously conducted sacrifices, of merits and of those of an auspicious lustre.

5-8a. O best brāhmaṇa, having consecrated Varuṇa (as the chief) among the waters and of places sacred to deities and of gems, and Vaiśravaṇa as the king of all other Yakṣas, the grandsire appointed Viṣṇu on the kingdom (i.e. as the king) of

*The relevance of these lines is not clear. They seem to have been inserted in wrong place. (Ed.)

Ādityas, for the good of the people, O you very intelligent one. He appointed the capable Dakṣa, conversant with all religious practices, the chief of the attendants of the lord of the beings, as the chief of all auspicious objects.

8b-15. He appointed Prahrāda, knowing all religious practices, on the kingdom (i.e. as the king) of the sons of Diti and Danu. He consecrated Yama, the son of Vivasvān, on the kingdom (i.e. as the king) of the dead ancestors, and (appointed) Śiva, having the trident in his hand, (as the king) of the Yakṣas, demons, ghosts, goblins, reptiles, of all female meditating sages, of magnanimous vampires, and also of all skeletons and spirits, and of all kings. (He appointed) the great mountain Himālaya (as the king) of all mountains. The lord of gods appointed the auspicious ocean, the best sacred place of all, on the kingdom (i.e. as the king) of rivers, lakes, small wells, of pools, and wells and other divine (sacred places). Then Brahmā, the lord of gods, consecrated Citraratha on the auspicious kingdom (i.e. as the king) of all the Gandharvas. Then the four-faced god (i.e. Brahmā) consecrated Vāsuki on the kingdom (i.e. as the king) of the snakes (nāgas) of auspicious vigour and Takṣaka (as the king) of the serpents (sarpas).

16-18. In the same way, he consecrated Airāvaṇa on the kingdom (i.e. as the king) of the elephants, and Uccaiḥśravas (as the king of) all the horses, and (Garuḍa) the son of Vinatā (as the king) of all the birds. He then appointed the lion on the kingdom (i.e. as the king) of all the beasts. The lord of beings consecrated an excellent bull (as the chief) of the bulls. The grandsire (appointed) the Indian fig-tree (as the king) of trees.

19. In this way the grandsire Brahmā, the best one, having founded all the kingdoms, appointed the regents of the quarters.

20-27. The best one consecrated Sudhanvan, Vairāja's son, as the regent —as the king— in (i.e. of) the eastern quarter. He consecrated the noble Śaṅkhapada, son of Kardama Prajāpati, as the king of the southern quarter. Similarly Brahmā, the lord of beings, consecrated the son of Varuṇa Prajāpati, named Puṣkara, in (i.e. as the chief of) the western quarter. In (i.e. as the regent of) the northern quarter, Brahmā consecrated Nalakūbara. Thus he consecrated the very powerful regents of the quarters, by whom even now the earth with the seven islands and (many) cities, is righteously protected according to (i.e. in) the regions (assigned to them). That illustrious Pṛthu also was consecrated as the king in accordance with the rites as seen (i.e. mentioned) in the Vedas and with all great sacrifices like the Rājasūya, in the pious period of Manu[1] called Cākṣuṣa, which has gone by, which had great splendour and which led to the good of gods and the righteous, O you illustrious one. Then he gave the kingdom to Vaisasvata Manu.

28-31. O best among the brāhmaṇas, if you desire to listen carefully, I shall also tell you the minute details about the magnanimous Pṛthu. This is the basis (*adhiṣṭhāna?*) (which is) said to be very meritorious. This (alone) is always determined (i.e. definitely told) in all the Purāṇas. That man, who, devoutly and with rapt attention, listens to this (account), which is meritorious, which leads to fame, gives long life, and an auspicious stay in heaven, which is blessed, pure, causing longevity, which bestows sons and prosperity, enjoys the fruit of (performing) the horse-sacrifice. There is no doubt about this.

CHAPTER TWENTYEIGHT

The Story of Pṛthu

The sages said:

1-7. O noble one, (please) tell us in detail (about) the birth of that magnanimous Pṛthu. We desire to hear it. (Tell us) how that noble king formerly milked this cow (i.e. the earth); how gods, manes, sages knowing the truth, demons, serpents, Yakṣas, trees and mountains, goblins and Gandharvas, brāhmaṇas doing auspicious acts, and how other magnanimous ones (did so). O you highly intelligent one, tell us especially how they held the pot of milk and the manner in which she was milked.

---

1. Manvantara—the period or age of Manu. This period comprises 4320000 human years or 1/14th day of Brahmā, the fourteen Manvantaras making up one whole day.

O Sūta's son, tell us why formerly the very meritorious and angry sages churned the hand even of that noble king Vena. This is a strange account which destroys all sins. We are desirous of hearing it; O noble one, (it is so interesting that) we are not at all content with (i.e. even though we hear) it.

Sūta said :

8-10a. O best brāhmaṇas, I shall tell you in detail about king Pṛthu's—Vena's son's—birth, power, his wife, also about the entire life of the intelligent (king). O noble and best brāhmaṇas, desire to hear it (i.e. listen to it).

10b-11. This account should not be narrated to one who is not a devotee, to one who is faithless, to a cheat, to a great fool, to one who is greatly deluded, to a bad disciple, to one who is void of faith, to one who is untruthful; do not narrate it to one who destroys everything.

12-13. He who recites it in a different way, goes to hell. You are full of devotion, and are intent upon behaving truthfully. In front of you (i.e. to you) I shall fully narrate the whole account that removes sins. O best brāhmaṇas, (please) listen.

14-17. O excellent brāhmaṇas, I shall tell you the secret, which leads (one) to heaven, to fame, which causes longevity, which is excellent, which is accepted by the Vedas and which is told by the sages. He, who, after saluting the brāhmaṇas, always narrates in detail this (account) of Pṛthu, the son of Vena, would never lament over what he has done and not done. The sin earned by him during seven births, perishes by just hearing it. A brāhmaṇa would know (the meaning of) the Vedas, a kṣatriya would be victorious, a vaiśya would be prosperous with wealth, and a śūdra would get happiness. One thus gets the fruit by reciting or listening to it.

18-26a. The biography of Pṛthu is pure and it removes sins. Formerly there was a Prajāpati, Aṅga by name, born in Atri's family and a lord resembling Atri. He preserved piety, was very intelligent and well-versed in the meaning of the Vedas and (other) branches of knowledge. His son was Vena, a lord of beings. Abandoning righteousness, he always proceeded (in all his acts). Mṛtyu had a highly virtuous daughter by name

Sunīthā. The noble Aṅga married that Sunīthā. On her he begot Vena, the destroyer of righteousness. Due to the blemishes of his maternal grandfather, Vena the son of the daughter of Kāla, gave up his own way of righteousness and became fondly attached to wickedness. Due to (sexual) desire, greed and infatuation he practised sin only. The lord of men gave up the virtuous practices as told in the Vedas, and being deluded by pride and jealousy, behaved sinfully. People at that time lived without Vedic studies. When he was the lord of the subjects, they were without the Vedic studies and Vaṣaṭkāra (i.e. they did not study the Vedas and did not offer oblations). Deities did not drink Soma that proceeded and was offered at sacrifices.

26b-30. The wicked one always said to the brāhmaṇas: "You should not study (the Vedas); you should not make offering into the fire. You should not give gifts; you should not perform sacrifices and should not make offerings into fire." When destruction was imminent, this was the declaration of that king. Again and again (he told): "Sacrifices are to be offered to me. I am the sacrificer as well as the sacrifice." (He) also (told them:) "Sacrifices should be offered to me; offerings should be made to me." Thus Vena always spoke. (He also said:) "I am the eternal Viṣṇu. I am Brahmā, I am Rudra, I am Indra. I am the wind. I am the enjoyer. I am the oblations offered to the deities and manes. There is no doubt about this."

31. Then all the very powerful sages, who got angry, got together and said to the king of a wicked mind:

The sages said :

32. The king is surely the lord of the earth (and) he always protects the subjects. The emperor is the image of righteousness, therefore he should protect it.

33. We are entering upon an initiation for a twelve-year sacrifice. Do not play a mischief with the sacrifice. Righteousness is the way of the good.

34. O great king, practise righteousness; practise truthfulness and merit. You have made an agreement that you would protect the subjects.

35. Vena, of a wicked mind, laughed and said this nonsensical thing to the sages, who were speaking like that:

Vena said :

36. Who else (but me) is the creator of Dharma (i.e. religious practices)? Whom else should I listen to? Who, on the earth, is like me in (point of) learning, power, penance or truth?

37. I am the source of all beings and especially of religious practices. You, who are confounded and ignorant do not know me.

38. If I desire, I would burn the earth or would inundate it with water. I would block up the heaven and the earth. There should be no discussion about this matter.

39-45a. O king, when they could not dissuade Vena from his infatuation and pride, the angry great sages, forcibly seized him with rage, and churned the left thigh of his, who was trembling with anger. The magnanimous ones saw (there a being) that was possessed of (=like) a heap of black collyrium, that was very short and strange, that had a long face and deformed eyes, that was bright due to an armour, that had a protruded belly and broad ears, that was very much frightened and that was a gamester. They then said to him, "sit down". Hearing those words of theirs, he, being distressed with fear, sat down. His race was settled in mountains and forests. (They are) the Niṣādas, the Kirātas, the Bhillas, the Nāhalakas, the Bhramaras, the Pulindas and those that belong to the other Mleccha species. From that part (i.e. left thigh) all those sinful ones were produced.

45b-52a. Then all the sages, with their minds pleased, (found) Vena, the best king, to be without a blemish. They churned the right hand of that magnanimous one only. When his hand was (thus) churned, sweat was produced. The sages again churned the right hand only. From that excellent hand a man was produced. He resembled twelve suns; the complexion of his body was like heated gold; he was covered with (i.e. he had put on) divine flowers; his body was shining due to divine ornaments; he had besmeared divine sandal on his body. He shone with a crown resembling the sun in colour (i.e. brilliance) and with a pair of ear-rings. His body was huge, his arms were large, he was matchless in form; the great lord had held a sword and arrows, a bow and had put on an armour. The highly intelligent one was endowed with all (auspicious) marks, and was decorated with all ornaments, and with a lustrous form and had a good complexion. The son of Vena was (i.e. shone) on the earth as Indra in heaven.

52b-53. When that magnanimous one was born, gods and spotless sages celebrated a festival to (i.e. in honour of) the son of Vena. With his body he was evidently bright like fire.

54-55. When, holding the first Ājagava bow (i.e. Śiva's bow) which was excellent, and divine arrows and a very bright armour for protection, the magnanimous and noble hero Pṛthu, was born, all the beings were happy, O best brāhmaṇa.

56-59. To consecrate him (with their water), all the best brāhmaṇas proceeded to all sacred places and various auspicious (places of) water. O best brāhmaṇa, gods led by the grandsire (i.e. Brahmā), various beings, the immobile and the mobile consecrated that king, the great hero, the protector of the subjects, viz. Pṛthu. That son of Vena, noble and brave, being approached by the mobile and the immobile, by all gods and brāhmaṇas, was consecrated by them as the emperor of (all) kings.

60-63. His father had never pleased his subjects; (but) pleased by him, they were very happy. The term Rājan (i.e. king) came about (i.e. was coined) because of the hero's pleasing (his subjects). Due to the fear of that magnanimous one, the entire water of the ocean stood still when the great hero approached the ocean. Cutting off difficult passage, the mountains offered easy passage. All those mountains never insulted his flag. Crops grew in unploughed land, and everywhere cows gave milk as desired (by those who milked them).

64. Rain(-fall) was as (much as) desired. All brāhmaṇas, kṣatriyas and others performed Vedic sacrifices and celebrated great festivals.

65. When that king was ruling, all trees bore fruits as desired, there was no famine, no disease and no untimely death of men.

66. When that un-assailable, noble king of kings was ruling, all people, intent on following religious practices, lived happily.

67. At this time only, (i.e. from) the auspicious sacrifice of the grandsire, on a grand, pleasing day, Sūta was born of Sūti.

68. In (i.e. from) the same sacrifice the wise Māgadha was also born. By the great sages the two were invited there for praising Pṛthu.

69. O best brāhmaṇas, I shall narrate the characteristics of Sūta: He is endowed with a lock of hair on the crown of his head and a sacred thread; he is devoted to Vedic studies.

70-73. He knows the meaning of all the sacred books; he maintains the sacred fire; he is endowed with (i.e. he gives) gifts and study; he is intent upon Brāhmaṇic practices. He is always engaged in worshipping gods and brāhmaṇas. He is a sacrificer and would perform sacrifices to the accompaniment of Vedic hymns. He was always intent upon Brāhmaṇic practices and always had friendship with brāhmaṇas. Māgadha was born like this (but was) without studies. All those bandins and cāraṇas should be known to be (i.e. were) magnanimous and were without Brāhmaṇic practices, and predominated as bards.

74-78a. Both the skilful Sūta and Māgadha were created for eulogising; all the sages said to them: "Praise this king; and also the deeds worthy of him, and (narrate) also how the king is." The Bandin (i.e. the Sūta) and Māgadha said to all the sages: "We two shall please all the gods and sages with our deeds; but we do not know his deeds, and also his characteristics and his glory. O best brāhmaṇas, we do not know that deed of this magnanimous (king) with which (i.e. taking which into consideration) we would praise him. This best king, whose merits are not known (to us), would be praised with (i.e. with reference to) his future auspicious qualities."

78b-86. All the sages told (them) the deeds which that very glorious Pṛthu performed, (and also) all the divine virtues of that magnanimous one. (The sages said:) "He (will be) truthful, endowed with knowledge, intelligent and of well-known valour; he (will) always (be) brave, (will) appreciate merits, (will be) meritorious, truth-speaking, and the best performer of sacrifices. He (will) speak pleasing words, (will) speak the truth, (will) have grains and wealth, (will) know and appreciate (others') merits, (will) know what is right, and (will) love truth, (will) be omnipresent, omniscient, friendly to brāhmaṇas, knower of the Vedas, and very intelligent. He (will) be wise, (will) have a sweet voice, and (will) master the Vedas and the Vedāṅgas. He will support and protect (his) subjects; he (will) be victorious on the battle-field. The best king will perform sacrifices like the Rājasūya, and is the only one on the earth who is endowed with all virtuous practices. The magnanimous one will possess these qualities." The two, viz. Sūta and Māgadha, were appointed by the sages to sing the praises of that magnanimous one with (reference to) the future qualities (i.e. qualities he will possess). O highly intelligent one, since then people are delighted with eulogies, and hereafter also the donors will be pleased with excellent praises.

87-93. Since then, O best brāhmaṇas, blessings are employed (i.e. included) in eulogies; and they (who sing praises) get excellent (i.e. abundant) wealth. The noble Pṛthu, out of graciousness, gave Sūta, Māgadha and Bandin, the prosperous and excellent country, viz. Tailaṅga, and also the Haihaya country. Having established a city named after himself on the bank of the Revā, he, performing sacrifices, formerly gave (gifts) to brāhmaṇas, O best brāhmaṇa. All the subjects, and also the sages of pure penance saw the best man, who was omniscient, gave all gifts, and whose strength lay in piousness. The meritorious ones said to one another: "He will give livelihood to gods and especially to us. He will protect the subjects and maintain them." O you very wise ones, it is said that formerly this earth became stable after the seed sown (in it) was eaten by the created beings for living.

94-98. Then the subjects ran to Pṛthu. Having heard (i.e. he heard) the words of the sages, 'Give us a good livelihood'. The Earth, having consumed all (kinds of) food, became very stable. The best king, seeing the very great fear of the subjects, and also by the word of the great sages, took his bow with an arrow, and the angry king speedily ran to the Earth. The Earth, through his fear, took up the form of an elephant, and concealing herself, moved through forests and inaccessible places. The very wise one did (i.e. could) not see (her in) the form of an elephant.

99-101. Then the king ran after her in the form of an elephant. Being struck by him with sharp arrows, she, taking up a lion's form, became wholly occupied in running. The king, observing that (Earth in a) lion's form, ran towards (i.e. after) her. That very wise one, who was extremely angry, and whose charming eyes were red due to anger, struck the Earth with whetted and sharp excellent arrows.

102. Struck with the arrows, she (i.e. the Earth) was

afflicted and alarmed. Taking up the form of a buffalo she became intent on fleeing.

103-120. The archer (i.e. Pṛthu), with an arrow in his hand, ran fast (after her). O you best brāhmaṇas, she became (i.e. turned herself into) a cow and verily went to heaven. She sought the shelter of Brahmā and of the noble Viṣṇu also. She did (i.e. could) not secure the refuge of gods like Rudra. Not getting a great (i.e. good) protection, she regarded Vena's son only (as her refuge). Afflicted with (the injury caused by) the stroke of the arrow, she came to his side (i.e. to him). With her hands joined in humble entreaty, she spoke (these) words to Pṛthu. She said to the king: "O king of kings, protect me, protect me. O magnanimous one, I am mother Earth, the support of all. O king, when I am killed, (all) the seven worlds are destroyed. I am always to be worshipped by the three worlds, with the palms of their hands joined in obeisance." She also said to the king: "O king, a woman is always exempt from death (i.e. is never to be killed). The best brāhmaṇas have considered killing a woman to be a great sin. The best brāhmaṇas have also considered killing a cow to be a great sin. O great king how will you support the subjects without me? O king, when I am stable, then (only) the mobile and immobile worlds become stable. These mobile and immobile worlds will perish without me. When I perish, the beings will perish. O king, how will you support your subjects without me? The people are steady on me, the world is supported by me. There is no doubt that when I perish all the beings will perish. If you desire bliss, then (please) do not destroy me. O lord of beings, O king, listen to my words. Undertakings become highly successful through efforts, O noble one. Properly consider that effort by which you will support (your) subjects. O you very wise great king, by destroying me, i.e. without me, how will you always support, maintain, nourish and hold in your possession these subjects? Control your anger. I shall be full of food and will support these subjects. As a woman I am not to be killed; (if you kill me) you will have to atone (for having killed me). They say that a female, even of the lower species, is not to be killed. Considering in this way, you should not give up your proper conduct." Thus the earth spoke many words to the king: "O great king, give up this terrible wrath. O king of kings, if you are pleased then (only) I shall be happy."

121. Thus addressed by her, king Pṛthu, the lord of subjects and the son of Vena, said (these words) to the noble Earth, O best brāhmaṇas:

CHAPTER TWENTYNINE

The Story of Pṛthu (Contd.)

Pṛthu said :

1-13a. If a very sinful one is killed, O you of sinful conduct, good people rich in merit live happily. Therefore one that is most sinful and of a wicked mind should be killed. Now you have suppressed all seeds by devouring them. Where will you go by being stable after having destroyed the beings? When a sinful one of a bad conduct is killed, the good live happily. Therefore sin should be destroyed; this is the truth; there is no doubt about it. That from which merit proceeds, should be carefully preserved. You have committed a great sin causing the destruction of the beings. He who for himself or for someone else kills one who torments the world, does not incur sin. O auspicious Earth, when many people become happy by a wicked one having been killed, there is neither a (major) sin nor a minor sin. There is no doubt that (i.e. certainly) I shall kill you. If, O Earth, for the good of this world (i.e. these beings), you do not act according to these meritorious and good words of (i.e. uttered by) me, I shall kill you with sharp arrows, if you are averse to my words. There is no doubt that I shall sustain, by means of my lustre and merit, the virtuous beings living in the three worlds. Accepting my meritorious rule, and obeying my order always rejuvenate these beings, O Earth. If, O you good one, you today obey this order of mine, then I shall be pleased with you, and will always protect you, and also other best kings (will protect you); there is no doubt about this.

13b-14a. That Earth, in the form of a cow, with her body adorned (i.e. covered) with arrows, said these (words) to the highly intelligent Pṛthu, Vena's son, who was the support of righteousness:

The Earth said :

14b-18. O great king, I shall carry out your order, full of truth and merit, for the well-being of the beings; there is no doubt about it. O best king, enterprises and meritorious undertakings become successful by means of exertion and resourcefulness. O king of kings, find out a means by which you would be upright. Support all the subjects in such a way that you make all of them prosperous. Your stone-like (i.e. hard) and sharp arrows have stuck to my body. O king, you yourself extract them. They very much prick me. Make me (turned into) such (a shape) that the water would remain on me.

Sūta said :

19-24. Extracting those big and stone(-like arrows) of various forms with the end of his bow, he made the Earth even. Since then, O best brāhmaṇas, those stones grew in size. The son of king Vena, with pleased mind, having extracted his arrows from her body, made even the ditches and the caves with the strokes of his arrows. Thus, he, prospering with merit, made even the entire Earth. Having made her even, and having thought repeatedly, the noble one made Svāyambhuva Manu as the first calf. O best ones, during the Manu-periods that had passed, the Earth had become uneven; and there was no path anywhere, O best brāhmaṇas, even and uneven portions were naturally there.

25-32a. When the first period of Cākṣuṣa Manu arrived, and when the first creation came up, and when the surface of the Earth was uneven, the boundries of villages, cities, towns, countries, and fields that were seized (*kṣetrapannānām?*) were not noticed. There was no agriculture, no trade and no cow-keeping. No one told lies; there was neither greed nor jealousy. It is said that nobody ever entertained pride or committed sin. O best brāhmaṇa, when the Vaivasvata period came, the beings were born even before the birth of Vena's son. All these beings desired to have an abode. All the beings, through their merit, lived at some places on the ground, or on a mountain, or on the banks of rivers, or in bowers, or at all sacred places, or on the sea-beaches. Fruits, roots and honey was their food. O best brāhmaṇas, (they got) their food with great difficulty.

32b-43. Having seen the misery of the beings, the king Pṛthu, Vena's son, made Svāyambhuva Manu the calf. O you highly intelligent one, he used his own hand as the vessel. That Pṛthu, the tiger (i.e. the best) among men, then milked the Earth, (and) the milk (was) all the crops and all food of a good quality. Those beings satisfied by means of that auspicious food, resembling nectar, all gods and others (like) the manes. Those beings lived happily by the favour of that son of Vena. O best brāhmaṇas, all the virtuous beings, after offering food first to gods, then to brāhmaṇas and especially to guests, enjoyed food. Some offered oblations in sacrifices, and pleased Viṣṇu only, the lord of gods with the same food. The deities also were satisfied (with the food). Rain sent by Viṣṇu showered. By virtue of that great auspicious trees sprang up. All kinds of crops (grew when) Pṛthu, Vena's son, was the king. Due to that food even now all beings live. The sages also, coming together, milked this Earth. It was again milked by the very blessed sages and the truthful gods. Soma was the calf and the lord of gods himself was the milkman. Energy was the milk, resembling water, by which the gods live. All the beings live due to their truthfulness and merit. They follow truth and merit. (Thus) the Earth was milked by the sages.

44-49. Now I shall narrate how formerly the Earth was milked by the manes and who was made the calf. Making a silver pot and svadhā, with nectar, the milk, and making Yama the calf, Antaka (i.e. Yama) himself became the milkman. O best brāhmaṇas, then the snakes (Nāga) and serpents (Sarpa) milked (the Earth) and (made) Takṣaka the calf. Taking a vessel made of gourd (they collected) the milk i.e. the poison (in it). The valorous Dhṛtarāṣṭra was the milkman for the snakes. O best brāhmaṇas, the matchless serpents and snakes live by that. O best brāhmaṇas, the snakes and the fearful serpents also live by that very poignant poison of a fierce nature,

The fierce, huge-bodied and very powerful ones live by that only. They eat it, move with it; that is their power and valour.

50-59. O best brāhmaṇas, now I shall narrate to you as to how all the demons and the goblins milked the Earth, making, at that time, an iron-pot, and making the milk of the nature of illusion, useful for all purposes, resembling food and destroying all the enemies. The calf of the demons was that powerful Virocana. The priest was Dvimūrdhan, and the very mighty Madhu was the milkman. Due to that illusion, the very strong, very wise, huge-bodied and very lustrous and valorous demons thrive. That is their power; that is their manliness; the demons live by that. O best brāhmaṇas, even now they, of limited intellect, live with that illusion. That is their strength. In the same way the Yakṣas milked the good Earth, the support of all. O best brāhmaṇas, thus we have heard. Formerly the noble ones (milked the Earth) in the former kalpa (when) the milk was of the nature of obscurity (*antardhānamayam*?). The very intelligent Vaiśravaṇa was made the calf; and the milkman of her (i.e. the Earth) was the meritorious, wisest and best among the intelligent viz. Rajatanābha, father of the Yakṣa Maṇibhadra. He was omniscient; he knew all the ways of good conduct; he was the powerful son of the king of Yakṣas; he had eight arms, two heads, and had great lustre and had very great (i.e. severe) penance (to his credit). O best brāhmaṇas, the Yakṣas always stood by him.

60-82. This Earth was again milked by the very strong demons; in the same way she (was milked) by the eager goblins who had consumed water. A human skull—a vessel that came up from a dead body—and one made of iron (were the pots used by them). They of strong anger and valor wanted to enjoy (i.e. to have) good progeny. The very strong Rajatanābha was their milkman, the calf was (one) by name Sumālin, and blood was the milk. The demons, evil spirits, and powerful goblins, Yakṣas and fearful groups of ghosts live by that (milk). Gandharvas and the celestial nymphs, making the learned Citraratha the calf, milked the Earth again. They milked her (milk) full of the music of Gandharvas. O best brāhmaṇas, the very intelligent and most meritorious Gandharva, Suruci, was their milkman. The noble ones milked pure songs as the good milk at that time. The Gandharvas and others (i.e.) the celestial nymphs also live by that. The auspicious mountains also milked this Earth. They (obtained as milk) various gems and herbs like nectar. The noble Himālaya (mountain) was made the calf. Meru was the milkman, and the pot was made from a big rock. All the very powerful mountains grew (strong) by (drinking) that milk. The great auspicious trees like Kalpa (i.e. the desire-yielding) tree again milked (the Earth). They had brought the pot made of Palāśa tree with its sprouts cut off and burnt. At that time Śāla, of a flowery body milked (the Earth) and Plakṣa was the calf. This (Earth) the supporter of all and the giver of everything was also milked by Guhyakas, Cāraṇas, Siddhas and groups of the Vidyādharas. Whatever the worlds desired with (i.e. by employing) particular vessels and calves, all that she just gave to them, (and) like this (she also gave) them milk with a good mind. This Earth is the supporter, the creator; she is the greatest. She is a cow yielding all desires and is adorned with the auspicious ones. She is the eldest, she is the prop. She is the creation and the beings. She is purifying, she gives merit, she is virtuous, she causes all the crops to grow, she is the supporter and the origin of all the mobile and the immobile. This (Earth) is great fortune, is learning, and is always full of everything. She yields (i.e. satisfies) all desires; she is a cow yielding milk; she causes all seeds to grow. This (Earth), the supporter of all the human race, is the mother (i.e. the origin) of all righteous deeds. She is the light and the form of even the five elements. She was bounded by the ocean and was known as *Medinī*. The entire Earth was submerged with (i.e. in) the marrow (*medas*) of Madhu and Kaiṭabha. Therefore she is called *Medinī* by the expounders of the Vedas. Then, O best ones, due to the arrival of Pṛthu, the wise son of Vena, she became his daughter, and is called *Pṛthivī*. O best brāhmaṇas, that king protected this Earth that is the support of villages and houses, and that is crowned with cities and towns, that has crops and mines, that is bulky and full of all crops, O brāhmaṇas. Thus this goddess Earth is full of all people; (her) prowess like this is mentioned in the Purāṇas.

83-91. The noble Pṛthu, Vena's son, was noted for all (good) deeds. He was like Viṣṇu, like Brahmā (or) like the ancient Rudra. The three gods deserve to be saluted by the expounders of the Vedas led by gods. The best king who is the founder of the castes and the stages of life, and who supports all the worlds, deserves to be saluted by brāhmaṇas and sages. Also the first, valorous king Pṛthu, Vena's son, deserves to be saluted by noble kings, and by those desiring to be kings. (Pṛthu) who has given livelihood to kings deserves to be saluted by warriors who desire (to master) archery and who always desire victory. O best brāhmaṇas, in this way I have narrated to you the particular vessels, the special properties of calves and of the milkmen in particular. I have also properly told you the speciality of the milk as desired by the king. O best brāhmaṇas, he, who listens to the account of Pṛthu, Vena's son, which is blessed, which leads to glory and good health, which is meritorious and which destroys sins, has (the credit of) a daily bath in the Bhāgīrathī. He, with all his sins purified, goes to Viṣṇu's world.

CHAPTER THIRTY

Sulobha and Śapharahā; Suśaṅkha and Sunīthā

The sages said :

1-2. O brāhmaṇa, what was the course of conduct of that sinful Vena, whom you mentioned as behaving sinfully, and what fruit did he get ? O you wisest and very intelligent one, tell us in detail the account of that Vena (as it) formerly (took place).

Sūta said :

3-9a. I shall properly tell you the story of that Vena and also the very meritorious account of his noble son, as I have heard it before. When that magnanimous son, Pṛthu, was born, the king (Vena) became spotless and again became religious. All the major sins earned (i.e. committed) by mean persons vanish with their close contact with the sacred places. There is no doubt that merit alone is produced in the company of the good; and sin alone is produced in the company of sinners. Sin would spread around by talking with, seeing, touching, sitting and taking food with and by the company of sinners. In the same way merit alone would spread in the company of the meritorious. The sinners are purified by their contact with great sacred place (only) and in no other way; and ultimately, with all their sins completely washed, they obtain a holy status.

The sages said :

9b-16a. O best brāhmaṇa, how do the sinners reach the highest attainment ? Tell that in detail; faith is produced (in us).

Sūta said :

There were very sinful hunters, slaves and fishermen, who remained in the water of Revā, Yamunā and Gaṅgā. By chance they knowingly or unknowingly bathed and sported in the water of the great river and obtained the highest position. Casting off their slavish life—the heap of sins—they went to the highest position. Due to their contact with the holy water they all crossed (the ocean of mundane existence). (This was) due to (their) contact with the great river, and not due to contact with other rivers, O best ones. By the contact of a highly meritorious person, and also by seeing and touching him, the sin of even the sinners perishes. No doubt should be raised about this. O brāhmaṇas, in this matter an account, destroying sins, is heard. I shall today tell you that (account) giving great merit.

16b-24a. In a great forest there was a deer-hunter named Sulobha. Greedy of tasting flesh, he everyday killed deer with (the help of) dogs, and with traps and snares. Once that very wicked one, holding a bow and arrows in his hand, being surrounded by dogs went to Vindhya-forest. He killed many beasts, deer and pigs that were frightened. A man, the killer (i.e. hunter) of śaphara (a kind of small glittering fish), resorting to the bank of Revā, and killing many śaphara, came out of the water. Then a female deer, afflicted with fear of that deer-hunter Lobha, and intent upon saving her life, distressed, frightened and with her mind unsettled, fleeing hurriedly, resorted (i.e. came) to the bank of Revā. She that was hurt by the stroke of an arrow, was attacked by dogs. Sulobha, the deer-hunter, pursued her with the speed of wind, and the female deer ran before him. The śaphara-killer, with an arrow in his hand and ready (to strike), bent his bow quickly and checked the female deer.

24b-30. Just then the hunter called Lobha came there with his dogs. "Do not kill her, she is my (game), she has come in the range of my hunt." Hearing (these) words of him (i.e. of Lobha), the wicked and very powerful fish-killer, greedy of flesh, discharged an arrow directed towards her. Struck by the deer-hunter with an arrow, the female deer who was (thus) struck with the two arrows of (i.e. discharged by) the two wicked ones, died there. (Trying) to run away in a hurry, she, being attacked by the dogs, fell from the peak into the Revā-pool that destroyed sins. The dogs also hurrying (to attack her) fell into the sacred pool. Overpowered with anger, the deer-hunter (i.e. Lobha) said to the fisherman: "O wicked one, this female deer is my (game); why did you strike her with arrows?" Then the fish-killer too said to the deer-hunter: "She is my (game); there is no doubt; why are you talking (like this), O proud one (i.e. proudly)."

31-35. Then the two lucky ones, fighting with each other through anger and greed, fell into the sacred water (of Revā). At that time the great parvan, giving a great religious merit and leading to an (excellent) position, viz. Amāvāsyā (i.e. the new-moon day) arrived. All of them, bereft of muttering prayers and meditation and of truthfulness fell (into the water) during the period of the parvan, O best one. On account of the bath of the holy place, the female deer, a dog and the hunter, being freed from all sins, attained the highest position (i.e. went to heaven). O best brāhmaṇa, due to the power of the sacred place and the company of the good, the sin of the sinners would be destroyed as fire would burn fuel.

Sūta said :

36-38. By the company of the noble sages, by talking with them, by seeing and touching them, by the company of the good, formerly the sin of king Vena perished. The sin of sinners perishes by the contact of very great merit (i.e. very meritorious persons). Sin alone would spread by the company of very great sinners. Vena was stained with the sin of his maternal grandfather.

The sages said:

39-44a. Tell us in detail what the fault of the maternal

grandfather was. He is death, he is Kāla (i.e. god of death) and is Yama and Dharma. He does not harm anyone. He is well-settled in his position. All mobile and immobile worlds, influenced by their own deeds, live and die due to their own deeds, and also enjoy due to their own deeds. On the ripening of their deeds, the sinners meet the fierce one. O Sūta, it is this very meritorious Yama, who, everyday would employ or punish (beings), according to their deeds, in all the hells. The pious-minded and righteous one employs (beings) in all very meritorious deeds. No fault of his is observed (in this). Due to what fault of Mṛtyu (i.e. Yama) was that sinful Vena born ?

Sūta said :

44b-56. That Mṛtyu remains in the form of Kāla (i.e. god of death) as the ruler of the wicked-minded. He reflects opon their deeds. He would destroy a person, who has (done) a wicked deed, with (i.e. as a result of) that deed. Knowing his sin this Yama takes him. A righteous soul, through his merit would obtain (i.e. go to) heaven. Mṛtyu alone, through his good messengers, unites all of them (with proper reward). He unites the blessed souls with great happiness, auspicious songs and gifts, and enjoyments. That Mṛtyu, being angry would frighten them only with various kinds of afflictions and distresses and beat them with terrible (clubs) of wood. O noble one, his function remains in (i.e. with reference to) the deeds, and that is due to one's greed of merit. A daughter by name Sunīthā was born to that magnanimous one. Always sporting and observing the deeds of her father, she advised him who observed the good and bad deeds of the subjects. That glorious daughter of him, Sunīthā by name, sporting and surrounded by (her) friends came to a forest. There she saw an excellent distinguished son of a Gandharva, by name Suśaṅkha, with all his body charming, practising penance, and meditating on Sarasvatī, for obtaining great competence in the science of music, in spite of (i.e. even though there was) a loud and confused sound of music. Everyday she created an obstruction in his (penance and meditation). Everyday Suśaṅkha, saying "Go, go (away)", pardoned her. Though thus sent away (i.e. asked to go away) she would still cause harm to him. (Thus) told by him, she, too, getting angry, struck him, who remained in (i.e. practising) penance.

57-62. Then that Suśaṅkha angry and overcome with wrath said to her: "O wicked, sinful one, why did you obstruct (my penance)? Great people do not beat (back) a wicked person when beaten (by him). Though abused they do not get angry. This is the restraint (brought about) by righteousness. O wicked one, you struck me who am faultless and endowed with penance." Speaking this to that sinful Sunīthā, that pious one, ceased (to speak) and knowing her to be a female, kept himself away from anger. Then she, through sinful delusion and immaturity, spoke to that noble Suśaṅkha, who remained in (i.e. was practising) penance: "My father himself is the destroyer of the residents of the three worlds; he would always destroy the bad ones and would protect the truthful ones. There would be no fault on his part, he would behave very meritoriously."

63-66. Saying so, she went to her father and said to him: "O father, in the forest I struck a Gandharva's son, who was always practising penance in a secluded place and was free from desire and anger. He, the righteous one, endowed with anger and love said to me: 'One should not beat him who beats one, nor should one make him weep, who makes one weep.' Thus, O father, he spoke to me. Tell me the reason (for this)." O best brāhmaṇas, that righteous Mṛtyu, thus addressed, did not say anything to Sunīthā, in reply to (her) question.

67-71. She again came to the forest where that Suśaṅkha remained. Through wickedness she struck him, the best among those who practised penance, with the blows of her hands. O brāhmaṇas, the daughter of Mṛtyu beat Suśaṅkha. Then the highly lustrous one got angry and cursed her of a slender waist: "O wicked one, since you beat me, who am faultless and who remained in this forest, therefore I shall give (you) a curse. Listen, O wicked one, when, with your husband, you will lead the life of a housewife a son, full of evil conduct, censurer of gods and brāhmaṇas, engrossed in all sinful acts, will be (conceived) in your womb." Cursing like this, he too left, and resorted to penance only.

72-75. When that glorious one had left, Sunīthā went home. With her mind burning (with anger) she told her noble father as (to how) she was then cursed by the son of a Gandharva. Mṛtyu listened to all that, and said: "Why did you harm him, who was practising penance and who was innocent? O (my) daughter, you have not done a proper thing in beating a truthful person." Saying so, the righteous Mṛtyu, reflecting upon what she had told him, became extremely pained.

Sūta said :

76-85. O brāhmaṇas, once the brāhmaṇa, the very lustrous and vigorous son of Atri went to the Nandana (garden); there he saw Indra, Pākaśāsana. He saw Indra, who was accompanied by hosts of celestial nymphs and Gandharvas and Kinnaras, who was (i.e. whose praise was) being sung by singers with seven very melodious notes, who was being fanned by beautiful women walking like swans with fragrant fans, and with chowries, who, the thousand-eyed one, shone with an umbrella (white) in colour like swans and (round) like the disc of the moon, who was adorned with all ornaments, who was engaged in sexual sports, who possessed an unlimited prowess. By his side he saw the blessed virtuous Paulomī, charming and auspicious, glorious with beauty, lustre and penance, shining with good fortune and chastity. With her that Indra enjoyed in the Nandana forest. Seeing his sport, the best brāhmaṇa Aṅga (thought): 'Lucky is the king of gods who is surrounded by such (beings). Oh, (great) is the power of his penance, due to which he has obtained such a great (i.e. high) position. When I shall have such a son, the great support of all the worlds, I shall obtain great happiness. There is no doubt about it.' Thus engaged in thinking he quickly came home.

CHAPTER THIRTYONE

The Account of Suvrata

Sūta said :

1-5. Then Aṅga, the very lustrous one, seeing noble Indra's wealth, enjoyment of amorous pleasures and sports (thought:)

'How shall I have a son, endowed with piety, like Indra?' Aṅga, the best among the righteous, thinking like this, came to his own house. Bowing down and with his neck (i.e. head) bent down (in respect) he asked Atri, his father: "Who enjoys this high position of Indra by doing pious deeds? Of what merit is this the result ? What deed did he do? And of what kind was it? What kind of penance did he have (i.e. practise)? Whom did he propitiate formerly? O best among the truthful ones, tell me in detail (about) this."

Atri said :

6-8. Bravo ! O noble one, you are asking me like this (a good question). O child, listen to me, who will tell you the account of Indra. Formerly there was an intelligent, excellent brāhmaṇa by name Suvrata. He pleased Kṛṣṇa, Hṛṣīkeśa, with penance. He again reached the meritorious womb of Aditi through Kaśyapa; and through Viṣṇu's grace, he became the king of gods.

Aṅga said :

9. O you affectionate towards your sons, how shall I have a son like Indra? Tell me a means for that, O best among the wise.

Atri said :

10-17. O you highly intelligent one, listen to the entire account of that illustrious Suvrata, in brief—as to how that intelligent Suvrata formerly propitiated Hari. The lord of the world (i.e. Viṣṇu) having observed his sincerity, devotion and meditation, gave him a great position. That Indra, sustaining the three worlds, enjoys the three worlds with the mobile and the immobile, and the (high) position, through Viṣṇu's favour only. All this I have told you, so also Indra's acts. O best one, Govinda (i.e. Viṣṇu) is pleased with devotion and sincere meditation. Hari, pleased with devotion, being delighted, gives everything. Therefore, O (my) son, having propitiated Govinda, who gives everything, who is the cause of everything, who is omniscient, who knows everything, who is the best man among all, you will obtain from him whatever you desire. He is the giver of happiness, of the highest truth, of salvation, and is the lord of the worlds. Therefore, O son, go (and) propitiate him; you will obtain a son like Indra.

18-19. He, having heard the words uttered by that illustrious sage, which contained the highest truth, and having understood the import of these words, he, having saluted that eternal one, left (the place). That noble Aṅga, having taken his leave of his father, Brahmā's son, and resembling Brahmā, reached the peak of the Meru mountain, which was full of gold and gems.

CHAPTER THIRTYTWO

Aṅga Gets a Boon from Vāsudeva

Sūta said :

1-20. The best mountain (i.e. Meru), with its regions very bright with various gems and gold on all sides, shone like the Sun with his rays. All the meditating saints, seated on firm seats after resorting to very pleasing, cool, comfortable shades, meditated. At some places the sages practised penance; at some places Kinnaras sang (songs). Gandharvas, being delighted, (sang songs), beating time with their hands. Delightful songs were presented by them, who were engrossed in beating (and) measuring time in music, and with the seven musical notes; and with melody and closed fists. On that greatest mountain, Gandharvas, knowing the essential nature of songs, and being intent on singing, sang them, after having resorted to the shades of sandal-trees. The divine women danced there on the excellent mountain. The sound (of the recitation) of the Vedas, which destroyed sins, gave religious merit, which was divine, which bestowed great bliss, and which was very sweet, was heard on the best mountain. The excellent mountain shone with (trees like) sandal, Aśoka, Punnāga, Śāla, Tāla, and bunyan, resembling clouds. The lord of mountains shone at every place with Santānaka[1] trees, desire-yielding trees crowded with Ambhā (?) trees and well-blossomed divine trees. The mountain was full of many minerals and full of heaps of gems. It was full of many wonders and of various auspicious things. It was resorted to by groups of Vedas and was full of the groups of celestial nymphs. It

1. Santānaka—One of the five trees of Indra's paradise.

shone with sages, ascetics, Siddhas and Gandharvas. It looked beautiful with elephants resembling mountains and with the roars of lions. It was adorned with Śarabhas[1], with furious tigers and cunning beasts. Everywhere it looked charming with wells, pools and tanks containing spotless water and crowded with swans and ducks. It looked beautiful with golden, white and red lotuses. The lord of mountains looked charming with groups of rivers and streams having clear water, with Śāla and Tāla trees, and with crystal forms and elephants, and with slabs of stone which were extensive, golden, divine and which resembled the sun and fire. It was adorned with the mansions of deities, and palaces (resembling) excellent mountains, and with golden staffs resembling swans and the moon. It was also decorated with pitchers, chowries and palaces. It was also adorned with hosts of gods delighted by various excellences (of the mountain). That holy, best mountain Meru shone all round with many hosts of gods, Gandharvas and bards. That great river, which is very holy, which contains sacred water, which is rich with holy places, which is crowded with swans and lotuses, and which is resorted to by ascetics and hosts of sages, has risen from it.

21-31. Aṅga, the great meritorious sage, the son of Atri, (went to) that best mountain having such excellences and auspicious on account of holy wonders. He entered a beautiful cave on the very sacred and secluded bank of the Gaṅgā. The intelligent one, free from desire and anger, sat there after having controlled all his senses, and meditated upon the pious Viṣṇu-Kṛṣṇa, the lord who removes all afflictions and who remained in his mind. He, being attentive, full of deep meditation and with his senses conquered (i.e. controlled) always saw Madhusūdana (i.e. Viṣṇu) on a seat or bed or in a vehicle or in meditation. He saw Viṣṇu in the beings—mobile and immobile. That brāhmaṇa (saw Viṣṇu) in all wet, dry and other things. In this way a hundred years passed, while he was practising penance. Seeing the best brāhmaṇa (practising penance like this), the lord of the world, with the disc in his hand, always presented before him many very fearful dangers. With that lustre of the glorious god Nṛsiṁha, the pious and fearless (brāhmaṇa) burnt (himself) as

1. Śarabha—a fabulous animal said to have eight legs and to be stronger than a lion.

fire burns the fuel. The best brāhmaṇa Aṅga was getting emaciated by observances and restraints; yet by means of his own lustre he appeared shining like the sun and fire. The god appeared before him who was thus deeply engrossed in penances and was meditating upon Janārdana, and said to him, "O you who show respect, choose a boon." Seeing that Hṛṣīkeśa, Aṅga, who was highly delighted, with his mind pleased, and bowing down, praised him.

Aṅga said :

32-54. O you origin of beings, O you purifier, you are the refuge of all beings; O you lord of all beings, you are the soul of beings. My salutation to you who are full of merit. My salutation to you who are of the nature of merit, who are a mystery and are beyond all qualities; to you who are merit (itself), who are the cause of merit, who are endowed with merit and are of the nature of merit; to you who are the worldly life, the cause of the worldly life and who remove (i.e. free) your devotees from the worldly existence; to you from whom the worldly life has sprung up, to you who are a mystery, and the destroyer of the worldly life. Salutation to you, who are the sacrifice, who are of the form of sacrifices and the lord of sacrifice; who are connected with the sacrificial act and the holder of the conch. My repeated salutations to (you who are) gold, who hold a disc, to you who are truth, and are of true thoughts and are full of all truth. My salutation to you who are Dharma (i.e. Piety), the cause of Dharma and the cause of everything. My salutation to you whose body is Dharma, who are a great hero and who are the prop of righteousness. My salutation to you who are a meritorious and noble son and not a son; to you who destroy illusion and delusion and who bring about entire illusion. My repeated salutations to you who sustain illusion, who are embodied and formless. My salutation to you who take up all forms and are Śaṅkara (i.e. you who bring about blisses). My salutation to you, who are Brahman, of the nature of Brahman and identical with the highest Brahman; to you who are all lustre and possess lustre. My salutation to you who possess glory, who live in glory and sustain glory; to you who live in the ocean and are immortal. My salutation to you who are a great mineral, who are fierce and are beyond great wisdom; to you who are not cruel, who are pure and the lord of sacred things. My salutations to you, the unlimited one, the complete one, and to the sinless one. Salutation to you who are the light of the sky and are of the form of a bird. Salutation to you who are the one to whom oblations are offered, who enjoys the oblations and who are of the form of oblations. Salutation to you who are Buddha (i.e. enlightened), who are a god, and you who are ever enlightened. Salutation to you, who are the oblation offered to the gods and to the manes; to you who are the utterance svadhā (used at the time of offering oblation to the manes) and svāhā (the utterance used at the time of offering oblation to the gods), to you who are pure, who are unmanifest and glorious. Salutation to you who are Vyāsa, Indra and of the nature of the Vasus; to you who are Vāsudeva, who are everything and to you who are of the form of fire; repeated salutations to you, who alone are Hari, Vāmana (i.e. Viṣṇu). Salutation to the god Nṛsiṁha and to you who maintain righteousness. My salutation to the cowherd Govinda and to the one-syllabled one. My salutation to you who are omni-syllabled and of the nature of the Supreme Soul. My salutation to you who are of the nature of the three principles or of the nature of the five elements; salutation to you who are (of the form of) the twentyfive principles and the support of the elements. Salutation to you who are Kṛṣna (i.e. Viṣṇu or dark), who are of the nature of Kṛṣna and are the lord of Lakṣmī. My salutation to you who are (charming) like a lotus-petal and are the highest bliss. My salutation to you who are the supporter of all and the destroyer of sins. My salutation to you who are the very great merit and you who practise truth. O eternal one, my repeated salutations to you who are immutable and a misty heap; to you having a lotus in (i.e. rising from) your navel; to you who are the great god. O Keśava, I salute your lotus-like feet. O you root of joy, O you dear to Lakṣmī, O Vāsudeva, O lord of all, O god, O Madhusūdana, make me your slave. O Keśava, I salute your feet. Be gracious to me in existence after existence, O you who give tranquility and who have a conch in your hand. Sprinkle me with water of knowledge, who am burnt by the heat of the fierce fire of the worldly existence and by many (kinds of) anguish and agony due to the deaths of sons etc. and of kinsmen; O lord Padmanābha, be a refuge to me.

55-58. Having heard this hymn of praise of (i.e. recited by) the noble Aṅga, Hṛṣīkeśa, shining with great lustre, and with the holy Kaustubha, marked with the Śrīvatsa, presented before Aṅga his own and very superior form having the conch, the disc and the mace in his hands, (and also) a lotus in his hand, and mounted upon Garuḍa, and with all limbs of his body beautified with a necklace, bracelets, and ear-rings, and looking great, divine and spotless, and charming due to the sylvan garland.

59-70a. Having thus manifested his own form, Hari, of the nature of all gods, said to that best noble sage, Aṅga : "O blessed brāhmaṇa, listen to (these) auspicious words." With a sound deep like (the thundering of) clouds, he spoke to the best brāhmaṇa : "I am pleased with this penance (practised by you). Choose an auspicious boon." He, full of great joy, again and again saluted the feet of Janārdana, who was shining, looking bright, who was the lord of people, who was of a universal form, who, the lord of Lakṣmī, was pleased, and said to him : "O you god of gods, O you holder of the conch, the disc and the mace, I am your slave. (If) you desire to grant me a boon, then give me a son born in my family (i.e. of my blood). Give me a son, the protector of all the people, and one full of all lustre shining like Indra in heaven. When you desire to grant me a boon, (then) (give me) a son, who is dear to all gods, who knows the Vedas, who is well-versed in the code of conduct, who is a donor, who is endowed with knowledge, and with the lustre of piety, who is the protector of the three worlds, who is Kṛṣṇa, who protects the truthful conduct, who is the best among the sacrificers, who is a unique hero, and who is the ornament of the three worlds, who is hospitable to brāhmaṇas, who knows the Vedas, whose promises are true, who has curbed his senses, who is unconquerable, who is the conqueror of all, whose lustre is like that of Viṣṇu, who is a devotee of Viṣṇu, who performs meritorious deeds, who is born due to merit, who has auspicious marks, who is tranquil, who is endowed with penance, who has mastered all branches of knowledge, who knows the Vedas, who is best among the meditating sages, and who is like you in point of virtues. Give me such a son."

Vāsudeva said :

70b-72. O you very intelligent one, you will have a son

endowed with all these qualities. He will support the family of Atri, and also this universe. He will also emancipate his father by means of his lustre, glory and merit; with his truthfulness he will emancipate his father (i.e. you) and his grandfather; you will reach my place, that is Viṣṇu's highest position.

73-75. The lord of gods, spoke like this to that Aṅga, O brāhmaṇa. (He said to him): "Marry the auspicious daughter of someone of virtuous power. Generate on her a son, who will be auspicious, bringing merit and dear (to you). O you very intelligent one, by my favour, he will be religious-minded, omniscient, knowing all, (that is) as desired by you." Thus giving (Aṅga) a boon Hari then vanished.

CHAPTER THIRTYTHREE

Sunīthā's Story

The sages said :

1. She (i.e. Sunīthā) was cursed by that Suśaṅkha, the noble son of a Gandharva. Due to his curse how did she become (i.e. what happened to her)? What deeds did she do?

2. O best brāhmaṇa, what kind of son did she obtain due to his curse? (Please) narrate to us in detail the account of Sunīthā also.

Sūta said :

3-14a. That Sunīthā, of a slender waist, who was cursed by him, being tormented by grief, went to her father's place. She disclosed her deeds to her father, Mṛtyu, the best among the truthful and the righteous ones. He spoke to Sunīthā, his daughter, who was cursed by that magnanimous one: "You committed a sin that destroys merit and lustre. O you noble one, why did you beat him, who was very tranquil? You did that which is contrary to (the ways of) all the world. Listen, what sin is committed by him who would kill him who is free from desire and wrath, who is very tranquil, who loves piety, who is fully engrossed in the path of penance, and is settled in the highest Brahman. His son is born wicked, and gets (i.e. accumulates) much sin. There is no doubt that he who beats a person who beats him and makes him cry who is crying, suffers for his sin (i.e. of the other person). He (alone) is tranquil, he (alone) is one who has conquered (i.e. controlled) his mind, who does not beat him (i.e. the person) who beats him. O you (my) daughter, he who has beaten an innocent person, would (thus) later beat, through delusion and in sin, even an innocent man (?). He, the sinner, who, without any reason, causes anxiety to an innocent man or would later beat an innocent man through delusion or some sin, obtains the sin produced in the body of the innocent one. If the innocent person would beat the wicked-hearted person that beats him rashly after suddenly getting up, the sin of the sinner goes to the innocent person.

14b-19a. Therefore, one should not beat even a sinner. O (my) daughter, you have done, a very wicked deed. As you are today cursed by him, therefore practise meritorious deeds. Secure the company of the good, and behave (properly). O you (my) daughter, behave taking to profound abstract meditation and knowledge. The company of the good is greatly meritorious, and causes great bliss. O (my) daughter, note that merit, well-observed, of the company of the good. Highly intelligent sages, cleansed from within and without by touching, drinking and bathing in the water, obtain perfection. All these worlds—mobile and immobile—become pure (due to the company of the good).

19b-20. Water is calm, very cold, soft for the body, causing pleasure, clear, tasty, of a meritorious power, removing dirt; you should know that the saints are like that, and should wait upon them carefully.

21. As gold gives up its impurity by its contact with fire, similarly a man casts off his sin by the contact of the good.

22-24. The fire of truth would burn brightly only with the lustre of merit. A man whose lustre blazes with truth, who is very spotless due to knowledge and very hot due to meditation, cannot be touched by men born of sin. By the contact of the fire of truth, all (one's) sin perishes. Therefore, you should, by all means, have contact with truth. Giving up your burden of sin, resort to merit in this way."

Sūta said :

25-26. In this way that Sunīthā, who was distressed, was advised by her father. Having saluted her father's feet, she went to a lonely forest. The devout one, giving up desire and anger and her childishness, and also abandoning tricks, malice and deceit, resorted to a secluded place.

27-28a. Her friends, endowed with grace, came there to sport. The large-eyed ones saw Sunīthā afflicted and meditating. Seeing her reflecting, they, full of anxiety, said to her:

28b-30. "O good one, full of anxiety why are you brooding? You, are causing anxiety and worry to us; tell us the cause (of your anxiety). Only one anxiety, entertained for piety (alone), is significant. The other kind of anxiety, viz. giving delight to the meditating sages in matters of piety is important. (I.e. the other kind of anxiety that is important is one which gives delight to the meditating sages in matters of piety.) (Any) other anxiety is worthless. One should not at all entertain it.

31-33. Anxiety withers the body; it destroys strength and lustre; it would destroy all happiness, and would show (i.e. bring about) loss of beauty. Anxiety would bring these, viz. thirst (i.e. desire), delusion and greed (to a person). Anxiety, when entertained, would produce sin day by day. Anxiety would show (i.e. bring about) bodily diseases, and would lead (one) to hell. Therefore, O beautiful one, behave by giving up anxiety.

34-35a. A man enjoys (or suffers) only what he has earned by means of his former deeds. A wise person should not mind them. Therefore give up your anxiety, and talk about happiness, unhappiness etc."

35b. Hearing those words of them, Sunīthā spoke these words.

CHAPTER THIRTYFOUR

Sunithā's Problem

Sūta said :

1-2a. She, the noble one, who was very much afflicted with grief, told her friends how she was formerly cursed by the magnanimous Suśaṅkha, and all that she did.

Sunithā said :

2b-5. O friends, listen now; I shall tell you something else. Seeing my wealth of beauty and excellence in age (i. e. youth) and good qualities, my father became worried about me. The very glorious one desired to give me (in marriage) to (one of the) gods or sages. Holding me by the hand, he said these words to them all : "This is my young daughter, full of good qualities and having charming eyes. Well-being to you, I desire to give her (in marriage) to a virtuous and very magnanimous (god or sage)."

6-8. At that time gods and sages heard the words of Mṛtyu. Gods, led by Indra, spoke to him, who was (thus) speaking: "This your daughter is endowed with virtues, and is a great treasure of good character; but she is defiled by one fault, viz. the curse of (i.e. given by) the sage. On her will be born a son, from whose semen a man will be (born) who will be a great sinner and the destroyer of the virtuous family.

9-14. A pitcher that is seen to be full of the water of the Gaṅgā, becomes a pitcher (full) of liquor when polluted with a drop of liquor. Due to the sinful contact of a sinner, the family becomes sinful. If a drop of the sour gruel made from the fermentation of boiled rice would go to (i.e. would get mixed with) milk, it would later destroy (i.e. spoil) the milk and would present its own nature. In the same way a sinful son would destroy the family; there is no doubt about it. This your sinful (daughter) is (soiled) with this blemish. Give her to someone else. (Please) go." Thus was my father told by gods. My father, afflicted with the grief was abandoned even by the noble gods, Gandharvas and sages; and the good men also did not accept me. Thus formerly I have committed a sinful act.

15-16. Tormented by agony and grief I have just resorted to the forest. I shall practise penance only, and shall wither my body. You have well asked me the effect and the cause. The deed, following my anxiety, has also been disclosed to you.

17. Speaking thus, that Sunīthā, Mṛtyu's glorious daughter, afflicted with grief, ceased speaking; and then did not say anything.

The friends said :

18-27. O you noble one, give up the grief, destroying your body. There is a blemish in the family of an atheist. (Even) gods have resorted to (i.e. committed) sin. Formerly (even) that Brahmā told a lie in the presence of Viṣṇu. That Brahmā (though) abandoned by gods, became most adorable. O (you), look at the king of gods (i.e. Indra) who was engaged in killing a brāhmaṇa. The noble one enjoys, along with the gods (the kingdom of) the three worlds. Formerly he went to (i.e. cohabited with) Ahalyā, Gautama's wife. He, who was an adulterer, has become the lord (of gods). Hara (i.e. Śiva) committed a fierce deed like killing a brāhmaṇa. Even now he lives with the skull of Brahmā. Gods and sages who have mastered the Vedas salute that god. The Sun, full of (i.e. suffering from) leprosy would illuminate (i.e. illuminates) the three worlds. All the worlds, including the mobile and the immobile, and led by the gods, salute him. Kṛṣṇa enjoys (i.e. suffers from) the curse given formerly by Bhārgava. Candra (i.e. the Moon), who went to (i.e. copulated with) Guru's (i.e. Jupiter's) wife, has become emaciated due to that. There will be (born) a very lustrous, valorous, very intelligent son of Pāṇḍu, viz. Yudhiṣṭhira, the king of kings. For the murder of his teacher, he will tell a lie. Great sin resides in (i.e. is committed by) these great ones. There is no defect in anyone of them nor any stigma.

28-29. O you beautiful one, you are smeared with a small sin. O you of an excellent complexion, we shall oblige you. O you of charming eyes, O you auspicious one, we do not find the qualities which you possess anywhere else (i.e. in any other woman).

30-35a. O you auspicious one, the virtue of beauty is the first ornament of women. The second one is good character; and the third one is truthfulness. The fourth one is honesty; the fifth one is piety itself. Then, O you beautiful one, sweetness is said to be the sixth one. O you young girl; internal and external purity of women is the seventh (ornament). Devotion to the father is the eighth (one). Service (to others) is the ninth one. Tolerance is said to be the tenth one, and love is the eleventh (one). O you of an excellent complexion, loyalty to husband is said to be the twelfth (one). O you young girl, you are adorned with those (ornaments); O you beautiful one, do not get frightened. We shall find out that remedy by which that highly meritorious one will be your husband; for, we are (living) for you only.

35b. The excellent friends said to her: "Do not indulge in a rash act."

Sūta said :

36. Sunīthā, who was thus addressed, again said to those friends: "Tell me the remedy by which (he) will be my husband."

37-41a. The excellent ladies of charming eyes, led by Rambhā, said to her: "You are endowed with beauty and sweetness; you would lead (your husband) to prosperity. You were frightened by a brāhmaṇa's curse. (Therefore) we have come here." They spoke to that Mṛtyu's daughter having large and charming eyes: "We shall give you, O good one, an incantation (having the power of) giving all good and alluring men knowing all tricks." Then these (ladies) gave her the powerful incantation giving happiness. (They said :) "Instantly allure him, whomsoever god (or other) you desire to allure , O good lady."

41b-46. That Sunīthā, being very happy when well-equipped with the incantation, thus wandered with her friends, and observed men. While wandering she went to Indra's paradise. (There) on the bank of the Gaṅgā, she then saw the brāhmaṇa, who was the ornament of the Atri-family, who was handsome, who was endowed with all (auspicious) marks, who resembled the sun in lustre, who was matchless in form in the world, who was, as it were, another god of love, who had god-like form, who was noble and fortunate, who bestowed bliss (on others), who had no match, who was magnanimous, who resembled Viṣṇu in lustre, who was a devotee of Viṣṇu, who destroyed all sins, whose valour was like that of Viṣṇu, and who was free from desire and anger.

47. Seeing him, who was handsome, the very form of penance, of a divine prowess, and who was tormenting himself (by austerities), she asked Rambhā, her good friend: "Who is this excellent, magnanimous one, remaining in heaven (i.e. possessing divine qualities)?"

CHAPTER THIRTYFIVE

Rambhā Helps by a Suggestion

Rambhā said :

1-6a. Brahmā was born from the Unmanifest one, and from him was born the lord of created beings, viz. the religious-minded Atri. O good lady, his son, viz. this Aṅga of a noble mind, came to Nandanavana. Seeing Indra's glory excellent with graceful lustre, he too longed for a position similar to that of Indra: 'If I would have such a son endowed with righteousness, (then) my existence, endowed with fame and glory, will be very blessed.' Then he propitiated Hṛṣīkeśa with austerities and restraints. When Hṛṣīkeśa was very much pleased, he asked for a boon : "O Madhusūdana, give me a son who resembles Indra, whose lustre and valour are like that of Viṣṇu, who is a devotee of Viṣṇu, and who destroys all sins."

6b. Then he gave (him) a son possessing all such (qualities).

7-12. Since then the best brāhmaṇa looked (for) an auspicious maiden. He saw you as you are beautiful in all limbs. O you beautiful lady, go to (i.e. accept) him; from him you will have a son, who will be righteous, who will be knowing pious ways of behaviour and whose lustre and valour will be like that of Viṣṇu. All this has been told to you, since you had asked me like (i.e. about) that. There is no doubt that this one will be a suitable groom for you. That curse of (i.e. given by) Suśaṅkha also will be ineffective. O good noble lady, when from him a son propagating righteous conduct will be born, you will be happy. I am telling you the truth, (and) the truth (only). A farmer, with great sincerity, sows the seed. O respectable lady, he enjoys (i.e.

reaps) the fruit as he sows the seed. It shall never be otherwise. It would all be just like that.

13-14. This noble one is devout and possesses merit and strength; a son born from his semen will be endowed with his wealth of virtues, will be very lustrous, will be best among all human beings, will be very fortunate, of a devout disposition, and will be conversant with the principles of deep and abstract meditation.

15. Hearing these words of Rambhā, uttered affectionately and bestowing well-being, Sunīthā entertained the notion : This is the truth, the entire truth.

CHAPTER THIRTYSIX

Sunīthā Gets Married and Vena is Born

Sunīthā said :

1-2a. O good lady, you have spoken the truth; I shall do like this. I shall allure the brāhmaṇa with this incantation, and not in any other way. Give me help so that I shall go to the meritorious one.

2b. Ramhbā, who was thus addressed by her, said to the high-minded one (i.e. Sunīthā):

3-5a. "O you beautiful young lady, tell me what kind of help I can give (you)." (Sunīthā said:) "O good lady, now go to him as my messenger." Thus she spoke to that Rambhā of charming eyes. That celestial nymph Rambhā promised (her) like this only: "I shall help you; give me instructions."

5b-13. Due to (her) good temperament, the beautiful lady, of large eyes and possessing beauty and youth, became of (i.e. took up) a divine form through a device. She was matchless in beauty in the world, and allured the three worlds. The charmingly smiling Rambhā, lovely in an all-elegant dress, was seated upon a swing on a very auspicious peak of Meru, which had lovely caves, which was covered with many minerals, which was adorned with various gems, which was covered with divine trees, which looked lovely due to abundant flowers, which was covered (i.e. crowded) with hosts of gods, which was resorted to by Gandharvas and celestial nymphs, which was attractive, very charming, and full of the shadows of the sandal and the aśoka trees. The beautiful lady looked lovely with the dark-blue silken garment, and with a bodice, having the colour of a bandhūka-flower, O best brāhmaṇa. The young lady, with all her limbs beautiful, had her hands engaged in (playing upon) the lute, (properly) beating the time, and was singing an excellent, very melodious song, alluring the universe. The very beautiful young woman was surrounded by her friends; and Aṅga had resorted to meditation in an auspicious secluded cave. He, free from desire and anger, meditated upon Janārdana.

14-15a. The bright one (i.e. Aṅga), hearing that very melodious, sweet and very charming song, accompanied by beating time and (proper) measure, and attractive to all beings, swerved from his meditation, as he was fascinated by that enchanting song.

15b-17. With his mind swerving due to that fascination, looking repeatedly (at her) quickly got up from his seat, speedily went there; the very glorious one, seeing her seated on a swing, and with her hand full of the neck of the lute, laughing, singing well and with her face resembling the moon, was allured by the song and (her) beauty.

18-19. The best brāhmaṇa, the son of a sage, was struck with Cupid's arrows (i.e. was overpowered by passion) due to her beauty, and with his mind perturbed and disturbed, talked through infatuation, and recoiled repeatedly. That moment only he perspired, shivered and was distressed.

20. Then Aṅga, as it were being allured by great fascination, languid, and with his mind unsteady, trembling and being afflicted, came (there).

21. Seeing that Sunīthā, Mṛtyu's daughter, of large eyes, glorious and smiling charmingly, the noble one said to her:

22. "O you beautiful lady, who are you? To whom do you belong? Surrounded by (your) friends, for what mission have you come (here)? Who has sent you to the forest?

23. In (this) large forest, your beautiful body is shining everywhere. Tell me (all about it) today only; be gracious to me."

24. The great sage, pierced with the arrows of Cupid, and infatuated by her fascinating device, did not grasp her actions.

25. Hearing these great (i.e. significant) words of that very intelligent one, she (just) looked at the face of her friend, and did not say anything to that brāhmaṇa.

26. Sunīthā, with a sign, set on her friend, Rambhā. Then Rambhā respectfully said to the brāhmaṇa:

27. "This noble one is the daughter of the glorious Mṛtyu, known as Sunīthā, and adorned with the wealth of all (good) marks.

28. The young girl is looking for a groom, who is a treasure of penance, who is tranquil and restrained, who is very intelligent and well-versed in Vedic lore."

29-34. Having heard these very significant words, the great sage said to that Rambhā, the best among the celestial nymphs: "I have propitiated Viṣṇu, Hari, of the form of all gods. He has given me a boon (granting) a son, and giving all prosperity. For that, O good lady, and for having a son, I am everyday thinking of the daughter of someone of an auspicious power. And for ever I am really not finding a good bride. Let this daughter, of Mṛtyu, whose conduct is righteous, and who is beautiful take me (as her groom) here, if she desires a husband. There is no doubt that I shall give whatever this young girl asks for. For having union with her I say that I (shall) give (even) what cannot be given." (Rambhā said:) "O best brāhmaṇa, listen, what one thing you should just give."

Rambhā said :

35-37. O best brāhmaṇa, listen to the pledge which I (shall) tell now. She is never to be abandoned by you. She is your lawful wife. You have never to assume either a blemish or a merit of her; (and) for this, O best brāhmaṇa, show (us) actually (some) convincing proof. O best brāhmaṇa, give her your hand giving a convincing proof.

(He said) : "Let it be so. I have given my hand to her. There should be no doubt about it."

Sūta said :

38-45. Thus establishing a relation showing a convincing proof, he married Sunīthā by means of the Gāndharva (type of) marriage. Having given that Sunīthā (in marriage) Rambhā, with her mind delighted, took leave of her, and went to her own abode. The friends, with their minds very much delighted, went to their own abodes. When all the friends had (thus) left, Aṅga sported with his dear wife. Having generated on her a son possessing all (auspicious) marks, he named the son 'Vena'. Then that son of Sunīthā (viz. Vena), of a great lustre, grew. The intelligent one, having studied the branches of the Veda, along with archery, mastered all the lores. Vena, the son of Aṅga, abided by good manners. That Vena, the best among the brāhmaṇas, took to the behaviour of kṣatriyas. As Indra, endowed with all lustre, shines in heaven, the very intelligent one shone with his own might and valour.

46-50a. When following the period of Cākṣuṣa[1] Manu that of Vaivasvata arrived, the beings were sinking in the world without a protector of the beings (i.e. without a king). The sages, having penance as their wealth, and knowing the essence of righteousness, thought of a king knowing righteousness and well-versed in truth. They just saw Vena, prosperous and endowed with (auspicious) marks. The best brāhmaṇas consecrated him in the position of the lord of created beings. When that noble king (Vena), the son of Aṅga, was consecrated, all the lords of created beings went to a penance-grove. When they had left, Vena ruled over the kingdom.

Sūta said :

50b-57. That Sunīthā, seeing her son looking well after the entire kingdom, thought: 'Due to the prowess and the curse of that noble one, my glorious son will be the protector of righteousness.' Thinking like this, she was everyday afraid of her former sins. She would present (i.e. she presented) before her son the very meritorious essential requisites of Dharma. She would throw (i.e. she threw) light on such virtues as truthfulness etc. She said to her son like this: "O son, I am the daughter of Dharma; (and) your father knows the essence of piety; therefore, practise piety."

1. Cākṣuṣa is the sixth Manu and Vaivasvata is the seventh. Manvanatara is a period or age of a Manu. This period comprises 4, 320, 000 human years or 1/14th day of Brahmā, the fourteen Manvantaras making up one whole day.

Thus that good lady would always advise her son, Vena. He would obey (i.e. obeyed) the words, proper for (i.e. leading to the well-being of) his subjects. Thus on the globe Vena had become a king. The people lived happily. The subjects were pleased. Thus was the greatness of the kingdom of noble Vena. When the king was ruling, the ways of Dharma prevailed.

CHAPTER THIRTYSEVEN

A Heretic Meets Vena

The sages said :

1. (If) thus was the creation of the noble Vena, how is it that giving up righteous conduct he would be (i.e. became) (a man) of wicked mind?

Sūta said :

2. Sages endowed with spiritual and worldly knowledge, and knowing the truth, tell what is good and what is bad; that would never become otherwise in the world.

3. O brāhmaṇas, how can the curse, given by that noble Suśaṅkha, who was practising penance, not turn true?

4-8. I shall tell (you) all the sinful conduct of Vena. When he—a noble king knowing righteousness—was ruling, a man, having put on a guise, naked, of a huge body, with his head clean-shaved, of a great lustre, holding under his armpit a broom of peacock's feathers, and a drinking-pot made of cocoa-nut in his hand reciting (texts containing) wrong doctrines, vilifying the Vedic religion, came (there). He quickly came to (the place) where Vena was (seated). The sinner entered the court of that Vena. Seeing him having arrived (there) Vena asked him a question:

9-11. "Who are you, taking up such a form, that have come into my court? Why have you come before me who am (seated) in the court? What (kind of) dress (do you have)? What is your name? What is your faith? Tell me (all this). What is your Veda (i.e. which Veda do you follow)? What are your practices? What (kind of) penance (do you practise)? What abstract meditation (do you possess)? What (kind of) prowess (do you have)? What are the real characteristics of your faith? Tell me all that and the truth before me."

12a. Hearing those words of Vena the sinful man said these words.

The sinful man said :

12b-15. In vain you are ruling. You are a great fool, there is no doubt about it. I am all-in-all of Dharma (i.e. religious practices). I am most adored by gods. I am knowledge, I am truth, I am the eternal supporter. I am Dharma (i.e. religious practices), I am salvation, I am full of all gods. I have sprung from the body of Brahmā; I am faithful to my promise, and not otherwise. Know me to be the chief Jaina saint, having the body of true religion. The meditating sages, intent on (obtaining) knowledge, run to me only.

Vena said :

16. What kind of acts (do you do)? What is your doctrine? What are your practices? Tell (all this to me).

The sinful man said :

17-21. (That is my faith) where Arhats are the gods, and Nirgrantha is looked upon as the preceptor. Compassion is said to be the best way of life and in it is seen (to lie) salvation in (i.e. according to) this faith. There is no doubt about this. I shall (now) narrate the practices. (In this faith) there is no performance of sacrifices; there is no officiating at sacrifices; there is no recital of the Vedas; there is no offering of the three daily prayers; there is no penance; there is no charity; it is without (the exclamations viz.) svadhā and svāhā; there is no offering to gods or manes; there are no rites like sacrifices; there is no gratification of the manes; there is no (worship offered to a) guest; there is no offering to all the deities. The best worship is that of a Jaina mendicant, and the best meditation is that of an Arhat. This way of life is seen in the Jaina faith. I have told you all this i.e. the characteristics of my faith.

Vena said :

22-23. (In your faith) the way of life as told in the Vedas is not seen, nor are rites like sacrifices seen; no oblations to manes, no śrāddha, no sacrifice offered to all gods, and also no charity and penance are seen. Where (then) are the characteristics of the pious way of life to be (seen)? Tell me what kind of the way of life based on compassion (you advocate).

The sinful one said :

24-32a. This body of (human) beings is nourished by the five elements. This soul is of the nature of air, so they have no association. Even as in the water there is a contact of the form of bubbles, in the same way there is a contact among the beings. The earthly state is (present) in the matter; water also remains there only; fire also is seen there; powerful wind is also seen in (these) three. The state of bubbles covering the space is then produced in water, where a very bright, excellent circle is produced. It is seen just for a moment, and just after a moment it is not seen. In the same way contact among beings is seen. At the time of death, the soul departs, and the five (elements in the body) go to (i.e. merge into) the five (gross elements). Moreover the mortals being confounded by ignorance behave with one another (foolishly). Through folly they perform śrāddha and offer oblations to the manes in the evening. O best king, where is the dead person (at that time)? Of what nature does he eat? (i.e. what is his state when he eats?). What is knowledge? What kind is the body (after death)? By whom is it seen? Tell us (all about it). (Only) the brāhmaṇas, being fed with sweet food go satisfied. To whom would the śrāddha be offered? The faith (due to which a śrāddha is offered) has no meaning.

32b-42. I shall tell you another fierce act (mentioned) in the Vedas. When a guest goes (i.e. arrives) to the house, a brāhmaṇa (kills and) cooks (the flesh of) a great bull; or O king of kings, he would feed the guest (with the flesh of) a goat. (They kill) a horse in a horse-sacrifice, and a bull in a bull-sacrifice; a man in a human sacrifice and goats in a Vājapeya sacrifice. O great king, a great slaughter of many animals is done at a Rājasūya sacrifice. At a Puṇḍarīka sacrifice one would kill (i.e. one kills) an elephant, and at an elephant-sacrifice (they kill) an elephant. At the Sautrāmaṇī sacrifice a beast is seen to be fit for being sacrificed. Thus, O prince, listen how at rites of various forms killing of beasts of various species is laid down. What are the characteristics of gifts that are given? That food should be known as left-over, (where) sumptuous food is had, and (when) in a great sacrifice they kill those (beasts) that are extremely impure. What righteousness is seen there or what fruit is seen there where those who are learned in the Vedas have prescribed the killing of beasts? Due to that (i.e. the killing of beasts) merit perishes and the (so-called) religious merit does not give (i.e. lead to) salvation. That way of life which is without compassion is fruitless. There is no doubt that the right way of life lies there where lives of beings are protected. It is not the right way of life (or righteousness) where there are offerings to gods, manes, penance, truth, and rashness without compassion, O best king. The Vedas are not Vedas where compassion is not (prescribed).

43-52a. Even a cāṇḍāla or a śūdra, who, being intent upon the gift of kindness, would protect a life, is said to be a brāhmaṇa. But that cruel brāhmaṇa who is intent upon killing beasts, is very ruthless, sinful, hard-hearted and of a cruel mind. That Veda which is without knowledge, is said to be a Veda (only) by the rogues. Veda stands firmly there where there would be knowledge. O you very intelligent one, neither truth nor rite is seen in the merciless Vedas and Brāhmaṇas and also in the brāhmaṇas who follow the Vedas. O best king, the Vedas, void of truth are not Vedas and the brāhmaṇas who are not truthful (are not brāhmaṇas). There is no fruit of charity, so gifts also are not given. As are the characteristics of śrāddha, same are those of charity. Whatever is the faith of Jīva is the giver of enjoyment and salvation—that I shall tell you. First, one with his mind being tranquil, should show kindness. One should devoutly propitiate god Jina who (has pervaded) the mobile and immobile. With one's mind having pure thoughts, one should worship Jina alone. Salutation should be offered to that god, and not otherwise (i.e. not to anyone else). One should never salute the feet of one's mother and father. Then what should be told about others, O best king?

Vena said :

52b-53. (They say) that these brāhmaṇas, preceptors and others, and also the rivers like Gaṅgā, are holy places giving great religious merit. Is that the truth? Tell me if you desire piety (to flourish) here.

The sinful man said :

54-60. O great king, from the sky the clouds shower water. Having floated in the water which has fallen everywhere on the ground and on the mountains, he would stand, and produce compassion everywhere. Rivers are but the streams of blemish. How have you heard (i.e. how is it told in the scriptures) that the holy places are (situated) in (i.e. on the banks of) them? O great king, ponds, lakes, seas, and mountains—the heaps of stones—support the earth. No sacred place can be situated in (or on) them. A cloud is the best (holy place) due to its (containing) water. If a bath (i.e. a dip in water) causes great religious merit, then why is it not (found) in the fish? If by bath purity is produced, then the fish are purified. It cannot be otherwise (i.e. it is quite certain). Sacred place and eternal Dharma (i.e. way of life) are to be found where Jina remains. Penance and all merit due to bath etc. is settled there. O lord of kings, Jina alone is full of everything. There is no other (Dharma) than that; that is the holiest place. This is the greatest gain. So always meditate on him; you will be very happy.

61. Censuring by (indicating) the sinful nature of the entire (Vedic) religion, the Vedas, and charity of the form of sacrifices, along with (i.e. causing) merit, the sinful one advised Aṅga's son in various ways.

CHAPTER THIRTYEIGHT

The End of Vena's Reign

Sūta said :

1-2. Vena, thus advised by that very sinful Jina, and deluded by him, attained to a sinful attitude. Abandoning the Vedic faith and rites of a truthful conduct, he saluted the feet of that very wicked one.

3-5a. There was cessation of good sacrifices, and also of the Vedas. Religious practices full of holy scriptures (i.e. as told in the holy scriptures) did not proceed at that time. As a result of his (bad) rule, the world became full of all sins. When that king ruled, there were no sacrifices, no (recitations of) the Vedas, no excellent purport of the holy texts, no charity and no study, O brāhmaṇas.

5b-9. Thus there was the cessation of religious conduct, and great sin proceeded uninterruptedly. Though warded off by Aṅga, he very much acted otherwise. The wicked-minded one saluted neither the feet of his father nor of his mother. (He did) not (salute) the feet of any brāhmaṇa also. (He thought:) 'I alone am valorous.' Though warded off by his father and by his mother, the wicked-minded one did not perform auspicious, meritorious (acts) like giving gifts at a holy place. The very glorious one (lived) for a long time according to his own ideas. They all thought: 'For what reason has he become a sinner? The son of Aṅga Prajāpati is a bane to his family.'

10. The religious-minded (Aṅga) again asked the daughter of magnanimous Mṛtyu: "O dear one, tell me the truth: Due to whose fault is he born (like this)?"

Sunithā said :

11-13. O you highly intelligent one, [the daughter (of Yama) formerly only told Aṅga her own account and her merit and faults: (She said:)] in my childhood I committed a sin towards the magnanimous Suśaṅkha. I have not done anything else. The angry one cursed me: "Your progeny would be wicked." Thus, I think, O glorious one, this (Vena) has become wicked due to that (curse of Suśaṅkha).

14-15. The very lustrous one, having heard this, went to a forest with her. When the glorious one went to a forest along with his wife, the Seven Sages then approached Vena. Calling him they thus spoke to (him) the son of Aṅga :

The Sages said :

16-17. O Vena, do not act rashly; you are the guardian of the subjects. You yourself have put all this world and the three worlds along with the mobile and the immobile on the righteous path, O glorious one. Give up evil deeds, and perform auspicious deeds.

18a. When they had spoken like this, Vena laughed and said :

Vena said :

18b-20a. I alone am the highest (form of) religion; I alone deserve to be worshipped; I am eternal; I am the supporter; I am the protector; I alone am the import of the Veda; I am religious; I am the ancient, very holy, Jaina religion. O brāhmaṇas, by means of your actions, resort to me, who am of the form of religion.

The Sages said :

20b-24. The three castes viz. brāhmaṇas, kṣatriyas and vaiśyas are twice-born.[1] This (i.e. the Veda) is an ancient sacred text meant for all the castes. The beings behave according to the Vedic practices; therefore they (continue to) live. You are born in the family of Brahman. (So) you are a brāhmaṇa only. Then you, who had performed valorous deeds, were made the king of the earth. O best king, brāhmaṇas live happily due to the religious merit of the king. They perish due to his sin. Therefore practise righteous deeds. O king, you honoured and practised righteous deeds; but (did) not (do) the deeds of (i.e. proper for) Tretā and Dvāpara-yuga.

25-30. When Kali (-yuga) sets in, all men, deluded by sins, will act after having resorted to the Jaina faith. Men will abandon Vedic practices, and will commit sins. There is no doubt that the

1. Dvijātayaḥ—Men of any of the first three castes of the Hindus.

Jaina faith is the root of sin. O best king, the fall of those men, who are heaps of sins, is brought about by this great delusion. Govinda (i.e. Viṣṇu), the destroyer of all sins, will be (appearing) for their destruction and for nothing else. Taking the form of his liking he will restrain (them) from sins. When sins will have thus accumulated, he, the god will be (appearing) as Kalki[1] for the destruction of the Mlecchas; there is no doubt about it. Give up the behaviour of (i.e. proper for) Kali (-yuga) and resort to merit. Behave truthfully; become the guardian of your subjects.

Vena said :

31. I am the best among the wise; I have known everything here. He who behaves in a different way will certainly be punished.

32-37a. All the magnanimous sons of Brahman got angry with that wicked-hearted king who was talking too much. When the high-souled brāhmaṇas were angry, king Vena, through the fear of a curse from the brāhmaṇas, entered an ant-hill. Then the angry sages looked for Vena everywhere. Knowing that the king who had fled, was well-settled in an ant-hill, the brāhmaṇas, forcibly brought (out) the cruel and wicked (king). Seeing the sinner the sages were well-composed. Getting angry, they churned the left hand of the king. From it sprang up a very short, terrible barbarian, whose complexion was dark-blue, whose eyes were red, who had arrows in his hand, and held a bow (in his hands).

37b-41. He became the king, supporter and the protector of all sinful Niṣādas, especially of the Mlecchas. O highly intelligent one, seeing that sinful one, the sages also churned the right hand of that noble Vena. From it sprang up very intelligent and very powerful and noble king of kings, viz. Pṛthu, who milked the earth. By the power of his merit, and by the favour of that disc-holder (i.e. Viṣṇu), Vena, having enjoyed the position of a sovereign emperor, went to Viṣṇu's heaven. That is the highest position of Viṣṇu.

---

1. Kalki—The tenth and last incarnation of Viṣṇu in his capacity of the destroyer of the wicked and liberator of the world from its enemies.

CHAPTER THIRTYNINE

On Gifts and Worthy Recipients of Gifts

The sages said :

1. O you best among the truthful ones, tell us in detail, how Vena casting off his sin went to heaven.

Sūta said :

2-6a. O best brāhmaṇa, by the contact of the merit of the sages, by their concurrence, the sin went out of his body as a result of the churning of his body. Then that Vena of a righteous mind obtained eternal knowledge. O brāhmaṇas, free from desire and anger, he practised penance for a full hundred years in the hermitage of the sage Tṛṇabindu, which destroyed sins, and (which was situated) on the right bank of Revā. O glorious ones, god (Viṣṇu), the holder of the conch, disc and mace, was pleased with the sinless king due to his severe penance. Being pleased with him, he said to him: "I am pleased. Choose an excellent boon."

Vena said :

6b-7. O god, if you are pleased with me, give me an excellent boon: I desire to go, by your power, with this body, and along with my father and mother, to your abode, to the highest abode of Viṣṇu, O god of gods.

Śrī Vāsudeva said :

8. O king, where has that great infatuation, by which you were deluded, gone? You were caused to fall on the path of darkness by greed united with infatuation.

Vena said :

9-10a. O lord, I was deluded by the sin which I had formerly committed. Therefore (please) emancipate me from this very fierce sin. Tell me through your grace what (i.e. which hymn) I should mutter or recite.

The lord said :

10b-15. Well, O blessed king, your sin has perished. By means of your penance you have become pure. So I shall tell you (what) merit (is). O dear, formerly Brahmā had asked me as (i.e. what) you have asked. I (shall) tell you all that I had told him. When once, Brahmā staying in the lotus sprung from (my) navel was engrossed in meditation, Viṣṇu (i.e. I) appeared before him for granting him a boon, O you of a good vow. Desiring a good state (i.e. salvation), he asked him about a hymn, of a great religious merit, destroying sin, and called Vāsudeva. O glorious one, he (i.e. I) taught him the hymn, best among all hymns, called Vāsudeva very much pleasing to Viṣṇu, and giving all happiness to men who always recited and muttered it.

Viṣṇu said :

16-19. This entire world is pervaded by me of an unmanifest form. Therefore sages devoted to Viṣṇu call me Viṣṇu (i.e. one who pervades). I should be respectfully known to be that Vāsudeva, in whom the beings live, and who lives in the beings. Since, at the end (of the world) the lord leads the beings to the unmanifest one, therefore, he (i.e. I) should be known, by those who seek his (i.e. my) refuge, by the name Saṅkarṣaṇa. With the desire 'Let me be many', I take up any form I intend (to take up). Therefore, I should be known as Pradyumna by those who desire (to have) sons.

20-25. In this world I am not restrained by anyone except the lords of all, viz. Hara and Keśava, by means of the prowess of deep and abstract meditation; therefore I have (the epithet) Aniruddha. To the world, I, possessing spiritual and material knowledge, am known as Viśva. Being awake and full of reflection, I am possessed of self-consciousness. Full of the movements of the world and possessed of sense-organs and form I am (called) Taijasa (i.e. bright); I am in the state of sleep when I am without understanding and action. When I am the presiding deity I move (everywhere) occupying all. I am supposed to be unconcerned with the world when I am in the state of deep sleep. As Turīya (i.e. in the fourth state) I am without any modification and void of properties. With my form reflected everywhere I am unattached and (am just) like a witness. I am the individual soul still sticking to the worldly defilements; I am consciousness and joy; I am full of consciousness; and have the form of consciousness. I am eternal, immutable; I am of the form of Brahman; know me to be Brahman only.

The lord said :

26. Speaking so to Brahmā about his own form formerly, Viṣṇu vanished. He too knowing his universality, in a moment became self-possessed.

27. O king, you too are pure due to the birth of Pṛthu only. Still, O you of a good vow, propitiate the lord with this hymn.

28a. Viṣṇu, being pleased, said to him: "O you, who give respect to others, choose a boon."

Vena said :

28b-29a. O Viṣṇu, give me the best refuge; (please) protect me from the sin. I have sought your refuge. Tell (i.e. show) me the cause (i.e. way to) the best state (i.e. beatitude).

Viṣṇu said :

29b-39. O you blessed one, formerly only the noble Aṅga had propitiated me, (and) I had granted him a boon. O you illustrious one, O you best brāhmaṇa, O you prince, you will go to the best heaven of Viṣṇu by means of your own deeds. O noble one, just ask for a boon for yourself. O illustrious Vena, listen to the account that took place formerly. Formerly the glorious Suśaṅkha, getting angry, gave a curse to your mother, Sunīthā, in her childhood, O king. Then I, who had known (Aṅga's) mind, and who desired to emancipate you, gave a boon to Aṅga: 'You will have a good son.' O you who love virtues, having thus spoken to your father I will, having sprung up from your body, protect the world. I remain on the earth as Indra shines in heaven. The sacred text: 'Oneself is born as (one's) son', is true. So, O dear, you will get the highest position as a result of my boon. For getting the (best) position (i.e. salvation), O king, O hero, give a gift; I (am the one), who in the form of the sinful naked one, spoke to you, to cause you deviate from righteousness;

otherwise the words of Suśaṅkha would have become untrue. I myself am injunction and prohibition both. I am the one who gives the fruit (to one) according to one's deeds, who is beyond comprehension and who insists on virtues.

40-46a. (Giving) a gift is the highest, the best. It is the cause of everything. Therefore you give gifts. Merit proceeds from (giving) gifts. Sin perishes due to (the giving of) gifts; therefore, do give gifts. O best king, perform sacrifices like the horse-sacrifice. Give gifts of land etc. to brāhmaṇas. Due to (giving) good gifts enjoyment is obtained, glory is obtained; fame takes place (i.e. is obtained) due to good gifts and happiness is secured through good gifts. A man obtains (i.e. goes to) heaven by means of (giving) gifts, and there enjoys the fruit (of his gifts). When the time of the maturity of a good gift that is given through faith arrives, O best one, the man (i.e. the giver of gifts) would go to a sacred place—this is also the fruit of (his) religious merit. To him, who, keeping faith in me, gives a great gift to a worthy brāhmaṇa, I give everything and whatever he desires with (i.e. in) his mind.

Vena said :

46b-48a. Tell me about the (proper) time of (i.e. for giving) a gift. What are the characteristics of the (proper) time (for giving a gift)? Being gracious to me, O lord of the world, if you have compassion for me, tell me in detail the nature of a sacred place, and also the good (i.e. proper) characteristics of a worthy recipient, and the procedure of (giving) a gift.

Śrikṛṣṇa said :

48b-57. O king, O great lord, I shall tell you the time for regular and occasional charity and also for the optional one, and for making daily and occasional gifts which would lead to the fourth (goal of life, i.e. salvation). At the time of sunrise, sin perishes everywhere. Very fierce darkness destroys men. This sun, my portion, is thought to be the treasure of lustre by day. Sins, burnt by the lustre of him only, are reduced to ashes. O king, what can be said about that which increases the religious merit of him who even gives water to my rising portion (i.e. the rising sun)? When an auspicious time comes, if a person, after having bathed and worshipped his parents and gods gives, according to his capacity and with his mind purified by faith, gifts of food, water, fruits, flowers, garments, tāmbūla, ornaments, gold, and gems etc., he has unending merit. O king, he, who would also offer water dedicated to me at midday and afternoon, has unending merit. Like this he regularly gives food, drink, sweets, ointment, sandal, flowers, camphor etc. along with garments and ornaments, (which) gives enjoyments and happiness. This is said to be the usual time (i.e. time for regular charity), auspicious for those who desire to give gifts or offer worship.

58-71a. Now I shall tell you about the excellent occasional (charity). There is no doubt that one should give gifts at all the three times. He, who desires his own well-being should not pass a day void (of gifts). O king due to the power of the time at which something is given, a man (becomes) very intelligent, full of great power, rich, virtuous, learned, wise and far-seeing. I keep the excellent man away from food for a fortnight, a month, or a day—that is, as long as he has not given food. One who has not given an excellent gift has eaten his own excrement. Being displeased (with such persons) I generate in their bodies a disease, which keeps off all enjoyments, which gives them great trouble, which is accompanied by weak digestion, and which causes fever and suffering. He who has not made a gift (of food) to Brahmins and deities, three times, and has himself eaten sweets, has committed a great sin. O great king, he should thus purify his body by a severe expiation, and also by fasts withering up the body. As a cobbler cleanses the hide in the bowl with exudations from trees and expands it, in the same way I certainly purify a sinner, by proper use of herbs, and also by means of astringent and bitter medicines; (thus I do) in the form of a physician, with hot water and heating, and in no other way; there is no doubt about it. Other people enjoy his excellent, auspicious enjoyments as desired(?) What can (even) a powerful man do if he has not given an excellent gift? I torment him through the form of a great sin. O king of kings, if the sinners, through selfishness, have not given the regular gifts with a mind purified with faith, then with terrible means I consume them.

Vāsudeva said :

71b-75. O best of men, I shall explain to you the occasional time (i.e. times for making occasional gifts) and the merit (obtained by giving such gifts); listen attentively and with a good mind. O king, when it is the new moon day or the full moon day or the Saṁkrānti day, or Vyatīpāta or when it is Vaidhṛti Ekādaśī, or when it is the full moon day in Māgha or Āṣāḍha, or Vaiśākha or Kārtika, or when the new moon day falls on Monday, or on the anniversary days of the Manu-age etc., when it is the day on which the elephant's shadow (falls towards the east), or it is a day called pitṛkṣaya—all these are explained (by me) to you, O best king.

76-83. I shall tell you the fruit of the gifts that are given on these (occasions). O best king, listen. To the man, who devoutly gives (a gift) intended for me to a brāhmaṇa, I give, without hesitation, a house, happiness, heaven and salvation and many (other things). There is no doubt about this, O great king. I shall (now) explain to you the optional time (i.e. time for optional charity) for giving a gift which is fruitful. The best sages have told about the auspicious time for all vows in honour of gods etc., and also for giving gifts. O king, I shall also tell you about the time leading to prosperity. Of all the sacrificial rites the nuptial one is the best; O king, so also the time when the rite of the birth of a son, his tonsure-ceremony or thread-ceremony is performed; so also the time of the installation of the palace-flag or of deities; so also that (of the fixing ceremony) of the site of wells, pools, lakes, houses, is called (the time) leading to prosperity, when the mothers are worshipped. At this time (a man) should give gifts which bring about all (kinds of) success. O best king, I have just told you the time leading to prosperity.

84-104. (Now) I shall tell you something else which removes affliction due to sin. When the time of death has come, a man, knowing (that this) death is (imminent), should give a gift, causing comfort on (his) way to Yama, O best man. O great king, I have told you the times called regular and occasional ones, and also those that lead to prosperity. I have (also) told you the time of death. I have told (you about) these times which give fruits of one's deeds. O king, (now) I shall tell you the characteristics of a sacred place. Among excellent holy places this Gaṅgā shines. (Others that are) mentioned are the holy (rivers) Sarasvatī, Revā, Yamunā, Tāpī; and river Carmaṇvatī, (and also the rivers) Sarayū, Ghargharā, and Venā destroying all sins, Kāverī, Kapilā and the big (river) Viśvatāriṇī, (and also) Godāvarī and Tuṅgabhadrā, O king. (The river) Bhīmarathyā is declared always to cause fear to the sinners. Other excellent rivers are Devikā, Kṛṣṇagaṅgā etc. (For offering gifts) on auspicious occasions there are many holy places of (i.e. on the banks of) these (rivers). Rivers, whether (they flow) through a village or a forest, are purifying everywhere. At these places acts like bath, charity etc. should be performed. O best ones, when the name of a holy place (on the banks) of those (rivers) is not known, the utterance of the (my) name should be done by saying: 'This is Viṣṇu's holy place', O king. O prince, a devotee should utter (the name of) me at the sacred places and (while presenting gifts) to gods. He gets the fruit of his merit due to (the utterance of) my name. O best king, at the time of bathing at unknown excellent holy places, and (offering presents) to unknown deities, one should just utter my name. O best king, the Creator has made these rivers the mothers of the all-meritorious sacred places, and they are (to be found) everywhere on the globe. O king, a man should not take bath etc. here and there (i.e. anywhere). Due to the grace of the excellent holy places, one gets an inexhaustible fruit. The seven oceans only are of the nature of sacred places and are very meritorious. O king, the lakes like Mānasa etc. are declared to be like them only. Streams and ponds are also said to be of the nature of sacred places. There is no doubt about it. (There are) O great king, (certain) very small rivers. A sacred place is said to exist in them (i.e. on their banks), so also in all ditches excepting (temporary) wells. On the surface of the earth, mountains like Meru are also of the nature of holy places. A sacrificial place, a sacrifice well-put (i.e. performed) in a fire-chamber, and also the place where a śrāddha is offered, is pure like that. Similarly a temple, a sacrificial chamber, a chamber where Vedas are studied (is pure). In the houses a cow-pen, possessing merit, is (said to be) the best. A sacred place exists there, where the performer of a Soma-sacrifice would be (present) and also a grove where the meritorious Aśvattha stands (is a sacred place). A sacred place exists there where there would be a palāśa or an udumbara tree or a bunyan tree; and also at a place where other sylvan marks (are present).

105-107a. These are said to be sacred places, and also father and mother; (the place) where a Purāṇa is being recited, or the one where (one's) preceptor resides (is also sacred). There is no doubt that that place where a good wife lives is a sacred place. The Place where a good son stays is a holy place—there is no doubt about it. These are said to be sacred places; and also a king's abode (is a sacred place).

Vena said :

107b-108a. O best god, O Mādhava, being gracious through compassion tell me the characteristics of a worthy person to whom a gift should be given.

Vāsudeva said :

108b-127. O very intelligent king, listen to the good (i.e. important) marks of a worthy recipient, to whom a gift should be given by the glorious ones purified by faith. A brāhmaṇa endowed with (i.e. born in) a good family, devoted to the study of the Vedas, tranquil, restrained, one having practised penance, especially pure, intelligent, wise, engrossed in the worship of deities, truthful, of a great religious merit, Viṣṇu's devotee, and learned, knowing religion, free from greediness, and avoided by heretics, is said to be a worthy recipient. O best man, O great king, other worthy recipients are these: sister's son—the best man, endowed with qualities like these; daughter's son; son-in-law having similar dispositions; also, O best man, a preceptor who is initiated. These are worthy recipients, fit for presenting gifts. One should avoid a brāhmaṇa who possessed conduct as laid down in the Vedas (yet) is not content. Also one should avoid a one-eyed or very dark-blue (brāhmaṇa), (a brāhmaṇa) who has black teeth, or has dark-blue or yellow teeth. O king, one should avoid a brāhmaṇa who has slaughtered a cow, who has very black teeth, who is a barbarian or is licentious or is short of a limb or has an extra one; also a lepor or one having bad nails, or bad skin; also a bald-headed brāhmaṇa, O great king. One should not give a gift to a brāhmaṇa, even if he is like Brahmā, if his wife is engaged in imporper (acts). O you highly intelligent one, a gift should not be given to a brāhmaṇa who is conquered by (i.e. under the thumb of) his wife, and also to him who is a traitor to his own school of the Vedas (Śākhā). O king, a gift should not be given to a diseased brāhmaṇa, or who eats the dead (i.e. meat eater). A gift should not be given to (a brāhmaṇa who is) a thief even though he is like Atri. A gift should not be given to a brāhmaṇa who is not content. One should also avoid a brāhmaṇa (doing rites) relating to a dead body. A gift should not be given to (a brāhmaṇa who is) very obstinate, and especially to a brāhmaṇa who is dishonest. O lord of kings, a brāhmaṇa, following Vedic practices, but void of good conduct, would not be proper at (the offering of) a śrāddha, or (giving) a gift. Now I shall tell you about the gift which is fruitful and meritorious. Faith is produced by association with a holy place and worthy recipients and (practising charity at an auspicious) time. There is no religious merit like faith, there is no happiness like faith for beings in the worldly existence, O king. A man should remember me with faith, O best king; a king should give even a small gift into the hand of a worthy recipient. He obtains an unlimited fruit of such a gift (given) according to the proper procedure; he would be happy by my grace.

CHAPTER FORTY

The Fruit of Occasional Charity

Vena said :

1-2. O god, I have heard from you the fruit of regular charity. By your grace (i.e. be gracious and) carefully tell me that fruit which is the fruit of occasional charity. I am not getting great satisfaction; my faith prompts me to hear it.

Viṣṇu said :

3-8a. O best king, I shall explain to you (gifts given called) the occasional. Listen to the fruit of the gifts given to worthy recipients by a person with faith, on a great parvan day. O best king, he, the best man, who gives an elephant, a chariot or a horse (to a brāhmaṇa) becomes the best king, accompanied by servants, in a holy country, O great king; there is no doubt about this. The religious-minded, powerful and very intelligent one becomes a very lustrous king and is unconquered by all beings. O great king, he, who gives a gift of land or a cow when the great parvan (day) arrives, would become the lord of all enjoyments. One should give a gift to a very meritorious brāhmaṇa with great care.

8b-11a. I shall tell you the characteristics of great gifts which a man gives at a sacred place on a parvan (day) : he becomes a king. He who gives a secret gift (to a brāhmaṇa) at a holy place on a parvan (day), quickly has an imperishable attainment of treasures (i.e. obtains imperishable treasures). When a great parvan (day) comes, (a man should give) a great gift with a garment and gold to a brāhmaṇa at sacred places.

11b-29a. O king, I shall tell you (about) the auspicious fruit of that gift : (to him) many very virtuous sons, proficient in the Vedas, long-lived, having progeny, and endowed with glory and merit are born. Many (such sons) are born. O you very intelligent one, ample wealth (also comes to him). He gets happiness and religious merit. He becomes religious. When the great parvan (day) arrives, a (man), having gone to a holy place with great effort, should present a golden cow to a glorious brāhmaṇa. O you very intelligent one, I shall tell you about the religious merit of (i.e. obtained by giving) that gift. O great king, the giver of a tawny cow enjoys all pleasures. He lives there as long as Brahmā would live. O king of kings, I (shall) tell you about the fruit and enjoyment of (i.e. due to) the gift of a cow given after adorning her, furnishing her with gold and with garments, ornaments and decorations. Ample glory full of gifts and enjoyments is produced. It is said that such a man (i.e. he who gives gifts) becoming a master of knowledge, would become a devotee of Viṣṇu. He would reside in Viṣṇu's world as long as the earth would remain. He, who, after going to a sacred place, would give an ornament to a brāhmaṇa, sports with Indra after having enjoyed many pleasures. He, who, endowed with faith, gives to the best brāhmaṇa, a deserving recipient, food along with land when a great parvan (day) arrives, having valour equal to that of Viṣṇu rejoices in Vaikuṇṭha. Giving (i.e. he who gives), according to his desire, gold along with garments to a brāhmaṇa for peace, he, resembling fire, would live happily in heaven. He should fill a big golden pitcher with ghee. He should adorn it with garments and garlands and cover it with (a) silver (lid). He should furnish it with a garland of flowers and make it adorned with a sacred thread. O highly intelligent one, worshipping it, consecrated with Vedic hymns, he should (then) worship it with sixteen pure articles of worship. Then well-adorning it, he should present it to a glorious brāhmaṇa. He should then give sixteen cows with bell-metal udders, along with garments; (he should) also (give) four (cows) and a gift (to a brāhmaṇa) along with gold. He should also give twelve cows adorned with garments, ornaments and decorations to a separated (living in a lonely place?) brāhmaṇa. There is no doubt about this. O prince, such and other gifts (should be given). Having properly found a sacred place and (the proper) time, and a brāhmaṇa's residence, he should give (gifts) with faith. That would lead to great religious merit. There is no doubt about it.

Viṣṇu said :

29b-46. A gift should be arranged (i.e. given) dedicating it to Viṣṇu. A man inspired by the feeling of love for that gift gets a fruit like that. There is no doubt about this. Now I shall explain good fortune. By giving the gift which proceeds (i.e. is given) in sacrifices etc., and even by having faith in (giving it), a man has increase in his intellect and does not get unhappiness, O best brāhmaṇa. The religious-minded one, while alive, enjoys pleasures properly. That donor, having obtained a divine position, enjoys pleasures of Indra. He takes his family to heaven for a thousand kalpas. I have thus explained (gifts) leading to good fortune. Now among the (gifts) I shall tell about (the gift to be given at the time of death). Knowing that the end of the body (i.e. death) has come near, and being afflicted by old age, he should give a gift. He should not entertain (any) hope about any one. (He should not entertain thoughts like:) 'What will happen to my sons, other relatives and friends in my absence after my death?' A man deluded by infatuation for them, does not give anything. He, with his mind confused, dies; friends and relatives weep (for him). All of them, afflicted by grief and by false attachment, resolve (to give) gifts, and reflect upon salvation. When he is dead, and when the false attachment is over, they, of greedy minds, forget the gifts and never give them, O great king. The one, O great king, who is dead, is extremely unhappy on the path to (the abode of) Yama, is overcome with thirst and hunger, and afflicted by gifts. O best king, to whom do sons and grandsons belong? To whom does the wife belong? In this worldly existence none belongs to none (else). Therefore gifts are given. O best king, O you highly intelligent one, a wise man should himself give food, drink, tāmbūla, water, gold, a pair (of) garments, an umbrella, many water-vessels with water, varied vehicles and carriages, various kinds of perfumes and camphor. If he would desire (if he desires) much happiness he should give (to a brāhmaṇa) shoes that give comfort on the path to (the abode of) Yama. O great king, by (giving) these gifts a man goes happily along Yama's path.

CHAPTER FORTYONE

The Story of Sukalā

Vena said :

1. Tell me how the son (or) the wife (or) the father (or) the mother is a holy place. Tell me also in detail how one's preceptor is a holy place.

Śrī Viṣṇu said :

2-8. There was a great city (named) Vārāṇasī along with (i.e. on the bank of) Gaṅgā. In it lived a vaiśya by name Kṛkala.

His wife, named Sukalā, was very chaste, devoted to her husband, always engaged in religious practices, and loyal to her husband. Her limbs were auspicious. She had a good son and she was charming and auspicious. She spoke the truth, she was always pure, she had a lovable form, and was dear to her husband. She, endowed with these qualities, was fortunate, and performed good deeds. The vaiśya (i.e. Kṛkala) was an excellent man; he knew various religious practices, was wise and virtuous. He was always intent upon listening to the Purāṇas and religious practices as told by the scriptures. With faith he set out, with the caravan of brāhmaṇas on a pilgrimage, meritorious and auspicious. He proceeded on the religious path (of the pilgrimage). The chaste wife (i.e. Sukalā), being stupefied by her love for her husband, said (these) words to her husband.

Sukalā said :

9-19a. O dear, I am your religiously wedded wife, and practise merit with you. Waiting (i.e. looking) for the path of (i.e. followed by) my husband, I propitiate the god i.e. my husband. O best brāhmaṇa, I shall never give up your proximity. Resorting to your shadow, I shall practise the excellent mode of behaviour called loyalty to my husband, which destroys the sins of women and gives them a good position. The woman, who would be solely devoted to her husband, is called meritorious. Except the husband, no other holy place befits young women, and no other holy place gives them heaven or salvation. O best one, a woman should look upon the right foot of her husband as Prayāga, and the left one as Puṣkara. Merit is produced by taking bath with the water (falling) from his feet. It is like taking a bath at Prayāga or Puṣkara. There is no doubt about it. The husband is full of all holy places. The husband is full of all religious merit. All that fruit—the religious merit, which an initiated man gets after the performance of sacrifices, is obtained by a wife through serving her husband. She obtains, through serving her husband that fruit which would accrue to one by having had pilgrimage to excellent holy places like Gayā. I am telling it in brief. Listen to me who am telling it. For them (i.e. for women) there is no other duty than serving the husband. Therefore, O dear one, I, helping you and giving you pleasure, shall, by resorting to your shadow (i.e. by following you), come (with you). This will not be otherwise.

Viṣṇu said :

19b-29a. Kṛkala, having considered her beauty, character, virtue and devotion and having again and again given a thought to her delicacy (thought): 'If like this (i.e. as she says) I shall take her (with me) along the difficult path causing great grief, her beauty will wither due to being shaken by cold and heat. Her body, of an excellent complexion, is like the interior of a lotus. It will be dark due to the cold stormy gale. The path is rough and has (i.e. is full of) stones. Her feet are very delicate. She will meet with severe pain; therefore she is unable to go (i.e. I cannot take her). What will be her plight, when her body would be encompassed by hunger and thirst? This woman of a beautiful body is my support. (This) woman of a beautiful face is the abode of my pleasure. She is always dear to my life. She is always the abode of religious merit. When this young woman will perish, I shall (also certainly) perish in this world. This one is always my livelihood. She is the ruler of my life. I shall not take her to the forest (and) to the holy place. I shall (just) go all alone.' The glorious Kṛkala thought (like this) for a moment. O best king, she knew (i.e. read) the thought in his mind. The glorious one again said to her husband who had started: "O best one, listen, men should not leave (back) their innocent wives. O you highly intelligent one, this is the root of Dharma (duty, righteousness) of a man. Realising this, O illustrious one, now take me (with you)".

Viṣṇu said :

29b-32a. Having heard all those many words uttered by his beloved (wife), Kṛkala laughed and again said to her : "O dear one, the wife who is religiously obtained is not to be abandoned. O you of a beautiful face, he, who has abandoned his well-behaved and religious wife, has even given up the Dharma of ten constituents.[1] Therefore, well-being to you, O dear one, I shall never abandon you".

1. Daśāṅga Dharma—The ten constituents of Dharma as mentioned in the Vāmana Purāṇa (14.1-2) are: harmlessness, truthfulness, non-stealing, charity, forbearance, restraint, quiescence, not demeaning oneself, purity and penance.

Viṣṇu said :

32b-50a. Having thus spoken to her, and having repeatedly advised his wife, he went with the caravan without her knowledge. When thus that glorious Kṛkala had left, the lady of an auspicious face did not at all see her husband Kṛkala, of meritorious deeds, at the auspicious time of the worship of deities and at (other) auspicious time. Weeping, and very much afflicted, oppressed by grief and sorrow for her husband, she quickly got up and asked her friends. (She said to them:) "O you illustrious ones, have you seen that Kṛkala, the lord of my life? He has gone somewhere. You are my relatives. O you glorious ones, if you have seen that magnanimous, very intelligent, meritorious, omniscient, truthful and wise Kṛkala of me (i.e. my husband), (then) tell me." Hearing those words of (i.e. uttered by) her, they said to the very intelligent one: "O you auspicious one of a good vow, your husband Kṛkala has, on the occasion of a pilgrimage, visited a sacred place. Why do you weep? Having visited a great sacred place, he will come (back), O you beautiful one." That Sukalā of a charming speech, thus addressed by the intimate persons, again went home, O king. That devout Sukalā wept piteously in agony. (She said:) "Till my husband comes, I shall sleep on a bed on the ground. I shall not eat ghee, oil, curd and milk." She gave up (eating) salt, and also (chewing) tāmbūla. O king, she also gave up (eating) sweet (things) like jaggery etc. (She said:) "Till my husband returns I shall eat once a day or will not eat anything at all. There is no doubt about this." Thus she was full of grief; she wore a single braid of hair; she put on one bodiçe (only), and was unclean. She also remained with only one garment (on her person). She gave out sounds like 'hā hā', sighed, and was extremely afflicted. She was parched up by the fire of separation; her body (had become) black; and she became unclean. Thus being unhappy, very much emaciated, and perturbed, and weeping day and night, she did not get sleep at night. O king, broken (down) by grief, she (even) did not feel hungry. Then (her) friends came there, and asked Sukalā. (They said:) "O Sukalā, beautiful in all limbs, why are you weeping now? O you of a beautiful face, tell (us) the cause of your grief."

Sukalā said :

50b-56a. That my righteous husband has gone for (obtaining) religious merit. He is roaming over the earth for pilgrimage. That my lord has gone after leaving me who am faultless and sinless. I am a chaste woman of good behaviour, always meritorious and loyal to my husband. That (my) husband intent on getting (i.e. visiting) a sacred place, has left me and gone. Therefore, O friends, being extremely afflicted by separation (from him) I am grieving. When a very cruel husband (like mine) leaves his dear wife and goes (away), it is better (for the wife like me) to destroy my life (i.e. to commit suicide); it is better to eat poison; it is better to enter fire; it is better to destroy (my) body. O friends, It is better to end my life; but forsaking the husband is not better. I am unable to put up with the ever-terrible separation from him. O friends, I am always afflicted by that separation.

The friends said :

56b-60. Your lord, your husband, who has gone on a pilgrimage, will come (back). You are unnecessarily drying up your body, you are grieving in vain. O young lady, you are tormenting yourself to no purpose; you are uselessly giving up pleasures. Drink drinks, enjoy (the fruit of) what you yourself have given before. Whose is the husband? (i.e. to whom does the husband belong?) To whom do the sons, relatives and kinsmen belong? In this mundane existence nobody belongs to anybody else. One has connection with none else. (People) eat, enjoy. O young lady, that is (just) the fruit of the worldly existence. When a being is dead, who would enjoy or see its fruit? O young lady, what (people) drink, enjoy is the fruit (that is got) from the worldly existence.

Sukalā said :

61-83. Whatever you have said is not approved by the Vedas; but that woman, who, separated from her husband, always lives all alone, would be a sinful one. Good people do not honour her. In the Vedas she is always said to be with her husband. A relation is produced due to the power of religious merit.

In the scriptures the husband is always described as the sacred place for women. She should always invoke him by means of speech, body and deeds. Intent upon truthful thoughts, she should always mentally worship him. The side of the husband—(especially) his right side— is always a great holy place. When a woman, having resorted to him, lives in the house, she gets the fruit of the gifts which he gives and the merit (he collects) when he performs a sacrifice, and the fruit that he gets (by bathing) at Vārāṇasi in Gaṅgā, or at Puṣkara, or at Dvārakā or at Avanti, or Kedāra at (the temple of) Śiva; (and) not that woman who always performs sacrifices. O friends, such a fruit she never obtains. (By resorting to her husband) the woman of an excellent complexion always obtains a beautiful face, good fortune in the form of a son, bath, gifts, decorations, garments, ornaments, good fortune (in the form of her husband being alive), form, lustre, glory, fame and merit. There is no doubt that she gets all (this) through the grace of her husband. When a woman, when her husband is alive, practises another mode of life (than the one that is prescribed), (all that) becomes fruitless, and she is called an unchaste woman. On the globe (i.e. the earth) the youth, beauty and form of women is certainly said to be for the husband alone. A wife is said to be one who has good sons and good reputation. There is no doubt that when the husband is pleased in the existence, the wife is pleasing to the sight. If on the globe there would be a wife without (i.e. segregated from) her husband, how can she have happiness, beauty, glory, fame and sons on the earth? She experiences great misfortune and unhappiness in the worldly existence. She would always be sinful and would behave unpleasantly. When her husband is pleased with her, all the deities are pleased. When her husband is pleased, sages, gods and men are pleased (with her). The husband is the lord, the husband is the preceptor, the husband is the deity along with other deities. O prince, the husband is a holy place, and (is) sacred for the wives (i.e. the wife). He is also her sentiment of love, ornament, form, complexion and fragrance. She puts on an elegant dress, ornaments (etc.) except on the auspicious parvan days; she shines with elegant dresses and ornaments when her husband is (with her). Without the husband she is like milk in the mouth of a serpent. The glorious, charming and auspicious wife practises good vow for her husband (only). If a woman puts on an elegant dress (etc.) when her husband is dead, all her beauty, complexion (etc.) is reduced to the form of a dead body. People call her a prostitute on the earth. Therefore, listen, that woman who desires great happiness on the earth, should never remain without her husband. The husband is described in the scriptures to be the highest Dharma of the wife. Therefore, a wife should not abandon that eternal Dharma. This, I know, to be the Dharma. How would (my) husband forsake (me)? In this connection, O friends, an ancient account is heard. It is the meritorious account of Sudevā, that (i.e. listening to which) destroys sins.

CHAPTER FORTYTWO

Ikṣvāku Goes Ahunting

The friends said :

1. Who is that Sudevā about whom you talked? Tell us as to how she behaved. You have told (about her). Tell us the truth.

Sukalā said :

2-7a. The great, glorious king, Manu's son, Ikṣvāku by name, lived in Ayodhyā. He knew the rules of conduct; he was exclusively devoted to religious ends; he knew everything, and he honoured gods and brāhmaṇas; his wife was ever meritorious and devoted to her husband. With her he performed many sacrifices and (visited) various holy places. Sudevā, devoted to truthful conduct, was the daughter of Vedarāja, the brave and illustrious king of Kāśī. King Ikṣvāku married her. Sudevā was beautiful in all limbs, and was devoted to the vow of truth. With her, his beloved, the best king, the meritorious leader of people, enjoyed.

7b-17. Once that great king went with her to a forest. Having reached a forest (on the bank) of Gaṅgā, he always enjoyed hunting, (by) killing lions, boars, elephants and buffaloes. In front of him, who was (thus) sporting, a boar, adorned with (i.e. accompanied by) a large herd of boars and (his) sons and grandsons, arrived. His only beloved female hog remained by his side. With (other) boars and hogs she surrounded him only. The hog, seeing the king of kings who was difficult to conquer and who was engaged in hunting, remained very courageously with his wife and by his sons, grandsons, elders and young ones after having taken the shelter of a mountain. O great king, knowing the great slaughter of those beasts (in the forest), the hog said to his sons, grandsons and wife : "O darling, the very powerful and brave lord of Kosala, Manu's son, is enjoying hunting, and is destroying many beasts. There is no doubt that the great king, after seeing me, will come here. I have certainly no danger to my life from other hunters; (but) the king, seeing my form, will not forgive me. O dear one, there is no doubt that he, the very lustrous one, full of great joy, with arrows in his hand, holding a bow, accompanied by dogs and surrounded by hunters, will kill me."

The female hog said :

18-19. O dear one, whenever, in this great forest, you see many hunters equipped with many weapons, you give up your great courage, power and valour, and with your heart dejected through great fear, run away, along with these my sons and grandsons. (Now) seeing this lord of kings and the best of men, what will you do? O dear one, tell me the reason.

20-32. Hearing her words, the boar, the king of hogs, gave the (following) answer to her: "O dear one, listen why I am afraid of a great hunter and go away. Hearing the (sound of) hogs, the great hunters, who are sinful and cunning, commit evils in the inaccessible caves of the mountain. They all are always wicked, always conceive many sins, and are born in the families of sinners. I am scared of dying at their hands; (for) though I die (after being shot by them), I shall again go to a sinful (existence). O darling, scared of an untimely death, I shall go away to a mountain or a mountain-cave. This king, greater than the world, a king of the nature of Viṣṇu, has come.

O dear one, on the battlefield I shall fight with valour and bravery with the glorious one. If, by means of my own lustre I shall conquer the king, I shall enjoy incomparable fame on the earth. (If I am) killed in the battle by that best hero, I shall go to Viṣṇu's heaven. The lord of the earth will be highly satisfied with the flesh and marrow of my body. Due to him the deities of the good worlds will be gratified. This one, with the thunderbolt in his hand, has come. O beautiful one, when I meet with death at his hands, it will be a gain and excellent fame for me. Due to him I shall have glory on the earth and in the three worlds; (and) I (shall) go to Viṣṇu's world. I was not scared like this; I went agitated, (so) I went to the mountain-peaks. I went there as I was afraid of a sinful (hunter), O dear one; (and) on seeing (this king practising) piety, I have remained (here). I do not know my former sin, committed in another (i.e. former) existence, by the accumulation of which, I went to (i.e. was born in) the species of hogs. I shall (now) wash the former, terrible accumulation of sins with the water of hundreds of very sharp and whetted arrows. O you female hog, giving up your love for me, and taking with you our sons, grandsons, daughters and children in the family, go to the mountain, Give up your folly (i.e. foolish love) for me. This Viṣṇu has come. By his hand (i.e. killed by him) I shall go to that highest position of Viṣṇu. Fortune also has laid open the gates of heaven for me. I shall go to the best heaven."

Sukalā said :

33. O friends, having heard those words of the magnanimous hog, his beloved, with her heart sinking, then spoke.

The female hog said :

34-51. The herd, of which you are the lord, (shines) being adorned by sons, grandsons, friends, brothers and other kinsmen and relatives. The herd, adorned by you only, shines. O you glorious one, what will be the condition of this herd without you? O dear one, due to your power only these roaring boars, my young sons, roam on the mountain. Fearless on account of your lustre, they eat well the bulbs and roots. Due to your lustre, they are not very much scared of lions and men in inaccessible places, forest-bowers, villages and cities and on this mountain, as they are protected by your lustre, O you very valorous one. Abandoned by you, all these young sons of me will be afflicted, confounded and senseless. All these young ones will never see (i.e. have) a happy course after going (from here). A beautiful woman does not at all look charming without her husband. (Even though she is) decorated with divine, golden ornaments, garments, food, clothes, father, mother, brothers and sisters, mother-in-law, father-in-law and others, she does not shine without her husband, as the night without the moon, (or) a family without a son (does not shine), (or) as a house without a lamp never shines. Similarly, O you, who cut off (i.e. remove) the pride (of your enemies), the herd does not at all shine without you. As a man does not shine without (good) behaviour, (or) an ascetic does not shine without knowledge, (or) as a king does not shine without (good) counsel, in the same way this (herd) does not shine (without you). As a boat full (of goods) does not (go on well) in an ocean without a fisherman, (or) as a caravan does not (shine) without its leader, similarly this (herd) does not (shine without you). As an army does not shine without a general, similarly this army of hogs (does not shine) without you, O you highly intelligent one. It will be helpless like a brāhmaṇa without (the study of) the Veda. Having entrusted the responsibility of the family to me you are going (to fight). Knowing that death is easy (i.e. would come easily) how are you having such a pledge? O dear lord, I shall not be able to sustain my life without you. O you highly intelligent one, with you alone I shall enjoy heaven, earth or even hell. I am telling you the truth and the truth only. O lord of the herd, we two—you and I—taking the sons and grandsons and the excellent herd (with us) shall go to an inaccessible place with a big cave. One goes to fight (only) after abandoning (i.e. being prepared to abandon) one's life. Tell me now what gain will there be in death (i.e. dying at the hands of the king)?

The boar said :

52-60a. You do not know the excellent way of life of the brave. Now listen to it. If a warrior desiring to fight with another warrior, goes to him (and says) : 'Fight with me, I have come (here) to fight (with you)', (and if the man) does not give (i.e. is not ready to have) a fight with (that) other man through desire, greed or delusion, then, listen, O dear one, he would dwell in the Kumbhīpāka hell for a thousand yugas. There is no doubt that it is the highest duty of kṣatriyas to fight (when challenged to fight). If the fight fought by him after going to the battlefield is won by him, he enjoys great glory and fame. If he, extremely fearless due to his valour, is killed while fighting, he obtains (i.e. goes to) the world of the brave and enjoys divine pleasures. O dear one, listen, he would dwell in the world of the brave for twenty thousand years, and during that period he is honoured with the practices of gods. There is no doubt. Here comes the brave son of Manu, asking for a fight. I must certainly give it. The welcome guest asking for a fight, and of the form of the eternal Viṣṇu has arrived. O auspicious one, I must offer him a reception in the form of a fight.

The female hog said :

60b-61a. O dear one, how shall I (be able to) see your valour when you would fight with the magnanimous king ?

61b-66. Saying so, and hurriedly calling her dear sons, she said (to them) : "O sons, listen to my words. The welcome guest in the form of the eternal Viṣṇu asking for a fight, has come. I have to go where this (my lord) will go. As long as (this my) lord, your protector, remains here, you go away to the inaccessible opening of a mountain-cave. O (my) children, live there happily, avoiding skilful hunters. I must go there only where he (i.e. my lord) will go. This your eldest brother will protect the herd. All these (your) uncles will protect you. O my good sons, leaving me (here), go away, all of you."

The sons said :

67-68. This best mountain is full of many roots, fruits and much water. There is no fear for anyone. Life is happy. You have both, all of a sudden, uttered these, fearful (words). O mother, tell us the reason for all this.

The female hog said :

69-70. This very terrible king, of the form of Kāla (i.e. god of death) has arrived. Longing for hunting, he sports in the forest by killing many beasts. He is the very powerful and unassailable son of Manu, named Ikṣvāku. O my good sons, this (god of) death will kill (you). My good sons, go away.

The sons said :

71-73. He, who goes (away) after abandoning his mother and father is wicked-hearted. He goes to a very terrible and fearful hell. He who, after drinking the holy milk of his mother, becomes shameless and spiritless, and goes (away) leaving his mother and father, goes to a pussy hell, stinking with the bad smell of insects. Therefore, we shall leave (our) father here only, but shall take our mother (with us).

74-75. In this way depression of spirits for the sake of Dharma and Artha (moral duty and worldly interest) overcame them. All of them full of power and lustre remained after having grouped themselves into an array. Full of daring courage and energy, and with valour, they, roaring and sporting, saw (there) the king's son.

CHAPTER FORTYTHREE

The Boar Gives a Tough Fight to Ikṣvāku

Sukalā said :

1-8. Thus those boars stood up for fighting. The hunters stood by the king standing before them. O best king, the great hog resorted to the mountain-peak. He stood after arranging his great herd in an array. The tawny, fat, plump-bodied, irresistible hog having large fangs and mouth, roared very fearfully, O king. The great king saw them resorting to the groves of śāla and tāla. Hearing those words of them the brave son of Manu (said): "Seize the brave hog, kill him who is proud of his strength." Thus the hero, the brave son of Manu, spoke to them. Then all the hunters, fascinated by the rapture of hunting became ready and furnished with armours, and proceeded with the dogs. The great and very mighty king was full of great joy. Mounted upon a horse, he was ready with his army having four constituents. He came to the bank of Gaṅgā on the best mountain Meru, full of gems and minerals and adorned with various kinds of trees.

Sukalā said :

9-19. (He came to the mountain) which best mountain, having the heap of the rays of the sun, was very lofty and high, had reached the sky itself, was beautified by many elephants that moved (on it); which shone with pure drops of water, resembling pearls, (and caused by) waves and ripples on the banks, rising from the pure stream of the Gaṅgā due to the crowds of people. The best mountain with its white slabs of stone washed everywhere, was endowed with excellent beauty. Surrounded (i.e. covered) by gods, Cāraṇas, Kinnaras and Gandharvas, Vidyādharas, Siddhas, bevies of celestial nymphs, sages, best elephants, Vidyādharas the mountain shone with (trees) like śrīkhaṇḍa, candana, sarala, śāla, tamāla, rudrākṣa, and desire-yielding trees giving divine powers. It was variegated with minerals of various kinds. It shone with aerial cars, variegated with various gems, with golden staffs and wives (i.e. women). It shone by the groves of coconut trees and divine betal-nut trees. It was adorned with flowers of divine white lotuses, bakula, and decorated with pieces of plantain trees, (also) with campaka-flowers. The mountain was decorated with reddish ketaka-flowers, and also the extensions of many creepers and with lotuses. It was adorned with beautiful flowers of many colours and with various trees. It was full of divine trees and crystal-slabs. It shone with the meditating saints, best meditating saints who had attained divine powers and who lived in its caves; and also with charming streams and many fountains. The mountain shone with the confluences bristling with the streams of rivers. The lord of mountains looked beautiful with deep lakes, small pools, having pure water and with peaks standing together. It was adorned with śarabhas, tigers and herds of deer. That lord of mountains always shone with highly intoxicated elephants, buffaloes and the ruru deer, and also with many divine substances.

20-22. Manu's son, the brave lord of Ayodhyā, (named)

Ikṣvāku, (was there) with his wife and the army having four constituents. In front (of him) the brave hunters and the fast dogs were going to the place where the brave, strong boar (remained) with his wife. He remained, after having resorted to the bank of Gaṅgā on the Meru-land, protected by many old and young hogs.

Sukalā said :

23-27. The delighted hog said to her very dear wife : "O dear one, see, the mighty lord of the Kośala country has come. The king is having the sport of hunting with me as the target. I shall just have the battle delighting gods and demons." Then the very lustrous king, the archer with arrows in his hands, who was delighted, said to (his wife) Sudevā, of a truthful behaviour : "O darling, see the very powerful, roaring hog, accompanied by his attendants and irresistible for the hunters. O dear one, today only I shall kill him with good, sharp arrows. The very brave one will come to me only to fight (with me)."

28-31. The pleasing, brave (king), speaking thus to his wife, said to the hunters : "O very brave ones, urge on the hog." The brave ones, having power, lustre and valour, and roaring, ran fast. All of them went to the hog with the speed of wind. The foresters pierced the hog of a brave form with volleys of sharp arrows and various weapons and missiles.

Sukalā said :

32-35. Arrows and javelins were discharged by the hunters; the arrows (discharged by them) showered on the mountain as clouds would shower on the earth. Struck by (hunters) giving strong strokes, the hog, the protector of the herd, who had gone to fight, was completely vanquished by hundred (of hunters). With his sons and grandsons he would destroy (i.e. he destroyed) his enemies. The hunters struck by his fang in the war fell down. Due to his speedy whirlings the hands and feet of a steady (person) dropped down. The hog saw the roar of (i.e. the roaring) hunter coming to him; and the lustre on his face was destroyed when struck with his fang. He went to the place where the king was. He (i.e. the king) did not want to fight. The lordly hog very much resisted and frightened the lord of the Ikṣvākus and was angry. Delighted with fighting, he desired to fight with Ikṣvāku (king) in the forest.

36-43. The hog skilled in fighting again desired to fight (with Ikṣvāku). The angry hog, shaking the earth with the front part of his mouth, sharp teeth and claws, and proudly making the huṁkāra sound, struck the sinless king. O king, finding him to have the valour like that of Viṣṇu, the son of Manu was thrilled with joy. The divine king, seeing the valour of the boar regarded him like Yama. Thinking that he was the enemy of gods in the form of a hog, and seeing the very powerful and huge opposing army, he suddenly collected (his army) for the destruction of the boar. He sent elephants, speedy chariots and hunters holding arrows and swords along with (missiles called) bhuśuṇḍi and mallets and having nooses in their hands. They were delighted and aimed at him. The horses and elephants that had gone to him, though warded off, remained (there only). At places he was seen, at places he was not seen. At times he would show (i.e. cause) fear, at times he would crush the horses. The hog, invincible in the battle, and with his eyes red due to anger, crushed the brave soldiers and made an inviolable sound. The brave lord of Kośala, seeing that boar, fighting, unconquerable in war, of a huge body and giving out a sound (i.e. thundering) like the clouds, roared; moved on the battlefield; and the brave one illumined the heroes with his own lustre. The fangs in his (i.e. the hog's) mouth shone and flashed like lightning. The son of Manu saw the hog in that condition, and pierced him with sharp arrows, and each one of the rest was pierced by his relatives (i.e. fellow-warriors).

44. The king said : "O (my) armies (i.e. my soldiers), why should you, who are brave, not seize him through your prowess? (Just) fight there with him with (your) whetted and sharp arrows."

45-59. Hearing the words of that noble one who was angry, all the soldiers stood together to fight. Many thousands of warriors, struck in all directions, and pierced the hog in battle, who had remained on the battlefield. On the battlefield, he was pierced with volleys of arrows by certain huge excellent warriors. The mighty ones hit the hog difficult to conquer in battle with the strokes of discs and throws of bolts. Then the angry hog having bravely cut off the nooses, remained in the battlefield. He went forth along with great boars. Then the brave hog, wet with the streams of blood, struck with his mouth and cut off the horses and elephants of the brave (soldiers). Angrily he struck the brave footsoldiers with the sharp fore-part of his fang. Being angry he struck the trunk of an elephant and being delighted, hit, with the nails of his toes, the warriors that were struck (down). Then all the hogs and hunters, with their eyes red with anger, resorting to fighting, fought with one another. The boars were killed by the hunters, and many hunters were killed by the boars. Being struck and red with blood, they dropped on the ground. The boars, giving up (i.e. at the cost of) their life, killed the hunters, and they fell on the battlefield. There the boars died and dogs gave up their life (i.e. died). Here and there, the hunters that were dead (i.e. that were killed), lay on the ground. The king, with the strokes of his sword, killed many boars. Some boars fled away; some were killed; some, being frightened, resorted to inaccessible places, bowers and interiors of caves, O best king. Some hunters, pierced by hogs with the tips of their fangs, and some, cut off into pieces, died and went to heaven. On all sides snares, nooses, traps and tubular organs of the body had fallen here and there. The hog, proud of his strength, remained only with his wife and five or seven grandsons (ready) to fight. The female hog again spoke to that hog, dear to her :"O dear one, with me and these children move (to a safe place)."

60-77a. The pleased hog said to his very dear wife, who was afflicted : "Broken (like this) where shall I go ? (Now) there is no place (for me) on the earth. When I run away, the herd of boars will perish. A hog drinks water by (remaining) between two lions; (but) a lion does (i.e. can) not drink water by (remaining) between two hogs. Thus excellent power is observed in the species of boars. Therefore I shall kill (the enemies); when broken I shall go (away). O you glorious one, I know piety causing many auspicious results. When a man, who is fighting, flees, leaving the holy battlefield through greed or fear, he would be a sinner. There is no doubt about it. He (who) is delighted at seeing the array of sharp arms, dives into the divine river and goes to the other end of the holy place. He goes to Viṣṇu's world, and would, emancipate the men (of his family). When now that (fight) has come by, how should I, being broken, go (away from it)? Listen to the fruit of him (i.e. which he gets), who, on seeing the battle, crowded with weapons, and giving delight to great heroes, is delighted and goes forth (to fight). For him a great (i.e. sacred) bath in Bhāgīrathī is had at every step. O dear one, (now) listen (to the description of him), who, fleeing from the battle through greed, goes home. He would manifest his mother's blemish, and is called a woman. O dear one, here (i.e. in a battle) are present sacrifices and holy places. Here (i.e. in a battle), gods of great prowess, sages, Siddhas and Cāraṇas witness (things creating) delight. All the three worlds are present there, where the heroes present themselves. The inhabitants of the three worlds watch him who has fled from the battle(-field), and curse and again and again laugh at the shameless sinner. King Dharma (i.e. Yama) would put him to pain (i.e. inflict pain upon him). There is no doubt about it. He, who faces (the enemy) and would drink blood from his own head (i.e. whose head would bleed while fighting), obtains the fruit of performing a horse-sacrifice and goes to Indra's heaven. There is no doubt that when the brave one conquers his enemies in a battle, he enjoys glory and many pleasures, O you beautiful one. When, unsupported (i.e. all alone) he, facing (his enemy), gives up his life, he would go to the highest place, and enjoys a divine maiden. Thus I know piety; how should I flee (from battle) and go (away)? There is no doubt that on the battle-field I shall fight with this courageous Ikṣvāku-king, the son of Manu. O you beautiful one, take these young ones with you, and go. Live happily."

77b-82. Hearing the words of him, she said : "I am bound by your bonds, called the sentiment of love, and which are the playthings of joy, O dear one. O you, who remove the pride (of others), with my sons I shall cast my life in front of you." Thus the two desiring the good of each other, and having well conversed with each other, decided to fight, and observed the enemies, (and) the very intelligent, brave Ikṣvāku, the lord of Kośala. As the cloud thunders in the sky in the rainy season, he roared along with his beloved and would challenge (i.e. challenged), with the tips of his hoofs, the excellent king. The noble one saw the roaring hog, endowed with valour. The courageous king, with a horse's speed, moved forward facing him (i.e. the hog).

CHAPTER FORTYFOUR

The Boar Dies Fighting

Sukalā said :

1-2. Seeing his own irresistible army completely vanquished by him (i.e. by the hog) who was difficult to be stopped, the king got angry with the cruel, unbearable hog. He, mounted upon a horse, and taking a bow and an arrow resembling the destructive fire at the end of the world, speedily moved in front of him.

3-7. When the lord of the herd of boars saw the king, the killer of his enemies, mounted upon the back of a horse and endowed with excellent valour, he went forth to him on the battle-field. The best hog, when struck with a sharp arrow of (i.e. by) the king, went to the soles of the feet of the horse. With a quick mind (i.e. decision) he overstepped him with a very sharp speed. The horse was afflicted by the hog. The hog did not go to (i.e. fall on) the ground. The horse, with his movement checked, and struck on the face, fell down on the ground. Then the king just went to (i.e. got into) a small chariot. He roared with sounds of (i.e. befitting) the species of a hog. The hog, who was in the midst of the battlefield, was speedily struck with a mace by the Kośala-king seated in his chariot; and then giving up his body, he just went to the excellent abode of Viṣṇu.

8-11. When the lord of hogs after fighting with the king in the battle, fell on the ground after being struck (by the king), best gods showered excellent flowers on him. On him a great heap of flowers was accumulated and the fragrance was as it were of the Santānaka flowers. Gods, being fully pleased, showered on him sandal with saffron. Being pondered over by the king, O king, he became one having four hands. He had (on his person) divine garments. His form was divine, and with his lustre he shone as the sun (shines). When, he being greatly honoured by the king of gods and (other) gods, went to heaven in a divine car, he, casting his former body here only, again became the lord of Gandharvas.

CHAPTER FORTYFIVE

The Female Hog Fights Back

Sukalā said :

1. Then all the hunters with nooses in their hands went to the female hog. Also the brave, fearful, terrible (dogs) came (to her).

2-8. Seeing her dear (husband) killed along with the family in the great war, the female hog took her four children (i.e. young ones) and remained (there). (She thought:) 'My husband got what he had thought (i.e. desired). He is honoured by sages and gods. The noble one has gone to heaven by means of (having performed) this act. I too shall go along the same path to heaven. The lord (i.e. my husband) waits (there for me).' Having well determined (like this) she thought about her sons: 'When my four sons, sustaining (i.e. continuing) our race live here, the noble, very brave hog also will have (the best position in heaven). By what means shall I protect my sons?' Thus being engrossed in thinking, and seeing the narrow passage on the mountain, she tried to find out an extensive (i.e. wide) path to go out. Having made up her mind about her sons, O great king, she said to those sons who were very much confused: "O sons, as long as I am (alive), go (away) quickly."

9-11. Out of them the eldest son (said): "How shall I with a strong desire to save my life go away abandoning my mother? How pitiable is my mother's good life? I shall retaliate my father's enmity. I shall overpower (my) enemies in the battle. He, who takes the three younger brothers to a mountain-cave by abandoning the father and the mother, is of a sinful mind. He goes only to hell crowded with crores of worms."

12-15. She, very much afflicted, said to him: "O son, how shall I, the great sinner, go by abandoning you (here)? (i.e. I shall be a great sinner if I abandon you here.) Let my three (younger) sons (only) go away (from here)." (Then) the three younger sons only went into the interior of the forest. When they were just witnessing, the two (i.e. the mother and the eldest son) again and again, roaring due to their lustre and great strength, went to the battlefield.

16-18. Then the hunters, having the speed of wind, came (there). O king, the three (younger sons) were sent (by her) along the difficult path; and the two—the mother and the (eldest) son, remained there by blocking the path. Then the hunters, holding swords, arrows and bows came there and struck (them) with javelins, sharp discs and pestles. Keeping his mother at the back, the son fought with them. He struck some with his fang; he hit some with his mouth. He also struck with the tips of his hoofs. The brave ones fell in the battle. The hog fought in the battle. The noble king saw him.

19-23. Knowing that he was brave like his father, the very lustrous, brave son of Manu, with arrows in his hand went in front of him. Struck by the noble (Ikṣvāku) king with a sharp crescent-shaped arrow, and with his chest pierced, he fell on the ground (i.e. the hog fell dead on the ground). She became very insensible due to (the death of) her son; she herself went towards him. O king, some brave hunters, hit by her with the strokes of her mouth, fell on the ground, and some fled (away) and some died. Then the female hog causing to flee (that) great army with her fang, appeared as (if) a female destructive deity, causing great fear, had sprung up.

24-27a. Then the queen said to him who resembled the son of the lord of gods: "O king, she has killed your large army. Tell me the reason why you are ignoring her, O dear one. To her the great king said : "I shall not kill this female (hog). O dear one, the deities have indeed seen a great sin in killing a female. Therefore one should not kill a woman. Nor shall I send anyone (to kill her). O beautiful one, I am afraid of committing a sin by killing her."

27b-31. Speaking thus, the king, the lord of the earth, ceased (to speak). A hunter by name Jhārjhara saw that female hog, creating a havoc amidst them, and irresistible even to excellent warriors. He pierced her with a very speedy and sharp arrow. She, with the arrow stuck into her (body), and covered with blood, endowed with the majesty of valour and looking charming, was hurrying. She again struck that Jhārjhara even with her mouth. Struck with a sharp sword by that Jhārjhara who was falling, she was rent asunder. Panting (heavily) due to (exertion of) the fight, she fainted, and (though) alive on the ground, she was overpowered with great grief.

CHAPTER FORTYSIX

The Story of Raṅgavidyādhara

Sukalā said :

1-3a. Seeing the female hog, who loved her sons, panting and fallen (on the ground), Sudevā, who was full of pity, went to her, who was afflicted, and having (first) sprinkled cold water over her face, she then sprinkled holy water over the entire body (who was) afflicted and resplendent with fighting. She (i.e. the female hog) spoke to her who was sprinkling.

3b-4. She spoke to the beloved (wife) of the king in a melodious human voice: "O respectable lady, may you be happy. When you sprinkled (holy water) over me, the heap of my sins left (me) by your contact and by my seeing you."

5-7. Hearing these great (i.e. significant) words (uttered) with a wonderful expression on her face (the queen said:) "I see a wonder, that you uttered words (like a human being). This one is born in the species of an animal, and clearly and elegantly speaks excellent Sanskrit with vowels and consonants (distinctly spoken) to me. She has done an excellent bold act with joy and (causing) amazement." Then the magnanimous (queen) who was there, said (these) words to her husband:

8. "O king, see, this extraordinary one who, though belon-

ging to a species of beasts, speaks great (i.e. excellent) Sanskrit, as a human being would speak."

9. Hearing that, the king, best of all the learned ones (said): "This (her speech) is wonderful and the expression on her face is (also) wonderful, which I have neither seen nor heard before."

10. Then the king spoke to that Sudevā, who was very dear to him : "O dear one, ask the auspicious one as to who she might be."

11-14. Hearing (these) words of the king, she (i.e. the queen) asked the female hog: "O good one, who are you? It is a great wonder that though born in a species of beasts you speak human language which is elegant and full of knowledge. Tell me your former acts. (Tell me) also about the noble warrior, your husband. What is the very valorous act that he did, due to which he has gone to heaven? Tell us all about you and your husband's former life." Saying so, the magnanimous beloved (wife) of the king ceased speaking.

The female hog said :

15-23a. O good lady, if you are asking about the life and former deeds of me and this noble one, I shall tell all that to you. This highly intelligent one is a Gandharva, skilled in singing. His name is Raṅgavidyādhara, and he is well-versed in all branches of knowledge. Pulastya, the very lustrous best sage, possessing brilliance, having resorted to the best mountain Meru having beautiful caves and streams, practised penance with a truthful mind. The Vidyādhara went there by his own will, O great lord. Resorting to that great mountain, he practised singing, which was accompanied by tunes and beating time, O you of a charming smile. Hearing his song, the mind of the sage was distracted from meditation. He said to that Gītavidyādhaa (or Raṅgavidyādhara), who was singing (there): "O learned one, by your very sweet, divine, holy song sung to beating time and measure, even gods are allured. This is not otherwise (i.e. it is quite true). O you of a good vow, due to your song, having (observed) the time in music, a sentiment and modulation, my mind has gone away (from) meditation. Therefore, leaving this place, (please) go to another spot."

Gītavidyādhara said :

23b-28a. Music is like spiritual knowledge; (then) why should I go to another place? I have never caused any unhappiness to anyone. I have always given happiness to people. All deities are pleased by means of this singing. O brāhmaṇa, even Śiva, delighted with the sound of a song, is brought (over here). Singing is said to be full of all emotions. Singing gives joy. All sentiments like that of love set up by singing, appear charming. The four excellent Vedas are elegant because of singing. All the deities are delighted because of singing, and not by anything else. You are censuring just that singing only, and are sending me away like this. O noble one, in this (in doing so) your injustice (i.e. injustice done by you) is noticed.

Pulastya said :

28b-35a. Today you have spoken the truth only. The meaning of a song gives much religious merit. O you very intelligent one, listen to my words; give up your pride. I am not condemning singing. I am honouring singing. It is not otherwise (i.e. I am not condemning it). The lores are fourteen[1]; together they bring about feelings. They bring success to beings through steady mind (i.e. if their minds are steady). By thinking about one (object only) penance and sacred hymns are highly successful. The great group of the organs of sense is, in my opinion, fickle. There is no doubt that leading the mind away from meditation, (i.e. even after the mind is taken away from meditation), it (again) very much takes the self to objects of sense. For this reason only, sages go to that place for the accomplishment of penance where there is no sound, no (beautiful) form or no young woman. This your singing is holy and gives great pleasure. We (i.e. I) would not look helplessly on it (since we are unable to prevent it), so, O hero, we (i.e. I) cannot remain in (this) forest. You (please) go to another place, or we (i.e. I) shall go.

Gītavidyādhara said :

35b-40. The noble one by whom is conquered the powerful group of the organs of sense is called a victor, a yogī, a brave one,

1. Vidyāḥ caturdaśa—The fourteen lores are: Four Vedas, six Aṅgas, Dharma, Mīmāṁsā, Tarka or Nyāya and the Purāṇas.

a sādhaka (one engaged in penance, spiritual practice). O you very intelligent one, he, who is not distracted from his meditation on hearing a sound or seeing a form, is a courageous (person) who accomplishes penance. Since you are void of lustre and conquered (i.e. overpowered) by organs of sense, you will not have the power to affront my singing even in heaven. All void of valour leave the forest. There is no doubt about it. O brāhmaṇa, this region of the forest is common to gods and all beings, it is as much mine as it is yours. There is no doubt about it. How (should) I go abandoning this excellent forest? You may go (or) you may stay. Whatever is to happen will not be otherwise.

41-44. After having heard these words of Gītavidyādhara, the intelligent sage thought : 'Doing what would merit accrue (to me).' Having forgiven him, the best brāhmaṇa went to another place. Always taking a posture suited to profound and abstract meditation, the righteous-minded (sage) practised penance, after giving up desire and anger, and also infatuation and greed. Thus Pulastya, the best meditating sage then remained like this, controlling all organs of sense along with his mind.

Sukalā said :

45-52. When that noble, best sage Pulastya left, that Gītavidyādhara also, ordained by destiny, thought : 'Due to my fear (i.e. fear caused by me) he is not to be seen for a long time. Where has he gone? Where does he live? What does he do and how does he do (it)?' Knowing that that son of Brahmā (i.e. Pulastya) was adorning (i.e. living in) a secluded (spot) in the forest, he (i.e. Gītavidyādhara), in the form of a hog, went to his excellent hermitage. O beautiful lady, having seen the eminent brāhmaṇa seated upon a seat, and obscured by lustrous flames, he disturbed him. With a wicked act he would certainly attack (i.e. he attacked) the brāhmaṇa with the tip of his mouth. O great king, he (i.e. Pulastya) knowing him to be a beast, pardoned him for his wicked act. He urinated before him, dropped his excrement before him, danced and sported before him, fell and again rose in front of him. O king, knowing him to be a beast, the sage let him go. When, once, he, again went (there) in the same form, he laughed a loud laughter. He also wept there and sang melodiously.

53-54. O king, having (once) seen Gītavidyādhara like that, and having seen his acts, the meditating saint (thought): 'This might not be a hog.' He knew (i.e. recalled) his account: '(He) had disturbed me, but I had let him go taking him to be a beast. He is wicked and very cruel.'

55. The highly intelligent, best sage, realising that glorious one to be the meanest Gandharva, got angry and cursed him:

56. "Since, in the form of a hog you are disturbing me like this, therefore, O you great sinner, go to (i.e. be born in) the sinful species of a hog."

57-62. (Thus) cursed by that brāhmaṇa he went to god Indra; and O you beautiful lady, he, trembling, said to the glorious (god) : "O thousand-eyed one, listen to my words. I have carried out your mission. That best sage, who was practising a severe penance, has been disturbed and agitated by me (rendering non-efficacious his penance). I have been cursed by that brāhmaṇa. My divine form is destroyed. O Śakra, protect me who am thus reduced to the existence of a beast." Knowing the account of that Gītavidyādhara, Indra went with him and said to the sage : "O you the best one of those born of a divine power, you who know divine faculties, grant favour , O lord. O best sage, pardon this (hog) and free him from your curse." Thus requested by Indra, the brāhmaṇa, with his mind pleased said :

Pulastya said :

63-65a. O lord of gods, on your word I should pardon (him). O great king, a very powerful son of Manu will be (born). (His name will be) Ikṣvāku; he will be righteous-minded, and a protector of all religions. When this (hog) will meet his death at his (i.e. Ikṣvāku's) hands, he will get (back) his own body. There is no doubt about this.

The female hog said :

65b. I have told you all this account of the hog. Now I shall also tell my (own account). With your husband, listen to it. (I shall) also (tell you about) the terrible sin I had committed formerly (i.e. in my former existence).

CHAPTER FORTYSEVEN

The Story of Vasudatta and His Daughter Sudevā

Sukalā said :

1. Sudevā, whose entire body was beautiful, said to the female hog: "How is it that you, who are born in a species of beasts, speak Sanskrit?

2. Tell me wherefrom you had such great knowledge. O you auspicious one, how do you know the account of your husband and of yourself?"

The female hog said :

3-7. Due to my being a beast I was enveloped by delusion, O you of an excellent complexion; and struck with swords and arrows, I fell on the battlefield. I was overpowered by swoon, and was unconscious, O you of an excellent face. O beautiful lady, with your pious hand you sprinkled (water on me). When my body was sprinkled over with the holy water by your hand, swoon left me and disappeared. As the darkness disappears due to lustre (i.e. light), similarly, O auspicious one, my sin disappeared due to your having sprinkled (over my body). O you of a charming body, by your favour I obtained old knowledge (i.e. knowledge of previous existence). O you auspicious one, I realised that I shall reach a holy position.

8. Listen, I shall narrate my former account. O you auspicious one (I shall tell you) what great sin, I, a sinner, had (formerly) committed.

9-12. In the great country called Kaliṅga, there was a city by name Śrīpura, which was full of all accomplishments, and was inhabited by (the people of) the four castes. There lived a certain brāhmaṇa, known as Vasudatta, who was always engaged in the duties of a brāhmaṇa, and always devoted to truthful acts. He knew the Vedas; he was erudite; he was pure, virtuous and rich.

He was full of (i.e. he had ample) wealth and grains, and was adorned (blessed) with sons and grandsons. O you auspicious lady, I am his daughter adorned (blessed) with brothers and sisters, kinsmen, relatives, ornaments and decorations, O you of a beautiful face.

13-17. My very intelligent father named me Sudevā. O you highly intelligent one, I was always dear to my father. I was matchless in beauty; and like that (i.e. like me) there was none in the (whole) world. I, of a charming smile, was puffed up with the pride of my beauty and youth. I was a maiden very beautiful and adorned with all ornaments. Seeing me, all the people—all relatives of my class (i.e. caste) solicited me in marriage, O you of a beautiful face. I (i.e. my hand) was solicited by all brāhmaṇas; (but) my father did not give me (in marriage to any brāhmaṇa). O you glorious one, the highly intelligent one (i.e. my father) was deluded through his affection (for me). That my magnanimous father did not give me (to anyone in marriage).

18-21. Youth with (all its accompanying) feelings set upon me, O you young lady. Seeing my beauty like that, my mother, being greatly afflicted, said to my father: "Why do you not give (our) daughter (in marriage to a brāhmaṇa)? O glorious one, give this daughter (in marriage) to a good, magnanimous brāhmaṇa (for) she has (now) attained youth." The best and excellent brāhmaṇa, Vasudatta, said to (my) mother: "O you noble one, listen to my words. O you of an excellent complexion, I am deluded by great fascination for (our) daughter.

22-23. O auspicious one, listen, I shall give my daughter to that son-in-law, who would be a householder. This Sudevā is dear to me like my own life. There is no doubt about it." Thus my father Sudatta spoke (to my mother).

24-27a. (There was a brāhmaṇa, who was) virtuous, pure, born in the family of Kauśika, and was well-versed in all lores, and was endowed with the qualities of brāhmaṇas. Seeing him, who did not have father and mother, who was endowed with the study of the Vedas, and who was reciting (them) melodiously, and seeing the form of him, who had come to (our) door for alms, my very intelligent father said : "Who are you? Tell me now your name; (tell me about your) family, lineage, your practices."

27b-29. Hearing (my) father's words he said to Vasudatta (my father) : "I am born in the family of Kauśika. I have, mastered the Vedas and the Vedāṅgas. My name is Śivaśarman. I do not have father and mother (i.e. I am an orphan). I have four other brothers, who have mastered the Vedas. I have thus told you (about) my family, and about the practices of my family."

30-35. Thus everything was told to my father by Śivaśarman. O you blessed one, when an auspicious time, date and the star of the deity presiding over marriage arrived, I was given (in marriage) to that brāhmaṇa by my father. With that glorious one I stayed alone in my father's house. Being very much deluded by the great wealth of my father and mother and pride, I, a sinner, did not serve my husband. O you auspicious one, I never shampooed his body through love or affection or (pleased him) with (sweet) words. A sinner that I was, I always looked at (i.e. treated) him cruelly. O auspicious one, due to my contact with unchaste women, I reached their condition. I did no good to my mother, father, husband and brothers. I went here and there.

36-38. Seeing such wicked behaviour of me, my husband, through his love for his father-in-law (and mother-in-law) my very intelligent husband did not say anything to me. I, a great sinner, was however, warded off by (the members of) my family. All those (members of the family like) my father and mother, knowing the character and goodness of Śivaśarman, were afflicted by my sin (-ful acts).

39-46. Seeing my wicked acts, my husband went out of the house. He left the country and the village and went (away) from it. When my husband had gone, my father was full of anxiety, and was afflicted with grief as one would be afflicted with a disease. My mother said to her husband (i.e. my father) who was afflicted with grief: "What for is your worry, O my dear (husband)? Tell me your worry." "O pleasing one, the brāhmaṇa, (our) son-in-law, has abandoned (our) daughter and gone. This one is of a sinful conduct, merciless and performs sinful acts. The very intelligent Śivaśarman has been forsaken by this one (only). The highly intelligent brāhmaṇa, O dear one, due to his courtesy towards our entire family and me, does not say anything at all to Sudevā. He lives peacefully and the intelligent, learned man does not condemn or censure Sudevā moving wantonly. This wicked Sudevā will destroy (our) family. O you housewife, leaving her, I (shall) go."

The brāhmaṇa's wife said :

47-65. O dear one, today you have understood the virtues and the vices of (our) daughter. She has now been spoiled because of your affection and love for her. One should fondle one's son till he is five years old. O dear one, one should always nourish him with the idea of training him (even) through affection also, by giving him bath, coverings, food, (other) eatables, drinks. There is no doubt about this. O dear one, one should urge the son in (i.e. to acquire) virtues and true learning. A father is always free from affection for the sake of teaching virtues (to his son). O dear one, affections take place (i.e. should be shown) in the protection and nourishment (of the son). (A father) should never describe his son as virtuous. Everyday he should censure him. He should always talk to him (with) sternness, and should afflict him with (harsh) words, so that the son, intent upon (acquiring) learning, will pursue true knowledge. Even through a device used to correct his pride, he leaves his sin far away. Perfection in learning and virtues is produced (in him). A mother should beat her daughter, and a mother-in-law should beat her daughter-in-law. A preceptor should beat his pupil. Thus they acquire perfection, not otherwise. A wife should flog her husband, a king should punish his minister. A soldier should beat his horse, and the elephant's driver should beat him. O lord, by means of being beaten and being protected, they are prepared with a thought for training. O lord, along with the good brāhmaṇa Śivaśarman, you yourself have foreover spoilt her. In the house she was made undisciplined (i.e. was not checked); therefore, O you highly intelligent one, she is spoilt. O dear one, listen to my words: The father should keep his daughter in his house till she becomes eight years old. He should not keep a strong (i.e. grown up) one. Both the parents get the (fruit of the) sin which a daughter, living in her father's house, commits. Therefore an able (i.e. a grown up) daughter is not kept in his house (by the father). She should get nourishment in the house of him to whom she is given. She, living there, should devoutly win over her virtuous husband. The family becomes famous; the father lives happily. The husband suffers due to the sin which she, living there (i.e. in the husband's house) commits. Living there, she always prospers with sons and grandsons. O dear one, the father obtains fame due to the good qualities of his daughter. Therefore, O dear one, one should not keep in one's house one's daughter with her husband (i.e. a married daughter). O dear one, in this context there is an account that is so heard: O brāhmaṇa, I shall tell you the account of the hero Ugrasena, the eldest Yadu, as it took place, when the great twenty-eighth Dvāpara yuga arrived. Listen to it with a concentrated mind.

CHAPTER FORTYEIGHT

The Story of Padmāvatī

The brāhmaṇa's wife said :

1. In the charming region of Māthura, in (the city of) Mathurā, lived the best Yādava king, the killer of his enemies, and well-known as Ugrasena.

2-7. The king knew the meaning and essentials of the whole religion; he knew the Vedas; he was learned and powerful; he was a donor, an enjoyer, an appreciator of virtues and a virtuous one. He, the intelligent one, ruled (over Māthura) and protected his subjects justly. Thus was that very lustrous and valorous Ugrasena. In the holy country of Vidarbha there lived a dignified (king named) Satyaketu. His glorious daughter, having eyes like lotuses and face like a lotus, and devoted to truthful behaviour, was Padmāvatī by name. That (Padmāvatī, the) daughter of the Vidarbha (-king) was endowed with feminine qualities and by means of her virtues based on truthfulness, she shone like another one born from the sea (i.e. like Lakṣmī). Ugrasena (the king) of the Māthura country married her, of beautiful eyes. O glorious one, with her the valorous one enjoyed himself happily. Being very much pleased with her qualities, he became happy with her (i.e. in her company).

8-9. The lord of the Māthura (country) was infatuated by her, due to her affection and love. The lucky Padmāvatī had become dearer to him than his own life. He did not eat without her, and sported with her (only). He did not at all enjoy any great pleasure without her.

10-12. O best brāhmaṇa, thus the best ones became affectionate towards each other, loved each other and gave great pleasure and joy to each other; and the glorious king of kings, Satyaketu, remembered his daughter Padmāvatī. Her mother (also) was very much afflicted. That king of Vidarbha (i.e. Satyaketu) respectfully sent his messengers to the brave king Ugrasena, O best brāhmaṇa.

13-18. The messenger said (these) words to the great king Ugrasena: "The brave lord of Vidarbha greeting you with devotion and affection, tells (i.e. informs) about his well-being, and inquires about your (well-being). O great king, Satyaketu has asked (i.e. requested) you like this : '(Please) send my daughter (to me) to see (so that I can see) her.' O lord, if you have regard for his love and affection, then send that glorious Padmāvatī, who delights you. O great king, he is very anxious and uneasy." Then, O best brāhmaṇa, having heard (these) words, the best and glorious king Ugrasena, due to love and affection for that magnanimous Satyaketu and through generosity, sent his dear wife Padmāvatī (to her father's —Satyaketu's— house).

19-27. That Padmāvatī, sent by him, was full of great joy, and went to her own former house. The charming and auspicious one saw (i.e. met the members of her) family led by her father. And she, devoted to truth, saluted her father's feet. O best brāhmaṇa, the great king, the lord of Vidarbha was full of great joy, when Padmāvatī had arrived (there). Greeted with presents and other respectful considerations, with garments, ornaments and decorations, Padmāvatī lived happily in her father's house. She lived with her friends without any apprehension. As before she at that time rejoiced in the chamber, tank and also in the palace. Having as it were become a young girl again, she stayed (there) without bashfulness. O brāhmaṇa, she always behaved without bashfulness with her friends. She, the glorious, loyal wife, full of great joy, knowing that the happiness obtained in the father's house is difficult to be obtained in the father-in-laws's house, sported (there). Wondering longingly 'When (again) could there by enjoyment like this' the beautiful lady everyday longed for sport in the groves with her friends.

CHAPTER FORTYNINE

Padmāvatī Succumbs to Gobhila's Fraudulent Approach

The brāhmaṇa's wife said :

1-9a. O you glorious one, once on the best mountain she saw a beautiful grove, adorned with groups of plantain-trees, with the śāla trees, tāla trees, tamāla trees, coconut trees, with big betelnut trees, mātuliṅga (i.e. citron) trees, orange trees, and charming jambu trees, with auspicious campaka trees and pāṭala trees that had blossomed, and also with kuṭaka and bunyan trees; it was full of aśoka and bakula trees, and was adorned with various other kinds of trees. She saw that holy mountain with trees that had blossomed. Everywhere it appeared beautiful, as it was full of many kinds of minerals. She also saw an excellent lake full of holy water on all sides, shining with fully developed lotuses and other fragrant golden lotuses, with white lotuses and fully developed red lotuses, with blue lotuses, white lotuses and with water-fowls, with other aquatic birds, and was full of various minerals. The lake was white all round, and was full of groups of many kinds of birds. The mountain was graced everywhere by auspicious and sweet cooings of cuckoos and was everywhere agreeable due to the sounds (produced) by madhura trees. It looked lovely by the excellent humming of the bees.

9b-13. The princess saw the mountain like this, charming and excellent, and the lake beautiful all round. Padmāvatī, the daughter of the Vidarbha-king, while playing and engaged in sporting in water, and on the bank of the lake with her friends, saw that auspicious forest full of flowers everywhere, and laughed and sang sportively due to fickleness and powerful feminine nature. O brāhmaṇa, that beautful lady, thus sporting in that lake moved happily.

Viṣṇu said :

14-15. The best demon Gobhila, the servant of Kubera, endowed with all enjoyments, was going in a divine aeroplane along an aerial path (i.e. in the air). At the time he saw the fearless, broad-eyed daughter of the Vidarbha-king.

16. She, the best of all women, the dear wife of Ugrasena, matchless in beauty in the world, shone beautifully in all her limbs.

17-25. (He thought:) 'Might she be Rati, (the spouse) of Cupid, or (Lakṣmī) the dear (wife) of Hari, or goddess Pārvatī or Śacī (the wife of Indra). No other woman like her, the best among women, is seen on the globe. The beautiful woman shines with her beauty and arts as the beautiful full moon shines among the stars. This woman with a charming smile (shines) as a swan in lakes. Oh, how beautiful does her form appear ! Oh, what an amorous gesture ! Who is this charming woman having beautiful round breasts? To whom does she belong?' The demon Gobhila thought like this about (that) beautiful Padmāvatī. O brāhmaṇa, for a moment he thought as to who she was and to whom she belonged. With superior knowledge he knew that she was the daughter of the Vidarbha-king. There was no doubt about it (in his mind). She was the wife of Ugrasena, devoted to her husband. She stood by her own power, and was not easily attainable even by men. Ugrasena, who has sent this young lady to her father's house, is a great fool. He is unfortunate. How would the (king) of a fraudulent mind ever live without her? Or is the king impotent that he would leave (i.e. he has left) her?

26-28a. Seeing her he instantly became enamoured. 'This chaste lady is difficult to be secured even by men. How can I go (near her) and enjoy her? Lust afflicts me very much. If I shall go without enjoying her, then I shall die today only. There is no doubt about it; since lust is very powerful.'

28b-35. Being anxious like this, Gobhila observed mentally (i.e. thought to himself). Taking up an illusory form of king Ugrasena, the demon Gobhila fully became as the great Ugrasena was in point of gait, voice and language; and putting on garments and apparel (like Ugrasena) and being of the same age, and putting on divine flowers and garments and having besmeared his body with divine sandal, and with his entire body (rendered) handsome as was the lord of Māthura, and thus being full of (i.e. exactly like) Ugrasena, and being equipped with great trickery and (fine) figure and handsomeness he remained on the top of the mountain, after having resorted to the shadow of an aśoka tree. Seated on a slab, the wicked-minded one with the neck of the lute (in his hand), was singing a melodious song, enchanting the universe. The wicked-minded one, enamoured of her beauty, sang a song equipped with the beating time, measure and execution, and adorned with the seven notes. O brāhmaṇa, he, seated on the mountain-top was full of great joy.

36. That beautiful Padmāvatī, who was in the midst of her friends, heard that melodious song, equipped with beating time, measure and the musical time.

37. 'Who is this pious one that is singing a song which gives great pleasure, which is full of fine execution and endowed with all ideas?'

38-42. The princess with curiosity went there with her friends and saw the mean demon Gobhila in the garb of the king, wearing divine flowers and garment and with his body besmeared with divine sandal, with all his limbs decorated with ornaments, seated on a spotless slab, resorting to (i.e. in) the shadow of an aśoka tree. The loyal wife Padmāvatī (thought): 'When did my glorious lord, the king of Māthura, and devoted to religious practices, come, after having left far behind his kingdom?' When she was thinking (like this), the sinful one called her hurriedly: "O my darling, come on." She was amazed and was doubtful as to how her lord had come (there).

43-46. She was ashamed, was afflicted, and then hung down her face (and thought:) 'I am sinful, of a bad conduct. I have turned fearless. There is no doubt that the glorious one will be just angry with me.' When she was thinking like this, that wicked one too hurriedly called her: "O my darling, come on, O dear one, O you of an excellent face (i.e. beautiful one), separated from you I cannot sustain my life; and life is very dear to me; I am longing for your love; I am greatly unable to leave you."

The brāhmaṇa's wife said :

47-48. Thus addressed, she, full of bashfulness, saw the handsome one. Then the demon Gobhila, having embraced that virtuous Padmāvatī, the daughter of Satyaketu, took her to a secluded place, and fully enjoyed her as he desired.

Sukalā said :

49-54. The beautiful one did not find the mark (known to her) on his testicle. Taking up her garment, she became afraid and afflicted. Angrily she spoke (these) words to that mean Gobhila: "Who are you of the form of a demon, who are acting wickedly and who are merciless?" O king, she, with her eyes full (of tears) due to grief, trembling, and oppressed with the burden of affliction was bent on cursing him: "O you wicked one, having come (here) in the guise of my husband, you have destroyed my excellent chastity—my best virtue. Having wailed melodiously, you have destroyed my existence. (Now) see my power; here (i.e. now) only I shall give you a very fearful curse." She, who desired to curse Gobhila, spoke like this.

CHAPTER FIFTY

Padmāvatī Is Grief-stricken

Sukalā said :

1-12. Hearing her words, Gobhila said (these) words: "Tell me the reason for which you desire to curse me. By what blemish am I defiled that you are ready to curse me? O auspicious one, I am a demon by name Gobhila, a warrior of Paulastya (i.e. Rāvaṇa). I act like a demon, I know excellent lore. I know the meaning of the Vedas and branches of knowledge, I am also skilled in arts. All this I know. (Now) listen about my demonish behaviour. I enjoy per force the wealth and the wives of others, and do so in no other way. Listen, we demons properly follow the demonish ways and do so knowingly. I am telling you the truth (and) the truth (only). Everyday we observe the loopholes of brāhmaṇas. By (putting in) difficulties we destroy their penance; there is no doubt about this. Finding a loophole in the brāhmaṇas we destroy them, O respectable lady. There is no doubt about this. O you of a beautiful face, listen. We destroy a sacrifice in honour of gods, (other) sacrifices and religious rites. There is no doubt about this. There is no doubt that we live by keeping far away excellent brāhmaṇas, the god Lord Nārāyaṇa, and a chaste, illustrious lady of a good mind and devoted to her husband. O respectable lady, demons cannot bear the lustre of a good brāhmaṇa, of glorious Hari (i.e. Viṣṇu), and of a lady loyal to her husband. The demons, the best evil spirits flee away due to the fear of a chaste lady, of Viṣṇu and of a good brāhmaṇa. I am roaming over the earth, according to the way of life of a demon. Why do you desire to curse me? What do you think my fault is?"

Padmāvatī said :

13-14. You alone have destroyed my dharma (chastity) and good body. O sinner, I am a chaste, pitiable, and virtuous woman, loving my husband. I remained on my own (i.e. followed my own) course (of life). You have defiled me through deceit. Therefore, O wicked one, I shall certainly burn you too.

Gobhila said :

15-16. If you agree I shall explain to you the way of the life of even a brāhmaṇa, who has kept the sacred fire. O princess, listen. Offering oblation (to fire), he should not leave the fire-chamber. He alone is one who has kept the sacred fire and who offers sacrifice everyday.

17-18. O you of an excellent face, I shall also tell you about another (thing)—the way of life of a servant. O respectable lady, he is called a meritorious servant, who is always pure in mind, deeds and speech, who always obeys (his master) and remains behind and in front of him.

19-20. That virtuous, learned and eminent son, who protects his father and especially his mother by his mind (i.e. willingly), by his body and his actions, has (the merit of) a bath in Bhāgīrathī everyday. He who does (i.e. behaves) in an opposite manner, is undoubtedly a sinner.

21-24a. I shall also narrate to you another excellent vow (in honour) of the husband. O you beautiful lady, listen. That lady alone, who everyday renders service to her husband by good words, mind (i.e. willingly) and actions, and she, who is pleased when her husband is pleased, she, who would not abandon her angry husband, she who does not find fault with him, and she who is contented (though) beaten (by him), and she who always stands in the forefront in all the deeds of her husband, is called a woman devoted to her husband.

24b-28. A father, though fallen, or full of many blemishes, or affected with leprosy or who is angry, is never to be abandoned on any account by his sons. Those sons (who) indeed serve their father or mother, go to the highest heaven. That is the highest place of Viṣṇu. The servants who in this way wait upon their masters go to the heaven of the lord through the grace of the master. A brāhmaṇa (who) does not abandon (keeping) fire, goes to Brahmā's heaven. A brāhmaṇa, who abandons (keeping) fire is called the husband of a śūdra woman. There is no doubt that a servant, by deserting his master, would be plotting against his master.

29. A brāhmaṇa should never give up (keeping) fire, a son should never abandon his father, and a servant should never desert his master. I am telling the truth (and) the truth (only).

30-34. Those who go away leaving (these), go to the ocean in the form of hell. If, O respectable lady, a woman desires her welfare here (i.e. in this world), she should never desert her husband who is fallen, diseased, languid, affected with leprosy, or who is void of (i.e. unable to do) all acts, and whose accumulation of wealth has been lost. A woman who would leave her husband and go and desire to work for someone else here (i.e. in this world), is looked upon as an unchaste woman and is fully excommunicated. People call that woman an unchaste one, who, through fickleness, enjoys pleasures and decorates herself when her husband has gone to (some other) village. Thus I know the dharma (which is) also approved by the Vedas and the sacred treatises.

35-45. There is no doubt that I shall tell you the entire reason about this, viz. as to why at the beginning the creator created demons, goblins and evil spirits. Brāhmaṇas, demons, fiends, goblins, have, O beautiful lady, studied all that is said about dharma. Demons know all (that), but do not practise it. Demons, void of knowledge, do (all acts) without the (proper) rite. Men abandoned by (i.e. not practising) rites go (i.e. act) unjustly. They (i.e. demons) are created for disciplining them (i.e. such men); and not for anything else. We discipline those mean men, who perform (various) acts without proper rites by severely punishing them. You have done a terrible and very cruel act. Why, abandoning your state of a housewife, did you come here? And with your own mouth (i.e. you yourself) are saying that you are a lady loyal to your husband! But that your loyalty to your husband is not seen through your action. Leaving the husband, why have you come here? Decorating yourself, putting on ornaments and (attractive) dress, and (thus) being shameless, you are staying here. O sinful one, tell me why, for what purpose, you have done (this). Being fearless and wanton, you are living in the mountain-forest. Listen, I have subdued you, a sinner, with a great (i.e. severe) punishment. Behaving impiously, you, a wicked woman, have abandoned your husband, and come (here). Where is your loyalty to your husband? Show that before (i.e. to) me. You are indeed an unchaste woman, who have deserted your husband. When a woman occupies a separate bed (i.e. does not occupy the same bed as her husband does), she is looked upon as unchaste.

46. Your husband is at a distance of a hundred yojanas. Where is your loyalty to your husband? You are behaving like an unchaste woman.

47-48a. O you shameless woman, O you cruel one, O you wicked one, facing me (i.e. to me) what (will) you say (now)? Where does your penance exist? Where is your lustre? Where is your power? Show me, today only, your power, valour and prowess.

Padmāvati said :

48b-52a. O you mean demon, listen. My father brought me here from my husband's house through affection. What sin is there? I, who am devoted to my husband, have come (here) leaving my husband not through lust, or greed, or delusion or hostility (to him). You yourself, taking the guise of my husband, have deceived me. I went forth to you, taking you to be (the king of) Māthura. O you mean demon, (now) when I know you to be (a demon) using tricks, I shall reduce you to ashes just with one hum-sound.

Gobhila said :

52b-56a. Blind human beings do not (i.e. cannot) see. Now listen. How do you, bereft of the eye of dharma know me now? Listen; when a desire for (visiting) your father's house arose in you after you had stopped thinking about your husband, then, your eye of wisdom in your heart had evidently perished. (Now), with your eye of wisdom lost, how do you recognise me on the earth (i.e. here)? To which wife mother, father, brother, kinsmen and relatives belong? (i.e. none of them is related to her). In all (these) places (i.e. in the places of all these), the husband alone (remains); there is no doubt about this.

56b-58a. Saying so, and laughing loudly, the mean demon Gobhila (again spoke:) "O you unchaste woman, listen. Today I have no (cause of) fear from you. What would happen by means of your curse? You are unnecessarily trembling. Resorting to my house, enjoy pleasures as you like."

Padmāvatī said :

58b-59. Go (away), O you of wicked acts. What are you, being shameless, talking? I have (always) lived as a chaste woman, devoted to my husband. O you great sinner, if you talk (shamelessly) like this, I shall burn you.

60-62. Saying so, she sat on the ground in a secluded place. Gobhila said to her who was afflicted with great grief; "O you beautiful one, I have deposited my germ into your womb. From it will spring up a son who will agitate the three worlds." Speaking like this, the demon Gobhila then left.

63. When that demon of wicked acts and sinful behaviour had gone, the princess, full of great grief, wept.

CHAPTER FIFTYONE

Padmāvatī Returns to Her Husband's Place

The wife of the brāhmaṇa said :

1-2. When that wicked-hearted Gobhila of a bad conduct had left, Padmāvatī, being full of great grief, wept. O best brāhmaṇa, hearing her weeping, all her beautiful friends asked the princess.

3-4. (They said:) "Well-being to you, why are you weeping? Tell us your story (i.e. what you did). Tell us where the great king, your (husband) the lord of Māthura, who had invited you by addressing you (as) 'O dear one' is". Weeping again, again she spoke with grief.

5-6. She told (them) everything that had taken place through error. They took her who was weeping and was extremely afflicted to her father's house. Then the damsels told (the account) in the presence of (i.e. to) her mother. Hearing that the queen (i.e. her mother) went to her husband's mansion.

7-10a. She told the account of her daughter to her husband. Hearing it, the king was extremely grieved. Giving her a vehicle, clothes etc. he sent her, along with attendants, to Mathurā. She went to the mansion of her dear (husband). The father and the mother concealed the blemish of their daughter, O best brāhmaṇa; but the righteous-minded Ugrasena, seeing Padmāvatī who had arrived, was glad, and again quickly said these words to her:

10b-11. "O you beautiful lady, I cannot live without you. You are very lustrous; O dear one, you are always dear to me due to your virtues, character, devotion, truth and qualities like devotion to your husband."

12. Ugrasena, the lord of men, the best king, speaking (like this) to dear wife Padmāvatī, enjoyed in her company.

13-16. The fierce foetus, causing fear to all the worlds, grew. Padmāvatī knew the cause of that foetus. Night and day she thought about it growing in her womb: 'What is the use of this one, destroyer of the worlds, being born? Now I have nothing to do with this wicked son.' Everywhere she enquired about a herb that would cause abortion. The lady, secured (i.e. tried to secure) a great (i.e. effective) herb for abortion. Everyday she adopted many remedies for abortion.

17-21. The foetus, fearful to all the worlds, grew. Then the foetus said to his mother, Padmāvatī: "O mother, why do you trouble yourself by (using) the herbs everyday? (The span of) life increases due to religious merit, and life becomes short due to sin. (Beings) live or die according to the ripening of their deeds. Painful foetuses depart, while others, that are immature (i.e. not properly developed) die as soon as they are born on the earth. Some others are endowed with youth. All children, old men, young men, being under the sway of vital power, die and (i.e. or) live according to the ripening of their deeds. There is no doubt that medicinal herbs, formulae and deities are only a means.

22-24. You do not know me—what kind of (foetus) I am. Formerly you have seen and heard about the very powerful (demon) Kālanemi, who is a very mighty (demon) among the demons, causing fear to the three worlds. In the great war between gods and demons I was formerly killed by Viṣṇu. To finish enmity with (i.e. to take revenge on him, I have come to your womb. O mother, do not act rashly and do not exert yourself everyday."

25-31a. O best brāhmaṇa, speaking thus to his mother, he ceased (speaking). His mother then gave up her exertion, (but) became very much afflicted. When ten years had passed, he grew. Then he became very lustrous, and that Kaṁsa became very powerful, who harrassed the people, the residents of the three worlds; and who, killed by Vāsudeva, went to (i.e. obtained) salvation. There is no doubt about it. Thus O dear one, I have heard like this. Whatever will happen, will happen. I have told you what has been determined in all the Purāṇas. The daughter, who lives in her father's house, perishes. O dear one, a daughter should not have longing for staying in her father's house. Abandoning this wicked one, a great sinner, be composed. Great sin and terrible grief would be obtained (by us if we keep her here). O dear one, enjoy with me, that leads to felicity in the world.

The female hog said :

31b-41a. That best brāhmaṇa, hearing these words containing good advice, decided to forsake (his daughter). He then called me. He gave me everything like garments and decorations (and said to me). "O good one, listen. Due to your bad conduct, that best, intelligent brāhmaṇa went (away). O you wicked one, O you of a bad couduct in the family, go there where your husband is. There is no doubt about this (i.e. this cannot be otherwise); (or go to) the place which you like. Do as you are advised." O you glorious one, after my father had said like this, I, a shameless woman, abandoned by my father, mother and (other) members of the family, quickly went away, O you beautiful lady. O you good lady, I did (i.e. could) not secure a comfortable abode. People reproached me saying, '(Oh) this unchaste lady has arrived.' Void of the pride of my family, and wandering (here and there), I went from (my father's) country, to a holy Śiva-temple in Saurāṣṭra in the Gurjara-country. It was a city full of prosperity and known as Vanasthala. Listen, O queen, at that time I was very much oppressed by hunger. Taking a potsherd in my hand I started begging. Being extremely afflicted I entered the gates of householders. People saw my form and reproached it. They did not give me alms, (saying) 'this wicked one has come (here)'. I thus obtained proper food with difficulty, and was entirely oppressed with poverty.

41b-43. While wandering, I saw an excellent house, surrounded by a high rampart, with a chamber for (the recitation) of the Vedas, which was crowded with many brāhmaṇas; it was full of wealth and grains, and was adorned with male and female servants. I entered that beautiful house, affluent with glory.

44. That house which was auspicious all round was the house of that Śivaśarman only. Sudevā, afflicted with grief, said: "(Please) give (me) alms."

45-47. The best brāhmaṇa, Śivaśarman, heard the words: "Give (me) alms". That righteous-minded, very intelligent Śivaśarman, smiled and said to his beautiful wife Maṅgalā by name, who was of the nature of Lakṣmī: "O dear one, this enfeebled one has come to (our) door for alms. O auspicious and dear one, being full of great pity, call her and give her food. She has come to me after having recognised me."

48-50. Maṅgalā said to her dear husband: "I shall give her food dear to (i.e. liked by) her." Speaking like this to her husband Maṅgalā, endowed with auspiciousness, again fed me, the weak one, with sweet food. That righteous-minded, great sage Śivaśarman said to me: "Who are you that have come here? To whom do you belong? On what mission do you roam everywhere over the earth. Tell me."

51-53. Having thus heard the words of my glorious husband, I, the sinner, recognised him by his voice. When I saw my husband, I hung down my face through shame. Maṅgalā, beautiful in all limbs, said to (our) husband: "Tell me who she is, (since) on seeing you she is ashamed. Please favour me and tell me who she might be."

CHAPTER FIFTYTWO

Sudevā Goes to Heaven

Śivaśarman said :

1. O Maṅgalā, if you are now asking, then listen to (my) words. O you of an excellent face (i.e. O you beautiful one), know that for which you have asked (me).

2-5. O you of charming eyes, this miserable one who has now come in the form of a beggar, is the daughter of the brāhmaṇa Vasudatta. O good one, this one is Sudevā, my wife, always dear to me. Leaving her (father's) country for some reason, she has come (here). O you beautiful one, she is scorched by grief due to me and separation from me. Recognising me, she has come to you in the form of a beggar. Realising this, O good one, you, desiring what is very dear to me, should show her good hospitality. There is no doubt about it (i.e. you should certainly show her good hospitality).

(*The female hog said* :)

6-14. Maṅgalā, who looked upon her husband as a deity, and who herself was extremely auspicious, was full of great joy on just hearing the words of her husband. O you beautiful one, she made (arrangements for) my bath, clothes and food. O you good one, I, devoted to my husband, was adorned by her, dear to her husband, with golden ornaments decked with jewels. O queen, I was graced by her with respect, bath and food. I was (also) respected by my husband. In my heart there was endless, very poignant grief, fully destroying my life. I observed her respect for me; in the same way (I noted) my affliction. I had terrible anxiety due to which my life departed (i.e. was about to depart). I, a sinner, committing bad acts never gave a good answer to this best brāhmaṇa. I did not wash his feet, nor did I shampoo his body, nor did I give the glorious one (company) in solitude. How shall I, of a wicked resolution, talk to him? Then at night I fell there into the ocean of grief. When I was thinking like this, my heart burst; then O beautiful lady, my life, leaving my body, departed.

15-27a. Then there came brave, fierce messengers of Yama who held maces, discs and swords. O you illustrious one, I was, bound by them with chains binding strongly. I, who was weeping and who was very much afflicted, was taken by them to Yama's city. Being beaten with mallets I was harassed along the difficult path. Being reproached by them I was ushered into the presence of Yama. The noble and angry Yama looked at me. I was thrown into a heap of ashes; I was thrown into a heap of hells. An iron figure of man was made; it was heated in fire, and it was hurled on my breast for having deceived my husband. I was very much tormented with various troubles; I was burnt with the fire in hell; I was thrown into an oval vessel and on mud and sand. I was cut with blades of swords and dragged by a machine used for raising water. The noble one hurled me on Kūṭaśālmali trees. I fell into pus, blood and feces, full of insects. O princess, the same magnanimous one thus threw me into all poignant hells full of trouble. I was torn up with saw, and was very much struck with darts. O princess, I was also hurled into other hells; I was thrown into hollows like wombs, and into a painful narrow passage. That lord of Dharma (i.e. Yama) threw me into hells. Reaching (i.e. being born in) the species of goats, I experienced very terrible pain. I went to (i.e. was born in) the species of jackals and again that of a bitch; (then) I was born as a hen, a cat and a rat.

27b-32a. Thus that Yama threw me into different species,

and I was troubled in all births. O princes, he himself made (i.e. created) me a female hog on the earth. O you glorious one, there are many kinds of holy places in your hand. O you of an excellent complexion, you yourself sprinkled that (holy) water on me. O queen, O beautiful lady, by your favour, my sin has vanished, O you of an excellent face, by the lustrous religious merit of you only. Knowledge is produced in me. Now emancipate me, who have fallen into the hell-like peril. When (i.e. if) O queen, you do not emancipate me, I shall again go (back) to a terrible hell. O you illustrious one, protect me who am experiencing grief. Due to sinful thoughts I suffered. I am wretched, I am without a shelter.

Sudevā said :

32b-33a. O auspicious one, now tell me what good deed I have done that would give rise to religious merit, by which I would emancipate you.

The female hog said :

33b-39a. This illustrious Ikṣvāku-king, the son of Manu, the very wise one, is Viṣṇu, and you are Lakṣmī, not otherwise (i.e. and none else). O you auspicious one, you are devoted to your husband; you are glorious; you are a loyal wife; you are always chaste; you are full of all holy places; you are dear; O queen, you are full of everything and are always full of all gods. You alone are a great loyal wife in the world; you who have day and night rendered service to your husband, are dear to the king. O beautiful one, if you (desire to) do what I like, give me your merit earned by the service to your husband, even for a day. You are my mother, you are my father, you are my eternal preceptor. I am sinful, of wicked acts, given to falsehood and without knowledge. O glorious one, emancipate me. I am afraid of being beaten by Yama.

Sukalā said :

39b-40a. Having heard like this, she saw the king and said to him: "O great king, what do (i.e. should) I do? What does this beast say?"

Ikṣvāku (king) said :

40b-41a. O auspicious one, with your merit emancipate this one who is unhappy, helpless and gone to (i.e. born in) a sinful species. It will be very righteous.

41b-47. That very charming and auspicious lady Sudevā, when addressed like this, said "O you beautiful lady, I have given you (my) merit for a year." When the queen uttered these words, just at that moment the hog became endowed with beauty and youth, adorned with a divine garland, got a divine body covered with lustrous flames, was rich with the beauty of all ornaments, and adorned with many jewels. She had a divine form, besmeared with divine sandal. The good one got into a divine aeroplane, and went into the higher region. She saluting the queen with her neck bowed down (in respect for the queen) then said: "O you magnanimous one, well-being to you; O beautiful lady, due to your favour, I, being free from sin, am going to the holiest and auspicious heaven." O best one, listen, having thus saluted her, Sudevā went to heaven. I have (thus) told you all this as told by Sukalā.

CHAPTER FIFTYTHREE

Sukalā's Sickening Description of the Body

Sukalā said :

1-2a. Formerly, at that time I thus heard (about) the Dharma from the Purāṇas. How shall I, of a sinful resolve, enjoy pleasures without my husband? I cannot sustain my life with (i.e. in) my body without that husband.

Viṣṇu said :

2b-9. She thus narrated the excellent, great Dharma of the chastity of a wife; and those friends, excellent women, having heard the very meritorious Dharma for women, giving a great position (i.e. salvation) to women, praised that glorious Sukalā devoted to virtue. O king, all brāhmaṇas, gods and all virtuous women call her to mind due to her prowess caused by love for her husband. Indra, the lord of gods, having given a great (i.e. serious) thought to the firmness of Sukalā, and he, the lord of gods, having well pondered over her great devotion (thought): 'I shall certainly shake her fortitude and her love for her husband.' The lord of gods hurriedly recalled to mind god Cupid. He, the fish-bannered (god), holding his flowery bow came there. The very powerful one was seen to be accompanied by his beloved Rati. Joining the palms of his hands, he said to the thousand-eyed (Indra): "O you lord, O you eminent one, O you who cut off the pride (of your enemies), why have you remembered me now? With all your heart give me an order today."

Indra said :

10-11a. This illustrious Sukalā is greatly devoted to her husband. O god of love, listen, give me an excellent help. Move away (swerve) this glorious Sukalā, auspicious due to religious merit, (from her devotion).

11b-20. Having heard those words of Indra, he said to him: "Let it be so, O thousand-eyed god; there is no doubt that I shall gladly help you." Cupid, of great lustre, and difficult to be conquered (even) by sages, having said so (spoke again:) "O god, I am capable of conquering gods, ascetics and best sages; then what to say of this woman, who has no strength in her body (i.e. who is weak)? O god, I always live in the limbs of women. (I live) in the foreheads, eyes, on the tips of their breasts, in their navels, waists, backs, buttocks, vaginal area, lips, teeth, middle parts (of their bodies); there is no doubt about this. I live everywhere; in their limbs and minor limbs. O god, a woman is my abode. I always live there. Living there, I slay all men; there is no doubt about this. A woman, weak by nature (and) tormented by my arrows, on seeing a handsome and virtuous (person like her) father, mother, or other kinsman or relative, and being struck with my arrows, is disturbed; there is no doubt about it. She does not even think of the consequence. O lord of gods, the vulva, and also the tips of the breasts of women, throb. They do not have patience. O lord of gods, I shall undoubtedly ruin Sukalā."

Indra said :

21-23. O mind-born (god), I shall become (i.e. turn myself into) a handsome, virtuous, wealthy man; and through curiosity I shall disturb this woman. O you dear to Rati, (I shall disturb her only through curiosity; and) not through longing for her, nor for frightening her, nor through cupidity, nor through infatuation, nor again through anger. (I am telling) the truth (and) the truth (only). How can I see her true devotion to her husband? Going from here I shall turn her (away from her vow). The cause for that would be the infatuation (caused) by you.

24-29. Having thus ordered the god of love, the king of gods brought about a change in himself (i.e. took up a different form), became handsome and virtuous, made his body graceful by ornaments, was endowed with all possessions and all pleasures and amusements, and possessed all generosity. He would show (i.e. he showed) his sportive movements, handsomeness, virtues and sincerity at the place where, O king, that respectable woman, the dear (wife) of Kṛkala, stayed. But she did not at all look at the man possessing the wealth of handsomeness. O king, Indra would (follow her to) see her wherever she went. The thousand-eyed god looked at her only with a longing mind and with all expressions of lustful acts. Wherever the woman went—into a crossway, along a path or to a holy place, the thousand-eyed (god) saw her.

30-32. The female messenger sent by Indra went to Sukalā; and having smiled she said to the glorious Sukalā: "O (great are) your truthfulness, courage, charm and forbearance. In the world there is no other beautiful woman resembling a form like that of this one. O auspicious one, who are you? Whose wife are you? He, whose virtuous wife you are, is blessed and meritorious on the earth."

33-37. Hearing her words the high-minded lady said (to her:) "(Kṛkala) the religious-minded one, lover of truth, was born in the vaiśya caste. I am telling you the truth: I am the dear wife of that intelligent and veracious Kṛkala. That my very intelligent, righteous-minded husband has gone on a pilgrimage. O glorious one, listen; three years have passed since he, my lord, left (for the pilgrimage). Since then I have been afflicted without (i.e. due to separation from) the magnanimous one. Thus I have told you all this my account. Tell me who, that ask me ('who I am'), you are."

38-51a. Hearing the words of Sukalā, the messenger spoke again : "O good one, you are asking me like this. I shall tell you everything. O you of an excellent complexion, I have come to you for (i.e. on) some mission. Listen (as) I shall tell you; and having heard, know it accurately. O you of a beautiful face, your merciless husband has gone after abandoning you. What will you do with him, the sinful one, who does harm to his beloved, endowed with a good conduct? What, O you young lady, have you to do with him, who has gone (away) and is alive or dead? What will you do with him? You are thus grieving in vain. Why do you destroy your divine body, lustrous like gold? O you auspicious one, O you glorious one, a man does not get any pleasure except children's sports, when childhood is attained by him. In old age, unhappiness comes (to him), and old age completely destroys his body. O you beautiful lady, he gladly enjoys all pleasures in youth. As long as youth lasts, men enjoy all pleasures and enjoyments. A man enjoys as he likes. He enjoys pleasures as long as youth lasts. What will you do, O good lady, when youth has gone? O respectable lady, no occupation succeeds when old age comes (to him). An old man constantly thinks, (but) does not (i.e. cannot) easily do any job. O young lady, bridge is constructed after water has gone (i.e. flowed). In the same way, O auspicious lady, the body would be (useless) when youth has passed. Therefore, enjoy happily; and drink sweet wine. O you of charming eyes, these arrows of Cupid are burning your body. This handsome and virtuous man has come. O you of an excellent complexion, this best man, who knows everything, who is virtuous and wealthy, is ever full of love for you."

Sukalā said :

51b-60. The soul does not have childhood; in life there is no youth. He (i.e. the soul) does not have old age. He (has) accomplished (everything); he grants good divine attainments. He is immortal, unaging, pervading (everything), (has) well accomplished (everything), and is best among the omniscient ones. Himself being desireless,[1] he fulfils desires, and lives in the world in the form of the soul. The formation of the body is seen to be like that of a house. As the body is (weak) due to old age, so is a house with a thread. One should effect it with the heaps of many sticks and collections of pieces of wood, with clay and water also. Besmeared with variegated (objects) by plasterers, a (piece of wood) becomes agreeable. A house first bound by a thread gets a form; and they themselves everyday maintain it by smearing it. The house constantly rocked by wind gets dirty. This is said to be the middle period of the house. It would lose its form, and the master of the house would smear it. The lord of the house, by his own desire, would make the house beautiful. O messenger, the youth of the house is said (to be like this). After a long time due to the heaps of sticks it becomes old. They lose their positions, and move to the tips of the roots. It does not (i.e. is not able to) stand the burden of the smearing, and stands (only) with a prop.

61-70a. O messenger, listen, this is said to be the old age of the house. The lord of the house, seeing the house falling, would leave it. To enter another house he goes away quickly. Like that are the childhood, youth and old age of men. In childhood, he, being of the form of a child, would act senselessly. He would even decorate his body with garments, ornaments and jewels, and also with smearings with sandal (-pastes), and others produced from tāmbūla etc. The body becomes young, and he becomes very handsome. He would nourish his exterior and interior with all juices. Being nourished like that he becomes strong. Due to the juices, fresh and excellent, increase in flesh takes place. O king, the limbs also become extended and corpulent. The minor limbs also take their own form due to the intake of juices also. The teeth, lips, breasts, arms, waist, back, both the hands and the soles of the feet (also) similarly develop. Due to these two (i.e. juices and flesh) the limbs develop. They become beautiful due to the juices and flesh. O messenger, due to these forms, a mortal becomes one dependent on juices. A mortal is called handsome in the world. Due to what would he be liked?

1. The analogy occurring in verses 53, 54, 55, 57 etc. is not sufficiently clear; also the description in vv. 94, 95, 101b etc. is not clear (Tr.).

70b-78. O messenger, this body is the store of feces and urine. The impure, shameless body always exudes (sweat). O you auspicious one, what is (the use of) describing its beauty? It is like a bubble on water. Till he is fifty years old, he remains strong. Then after that, day by day, he loses (his strength). His teeth become loose, and his mouth has a flow of saliva. He would not (i.e. is unable to) see with his eyes, and does not (i.e. cannot) hear with his ears. O messenger, he is not able to make any movement with his hands and feet. Being afflicted with old age, the body becomes unfit. The juice, dried up with the fire of old age, withers. O messenger, he becomes unfit. Who desires handsomeness? As an old house perishes—there is no doubt about it, in the same way the body becomes weak in old age. Everyday you are describing that beauty has come to me (i.e. I am beautiful). Due to what am I endowed with beauty? Who desires my beauty? Due to what (i.e. in what way) is the man for whom, O messenger, you have come to me—as one goes to an old house—powerful? On account of what are you praising (me)?

79-97. O messenger, now tell me, what did you see in my body? There is nothing here (i.e. in my body) which is short or extra as compared to his body. There is no doubt that as he is, so you are, so also I am. Who would not have beauty? On the earth there is no one (who is really) handsome. All heights end in a fall; O auspicious one, trees and mountains are devastated by time. Beings are like them (only), not otherwise. O messenger, the divine, pure soul, formless (and yet) having a form, is present everywhere, in all immobile and mobile objects. The pure one lives (everywhere) as one (and the same) water remains in (many) pots. On the destruction of the pots, it becomes one. You do not know (this). This soul also becomes just one on the destruction of bodies. I have always seen this form (only) of those who live in the world. Speak like this, after knowing him for whom you have come here. (Tell him:) you should show me something new about the body that is afflicted by a disease, and covered with cough, if you desire to enjoy me here. Blood drops from the body, and he is removed from his position. There is unsteadiness in all the joints of the body and remaining within he singly perishes and would give up his own form. Quickly the condition of feces takes place (i.e. food quickly turns into feces) and (the body) would be (i.e. is full of) insects. He would then give up his own form painful like that. Listen, it later becomes full of bad odour due to insects. Then lice or worms are produced there; there is no doubt about this. The worm causes boils and terrible itch. The louse would produce disease, and would disturb the entire body. The itch scratched with the nail-tips is abated. Similarly hear about copulation (enjoyed) by them. There is no doubt that a mortal enjoys drinks and feasts on abundant supply of food. It is taken to the place of digestion by the breath (called) Prāṇa. O messenger, all that food taken to the place of digestion is covered there, and the wind (called Apāna) would make the fece fall (out of the body). The liquid which has become vigorous there, becomes red (blood). Being free from dirt and of a pure vigour it goes to Brahmā's place. Being dragged by the wind (called) Samāna, and taken by that very wind, he does not obtain a place. The semen remains unsteady. In the skulls of beings five (kinds of) insects live. Two of them live at the root of the ears, and (two) at the place of the eyes. Having the size of the small finger, they have red tails, O messenger. Having the (white) colour of butter, they have black tails. There is no doubt about this.

98-109. O good one, listen to their names being narrated by me: The two, named Piṅgalī and Śṛṅkhalī, remain at the root of the ears. The two Capala and Pippala remain on the tip of the nose. The two others, Śṛṅgalī and Jaṅgalī remain inside the eyes. There is no doubt that there are one hundred and fifty (varieties) of insects like that. All they remain at the border of the forehead and have the size of a mustard. All (these) carrying diseases deform (the body); there is no doubt about it. O messenger, listen, a pair of hair remains in his mouth. Know that the destruction of beings takes place just at that moment. There is no doubt about it. The vigour falls in the form of a fluid. There is no doubt about it. He drinks the vigour with his mouth, and by that becomes inebriated. It remains unsteady in the middle part of the palate. There remain (the two vessels of the body called) Iḍā and Piṅgalā and the artery called Suṣumnā. Due to the great power of it only, there is indeed the itch for sex in the cage formed by the net of arteries, in the case of all beings. O messenger, the organs of generation of the male and also of the female throb. Then the male and the female, being inflamed with passion, unite. The body (of the male) is rubbed with the body (of the female). Due to coitus a momentary pleasure is produced. Then again a similar itch is (produced). Such a condition is indeed observed everywhere, O messenger. Go to your own place. There is nothing new about it. I have nothing new, nor do I do anything new. This is certain.

CHAPTER FIFTYFOUR

Sukalā Gets Prepared For the Showdown

Viṣṇu said :

1-4. When the female messenger was thus addressed by that Sukalā she went (to Indra). Indra, having understood those significant and truthful words of her, well spoken in a brief manner, and having perceived her boldness, courage and knowledge (thought:) 'Who, (even) being a woman, would speak on the earth, words that are of the form of (i.e. endowed with) propriety and that are well-ordered and washed with the water of logic? This magnanimous one is pure and of a truthful nature. There is no doubt that she is capable of bearing the yoke (i.e. responsibility) of all the three worlds?'

5. Due to this Jiṣṇu (i.e. Indra) thought and said to Cupid: "With you I shall go to see that beloved (wife) of Kṛkala."

6-7. Cupid, proud of his power, replied to the thousand-eyed (Indra): "O lord of the gods, let us go (to the place) where the chaste lady is (staying). Having gone there, I shall destroy her self-respect, power, strength, courage, truthfulness and loyalty to her husband. Of what account is she (to me), O lord of gods?"

8-9. Having heard (these) words of Cupid, the thousand-eyed (Indra said:) "O Cupid, listen. Excessive talking is of no use. She is quite strong with true power. Due to religious rites she is quite firm. This Sukalā is inconquerable. Your valour is (of) no (use) there (i.e. against her)."

10-13. Hearing this, and getting angry, Cupid said to Indra:

"I have destroyed the power of sages and deities. Of what measure (i.e. how much) is her power (about which) you are telling me? You just see (i.e. in your very presence), I shall destroy the woman. As butter, on seeing (i.e. in the presence of) the lustre of fire, would melt, similarly I shall melt her with my form and lustre. Now certainly great mission has come up for me, who am going there. Why do you condemn my lustre (capable of) destroying the three worlds?"

Viṣṇu said :

14-17. Having heard the words of Cupid (Indra said:) "O Cupid, I know, (even) if you raise (i.e. augment) your courage, you cannot subdue her of a holy body, meritorious due to her virtue, and behaving piously. Going from here (with you) I shall observe your strong power." With the archer (i.e. Cupid) and with the female messenger Rati, he again went to that chaste lady, who of a great merit was (all) alone and attached to her husband's feet, as a meditative saint would place his heart (in meditation) and make it free from uncertainty. The glorious fish-bannered god (i.e. Cupid) made (i.e. took up) a form, extremely wonderful, endowed with an unlimited lustre, alluring the chaste lady, adorned with blue (garments) and full of objects of enjoyment. Also Indra (took up a similar form).

18-24. Seeing that great man, of many amorous sports and wandering like this, full of desires, the wife of the glorious Vaiśya did not highly think of him (who was) endowed with a handsome form and (was an) appreciator of merits. The nature of that chaste lady had become endowed with truth, as water going to a lotus-petal, gets the name 'pearl'. 'The female messenger, whom he had formerly sent, told (me) about this appreciator of merits. This one would show in various ways his sportive form and his nature. How far this very intelligent and mischievous lover, knowing my nature would live? (Now) my body is a vacuum, and is instantly free of movements and is as good as dead. The subjects of the village of the body, have, after performing the acts called good acts, fled away. Cupid has endowed him with charm, greater than, equal to or superior to my charm. I shall talk in a wonderful way to him, who longs for me, in such a way that he, dancing with his own knowledge, powerful and endowed with joy, dies.'

25. Thinking like this, that great chaste lady, binding her firmly with the string of truth entered her own house to know his mind definitely.

CHAPTER FIFTYFIVE

Indra Tries to Dissuade Kāma

Viṣṇu said :

1-3. Knowing her mind, the lord of gods said to Cupid standing before him: "O Cupid, she, who is well-equipped with the armour of meditation with truth as its soul, cannot be conquered by you. With a desire to conquer, and taking in her hand the bow called piety and an excellent arrow named knowledge, she has stood on the battlefield, like a hero proud of his valour, to fight (with you). (This is her) valour only. Now do (i.e. show) your valour. She is today capable of conquering you in the battle. What is going to happen should be thought just now.

4-5. Here only the glorious Śiva had formerly burnt you, who had opposed him. O Cupid, as a result of that evil (act of yours), you had become bodiless. (This is) just the truth. O Cupid, you had formerly obtained a horrible fruit in accordance with the deed you had performed. Certainly you will obtain a very contemptible birth (i.e. will be born in a very contemptible species). Here only you will be told (like this) along with this chaste lady.

6. Those wise men who, in the three worlds, entertain enmity with the magnanimous, have as its fruit, sin accompanied by misery and destroying their form.

7-14. O Cupid, having proclaimed ourselves to this chaste lady, and having urged her (to continue her pious acts), we shall go. Formerly due to my contact with a chaste lady I obtained a sinful, unbearable fruit. You know this account (that) I was cursed by that Gautama also. I became one having the scrotum of a ram for ever, and you went away, leaving me there. The power of the lustre of chaste women is matchless. (Even) the creator or the sun (also) is not able to bear it. The curse formerly pronounced by the sage (-husband) of Anasūyā would (continue to) preserve this contemptible form (of you). (The chaste lady) having stopped the forcible, rising sun, very bright with lustre, stopped the curse of Kauṇḍinya pronounced by Nāṇḍavya. Atri's wife was truthful and chaste. She made the three gods her sons. O Cupid, have you not formerly heard that chaste women are always purified by sacred rites. Sāvitrī was the daughter of Dyumatsena. She brought back here only the life of Satyavān, Aśvapati's good son, from Yama. Chastity of women is thus well known. Who would touch the flame of fire? Or, who, except a fool, would, tying stones round his neck, (try to) cross the ocean with his hands? Or who would (try to) subdue a chaste woman who is free from attachment?" When Indra thus spoke words of prudence for instructing Cupid well, he, Cupid, having heard (these) words said to the lord of gods.

Cupid said :

15-18. By your order I have come (here). Having given up patience, goodheartedness and manliness, you are telling me about her (something), which lacks energy and is full of great fear. When I shall entertain bad thoughts, O lord of gods, my fame in the world will perish. Subdued by her people will describe me, who bring about marriages to be without self-respect. The hosts of gods, demons, sages, and saints with austerity will instantly laugh at me (saying:) 'This fearful Cupid is subdued by a woman.' Therefore, O lord of gods, I shall go with you and shall destroy her power, self-respect, lustre and fortitude. O Indra, why are you (then) afraid here (i.e. in this matter)?

19-23. Having thus addressed the lord of gods, and having held his bow and flowery arrow, he said to Rati, standing before him: "Acting deceitfully you should go the vaiśya's wife Sukalā, who is meritorious, who remains in (i.e. practices) truth, who knows piety and appreciates virtues. O darling, going from here do the work, helpful (to my mission), as told (by me). (Please) obey (me)." Having thus spoken to Rati, he again called Rati, standing near. (He said:) "Do this excellent job for me; subdue her through great affection. (Act in such a way) that this beautiful woman would fall in love with Indra on seeing him. O friend, listen, by all means win her over with all miraculous powers; O friend, go quickly and effect an illusory grove, having the form of (i.e. resembling) Nandana-garden, full of flowers, abounding in fruits, and resounding with the cooings of the cuckoos and the hummings of the bees."

24-25. Having called the brave Elixir of Life, the very gratifying Flower-juice, endowed with sweet virtues, and sent him according to his wish along with Wind etc. engaged in their own duties and ordering the great army, infatuating three worlds, Cupid went with the lord of gods, to that great chaste lady, to allure (her).

CHAPTER FIFTYSIX

Satya & Dharma Come to Sukalā's Help

Viṣṇu said :

1-11a. Cupid, with the lord of gods, started to go to Sukalā to bring about a genuine destruction of her. At that time Satya (i.e. Truth) said to Dharma: "See, O very intelligent Dharma Cupid's misdeed. I create (i.e. have created) a great place, an excellent house, of the nature of an abode, causing (i.e. giving) happiness, and called Satya (truth), Supriya (very dear) and Sudeva (with good deities), for the sake of you, the righteous and magnanimous one, and for my sake. This wicked Cupid, of a blundering mind, and of an inimical nature, would go to it and certainly destroy that excellent house of us. There is no doubt that a Brāhmaṇa with penance as his wealth as the husband, a very poius chaste woman, and a very truthful king, are, O Dharma, my abodes. There is no doubt about it. You would reside there where I am nourished with prosperity. Puṇya (i.e. Merit) comes there and sports with Śraddhā (i.e. Faith). Kṣamā (i.e. Forbearance) accompanied by Śānti (i.e. Tranquility) comes to my abode. Real Dama (i.e. Restraint), and Dayā (i.e.

Pity) and Sauhārda (i.e. Good-heartedness), Nirlobha (i.e. Absence of greed), along with Intelligence are there where I live. Śuci Svabhāva (i.e. Pure Nature) (stays) there only. These are my kinsmen. Non-stealing, Harmlessness, Endurance and Prosperity have come to my house. O king Dharma, listen to my blessedness. Service of preceptors and elderly persons, Viṣṇu accompanied by Lakṣmī, gods led by Agni, come to my house. Jñāna (i.e. Knowledge) accompanied by Brilliance, that would illumine the path to salvation (has come to my house).

11b-14. I always live with these in chaste women, religious persons, and in all good people that are of the form of my house. Along with you I just live with the family about which I told you. They, who are virtuous and of a good nature, have been made my abode by the Creator. O magnanimous one, I move comfortably and at will. The lord, the master of the three worlds, the three-eyed one, having the bull (viz. Nandi) as his vehicle, lives, with Śivā (i.e. Pārvatī), in his own form in my house.

15-20. This, then, is the essence of the worldly existence, of the form of a house, of a lordly nature—an abode called Śaṅkara. That is destroyed by Cupid. This Cupid formerly subdued, after having taken resort to (i.e. the help of) Menakā, the magnanimous Viśvāmitra, practising excellent penance. That wicked Cupid led the chaste, loyal Ahalyā, the dear, auspicious wife of Gautama away from great truth. All sages, knowing the genuine Dharma, many chaste women—all these my abodes were burnt by the fire of Cupid. He is irresistible, unbearable, (all-) pervasive, and very harsh to great truths. He is looking for me (saying:) 'Where does Truth stay?' Knowing me (i.e. finding out my abode) he, the archer, with arrows in his hands, comes; and the sinful one would destroy my house with fires.

21-25. All those having bits of sins, who are cruel, who have resorted to heretics, who are malevolent in mind, will enter the house of Satya. Subdued by the generals of the army who are untruthful and by that Chadman (i.e. Dishonesty), the sinner would ruin (and) strike (my) house with sinful weapons. The wicked, very powerful Cupid will strike me like this. Burnt by his lustre I shall be a non-entity. I desire (to have) a new house called the woman looking upon her husband as her king. This one, good and auspicious, is the dear (wife) of the meritorious

Kṛkala. This wicked (Cupid) is intent on burning that house called Sukalā.

26-30a. How is it that the mighty thousand-eyed (Indra) does not know (i.e. remember) his former account (i.e. what happened to him) on account of Cupid? He became one having the scrotum of a ram due to his attachment to Ahalyā. The lord of gods (i.e. Indra), who had remained there (i.e. in Gautama's hermitage), had perished on seeing the manliness of the sage and due to the outrage of a chaste woman, as a result of Cupid's fault. He suffered a terrible curse, and was full of great grief. This thousand-eyed (Indra), along with Cupid, is eager to strike this Sukalā, Kṛkala's dear wife practising meritorious acts. O Dharmarāja, O very intelligent one, act in such a way that this Cupid would not come (to her) with Indra. You are the best among the intelligent ones."

Dharmarāja said :

30b-33a. I shall lessen the lustre of Cupid and bring about his death. I have found out one remedy. You may (please) examine it now only. This very intelligent Prajñā moving in the form of a bird, may tell (i.e. announce), from the sky, the auspicious arrival of (Sukalā's) husband. She, due to the prowess of the omen, and with her mind steady, would certainly not be ruined by the wicked.

33b-35a. He (then) sent Prajña. She went to the house of Sukalā. Making a great sound she shone like one who had been seen (i.e. favoured) by gods. Then she was worshipped and honoured with incense, lights etc. Sukalā asked the brāhmaṇa: "What would she (i.e. does she) say to me?"

The brāhmaṇa said :

35b-36. The steady one announces the arrival of your husband, O blessed one. He will arrive within seven days. This will not be otherwise.

37. Hearing these very auspicious words, she at once became very glad. (She thought that) her virtuous, dear husband, knowing righteousness, had arrived.

CHAPTER FIFTYSEVEN

The Trap Is Laid For Sukalā

Viṣṇu said :

1-3. Rati, taking up the form of a chaste lady, went to the house of the charming loyal wife. She (i.e. Sukalā) the blessed one, endowed with a truthful nature, respectfully spoke to her (i.e. Rati). Rati, the chaste lady, well-honoured with very auspicious words, smiled and spoke to Sukalā, words full of deceit, alluring all and containing a truthful topic: "(Please) listen, my husband, my lord, who is very strong, who appreciates virtues, who is wise and learned, who is endowed with greatness, who has a holy name, left me who am more (i.e. very) sinful and has gone away."

4-5. Sukalā, due to her feminine nature, after having heard all that she (i.e. Rati) said through agreeable words, took her to be of a very pure nature, and said to her: "O beautiful lady, why did your lord abandon your beautiful form and go away? Today tell me the truth about your good husband. You, endowed with meditation, who have come to my house, and being of the nature of my friend, are doing everything for me."

6-10. Rati said: "Listen to the real account of my lord. O dear one, I was always engaged (in giving him) what he desired, and thus appeased him. To carry out the auspicious words of my good lord, I did everything attentively. I am of an extremely good disposition, virtuous and worthy of him through my rendering service to him who is supreme for me in this world. This is the fruit of my former (deeds) which appears now only, and due to which my husband has thus gone away after abandoning me, who am luckless. O friend, I do not (i.e. cannot) sustain my life and my body. How do shameless women live well without their husbands? In the scriptures, a husband is described to be the beauty, decoration, good fortune, happiness and wealth, and not otherwise (i.e. and none else)."

11-14. She (i.e. Sukalā) having heard all that Rati said, and looking upon it as the truth, believed her talk. That magnanimous Sukalā, devoted to her husband, and confiding (in Rati), again spoke to her words describing her acts. She told in brief all her former account. "Since the husband, intent upon gaining religious merit, has gone on a pilgrimage, our grief is very true, and so is our suffering, O you virtuous lady." Having (thus) cheered up the chaste lady, Rati advised her.

Sūta said :

15-22. Once that Rati said to Sukalā : "O friend, see the pleasing wood adorned by divine trees. There is a very auspicious sacred place, destroying sins. It looks charming due to the spreading out of many creepers, and good flowers. O you of an excellent face, we too should go (there)." Hearing that Sukalā entered, with Rati, that divine forest, resembling Indra's garden. It was having flowers of all seasons, and was resounding with calls of hundreds of cuckoos; it was full of the music of bees' sweet hummings; it was full of the auspicious sounds of propitious birds; it shone with trees like the sandal and with fragrances. It was full of all pleasures and with the spring-creeper and the spring season. It was put up to allure Sukalā. With her she (i.e. Rati) entered the wood, pleasing to all. She saw the auspicious (grove) giving pleasure (but) did not know the fraudulent intention (of Rati), when, O lord of men, she saw the divine wood with her (i.e. Rati).

23-26a. Shining with his divine form, Indra also went to that place. Cupid also came there along with that messenger. (Indra) being the lord of all enjoyments, and full of amorous sports, called Cupid and said to him: "This Sukalā has come. O glorious one, strike her standing before you and brought by Rati through trickery near you. If you have valour show it today. Do it certainly."

Cupid said :

26b-27a. O you thousand-eyed (Indra), show your charming form, endowed with amorous sport, so that I shall strike (her) with (my) five arrows.

Indra said :

27b-28a. O fool, where is your valour with which you afflict people? Now you desire to fight after taking my support.

Cupid said :

28b-36a. Formerly only that trident-holder, Mahādeva (i.e. Śiva), the god of gods has snatched away my form. My body does not exist. Listen, when I desire to strike a woman, I manifest my form by resorting to a male body. O thousand-eyed (Indra), I shall now execute the mission by resorting to (the body of) a man. When a lady is repeatedly thinking about the form of a man (i.e. about a man) not seen before, I excite the man by resorting to him. In the same way, I shall certainly excite this one of the form of a woman (i.e. I shall certainly excite this woman). There is no doubt about it. O lord of gods, I got the name 'Smara' as I was thought of. Seeing her I shall, (being) like that, resort to the (particular) colour, object or form. My lustre would repel what is to be repelled by means of its brightness, and by resorting to the form of a woman it would allure (even) a strong-minded man; and resorting to a man (-form) I shall secure this woman for you. O Indra, I am formless. I would resort to my (original) form (and) resorting to your body I shall secure her as desired (by you).

36b-38. Having thus addressed the lord of gods, Cupid too, who was the friend of the Spring Season and who had flowers as his weapons, having resorted to the body of that magnanimous (Indra), was eager, looking, with his eyes, at the target of his arrows—the chaste, very meritorious wife of Kṛkala—to strike her.

CHAPTER FIFTYEIGHT

Sukalā Wins

Viṣṇu said :

1-2. Prompted by Rati, Sukalā, the beautiful wife of the vaiśya entered the beautiful grove. The chaste lady saw all the charming grove and then she asked her friend. (She said:) "O friend, to whom does this excellent, very meritorious, divine and charming grove, which is furnished with all excellent pleasures, belong?" Sukalā joyfully asked her friend (Rati).

Krīḍā (i.e. Rati) said :

3. This grove is endowed with all divine qualities of well-known inherent properties and decorations of flowers and perfumes; it is full of flowers and desired fruits; see, it is of (i.e. it belongs to) Cupid.

4-12. Having heard these words, and full of great joy, and observing the great account of the wicked Cupid, she smelt the fragrance carried by wind. (In it) wind, endowed with fragrance, blew naturally, in such a way that his (i.e. Cupid's) arrow very easily entered her nose; but that (Sukalā) of an excellent face (i.e. beautiful) did not smell the fragrance of the flowers; nor did the very chaste lady enjoy the excellent pleasures. The delightful friend of Cupid, vanquished (by her), was ashamed, and having turned away his face, fell on the ground with bits of leaves. Juice, of an excellent brightness, and decorated with flowers and shoots, fell on the ground from ripe fruits. The flower-juice, of a melancholy nature, fallen from the fruits, was eaten (i.e. drunk) by bees, as a dead man (is eaten up) on the battle-field. Being (thus) eaten (i.e. drunk) by bee, it flew in a stream. It flew slowly only; the birds laughed at it. With many notes, full of joy, they happily roamed (in the grove). The birds happily remained on the mountain in the forest. He, who had resorted to a mean course, was vanquished by Sukalā.

13-14. Cupid's wife Rati, accompanied by Prīti, went to Sukalā, and, with a smile, said to her: "O auspicious one, well-being to you; welcome to you; enjoy happily; your spotless form, delightful to the eyes, is liked by the magnanimous Indra. When you desire (something), tell (me); I shall certainly bring it."

Sūta said :

15-19. Seeing and hearing the two ladies (viz. Rati and Prīti) talking, she said (these) good words: "My very intelligent husband has gone away, taking with him my pleasure. I am united with my husband at the place where he remains. My desire (remains) there, so also my love. This body is without a prop." Both Rati and Prīti, having heard what (Sukalā) said, were ashamed. Being ashamed, they went to the place where the very mighty Kāma stood. They said to the great hero of a great might, who had drawn his bow, who had resorted to Indra's body (and therefore) who was visible to the eyes: "O you highly intelligent one, she is invincible. Give up (trying) your valour (against her). The magnanimous chaste lady always longs for her husband (only)."

Cupid said :

20. O respectable lady, if she looks at the form of this magnanimous Indra, then I shall certainly strike her.

21-24. Then that lord of gods, of a great form, who had put on a (different) garb, endowed with all pleasures, decorated with all ornaments, wearing divine flowers and garments, (with his body) smeared with divine sandal, and accompanied by that Rati, very sportively and quickly went to that place where the lady looking upon her husband as a deity (i.e. the lady loyal to her husband) stood. He spoke to the magnanimous Sukalā, behaving truthfully: "Formerly I had sent a messenger to you. Why, O auspicious one, do you not show regard for me, who have betaken myself to you?"

Sukalā said :

25-28a. Well-being to you. I am protected by the magnanimous sons of my husband, and by companions; so I am not at all alone. From whom (then) do I have fear? I am protected by brave men everywhere. I do not have much time to talk. I am engaged in my duty towards him. O you very intelligent one, why do you not feel ashamed of dallying with me while your eyes are trickling (i.e. while you are old). Who are you that have come here, and are not afraid even of death?

Indra said :

28b-29. I saw you having come into the grove; but you told me about the brave sons of your husband. How can I see them? Show them to me.

Sukalā said :

30-34. The pious-minded, magnanimous one, whose entire piety is firm, who is always devoted, who is powerful with love, having established Truth as the chief of his own group (of allies), and placing him (to protect me) along with qualities known as Courage, Resolution, Fate and Intelligence, always protected me. Dharma thus always protects me with the pure qualities of restraint. See, Truth, along with Tranquility and Forbearance, has come to me. Knowledge, who is very powerful and very famous, will never desert me. I am bound with firm bonds of his qualities. He has just come to my vicinity. All (the qualities) like Truth etc. had been now made my protectors. All (qualities like) Piety, Gain and Restraint, Knowledge, Valour protect me only. Why do you solicit me against my will? Who are you, being fearless, that have come here with a female messenger? Truth, Piety, so also Merit and Knowledge etc. are very powerful and are the companions of my husband. They protect me in the house.

35-37. I am always having protection, and am solely devoted to Restraint and Tranquility. Even the lord of Śacī (i.e. Indra) himself is not able to win me over. Even if that powerful Cupid comes, I am always furnished with the armour of truth, and not by anything else. There is no doubt that his arrows would be futile. The great warriors like Dharma (i.e. Piety) etc. will kill you only.

38-39. Go away, run (away); now do not stand here. If you stay (here), though warded off, you will be reduced to ashes. I shall just burn you, as fire would burn wood, and in no other way, when you look at my form without (i.e. in the absence of) my husband.

40-43. Hearing (these words) (uttered by her) in the presence of even Cupid, the thousand-eyed god (i.e. Indra said:) "See her valour. Fight with your valour (with her)." O great king, all those, Indra and others, being afflicted with fear of the great curse, went to their respective places, as they had come. When all of them had gone, that Sukalā, devoted to her husband, and endowed with merit, came to her own house, thinking of her husband (only). That lady, looking upon her husband as her god, then came to her own house, endowed with merit, full of (the merit of) all sacred places and all sacrifices.

CHAPTER FIFTYNINE

Riligious Observances Without One's Wife Are Fruitless

Viṣṇu said :

1-2. Having finished (i.e. having visited) all sacred places, Kṛkala, full of great joy, started for his house along with the leader of the caravan. He always thought like this: 'My worldly existence is fruitful. My dead ancestors, when gratified will go to heaven; not otherwise.'

3-5a. Just then having bound his grandsires (Dharma) spoke to him: "You do not have excellent religious merit." (Dharma) of a divine form and of a huge body said (these) words to Kṛkala: "You do not have the fruit of (your visits to) holy places. In vain have you exerted. You alone are happy (i.e. you have not gratified your dead ancestors etc.); (therefore) you do not have excellent religious merit."

5b-7. Hearing like this, the vaiśya, viz. Kṛkala, was afflicted with pain. (He said to Dharma:) "Who are you that are talking like this? Why are my grandsires bound? Due to the effect of what fault (of mine are they bound)? (Please) tell me the reason of it. Why do I not have the fruit of (my visits to) the holy places? How is my pilgrimage not (fruitful)? If you know, then tell me everything clearly."

Dharma said :

8-19. The entire fruit of the religious merit of him, who, leaving (behind) his pure and most meritorious wife, goes (on a pilgrimage), becomes worthless, not otherwise. All the religious deeds of him, who, leaving (behind) even his wife who is devoted to a pious conduct, who is meritorious, who is engrossed in the vow of loyalty to her husband, who is virtuous, who loves merit, goes to (holy places to) perform religious rites, are done in vain. Not otherwise. In the house of him, whose meritorious and very chaste wife has qualities like being devoted to all (good) practices, being worthy, being intent upon accomplishing moral merit, being devoted to her husband, always loving knowledge gods of great prowess always stay; and his dead ancestors, living in his house, desire bliss. There (i.e. in his house) are present auspicious rivers like the Ganges and Seas; (and) not at any other place. He, in whose house lives his chaste wife, entirely devoted to truth, has (the credit of having performed) sacrifices; cows and sages (live there), and at no other place. Due to the conduct of his wife all these sacred places and various religious merits (stay) there, and at no other place. The stage of householder is produced (i.e. is possible) due to the contact of a meritorious wife. Highest moral merit is (obtained) from the stage of a householder. There is no such stage on the earth. O vaiśya, the house of a householder is meritorious, is endowed with truth and religious merit, is full of all holy places and is attended by all gods. All beings live (only) after resorting to the stage of a householder. I do not see any other excellent stage (of life) like that. The man in whose house the sacred fire is maintained to the accompaniment of sacred hymns, all gods live, all old practices are followed, gifts are given (is blessed).

20-34. Similarly the house of him who is without a wife, becomes a forest. (In his house) sacrifices are not accomplished (i.e. performed) and various gifts (are not given). Any great vow of a man without a wife is not fruitful. So also no religious rites and no meritorious deeds (are fruitful). To accomplish religious merit there is no holy place like a wife. Listen to the way of the life of a householder. There is no other Dharma in the three worlds (like that of a householder). A man has a house where his wife lives, whether in villages or in a forest. She is the means of all moral merit. There is no holy place like a wife; there is no happiness like a wife. There is no religious merit for the emancipation and well-being (of the husband) like a wife. O you mean man, you go (i.e. you had gone) leaving (behind) your righteous and chaste wife. Leaving (i.e. when you leave) your house and proper course of conduct, where does the fruit of your moral merit remain? When (i.e. since), without her (i.e. in her absence), you offered a śrāddha, therefore, due to that fault only your grandsires are bound. You are a thief; these (grandsires) also are thieves who, being very greedy, enjoyed the food offered by you without her (i.e. in her absence). I shall tell you about the religious merit of a good son, who, full of faith, offers a śrāddha, with (i.e. in which) a piṇḍa (is) offered by his wife. As men are satisfied with drinking nectar, in the same way the dead ancestors are satisfied with a śrāddha. I am telling you the truth and truth only. A wife is the owner of the stage of a householder. O fool, you have deceived her. You have committed a theft. These your manes, who ate without her (i.e. in her absence) are great thieves. The dead ancestors eat with a pleased mind the food resembling nectar which the (son's) wife prepares with her own hands. With that only they are gratified and become pleased. Therefore, the religious practices of a man do not succeed without his wife. There is no holy place like a wife giving men a good position (i.e. leading them to salvation). The religious practices carried on without (i.e. in the absence of) the wife would become fruitless.

CHAPTER SIXTY

Sukalā's Story Ends

Kṛkala said :

1. O Dharmarāja, now tell me in detail how I would have final beatitude and how my dead ancestors would be liberated.

Dharma said :

2-6. O you noble one, go home. She (i.e. your wife) is experiencing grief without you. Inform your wife, Sukalā practising piety, (of your arrival). Having gone home, offer śrāddha with her hands. Win over the best gods by remembering the holy places. You will have the salvation obtained through pilgrimages to holy places. He who desires to accomplish religious merit without his wife (i.e. all alone), loses (the fruit of) the stage of the householder and would wander alone in a forest. He is unsuccessful in the world, (and) the deities do not respect him. The sacrifices become successful (only) when the housewife remains in the house. All alone (i.e. without his wife) he is not able to accomplish (the fruit of) piety and worldly prosperity.

Viṣṇu said :

7-11a. Having thus spoken to the vaiśya, Dharma left as he had come. That religious-minded Kṛkala also proceeded to his house. The intelligent one reached his house and saw that chaste wife (of him). The intelligent one reached his own abode along with the leader of the caravan. Seeing her husband, well-versed in Dharma, who had arrived, she performed very auspicious and meritorious (rites) on the arrival of her husband. The religious-minded one told her what Dharma did. The magnanimous one, having heard her husband's words causing delight, and having praised the words of Dharma, agreed with him.

Viṣṇu said:

11b-16a. Then that vaiśya Kṛkala remaining in the chamber of the (idol of the) deity (in his house) devotedly offered, with her, a śrāddha, giving great merit. The dead ancestors, gods, Gandharvas and sages came there in aeroplanes and praised the high-souled couple. I (i.e. *Viṣṇu*), also Brahmā and the great lord (i.e. Śiva) with the goddess (Pārvatī) and all (other) gods with Gandharvas arrived (there). I, Brahmā, and the great god (i.e. Śiva) with the goddess (i.e. Pārvatī), also all gods with Gandharvas, pleased with her truthfulness, said to the two who were well-versed in truth: "Well-being to you along with your wife. O you of a good vow, ask for a boon."

Kṛakala said :

16b-17a. O best gods, due to the association of the merit of which penance, have you come here to grant a boon to me with my wife?

Indra said :

17b-18a. This chaste, noble Sukalā is pleasing and auspicious. We were pleased with her truthfulness. We (therefore) desire to grant you a boon.

18b-23a. (Then) in brief they narrated her former account. Having heard of the magnanimity of her behaviour, the husband was delighted. With her the religious-minded one (i.e. Kṛkala) with his eyes full of joy saluted all the deities, and again and again said : "If now all the magnanimous, ancient three gods (i.e. Brahmā, Viṣṇu and Śiva) and other holy sages have favoured me and have come here, then I shall be devoted to gods like this (only) in existence after existence. Due to your grace let me have liking for piety and truth; and afterwards, O gods of great prowess, if you are pleased, I desire to go to Viṣṇu's heaven with my wife and grandsires."

Gods said :

23b. O noble one, let it be so. Everything will take place (like this) only.

24-32. Then, O king, they showered flowers on the two (i.e. Kṛkala and Sukalā). Gandharvas, knowing the essential nature of music, sang a charming, melodious song, giving great religious merit; and the groups of the celestial nymphs danced. Then the gods with the Gandharvas, praising the chaste lady, went, after giving (Kṛkala) a boon, to their respective abodes, O best king. I have told you (how) a woman is (called) a sacred place. (Now) I shall tell you something else. I have narrated to you this entire, excellent, meritorious account. O king, a man who listens to it is free from all sins. A woman who devoutly listens to the excellent account of Sukalā, is never deserted by good fortune, truth, sons and grandsons. She is delighted with wealth and grains and would be happy with her husband. In existence after existence she would be a loyal wife, and not otherwise. A brāhmaṇa (who listens to the account) would become well-versed in the Vedas; (and) a kṣatriya would be victorious. There is no doubt that there would be wealth and grains in the house of a vaiśya. O king, a man knowing piety would become one of good conduct and happy. A śūdra gets happiness and prospers with sons and grandsons. There is great prosperity adorned with wealth and grains.

CHAPTER SIXTYONE

Pippala's Penance

Vena said :

1. You have described the holy place in the form of wife, the best of all holy places. Now tell about the sacred place in the form of dead ancestors, which is a great emancipater of sons.

Viṣṇu said :

2-7. In the great sacred region (called) Kurukṣetra (there lived) a brāhmaṇa named Kuṇḍala. That noble Kuṇḍala had a good son by name Sukarman. His parents were very old, knew religious practices, and were proficient in sacred precepts. Both the noble ones were afflicted with old age. He, who knew piety, and who was full of sincerity, devotedly and continuously served them night and day. He, intent on (following) all (good) practices, knowing piety and a lover of knowledge, learnt from that (i.e. his) father, many sacred treatises; and he himself massaged the bodies of the two. He also washed their feet, bathed and fed them with devotion and naturally became thoughtful about them. O best king, he (thus) served his mother and father.

Sūta said :

8-11. At the time he lived there was a brāhmaṇa, (a descendent) of the noble Kaśyapa, O best king. He, void of passion, free from jealousy, endowed with pity, charity and restraint, having subdued lust and anger, practised penance without eating food. The intelligent one, solely devoted to knowledge and tranquility, went to Daśāraṇya, and the high-souled one having controlled his senses performed penance (there). Due to the power of his penance, the beings, free from fighting (with one another) lived there, in that age, as it were remaining in one (and the same) womb.

12-28. Seeing that (severe) penance of him, the sages were amazed. (They said:) 'None else has practised penance as this one is doing.' So gods led by Indra, were highly amazed. (They said:) 'Oh what severe penance he is practising? How great is his tranquility and restraint over senses?' Being free from emotion and agitation, and enduring cold, wind and heat, he remained (there) like a mountain. The best brāhmaṇa, disinclined to pleasures of senses, patient at heart, did not hoard anything and did not hear the sound of anyone. Having taken up a position like that, he, with a concentrated mind, meditating upon Brahman, remained there with his lotus-like face full of joy. Resembling stone and wood, he remained motionless like a mountain. Very firm and loving piety he appeared like a post.

His body was afflicted with penance. He was full of faith, and was free from jealousy. (Practising penance) in this way, the intelligent one passed a thousand years. Many ants constructed on this body a huge ant-hill with a heap of clay, as his abode. In the interior of the ant-hill he remained motionless. In this way that brāhmaṇa (named) Pippala practised very great (i.e. severe) penance. The best brāhmaṇa (Pippala) was surrounded on all sides by black serpents. (The serpents) of a strong poison bit that brāhmaṇa of an intense penance. Poison (even) after reaching the vulnerable points of his body did not harm it. Due to the brāhmaṇa's lustre the serpents became peaceful. From his body rose many flames of blazing lustre. They appeared separately. O best man (i.e. O king), they were just like the more (i.e. very) hot (flames) of fire. As the sun, having entered the interior of clouds, shines with his rays, in the same way the brāhmaṇa remaining in the ant-hill shone with his lustre. O best king, angry serpents bit the brāhmaṇa with their teeth, but even after piercing his skin, they did (i.e. could) not cleave (his body), with the tips of their teeth. O lord of kings, in this way the noble sage passed a thousand years in practising penance. The period, attended by cold, rain and heat was thus passed by the noble Pippala who subdued the three times, O great king. In the same way the noble one also ate (i.e. lived on) air.

29-31. He passed three thousand years in practising penance. Then soon the gods showered flowers on his head. (They said to him:) "O you noble one, you know Brahman, you know piety, there is no doubt about it. You have become full of all knowledge (i.e. omniscient) due to your deeds. You will certainly get (i.e. fulfil) whatever desire you have. You, on your own, will have all your desires accomplished (i.e. satisfied)."

32-37. Hearing (these) great words, that large-hearted Pippala, with his neck (i.e. head) devoutly bent down, and full of great joy, spoke (these) words: "O best gods, do that by which this entire world would be under my control. May I be a Vidyādhara." O best king, speaking like this, the intelligent one ceased (to speak). The gods then said to the best brāhmaṇa: "Let it be so." O noble one, having given the boon to that magnanimous (Pippala) they left. When the gods had left, that best brāhmaṇa Pippala was everyday devoted to sacred knowledge, and thought (as to how he would) control everything. O best king, since then Pippala, the best brāhmaṇa, obtained the status of a Vidyādhara, and was honoured as one moving according to his own desire.

38-41. In this way that brāhmaṇa Pippala attained the status of a Vidyādhara, and became well-versed in all branches of knowledge and the lord of gods. Once that Pippala of great lustre thought: 'I shall have everything under my control. I have been granted the best boon.' The best brāhmaṇa (Pippala) was eager to ascertain it. He would bring (i.e. brought) under control whatever he wanted to. When he thus became confident, he thought : 'In the world there is no other best brāhmaṇa like me.'

Sūta said :

42-46. O king, knowing the thought of that noble Pippala who was thinking like this, the crane which was on the bank of a lake said to Pippala in a melodious tone, charming and full of charity: "Why do you have this great pride? I do not think you have the power to bring everything under your control. This act of subjugating everything is recent (or is on this side). O Pippala, you, whose intellect is confounded, do not know what is ancient (or is on the other side). O brāhmaṇa, why do you in vain entertain pride when you have practised penance for three thousand years?

47-53a. That wise and very intelligent Sukarman, who was the son of Kuṇḍala had all the world under his control. Now listen. That intelligent one knew the recent (or on this side) and the ancient (or on the other side). O Pippala, listen, there is no one so very wise as he was. You are not like (that) Sukarman, the son of Kuṇḍala. He did not give gifts. He did not reflect on knowledge. He never performed acts like offering oblations or sacrifices. He never went on a pilgrimage, nor did he ever offer excellent service to fire for resorting to (i.e. obtaining) religious merit. He moved at will, he was ever a friend of (i.e. always loved) his father and mother. He was endowed with the knowledge of the Vedas, and was well-versed in the meaning of all branches of knowledge. You do not have that knowledge which even that child (i.e. even as a child) Sukarman had. In vain you are proud."

Pippala said :

53b-60. Who are you in the form of a bird, that are thus censuring me? Why do you condemn my knowledge? Of what kind is the ancient knowledge? Explain that to me in detail. How do you have knowledge (i.e. How have you come to possess knowledge)? Now tell me the scope of the recent (or inferior) as well as of the ancient (or superior knowledge), in detail and accompanied by learning, O best bird; and (tell me) whether you are Brahmā, or Viṣṇu, or Rudra.

The crane spoke :

Your penance does not exist; (therefore) you will not have its fruit. Hear now about the penance which you have not practised. You do not have the virtue which the child of Kuṇḍala had. Nor do you have the knowledge (which he had). Nor have you known the (highest) place (as he knew). O best brāhmaṇa, having gone from here you ask (him) about my form. He, the religious-minded one, will explain to you all knowledge.

Viṣṇu said :

Having heard all that which the crane said, he speedily went to the great hermitage in Daśāraṇya.

CHAPTER SIXTYTWO

Parents As Sacred Places of Pilgrimage

Viṣṇu said :

1-5. (Pippala) having gone to Kuṇḍala's hermitage, full of truthful practices, saw (there) noble Sukarman, greatly devoted to his father and mother, serving (them), possessing great prowess born of truth, of great form and lustre, having great knowledge, engaged in serving his parents and seated at their feet, tranquil, endowed with great devotion and the great treasure of all knowledge. That high-souled Sukarman, the son of Kuṇḍala, seeing the very intelligent Pippala who had come to the door, quickly got up from his seat and honoured him, (and said to him): "O you glorious, very intelligent Vidyādhara, (please) come."

6-10. The very intelligent (Sukarman) gave him water for washing his feet and a respectful offering, (and said to him): "O you highly intelligent one, are you free from difficulties? Are you all right?" He also asked Pippala that had come (to him) about his well-being. (He said to Pippala:) "I shall explain to you all about your arrival (here) today. You practised penance for three thousand years. O glorious one, you thus practised penance, and obtained a boon from the gods. You secured the power of subjugation, and also (the power of) moving according to your desire. Due to that you have become arrogant, and are unnecessarily proud. Seeing all your movements, the noble crane told you my name and about my excellent knowledge."

Pippala said :

11. Who is that lord, that god, the crane who directed me (to come to you) and told me about all knowledge on the bank of a lake?

Sukarman said :

12-13a. Know that crane who talked to you on the bank of the lake to be the highest god Brahmā, of great knowledge. Speak (out) what else you want to ask. I shall explain it to you.

Viṣṇu said :

13b. O prince, that religious-minded Sukarman thus spoke (to Pippala).

Pippala said :

14. On the earth we have heard that the entire world is under your control. O brāhmaṇa, carefully show me the spectacle.

15-18a. "Today see the spectacle—the cause of controlling the uncontrolable." (Thus) spoke the religious-minded Sukarman to Pippala. Then for convincing (Pippala), Sukarman called to mind the gods. The Guardians of the Quarters like Indra, and also gods led by Agni and many Vidyādharas that were invited came (there). Then the gods led by Agni said to Sukarman : "O brāhmaṇa, tell us the reason for which you remembered us."

Sukarman said :

18b-20a. Here has come this Vidyādhara (named) Pippala. He asks me the reason of my controlling the uncontrolable. I have invited you for convincing this high-souled one. (Please) go to your respective abodes.

20b-24. Thus he spoke to the gods. Then the gods said to that very intelligent Sukarman: "Your seeing us will not be fruitless. Well-being to you. Ask for a boon which you like. We shall grant it. There is no doubt about it." Thus the best gods spoke to him. The best brāhmaṇa having devoutly saluted those gods requested them: "O best gods, grant me always a sincere and firm devotion to my mother and father. This is the best boon (I desire to have). May my father go to Viṣṇu's heaven; similarly, O lords of gods, may my mother (also) go to Viṣṇu's heaven. This is the best boon (I desire to have). I do not solicit any other boon."

The gods spoke :

25. O best brāhmaṇa, you are devoted to your father. O Sukarman, listen, due to your devotion we are always pleased with you.

26-28. O prince, having said like this, the gods went to heaven. Then he (i.e. Sukarman) presented before him (i.e. Pippala) all his grandeur. Pippala also saw that great wonder. The religious-minded (Sukarman) also said to Pippala, the son of Kuṇḍala. (Then Pippala said:) "This is a recent (or interior) form; what kind of form is the ancient (or superior) one? O best among the speakers, tell me about the prowess of both."

29-37. I shall tell you the mark of the ancient form, due to which the worlds, the mobile and the immobile (and gods) led by Indra are delighted. This lord of the world himself, who pervades the entire earth, is the master (of everything). No meditating saint has seen his form. The scriptures, as it were afraid to speak, speak (about him) like this: "He is without hands, feet and nose. He is without ears and mouth." (Yet) he sees all the acts performed by the residents of the three worlds. (Even though he is) without ears he hears their talk. (Thus) he gives good (i.e. proper) evidence (of his omnipresence). Even without any movement, he would go; he is seen everywhere. Even being handless, he can seize (things); (though) footless, he runs. O brāhmaṇa, he, pervading everything though footless, is seen everywhere. He, whom the best gods and sages knowing the truth, do no see, sees them all, stationed in truthful and untruthful positions; whom, the (all-) pervader, pure, the divine being granting divine faculties, the leader of all, Vyāsa, the great meditating saint, knowing piety and material prosperity and of a lustrous form, knows. Vyāsa himself knows him to be the sky, of one colour and endless. (Vyāsa alone knows) this spotless form determined by what is told in the scriptures.

38-49. Mārkaṇḍeya also knows that station. I shall explain to you the recent (form). Listen with a concentrated mind. When the soul of the beings withdraws (everything into himself), he goes all alone; resorting to a bed in the water (i.e. in the ocean) he remains on the seat of the hood of Śeṣa. Resorting to him Janārdana sleeps for a long time. The great meditating sage Mārkaṇḍeya, tormented by the darkness in the water, and desiring a place (for him), dejected due to wandering, saw, while wandering, (Viṣṇu) who was lying on the bed of Śeṣa, who resembled a crore of suns, who was adorned with divine ornaments, who wore divine flowers and garments, who is the lord of all the pervading objects, who was enjoying his sleep at the end of a yuga, who held the conch, the disc and the mace. O best brāhmaṇa, (he also saw) a noble lady, resembling a heap of black collyrium, with her face terrible on account of large teeth, and of a fearful form. The best sage was addressed by her: "O great sage, do not get frightened." There was a very large lotus-leaf, extending over five yojanas. The great goddess put Mārkaṇḍeya on that leaf. (She said to him:) "Even though Keśava is asleep, you have no (cause for) fear here." The best of the meditating saints said to her: "O you beautiful lady, who are you? When this one is completely won over, you alone have grown." O brāhmaṇa, when thus asked by the sage, the goddess respectfully said: "I am the Vaiṣṇavi (i.e. belonging to Viṣṇu) power of this Keśava who is sleeping on the bed of the serpent. I am here called Kālarātri. O best brāhmaṇa, know me to be thus endowed with all (kinds of) illusion. In the Purāṇas I am described as the great illusion for (i.e. causing) infatuation of the world." O Pippala, speaking thus, that goddess vanished.

50-57a. When the goddess had gone, from his (i.e. Viṣṇu's) navel sprang up a lotus, shining like gold, while Mārkaṇḍeya was looking (at him). From him were born all the worlds, the immobile and the mobile, all the regents of the quarters like Indra, and gods led by Agni. O king, I have presented to you his recent (or inferior) form. This one of the recent (or inferior) form is without any support in his ancient (or superior form). When he would present his body then (only) all the recent (or inferior deities) like Brahmā and all worlds have bodies, O Pippala. All the regions that are there in the three worlds are recent. This soul of the beings is ancient. The meditating saints well see him, who is of the form of final beatitude, of the nature of Brahman—the highest place—, who is the universal soul, is pure and endowed with divine powers. O Vidyādhara, I have explained to you the entire nature of the ancient one. Tell me what more I (should) explain.

Pippala said :

57b-60a. O you of a good vow, how has this great knowledge risen in you? You know the recent (or inferior) as well as the ancient (or superior) station. The great knowledge of the three worlds abides in you. I (however) do not see (in you) great devotion to penance. Tell me the power of performing a sacrifice, of acting as a priest at a sacrifice, of (the visit to) a holy place, if you have done these. Due to what have you thus (obtained) all knowledge?

Sukarman said :

60b-78a. I do not at all know (what) penance (is). I have

not emaciated my body. I do not know performing a sacrifice, or acting as a priest at a sacrifice or going to holy places. I have not practised meditation, not attained the meritorious period as a result of good acts. One (thing) only I know clearly and well, (and that is) the worship of (my) father and (my) mother. With both my hands I myself everyday do the meritorious washing of the feet of my mother and father. Engaged in contemplation at three times everyday I massage their bodies, and bathe and feed them. With devotion I obtain the water with which the feet of those two only i.e. my mother and father are washed, and with great devotion I worship them. During that time a measureless gain comes to me. With my heart having pure thoughts I worship them thrice (a day). O Pippala, I am one who moves freely and comfortably. What is the use to me of any other penance or of emaciating my body? Now what good would acrue to me by good (i.e. meritorious) pilgrimages or by other (acts of) virtue? O brāhmaṇa, I have seen that to be the fruit of serving one's father, which is obtained by performing all sacrifices. Similarly serving the mother gives a good position (i.e. bliss) to the sons. It is the all-in-all and the essence of all acts in the three worlds. By serving his mother the son gets (i.e. goes to) a (good) world. Similarly great religious merit is produced due to the service to the father. There is no doubt that there (only lie) the Ganges, the holy place like Gayā, or like Puṣkara, where the father would live (i.e. lives) with the mother. By serving the father the son gets the merit of visiting these sacred places and other various holy and auspicious places. O brāhmaṇa, a good son obtains the fruit of charity and penance by serving his father (and mother). Any other customary observance leads to affliction. A son obtains excellent religious merit by serving his father (and mother), which is the all-in-all of his deeds in this and in the next world. Now listen to the auspicious merit when as a son he serves his elders—the mother and the father—when they are alive. Gods are pleased with him, and also the sages who love religious merit. Due to service of the father (and mother done) here (i.e. in this world) the three worlds are pleased. He, who everyday would wash (i.e. who washes) the feet of his mother and father, has everyday a bath in the Ganges.

78b-82. I shall (now) tell you about the religious merit of him who always devoutly feeds his father and mother with sweet food and drinks. The son gets that fruit which is got by performing the horse-sacrifice. He, who devoutly worships his elders (i.e. parents) with (i.e. by giving them) tāmbūla, coverings, drinks, eatables and pure food, would become omniscient, and would obtain glory and fame. A son, on seeing his mother or father, should talk to them with joy. They are the treasures,[1] that, being pleased, live in his house. They are the cows, that love the son and always give him happiness.

CHAPTER SIXTYTHREE

Merit Resulting from Service of Parents

Sukarman said :

1-6a. O best brāhmaṇa, the son properly gets (the religious merit of) a bath similar to the one in all the holy places when the drops of water, (falling from the bodies) of the mother and the father who have bathed, fall on the entire body of the son. I shall (now) tell you about the religious merit of the son who serves his father who is fallen, who is maimed, who is old, who is weak (in doing) all acts, who is ill, who is suffering from leprosy, and also his mother like that (i.e. in such a condition). There is no doubt that Viṣṇu has his mind pleased with him. He goes to Viṣṇu's heaven, unobtainable by (even) the meditating saints. That son of a sinful mind who abandons his parents who are maimed, helpless, old, or are suffering from a serious disease, obtains (i.e. goes to) a terrible hell, full of worms.

6b-22. I shall now tell you about the sin of (i.e. committed by) a son, who, when called by his old parents, does not go (to

---

1. Nidhayaḥ—Nidhis are the treasures of Kubera. They are nine: Mahāpadma, Padma, Śaṅkha, Makara, Kacchapa, Mukunda, Kunda, Nīla and Kharva.

them). There is no doubt that the fool becomes the eater of feces and a village-pig; and then again he is born as a dog for (the next) thousand existences. That son, who, without feeding his old mother and father living in his house, himself eats (i.e. eats alone), would eat (i.e. drink) urine, (and eat) feces for a thousand existences. The sinner would be (born) as a black serpent for two hundred existences. He, the sinner, who goes forward by neglecting his old mother or father, is born as a shark for crores of existences. That sinful son, who censures them with bitter words, would be (born as) a tiger and then would be born as a bear. That wicked-minded son who would not worship his mother or father would dwell in (the hell called) Kumbhīpāka for as long as a (period covered by) a thousand yugas. For a son there is no other holy place, that would emancipate him and would cause his well-being here and in the next world, like his mother or like his father. Therefore, O you very intelligent one, I worship the deity in the form of my father (and) the deity in the form of my mother. I have by that become a devotee devoted to all gods. Excellent knowledge is produced (in me) due to the grace of my mother and father. Which wise man does not worship his mother or father? O brāhmaṇa, what is the use of his having studied the Vedas, with the Aṅgas and the Upāṅgas, and along with scriptures and (other) branches of knowledge, who has not honoured his father? The Vedas are useless for him who has not honoured his mother. Also, O brāhmaṇa, what is the use of sacrifices, penance, (giving) gifts and worships (of deities)? (All this) becomes fruitless (in the case) of him, who, while living (as a householder) in his house, has not worshipped his mother and has not worshipped his father. This (i.e. honouring his parents) alone is the duty of a son; this (alone) is a holy place among (i.e. for) men. This alone is the final beatitude of a son; similarly (this alone) is the auspicious fruit of his existence. This (alone) is the sacrifice of (i.e. performed by) a son. There is no doubt about it.

23-29. Intent on worshipping the father (and the mother, a son) who everyday devoutly worships his father (and mother), has all that has been said before. He, who has worshipped his mother also, has undoubtedly obtained the fruit of giving gifts, or of (visiting) a holy place, or of (performing) a sacrifice. All the acts giving merit, like sacrifices etc., are well accomplished by him who has everyday worshipped his father with good (i.e. great) devotion. For this only I have studied and learnt the science of religious merit. O Pippala, a son should always be intensely devoted to his father. Formerly, king Yadu obtained happiness when his father was pleased; (and) listen, how formerly when the father was angry, Ruru, a Paurava (king), obtained great sin on the earth, when cursed by his father. When I served these two (i.e. my parents) I got knowledge like this. By the grace of these I obtained an excellent fruit.

CHAPTER SIXTYFOUR

Mātali's Discourse on Old Age

Pippala said :

1-2. Tell me in detail, how, by the grace of his father, Yadu obtained happiness and enjoyed well. O son of Kuṇḍala, tell me also in detail how Ruru suffered as a result of his sin, O best brāhmaṇa.

Sukarman said :

3-11a. Listen, I shall tell you the account of the very meritorious Nahuṣa, and the noble Yayāti, (the account) which destroys sin. Nahuṣa, the lord of the earth sprang from (i.e. was born in) the Soma dynasty. He made many matchless gifts. He performed an excellent century of the horse-sacrifices (i.e. performed a hundred excellent horse-sacrifices). He also performed a hundred Vājapeya sacrifices and many kinds of (other) sacrifices. By the power of his religious merit he obtained (i.e. went to) Indra's world. He made his very intelligent son Yayāti, endowed with truthfulness, having piety as his valour, the protector of his subjects (i.e. the king). The king (Nahuṣa) went to (i.e. obtained) Indra's position. His son Yayāti, endowed with truthfulness, who (occupied) his place (i.e. the throne), would protect (i.e. protected) the subjects religiously. He himself would look (i.e. looked) after his subjects and the respective duties. Having learnt about excellent duty, he, who knew righteousness got sacrifices performed. He did everything like performing sacrifices, (visiting) holy places, giving gifts (giving) religious merit. The intelligent son of the king (Nahuṣa) ruled truthfully for eighty thousand years in those days. The glorious Yayāti passed that much time (in truthfully ruling his subjects).

11b-15. He had four sons who were powerful and valorous like him. I shall tell (you) their names. Listen with a concentrated (i.e. attentive) mind. His eldest son was Ruru by name, who was very powerful. The second son was named Puru; the third one was Kuru; the fourth son of the king was Yadu by name, who was religious-minded. Thus the noble Yayāti had four sons. By means of their lustre and manliness, they resembled their father in valour. Thus Yayāti ruled his kingdom righteously. Great were his fame and glory in the three worlds.

Viṣṇu said :

16-18. Once the greatest brāhmaṇa, Nārada, the son of Brahmā, went to Indra's world to see Indra, O king. The thousand-eyed god (i.e. Indra) saw the brāhmaṇa (i.e. Nārada) who was omniscient, who was proficient in (all kinds of) knowledge, whose lustre was like fire, (when) he came there. With his neck bent in devotion (i.e. bowing in devotion), he seated the best sage, who was honoured with a respectful offering,[1] on an auspicious seat, and asked him:

Indra said :

19. Where have you come from today? For what purpose have you come here? O brāhmaṇa, O great sage, what very dear to you should I do today?

Nārada said :

20-21. O king of gods, O very intelligent one, I am pleased with all that you did devoutly and with what you said. I shall answer your questions. I have now safely come to your house

1. Madhuparka—a respectful offering made to a guest. Its usual ingredients are: Curds, ghee, water, honey and sugar.

from the earth. After having seen (Yayāti), the son of Nahuṣa, I have come to seek you.

Indra said :

22-23. Which king, being learned, wise, virtuous, and full of righteousness, always protects his subjects truthfully? On the earth, which is the king, who knows the Vedas, to whom the brāhmaṇas are dear, who is pious, who is conversant with the Vedas, who is a sacrificer, who is a donor, and who is a great devotee?

Nārada said :

24-30. With these qualities was endowed the powerful son of Nahuṣa, due to whose truthfulness and valour all people were well-settled. Yayāti, the son of Nahuṣa, is like you on the earth. As you are in the heaven, enhancing the prosperity (of your subjects), so he is on the earth enhancing the prosperity (of his subjects). O great king, that king Yayāti, superior to his father, performed a hundred horse-sacrifices, and also a hundred Vājapeya sacrifices. Devoutly he gave gifts in many forms like thousands of lakhs and hundreds of crores of cows. In the same way, he performed a crore of sacrifices, so also lakhs of sacrifices. He also gave gifts like grants of land to brāhmaṇas. He has protected Dharma in its full form. As you are ruling here in the heaven, so Yayāti, Nahuṣa's son, the best king, who was endowed with these qualities, truthfully ruled for eighty thousand years.

The intelligent Sukarman said :

31-47. The lord of gods, having heard like this from the best of sages, reflected, and was afraid of (his) protecting the Dharma. (He thought:) 'Formerly, by the power of hundred sacrifices, the brave Nahuṣa went to (i.e. obtained) my position of Indra, and became the king of gods. He fell from that as a result of Śacī's intelligence. This great king who is like his father in valour, will undoubtedly reach Indra's position. There is no doubt about it. With this or that means (i.e. by hook or crook) I shall bring the king to heaven.' The lord of gods, who was afraid of him, thought like this. Then the king of gods, O best king, due to the great fear of that king Yayāti, sent his messenger to bring him to heaven. (He sent) Nahuṣa's aeroplane endowed with all pleasures, and his charioteer Mātali with the aeroplane. Mātali, who was sent by the lord of gods to bring the very intelligent (Yayāti) went there where (Yayāti), Nahuṣa's son, stayed. As Indra, shines in his assembly, in the same way Yayāti, the religious-minded (king), shone in his own assembly. The charioteer of the king of gods said to that magnanimous king, whose ornament was truth: "O king, listen to my words. I have now been sent to you by the king of gods. Do, with a good (i.e. devoted) mind, all that the king of gods tells. O lord, you should come to Indra's world; (do) not (do) otherwise (i.e. do come), after having entrusted your kingdom to your son, and after having performed the best and the last sacrifice (in your life). O son of Nahuṣa, the very lustrous king lives there. Purūravas, of a great power, the noble-minded Vipracitti (also live there). Śibi lives there, Manu, king Ikṣvāku, the intelligent (king) named Sagara, and your father Nahuṣa (live there). The grateful Ṛtavīrya, and the noble Śantanu, and Bharata, Yuvanāśva, also king Kārtavīrya, —(all these) kings, after having offered various sacrifices are rejoicing in heaven. Many other kings also, very much devoted to the performance of sacrifices, are all rejoicing as a result of their meritorious acts in heaven with Indra; and you again know all the Dharma and are well established in Dharma. (Therefore,) O king, rejoice with Śakra (i.e. Indra) in heaven."

Yayāti said :

48. What deeds have I done due to which this request is made to me by you and by Indra, the lord of gods? Tell me all that.

Mātali said :

49-52. Since, O king, you performed meritorious acts like giving gifts, and performed sacrifices for eighty thousand years, (therefore) due to (i.e. as a result of) your deeds, go to heaven, O lord of the earth. Make friendship with the lord of gods. Go to the abode of gods (i.e. heaven). O you highly intelligent one, leave your body having the five (elements) as its constituents, on the earth; and taking up a divine form, enjoy pleasures after your heart (i.e. as you like). O lord of men, pleasures in heaven solicit (i.e. wait for) you in accordance with the sacrifices which are performed by you, or gifts which are given by you or penance which is practised by you, on the earth.

Yayāti said :

53. O Mātali, how should one go to the world obtained (according to one's deeds) by leaving the body with which good or bad deeds would be (i.e. are) accomplished on the earth?

Mātali said :

54-55. O king, men go to him due to divine (deeds) after leaving the body there (i.e. on the earth) only, where they have obtained this body of the nature of the five (elements). All other men also, who obtain merit or demerit, go down (i.e. to the hell) or up (i.e. to the heaven) after leaving the body (here).

Yayāti said :

56-60. O Mātali, having produced merit or demerit with the body of the nature of the five (elements), all other men do go up or down. What is the difference due to which one would leave (i.e. leaves) the body on the earth, O you who know moral virtue? (How do you say that) the body would fall (i.e. falls) as a result of (one's) sin or religious merit? In the mortal sphere, O charioteer, an example is directly seen. I, (therefore), do not see a greater difference between sinful or meritorious deeds. Why does a man, a mortal, leave the body with which he performs deeds like truthful behaviour? The soul and the body are both friends (of each other). The well-determined soul goes after leaving his friend viz. the body.

Mātali said :

61-65. O king, you have said the truth. He goes after leaving the body. There is (then) no connection of the soul with that body. Since this (body) of the nature of the five (elements) is always worn out in the joints, is troubled by old age, and always damaged by diseases, he (i.e. the soul) does not desire to stay here (i.e. in it). Being agitated and troubled, the soul leaving it (i.e. the body) departs. Due to truthfulness, acts of religious merit, gifts, religious observance and restraints, sacrifices like the horse-sacrifice, (visits to) holy places, and self-control, and also due to good deeds of great religious merit old age is not at all undergone. (On the other hand,) O great king, it attacks the body by means of sins.

Yayāti said :

66. O best one, please tell me in detail, from what old age has sprung up and why it troubles the body.

Mātali said :

67-95. I shall describe to you the cause of old age; and why it has sprung up in the body, O you best king. The body of the nature of the five elements, is resorted to by the five objects of sense. O king, when the soul leaves the body, it (i.e. the body) is burnt. O king, when blazing with fire the body burns along with the fluids. From it smoke is produced, and from smoke clouds are produced. Water proceeds from the clouds; the earth becomes ready for water as a chaste woman in her menses implores water. From that odour is produced, and fluid is produced from odour, O best king. From the fluid food is produced, and semen is produced from food. There is no doubt about this. From semen body is produced; and body is surely ugly. As the earth (element) would produce odour and it moves on the earth through fluids, similarly the body would always move. It is everywhere the substratum of fluids. From it odour is produced and again fluid would be (produced) from odour. From it is produced great fire; O king, mark the analogy. As fire is produced from wood, and would illumine wood, in the same way in the body fire is produced from fluid. It moves there (in the body) and, O king, it always nourishes the body. As long as there is preponderence of fluid (in the body) the soul is tranquil. Fire moving (in the body) like that remains in the form of hunger. Being sharp it desires food with water; O king, it receives the gift—food and water also. The fire consumes blood and semen also like that; there is no doubt about it. Due to that there would be consumption destroying the entire body. O king, when there would be preponderence of fluid, the fire is put down. Being troubled by the fluid, it is produced in the form of fever. The fire having arrested the neck, the back, the waist, the anus remains in all the joints. (Thus) the fire moves on in the body. Its preponderence always continues to exist, and nourishes the body on all sides. (When) the fluid is restrained it then becomes powerful. Being excessive due to power, it would move the vital parts of the body through the semen. Due to that lust is produced; and O king, it would become (i.e. becomes) of the nature of a dart. O king, it is called the fire of lust, which destroys strength. Due to addiction to coitus destruction (takes place) in the body. A being oppressed by the fire of lust would resort to a female. Due to addiction to sexual intercourse, the body which is made violent and emaciated by lust, would become void of lustre, and there is a loss of strength (in the body). The (already) weak body becomes (more) weak when urged on by fire. That fire would consume blood and semen in the body. Due to the consumption of semen and blood, the body becomes dispirited. A violent wind of a terrible form is produced; and then he would be pale, tormented with grief and of a vacant mind. He moves, having in his mind that woman whom he has seen or about whom he has heard. When the course of the mind (i.e. the mind) is greedy, there is no satisfaction in (i.e. of) the body. When the lustful man, ugly or handsome, becomes weak due to brooding and the loss of flesh and blood, there appears old age in the body (being) consumed by the fire of lust. Due to that, he being (more) lustful, becomes older and older day by day. As a usurer thinks of money, so he thinks of a woman in (i.e. for) coitus; so also, O lord of men, there is a loss of his lustre. From that a body is produced, and he perishes. Then undoubtedly fire in the form of old age is again produced; and then there is a terrible fever in the form of (i.e. of the nature of) consumption in the beings. All the immobile and the mobile ones being tormented by fever and by many other troubles, perish. All this I have told you; what else should I tell?

CHAPTER SIXTYFIVE

Mātali on Why the Body Is Left Behind

Yayāti said :

1. O Mātali, tell me the reason, why this body, the protector of Dharma, does not go to heaven with the soul.

Mātali said :

2-9. The five elements do not go together (with the soul); in the company of the soul, O king. All of them come together in the village of the body. All of them, afflicted by old age, go to their respective abodes. Since the earth is created with a preponderance of fluid, it being wet due to the fluids becomes soft, O king. It is pierced by ants and rats. Holes are formed into it, and also anthills with large interiors. In the same way inflammation of the glands of the neck and itch are produced in the body. O best of men, this body is also cleft by worms. Enlargements (of parts like the spleen), instantly troubling, are also produced in it. O son of Nahuṣa, this body is full of such defects. How will it go to heaven with the life, O lord of men? The earthly part is settled in the body for the vital air essential to digestion. The body does not come (i.e. go) to heaven. It remains here as the earth does. I have told you all this along with a heap of earthy blemishes.

CHAPTER SIXTYSIX

Mātali on the Universality of Suffering

Yayāti said :

1-2. O Mātali, listen, (we see that) the body falls due to sin and also due to religious merit. On the earth I do not see what difference religious merit makes. The body is produced again (just) as it fell before. Tell me in detail how the body is produced.

Mātali said :

3-16. In the case of the hellish beings, just in a moment, the (hellish) body is produced from the (five) elements due to impious acts only. In the same way, due to religious merit, a divine body (in the manner of that) of the gods is instantly produced from the essences of the elements. That body of the magnanimous ones, (which is produced) due to the mixture of the (fruits) of deeds should be known to be of four kinds according to the transformation of deeds. The immobile ones in the form of grass and bushes should be known as the ones born by sprouting up. Worms, insects and moths should be known to be born from the sweat of living beings. O king, all birds, serpents and crocodiles are oviparous. Human beings and quadrupeds should be known to be viviparous. When the earth is 'cooked' by heat, it is moistured by water and is scattered by wind (into loose particles). Then the seed approaches the soil in such a way that the seeds that are sown and are watered, become soft and attain the state of roots. From the root there is the rise of a shoot. From a shoot a leaf springs up. From a leaf a hollow stock comes up; from that a stem comes up; and from that the *prabhava* (power). From it would be (produced) *Kṣīra* (the sap), and from the sap there is the rise of *tandula*(the gram?), from the gram come up the ripened *oṣadhayaḥ* (herbs). They are said to be seventeen—the best ones—beginning with barley and ending with rice. The herbs are rich with the wealth of fruits. The remaining ones are said to be trifling. These were first cleansed and cut and crushed by the sages with winnowing baskets, mortars and (other) vessels. With water in a pan and fire, they, which have six varieties, undergo alteration, have many tastes due to the combinations of their respective tastes. O king, they have six varieties like that which is consumed, eaten, drunk, licked, sucked and bitten (and eaten). They have six tastes like the sweet (taste) etc. That food which is eaten by living beings through (i.e. in the form of) balls and mouthfuls, settles all the vital airs in the stomach one by one.

17-18. That (vital) air divides into two the food that is consumed (but) not digested. Having got into the food and having separated the digested food into (i.e. having created in it) various properties, having put water above fire and that food above the water, that (vital air) Prāṇa itself remains below the water and slowly blows the fire.

19-21. The fire being blown by the wind makes the water very hot. That food again, due to the contact of heat, is digested wholly. That (food) which is digested, becomes divided into two—the secretion is separated, and the liquid is separated. The useless divided into twelve (kinds of) impurity would go (i.e. goes) out of the body. (The outlets are:) ears, eyes, nose, tongue, teeth, lips, organ of generation, anus. (These) would pour out impurities (like) perspiration, faeces, urine. They are said to be twelve.

22-38. In the lotus of the heart, all around, the arteries are confined. (The vital air) Prāṇa places that subtle liquid into their openings; and then that prāṇa fills those arteries with that liquid. Those arteries wholly furnish that liquid to the body. Then that liquid remaining in the arteries is digested by the heat of the body. It is digested in two ways. Skin, flesh, bones, marrow, fat, blood are produced. Fine, soft, short hair and flesh are produced from blood; hair and sinews are produced from flesh. From the sinews are produced marrow and bones. Marrow of the flesh is due to bones. The healthy semen, of the nature of procreation is due to the strength of the marrow. These twelve are said to be the transformations of (i.e. brought about by) the satisfied one. Semen is its transformation, and the body is born from semen. When at the time favourable for conception defectless semen remains in the womb (of a woman), it, sent forth by that vital air, becomes one (i.e. united) with the blood of the woman. At the time of the emission of the semen, the soul, united with the organs of sense, and always being controlled by his own acts, enters the womb. The semen with the blood (of the woman) would be (turned into) a foetus in a day. Then within five nights bubbles would be formed in the foetus. It takes the form of flesh in the five forms; neck, head, shoulder(s), spine and belly; so also hands and feet, the two sides, waist, and (the other parts of) the body; the limbs are produced one by one within two months. After three months, hundreds of sharp joints are produced (i.e. formed). Fingers etc. are produced (i.e. are formed) one by one in four months. After five months mouth, nose and ears are produced (i.e. formed). Within six months, the row of teeth, so also tongue and nails are formed, so also cavities in the ears are formed. So also are formed anus, penis, organ of generation and the male organ of generation. The joints which (are present) in the limbs, are formed within seven months. In the eighth month the head with the entire body with limbs and with each limb clearly separated is formed. He is complete and endowed with the five. Due to the power of the food of (i.e. eaten by) the mother and by the tastes of six kinds, fixed in the umbilical cord, it (i.e. the foetus) grows day by day.

39-48. Then the soul would have recollection in this entire body (i.e. when the entire body is formed). He is conscious of (former) happiness and unhappiness and sleep and dream seen before: 'I, who was dead, am born again, I, who was born, died. I saw (i.e. was born in) many existences in many ways. Now I am just born, and have received (i.e. undergone) sacraments. I shall hereafter perform righteous deeds, by which I shall not be born (i.e. conceived) in a womb.' While remaining in the womb, he just thinks: 'After I come out from the womb (i.e. after I am born) I shall study (i.e. obtain) highest knowledge that would cause the cessation of the worldly existence.' The soul, certainly very much troubled by the great affliction in the womb, lives (there) and would think (i.e. thinks) of the means to salvation. As one who has gone over an excellent (i.e. high) mountain, stays there unhappily, in the same way, the soul, afflicted by the outer skin of the embryo, remains (in the womb) with the body wet with the fluid in the womb. As someone, being put into an iron-vessel is baked by fire, in the same way (the soul) put into the vessel of womb is baked by the digestive fire in the stomach. Its parts are continuously pierced by needles resembling the colour of fire. The pain he suffers (due to these), would be (i.e. is) eightfold in the womb. There is no other abode anywhere else like the one in the womb. The souls have immense suffering and a very fierce danger.

49-66a. Thus is narrated the suffering in the womb of (i.e. experienced by) all beings—mobile and immobile—according to the wombs (in which they are confined). The bewildered soul that is being born has (to suffer) a crore-fold more pain due to being pressed by the thong of the womb than he has experienced in the womb. Very great affliction takes place in the case of (i.e. is experienced by) (the soul) coming out of the womb, and being squeezed like a sugar-cane due to being pounded by destructive hammers, and by means of the air (passing out at the time) of delivery. He does not get any protection. As the sugar-canes being pressed by the machine become sapless, in the same way the body remaining in the womb is caused to fall (out of it) by the pressure of the thong. It has limbs; it is of a round shape; it is tied by the bonds of sinews. It is smeared with blood, flesh and marrow, and is the receptacle of substances like excrement and urine; it is covered with hair, down and nails; and it is the principal abode of diseases. It has one gate (in the form) of the mouth and is adorned with eight windows.[1] It has the (two) doors of the two lips, and is possessed of teeth, tongue and throat. It has the arteries and the stream of perspiration, and is overwhelmed with phlegm and bile. It is approached by old age and grief. It remains in the fire in the mouth of Death. It is overcome with lust and anger, and is pressed by winds; it is effected by desire for enjoyments; it is hidden, it is under the sway of attachment and hatred. Every limb, big and small, has a complexion; it is covered by the outer skin of the embryo; it comes out through the lonely and narrow passage of the womb. It is moistened with excretion, urine and blood; it is due to the six (kinds of) marrow. It should be known that there is collection of the bones in the skeleton numbering three hundred and a hundred more (i.e. four hundred). There are five hundred muscles. It is all around covered with small soft hair numbering three crores and half. The body is full of crores of these gross and subtle, visible and invisible, fleshy tubular organs from within. There is perspiration, and due to those it is eternally impure. The teeth were said to be thirty-two in number, and the nails are said to be twenty. It should be known that (the quantity of) bile (in the body) is one kuḍava; in the same way the quantity of phlegm is half an āḍhaka. (The quantity of) marrow is five palas; and the buttocks are half of it. The lump of flesh is five palas; fat is ten palas; thick blood is three palas; the quantity of marrow is four times that of the blood. Semen is half a kuḍava; and the power of men is half of it. It is said that

1. Gavākṣāṣṭaka—The eight apertures of the human body are: the two ears, the two eyes, the two nostrils, organ of excretion and organ of generation (the ninth is the mouth).

one thousand palas of flesh (exist in) a corporeal frame. It should be known that the quantity of blood is a hundred palas, and there is no (definite) measure (of the quantity) of faeces and urine.

66b-83a. Thus, O king, there always is the residence of the soul (in the body). The impure body is (the residence) of the soul, which is produced by the bondage of (his) deeds. The body is produced due to the combination of the semen (of the male) and the blood (of the female). It is always united with faeces and urine; therefore it is said to be impure, like an externally pure pot full of faeces from within. This body would be (i.e. is) impure even though it is cleansed by voiding of excrement. This body is impure because the very pure five products of the cow[1] and offering quickly become impure after reaching it. Agreeable and fragrant food and drinks quickly become impure on reaching it (i.e. on being consumed). Which other object is more impure than it (i.e. the body)? O men, do you not see that everyday the foul-smelling excrement, the companion of (i.e. living in) the body, goes out of it? Then how can its support be pure? Like a charcoal being rubbed, the body, though cleansed with the five products of the cow or with water containing darbhas, never becomes pure. How can that body, from which the streams of phlegm and urine flow everyday, as streams (of water) from a mountain, be cleansed? There is not a single part which is pure in the body, the receptacle of all impurity, except (the soul). Even though the hand is cleansed with clay and water, by day or at night, it can never be pure. (And yet) the men are not free from attachment. Though this body is carefully decorated with excellent incenses etc., yet, like the dog's tail that is bent, it does not give up its nature. Wool that is naturally black can never become white; similarly the body, though cleansed, does not become pure. This world, smelling its own bad odour, and seeing its excrement, does not get detached, though (by doing this) he (i.e. a man) troubles his nose. Oh! see the greatness of attachment, which has deluded the world? Smelling, seeing his own foul things, man has not lost interest in the body. What other cause for detachment can be pointed out to a man, who does not

1. Pañcagavya—The five products of the cow taken collectively: milk, curds, clarified butter or ghee, urine and cowdung.

become detached by the odour of his body? The entire world is pure, but the body is highly impure, by the touch of the dirty parts of which even a pure (object) would become impure. The cleansing of the body is said to be (i.e. recommended) for removing the application of sandal paste. When both (the sandal and the dirt) are removed, (a man) becomes pure by the purification of his thoughts.

83b-93a. This mortal, foul-smelling body, impure in thoughts, does not become pure with all the water of the Ganges and with besmearing the body with a large quantity of clay. The wicked heart is not purified by baths at holy places and austerities. The body of a man, whose mind is impure, does not become pure even though washed at a holy place or even after entering fire. There is neither heaven for him, nor hell (also). (The) best thing is burning the body. Purification of mind is the greatest purification, and is the main thing in all acts. A beloved (wife) is embraced with one thought, a daughter with another. The attitude varies even in the case of things that are not separate. A chaste woman would think about her son in one way, and about her husband in another way. In this way, O magnanimous one, the (variety) of nature is explained, since even though embraced by his wife, he should not make her void of thoughts. A man would not eat various kinds of food, so also fragrant tasty things, without interest. Therefore thought (or interest) is the cause everywhere (i.e. in all one's dealings). With effort purify your mind; what is the use of other external purifications? The soul, pure due to pure thoughts, obtains (i.e. goes to) heaven and salvation. The smearing with the excrement and urine of ignorance and attachment would perish (i.e. be removed) by means of purifiers (like) the spotless water of knowledge and the clay of detachment. Thus they know this body to be impure by its (very) nature. One should know it to be worthless and useless, like the essence of a plantain-tree.

93b-102a. He, who, knowing the body to be full of blemishes like this, becomes relaxed, crosses the worldly existence, and remains with (i.e. has) a firm conviction. Thus the affliction due to birth is said to be very painful. That sense which the human being has, due to the fault of ignorance, and due to various kinds of deeds, perishes when he is born. Feverish heat is produced in the case of human beings, when a human being is afflicted by being painfully pressed by the thong of the womb, and by the fearful external air due to his contact with delusion. Due to that feverish heat great delusion is caused. Then in the case of the deluded one, loss of memory takes place quickly. In the case of that being, attachment is produced during that existence only, due to the loss of his memory and due to his former deeds. The world (i.e. people) being attached and deluded, proceeds (proceed) to do what ought not to be done. They do not know themselves, nor do they know the highest deity. They do not listen to the (advice relating to) highest good, nor, though having eyes, do they see, like a person, tumbling at every step, even though walking slowly along an even path. Though they have intelligence, and though they are advised by the wise, they do not realise (the truth). Due to that a man going after (i.e. led by) greed is afflicted in the worldly existence.

102b-128. In the absence of a text (about the description of the soul's existence in) the womb, Śiva has propounded a sacred text to tell the affliction of (the soul's existence in) it (and) leading to salvation. It is a great wonder that even when a man has known that (text propounded by) Śiva, he does not accomplish what is good for himself. Since the sense-organs and intellect are not (properly) developed, there is great affliction even in childhood. The blessed (child), though desiring to speak or to act, is not able to do so. Cutting of teeth is very painful, and there is affliction also due to unsteadiness, wind, various child-diseases and planets harming children. With his body surrounded (i.e. overcome) by thirst and hunger, (the child) sometimes stays (at one place and sometimes) moves. A child would indulge in eating excretion, urine etc, due to ignorance. The child suffers pain due to his ears being pierced, due to being beaten by the mother and the father, due to learning the letters (i.e. the alphabet) and due to punishment (given by) teachers and others. How can there be happiness in youth, (to a young man) the functions of whose organs of sense are deluded, who is troubled with the disease of lust and who is always afflicted with diseases? Due to jealousy there is great affliction. Affliction is caused by delusion. The attachment in an angry (young man) leads to unhappiness only. Troubled with the fire of passion he does not get sleep at night. How can there be happiness even by day due to the anxiety to get money? The drops of semen of a man with his body prostrated (over the bodies) of women, do not lead to happiness like drops due to (i.e. of) perspiration. They know that the pleasure obtained from (union with) women is the same as (obtained by one) being struck (i.e. bitten) by insects, or as of a helpless lepor due to the trouble caused by the fire of scratching. It should be known that the pleasure in (i.e. obtained from) women is like that which one feels due to anxiety about getting money; it is not at all different. The same is the pang of a mortal; without that joy is had by one's mind. Then it goes from one to another to whom it had gone before. Ultimately it is the same; it does not change. Who else is more insensible than one who, seeing his dear one that is thus affected by old age, or that is sick, or his own extraordinary child troubled by old age, is not detached? A being, though overcome with old age, is treated with contempt due to his weakness by his wicked servants. An old man is not able to achieve (the four goals viz.) righteousness, worldly prosperity, sensual enjoyments and salvation. Therefore while young one should practise piety. Inequality (i.e. disturbance) in wind, bile and phlegm etc. is called a disease. This body is (so) called due to the congregation of wind etc. Therefore one should know that this body of the soul is full of diseases. In addition to (diseases caused by) wind etc. the human being meets with many kinds of afflictions due to the diseases of the body. They can be known by oneself. What else should I tell? In this body remain one hundred one (kinds of) death. Among them one is united with Kāla (i.e. god of death). Others are adventitious. Those that are said to be adventitious, are alleviated by means of medicines, muttering of sacred hymns, sacrifices and gifts; but death brought about by Kāla cannot be stopped. Untimely death might not occur by eating poison, (yet) a man would not eat it without fear, for he is afraid of an untimely death. For human beings there are various gates (leading) to death like many diseases; so also animals like serpents; poisons and employment of magical spells for malevolent purposes. Even the physician of gods[1] himself cannot cure a man who is afflicted

1. Dhanvantari—Name of the physician of the gods said to have been produced at the churning of the ocean with a cup of nectar in his hand.

by all diseases and whose death is imminent. This cannot be otherwise. No medicine, no penance, no charity, not the mother, no relatives can protect a man who is afflicted with Kāla (i.e. death). With (the help of) the magnanimous souls, who are equipped with medicines supposed to prolong life and prevent old age, and with penance and muttering of sacred hymns, he would only have intermediate (temporary) peace; he would (certainly) meet with death.

129-151a. He, who dies, is born in the species of insects due to his acts; he sees (i.e. meets with) death as a result of (i.e. which is a) change of the body. That is said to be death. It is not a real (i.e. total) destruction. In this world there is no analogy for the grief which a being has in death when he has entered great darkness (i.e. hell) and when his vitals are being cut off. Being extremely afflicted, he/she cries 'O father, O mother, O husband'. The world is swallowed by death as a frog is by a serpent. He is abandoned by kinsmen and is surrounded by his dear ones. Rolling on a bedstead and heaving deep and hot sighs, he, with his mouth parched, again and again faints. Being in a swoon, he throws his hands and feet here and there. From (i.e. when he is on) the bedstead he desires (to go to) the ground, and from (i.e. when he is on) the ground he again desires (to go to) the bedstead. He is helpless, is ashamed, is smeared with excretion and urine; he asks for water; his throat, lips and palate are dry; thinking about his wealth (as) 'to whom will it belong when I die?', being taken by the messengers of Yama and being dragged by the noose of (the god of) death, he dies, when (the relatives etc.) are watching. His throat makes a sound. Like a caterpillar the soul would enter (i.e. goes to) one after another body. He obtains the next body; he abandons the previous one. For the discriminating people, death is more painful than supplication. The grief in (i.e. due to) death is momentary, while in (i.e. due to) supplication it is unending. Viṣṇu, the lord of the worlds, became a dwarf through supplication. Who is greater than he who does not become mean (through supplication)? I have now understood this as to when one becomes superior to death. One should not repeatedly solicit another (man). Thirst (i.e. desire) is the cause of meanness. There is grief in the beginning, there is also grief in the middle; at the end there is terrible grief, due to nature (i.e. this is natural). Thus there is a series of griefs for beings. A man should not lament over these griefs for beings, which are present and which have gone by. Due to (even) that (i.e. these griefs) (a man) is not detached from existence. There is a great grief due to excessive eating; then there is grief due to eating less. While eating the throat breaks; (so) wherefrom is there pleasure from eating? Hunger is said to be the greatest disease of all the diseases. It is temporarily alleviated due to the application of soothing medicines. The pang of the disease of hunger is acute, and it euts off the entire strength (of a man). Overpowered by that a man dies as he would die of other diseases. What delight is there in its relish that lingers on the tip of the tongue? In a moment—in half of that time—it reaches the throat and returns. Thus for those who are tormented by the disease of hunger food is said to be (working) like a medicine. Wise men should not look upon it as actually leading to pleasure. In the case of him also, who, without (doing) any work, lies like a dead body, and whose mind is impelled by ignorance, wherefrom can there be pleasure? Wherefrom can there be happiness in the case of him whose mind is affected in (i.e. while performing) deeds, though he has knowledge? Beings though content, are troubled due to optional (deeds) by exertion in agriculture, trade, service, animal husbandry etc. and by (passing) urine and excretion in the morning, and by hunger and thirst in the noon, and by sleep at night.

151b-163. There is grief in earning money; there is grief in preserving what is earned. There is grief when wealth perishes; there is grief in spending it. Wherefrom (i.e. how) can there be happiness from wealth? As there is fear from death in the case of (i.e. to) men, similarly there is always fear to the wealthy persons from thieves, water, fire, their kinsmen, and even from the king. A wealthy person is everywhere eaten up (i.e. robbed) as flesh is eaten by birds in the sky, by wild beasts on the earth, and by fish in water. Wealth deludes a man in prosperity, keeps him away (from joy) in calamity, is painful when it is earned. (Then) when does it bring happiness? First (consider) a wealthy person; he is (always) sad; then (consider) one who is free from desire for all objects. Between the two, I think the wealthy person is unhappy, and the one, whose mind is detached, is happy. Due to heat there is suffering in the spring and summer seasons; in the rainy season there is suffering due to (stormy) wind, heat and showers. Thus wherefrom (can one get) happiness? There is suffering in the (so-called) glory of marriage; again there is suffering in pregnancy. There is suffering due to the difficulty in delivery, and also due to the acts like those of excretion etc. (In the same way) there is suffering due to the son suffering from diseases of teeth and eyes. (Then one says:) 'Alas! What shall I do (now)? My cows have perished; my husband has broken down; my wife has run away. These guests, indicating fear, have come to my house. My wife has a young child. Who will do the cooking? What kind of bridegroom will be (obtained) by my daughter at the time of her marriage?' How can there be happiness to householders who are overcome by this anxiety? The knowledge, (good) character, all virtues of a man distressed by the anxiety of the family, perish along with his body, like water put in an unbaked jar. Wherefrom can there be pleasure in (i.e. from) a kingdom due to (i.e. as there is) anxiety of peace and war? There is fear even from the son (to a king); (then) what kind of happiness is there?

164-173. Generally all beings have fear from (members of) their own species, as dogs have fear from one another, as all of them desire to have the same object. There is no king on the earth, who, having abandoned everything, has entered a forest and remained there happy and fearless. The brave son (viz. Paraśurāma) of the sage (viz. Jamadagni) knocked down on the ground the thousand arms of the famous Kārtavīrya in a battle. Rāma, the son of Daśaratha, destroyed the matchless, rising valour of the very magnanimous son of the sage (viz. Jamadagni). The glory of Rāma (i.e. Balarāma) was destroyed, with his splendour, by Jarāsandha. The glory of Jarāsandha was destroyed by Bhīma, and his glory too by (Hanumān) the son of Wind. Hanumān too, being tossed by the Sun, fell on the ground. The glorious Arjuna killed all the demons—the Nivātakavacas—who were proud of their strength. He (too) was vanquished by the cowherds. At times even the sun, full of glowing heat is screened by clouds. A cloud is tossed by wind, and the power of wind is vanquished by the mountains. The mountains are burnt by fire, and that fire is extinguished by water. That water is dried up by the suns; (and) all those suns, along with water and the three worlds, perish on (i.e. at the end of) Brahmā's day. Brahmā too, at the end of the period of two Parārdhas, is withdrawn along with the gods, by Śiva, the highest lord.

174-198a. Thus, in this worldly existence, there is no best power, excepting the highest soul, the immutable lord of the world. Realising that everything has a superior (object), one should avoid great pride. When the world is like this, who is a god, or who is even a learned man? There is no one (in the world) who is omniscient, or who is a total fool? A man is learned there (i.e. in a particular field) to that extent to which he knows it. By deep thinking, (it is found that) the power (of men) everywhere is similar. Someone has power in some field due to excess of wealth. Gods were vanquished by demons, and they were again (i.e. in their turn) vanquished by gods. Thus the beings in the world are dependent on one another through good fortune, success and defeat. Thus (even) for kings a pair of garments and water and food of the measure of a prastha, a vehicle, a bed and a seat (are enough). All the rest just leads to misery. He can even have a bedstead on the seventh floor; (but) there is the painful glory (of being consecrated by the water) from a thousand pitchers of water. In the early morning there is the sound of the musical instruments along with (that of) the citizens. There is just that pride in (i.e. due to) a kingdom, viz. 'This (musical instrument) is being beaten in my house.' All ornaments are (but) a burden; all anointing is dirt (only); all songs are (just) a prattle; dancing is (nothing but) the movement of a mad person. This (is the fruit) due to the enjoyments (obtained from) a kingdom. On reflection (one would see): 'wherefrom (i.e. how) is happiness (obtained?)'. Kings have anxiety about war (with one another) or due to the desire of conquering one another. Mostly great kings like Nahuṣa have fallen after reaching heaven due to the pride of wealth. Who gets happiness from wealth? Even in heaven, how can there be happiness when gods have observed the bright glory of other (gods) which remains more prominently in one than in another? When the foundation (of all ill acts) is cut off, men enjoy the fruit of their merit in heaven. Here the very terrible blemish is that no other act is performed. As a tree, with its roots cut off, falls on the ground after (a few) days, similarly the residents of heaven fall down due to the exhaustion of their religious merit. All of a sudden calamity befalls those who strongly desire happiness through the boats of enjoyment of pleasures etc. There is misery for the gods in heaven. Thus on reflection (it is seen) that even in heaven gods do not have happiness. When the objects of senses are not obtained, there is the exhaustion of the acts that lead to enjoyment in heaven. In the fires of hell there is a great affliction to the beings, due to various terrible objects produced from speech, mind and body. There is a severe cutting with axes; and the chopping off of the bark-garments. There is the fall of leaves, branches and fruits (caused) by terrible wind. There is suffering among the immobile species due to being uprooted by rivers, elephants and by other beings, and also by wild fire, snow and dryness. There is a terrible pain in (i.e. due to) the anger of snakes and serpents. In the world the wicked are killed, and are bound down with fetters. Repeatedly there are sudden birth and death in the case of insects and also (in the case of those) belonging to the class of reptiles. Thus there are many kinds of miseries. The beasts end themselves and are beaten with sticks. They are troubled due to their noses being pierced and are beaten with a whip. They are fettered with canes, wood, goad etc. Service causes affliction to the mind; the young etc. are troubled. Due to separation from their herds, and their eyes being tied (i.e. covered), beasts have thus many kinds of afflictions. Sharks and birds have a great affliction due to rain, cold and heat.

198b-210. Thus there are many kinds of afflictions for bodies. For men there is a great affliction while living in the womb, and also great affliction of (i.e. during) birth. Ignorance is a great affliction of childhood; in adolescence there is (the affliction of) the punishment by a teacher. There is affliction in youth due to lust and attachment, and due to jealousy; and also due to agriculture, trade, service etc., and acts like protection of the cattle. In old age (there is affliction) due to aging and diseases. There is great affliction in (i.e. at the time of) death; still greater (is the affliction) in solicitation. There is a great fear from the king, fire, strokes by clouds (like lightning), thieves and enemies. There is again a great fear in earning and preserving money and its destruction and spending. Miserliness, jealousy, and arrogance are greatly fearful results of the excess of wealth (i.e. when there is excessive wealth). There is a tendency for doing misdeeds. These are always the afflictions of the wealthy. (There are afflictions like) servitude, usury, slavery, dependence on others, connection with the desirable and undesirable, and many kinds of unions. (There are calamities like) famine, misfortune, folly, poverty, enjoying lower or higher (position), (going) to hell, and being overpowered by the king. There is affliction due to mutual subjugation. There is a great fear from one another; there is a great wrath towards one another; and a king has (to suffer) affliction from (other) kings. Here (i.e. in this world) the objects are transient, (so also) of a human being whose desires are satisfied. (There is affliction) due to the cutting of the vitals of one another, and due to the squeezing of the hands of one another. The greedy ones due to sin (indulge in) consuming one another. Since the mobile and the immobile (beings) beginning with (denizens of) hell and ending with human beings, are afraid of such and other afflictions, therefore a wise man should abandon everything. As when a burden is shifted from one shoulder to another it is regarded as rest, similarly in this world one grief is alleviated by another. The boats of enjoyment always excel one another.

211-225. Misery has settled with gods in the heaven due to the exhaustion of their religious merit. Due to the exhaustion of religious merit there is birth (i.e. a soul is born) in many species. Even in the world of gods there are said to be diseases of various forms. The head of Sacrifice was cut off; and it was rejoined by the Aśvins. Due to that defect the Sacrifice always has (i.e. suffers from) the disease of the head. The Sun has (i.e. suffers from) leprosy and Varuṇa has (i.e. suffers from) dropsy. Pūṣan has defect in his teeth, and Indra has (i.e. suffers from) stiffness of arms. Soma is known to have been suffering from a very severe disease of consumption. Even Dakṣa, the lord of created beings, suffers from acute fever. In every Kalpa even great gods perish. Even Brahmā becomes unstable after a period of two parārdhas. Brahmā again longed for his granddaughter, the daughter of Dakṣa. The lord angrily cursed goddess Jayā, who knew deep, abstract meditation. The defects of the nature of (i.e. due to) lust and anger remain there, where the two remain. (Thus) all miseries are stable. There is no doubt about it. The fire consumes everything shattered by birth and death. (Kṛṣṇa or Viṣṇu) murdered a woman, was lustful, and acted as a charioteer in the Pāṇḍava army. Rudra burnt the three cities (of Maya), and destroyed Dakṣa's sacrifice. The birth of Skanda is from the semen from (i.e. discharged during) sports in thousand ways. Thus all the three gods possess the faults like attachment. The lord superior to these is tranquil, perfect and giver of salvation. Thus the entire world lives on the excellence of one (over) another. One should go to (i.e. have) disgust, knowing that (the world) is full of miseries. From disgust there would arise detachment, and knowledge springs from detachment. Through knowledge one would get that highest propitious knowledge (and) salvation. He then is happy with his mind at ease (since he is) freed from all miseries. He who is omniscient, and perfect is called (a) free (soul).

Mātali said :

I have told you all that you had asked about. The discrimination between merit and demerit is due to omniscience. You should go to Indra's heaven at his bidding.

CHAPTER SIXTYSEVEN

Mātali on Three Kinds of Sin

Yayāti said :

1-2. O you charioteer of Indra, due to my good luck I have been able to see you. This gives me immense merit. Even in the mortal world human beings commit a terrible sin. O Mātali, now tell me about the ripening of their actions.

Mātali said :

3-12. Listen, I shall tell (you) the characteristics of a sinful behaviour. In this world great knowledge is produced when (things) are heard. People condemn the Vedas and censure brāhmaṇic practices. Those who are learned should also know what great sin is. He who causes harm to all the good persons (has committed) a major sin. It would go (i.e. its effect would be nullified only) by expiation. People give up the customs peculiar to their own family and practise those of others. Those who know what should be done (i.e. what is proper) have described this to be a major sin. Reviling one's mother and father, beating one's sisters, and abusing one's father's sister is certainly a sin. The dead ancestors of him, who, when the time for offering a śrāddha has come, proceeds (to offer the śrāddha and) feeds someone else through lust or anger or fear, ignoring his son-in-law living at a distance of five kośas, his daughter's son, his own sister and her son, do not enjoy (the oblations offered by him), nor do the gods enjoy (the offerings made to them). This sin, committed by him, is equal to patricide. When the time for giving gifts has come, and when a brāhmaṇa (-group) has come, he avoids giving gifts to many, and gives them (only) to a few. That a gift is given to one, and no gift is given to another, is also a terrible sin, and is said to destroy (the merit acquired from) gifts.

13-23a. That is not a distinctive mark of a gift which is given (to someone else) ignoring his own brāhmaṇas employed by the patron. O king, a (patron) should well nourish, with all means and good gifts, that brāhmaṇa of a religious conduct who has resorted to him. He should not consider whether he is a foolish or a learned brāhmaṇa. A brāhmaṇa is always to be fed. He should always worship a learned brāhmaṇa endowed with all religious merit, who has come to him, after honouring him with good gifts. There is no doubt that the gifts which he would give to some other brāhmaṇa by ignoring that (learned brāhmaṇa) or the offerings that he would make, would be fruitless. On all auspicious occasions a brāhmaṇa, a kṣatriya, a vaiśya and a śūdra as the fourth should worship a brāhmaṇa that has sought their shelter—whether he is a fool or a learned brāhmaṇa. Listen (I will tell you) the meritorious fruit of it. He obtains the fruit of a horse-sacrifice. O king, what is the reason for which (i.e. there is no reason why) he should not get done what is possible? If another brāhmaṇa comes at that time when the śrāddha-rite is going on, he should then honour both the brāhmaṇas by giving them food, shelter, tāmbūla and presents. (If he does this) his dead ancestors are pleased. One should always give gifts and make presents to (a brāhmaṇa) who has eaten at a śrāddha. The sin of that performer of a śrāddha who does not give gifts would be equal to that due to the killing of a cow. Therefore, O best king, these two should be honoured with faith. Or if he is poor he should honour one (of the two).

23b-30. Thus men belonging to the three castes such as brāhmaṇa etc. should perform a śrāddha on the day of a great calamity, or when the astronomical division of time called vaidhṛti has come, or on a new-moon day, or a day between two sunrises in the next half. O great king, he should employ priests officiating at sacrifices. In the same way he should always employ brāhmaṇas for offering a śrāddha. A wise man should never employ an unknown brāhmaṇa. He should invite that brāhmaṇa whose family up to the third (previous) generation from him is known and whose conduct is known, O king. He should consider the conduct of a brāhmaṇa whose family is not known. When the śrāddha-offering is to be made, it may not be known whether a brāhmaṇa is pure or foolish, or is one who has mastered the Vedas and the Vedāṅgas. A śrāddha-offering ought to be done; so he should invite a brāhmaṇa (for that); O best king, first hospitable reception should be given (to him). If a sinful (host) does otherwise he certainly goes to hell. Therefore a brāhmaṇa should be engaged at a presentation of gifts or a śrāddha on the parvan-days.

31-33. At the time of presentation of gifts or a śrāddha, he should engage a brāhmaṇa after examining him. In his house the dead ancestors do not eat without a brāhmaṇa. They go away after cursing (him who offers the śrāddha) from a śrāddha (performed) without a brāhmaṇa. He (who offers such a śrāddha) is a great sinner even if he resembles Brahmā. O king, he who lives by abandoning the performance (of rites) to the dead ancestors, should be known to be a great sinner to be excommunicated.

34-39. Those who give up auspicious practices relating to Viṣṇu and giving (i.e. bringing) enjoyments, and who condemn the brāhmaṇic way of conduct should be known as men of increasing sins. Those, who give up auspicious practices (or practices relating to Śiva), who hate the devotees of Śiva, who, the sinners, abuse Hari (i.e. Viṣṇu), who always hate Brahmā (or brāhmaṇas), who condemn the (religious) practices, are the greatest sinners. I shall now tell (you) about the religious merit of those who worship the first, venerable, the highest knowledge, the meritorious Bhāgavata and (other Purāṇas like) Viṣṇu, Harivaṁśa, Matsya or Padma. He (i.e. such a person) has actually worshipped god Viṣṇu. Therefore one should worship the knowledge, contained in the Viṣṇu (Purāṇa), (and) dear to Viṣṇu. O king, there is always (kept) a book (i.e. a copy) of the Viṣṇu (Purāṇa). When it is worshipped, Lakṣmī's lord (i.e. Viṣṇu) is worshipped.

40-58. Those who, without worshipping (the Purāṇa containing) knowledge about Hari, sing or write, or without knowing it, present it, or listen to or recite it, or sell it through greed and devotion to bad (i.e. wrong) knowledge, or place it, as they will, at places that are not purified, or one who would declare it explicitly in accordance with (i.e. helping) his welfare, or he who, being capable, commits mistakes after having studied it, or he who being impure explains or listens to it at an impure place (all these condemn knowledge). This, in brief, is said to be the condemnation of knowledge. I (shall now) tell (you) about the sin of him who, the sinful one, desires to learn sacred texts without worshipping his preceptor, who does not render service (to his preceptor and) deliberately disobeys him, (and who) does not approve of the words (of the preceptor), does not respond to him, ignores when (some) work of the preceptor is to be done, (and he, who) abandons his preceptor who is afflicted and weak, or is proceeding to a foreign country or has been humiliated by adversaries or while he is reciting a Purāṇa. Till (the period during which) fourteen Indras have ruled, he would live in (the hell called) Kumbhīpāka. Also one who, of a sinful mind, ignores his preceptor reading the Purāṇa, has (committed) a terrible sin, giving (i.e. taking him to) hell. Also the sin (of him) who condemns his wife, sons and friends is as great as (that of) the condemnation of one's preceptor. One who kills a brāhmaṇa, one who steals gold, one who drinks liquor, one who violates his teacher's bed (i.e. his teacher's wife)—all these are great sinners; so also the one who joins (i.e. abets) them. He, who very much cuts the vitals especially of a brāhmaṇa through anger, hatred or greed, is declared to be the killer of a brāhmaṇa. O king, he also is the killer of a brāhmaṇa, who, having invited a poor, soliciting brāhmaṇa, says 'no' (i.e. refuses to give any gift) to him. He is declared to be killer of a brāhmaṇa, who, due to the pride of his own knowledge, renders lustreless (i.e. humiliates) a neutral brāhmaṇa in an assembly. He is said to be the killer of a brāhmaṇa, who elevates himself by means of pretended virtues, and who opposes his preceptor. They call him to be the killer of a brāhmaṇa, who creates an obstacle to them, who, with their bodies tormented by hunger and thirst, seek food or meal. He also is said to be the killer of a brāhmaṇa, who, a wicked one, is intent upon finding out the weak points of all the people, who causes torture and is cruel. They call him the killer of a brāhmaṇa, who would snatch back the land, though destroyed, in course of time, which was formerly given to a deity, a brāhmaṇa, or cows. That sin of taking away the wealth of a brāhmaṇa obtained as (i.e. which was put as) a deposit should be known to be as great as that of killing a brāhmaṇa.

59-66. He who gives up making an oblation to the fire in the rite of the five daily sacrifices; he who stands as a false witness against his mother, father and preceptor (is, a great sinner). (This sin and) eating what is not dear to Śiva's devotees and what ought not to be eaten, also killing innocent beasts in the forest, and setting fire to a cow-pen, a city or a village—all these are terrible sins equal to the sin (involved) in drinking liquor. Taking away all the possessions of a poor man, kidnapping another's wife, snatching elephants and horses, or cows, land, silver, garments, herbs and minerals, sandal, aloe wood, camphor, musk, woven silk, or taking away the deposits (made) by others is said to be like the stealing of gold. Not giving (in marriage) his marriageable daughter to a befitting groom, having an illicit connection with the wife of his son or friend or his own sister, fearful violating of a maiden, attachment to a śūdra-woman, cohabiting with a woman of the same caste is said to be like violating one's teacher's bed (i.e. teacher's wife). Those sins, which have been enumerated as sins, resemble major sins.

67-70. When a brāhmaṇa having promised money to a brāhmaṇa does not give it and forgets about it—that is equal to a minor sin. (Some other minor sins are:) snatching the wealth of a brāhmaṇa, crossing one's limit, too much pride, too much anger, hypocrisy, ingratitude, lust for someone other (than one's own wife), miserliness, wickedness, jealousy, sexual intercourse with the wife of someone else, violating a chaste maiden. The elder brother before whom his younger brother gets married, the younger brother married before the elder brother, the girl whom he marries (are sinners). (It is a sin) to offer a girl to them, or to act as a priest at sacrifices performed by them. (Other sins are:)

71-80. Abandoning one's son, friend, wife, also one's master when he is reduced to poverty, and one's wife and good people and ascetics; killing a cow, a kṣatriya, a vaiśya, a woman or a śūdra; destruction of a Śiva-temple, trees, and lovely groves. (He) who causes even a small damage to hermitages or harms the group of servents there, or the beasts (living there), or the grains or wild crops, or steals ploughs, corn or beasts, or acts as a priest at a sacrifice of those who do not deserve to perform a sacrifice (is a sinner). The sale of (the merit due to) a sacrifice, of a grove or a lake, one's wife and children, of (the merit of) pilgrimage, fasts, vows and (other) pious acts (is a sin). (They are sinners) who live by the wealth of women and he who lives for a large part on the affluence of a woman (are sinners). O prince, he who would sell off his own faith, and he who would praise unrighteousness, he who mentions the faults of others, he who observes the weak points of others, he who longs for other's wealth, he who (passionately) gazes on another's wife—all these should be looked upon as resembling the killers of cows. (He is a sinner) who condemns all sacred texts, who snatches a cow, who sells the beasts, who tells lies or listens to the lies (uttered) by others; (he is a sinner) who plots against his master, or preceptor, who is deceitful, who is fickle or wicked. (He is a sinner) who eats (alone) leaving his hungry wife, sons, friends, children, old people, weak and afflicted persons, and also servants, guests and relatives.

81-87a. Those who eat savory (food) and do not give it to him who desires it should be known as ones cooking separately (for themselves only) and such a person is condemned by the teachers of the Vedas. Those who take up restrictions and (later), with their organs of sense not conquered, give them up, and also those who have given up the life of a recluse, and those who are in the company of drunkards, and those who do not protect a cow that is afflicted with consumption or with thirst and hunger, are the killers of cows and are said to be hellish beings. Those who are engrossed (in committing) all (kinds of) sins, those who destroy the (grazing) field of the quadrupeds, or he who would beat (i.e. beats) saints, brāhmaṇas, preceptors or a cow, and also those who beat a faultless woman settled in a good position (i.e. behaving properly), and he, who, with his entire body bound with laziness, sleeps again and again; those who do not feed the weak or who do not look for the missing ones, or who trouble (the bullocks) by (putting) large burdens on them or drive them (even) when they are wounded are involved in (i.e. have committed) all (kinds of) sins. So also those who eat together (i.e. from the same plate).

87b-95a. Those men, who do not protect a cow with her limbs broken, and afflicted with wounds and (other) diseases and with hunger, are said to be hellish beings. Those men, who, the most sinful ones, strike the scrotum of bulls (i.e. castrate them), and also who harm cow's calves are beings living in a great (i.e. very painful) hell. Those (men) also, who do not honour a guest who has come to them with hope, and who is oppressed with hunger and exertion, go to hell. Those fools who do not show pity for a helpless, or maimed, or poor or young, or old or very much afflicted person, go to the ocean of (i.e. in the form of) hell. One who keeps goats, one who keeps buffaloes, one who is the husband of a śūdra or a barren woman, or a śūdra behaving like (i.e. following the profession of) a brāhmaṇa or a kṣatriya, also architects, artisans, physicians and devalakas,[1] and those who make their servants work hard, go to hell. He, who, having transgressed what is prescribed, would charge arbitrarily (more) tax, also he who would inflict punishment without a (proper) cause, would be roasted in hells. That king

1. Devalaka—A low brāhmaṇa who subsists upon the offerings made to an idol.

whose subjects are harassed by officials receiving bribes, by thieves in his kingdom, is roasted in hells.

95b-103a. There is no doubt that those brāhmaṇas who accept (gifts) from a king of a bad conduct also go to fearful hells. The king has (committed) that sin which is (committed) by men cohabiting with others' wives or by thieves. Being favoured by a king who does not protect, is fearful. That king, who, without thinking (properly), behaves with a person, who is not a thief, as (he would behave) with a thief, or who behaves with a thief, as he would behave with one who is not a thief, would also go to hell. Men (go to hell, who) through greed, snatch such objects as ghee, oil, food, drink, honey, flesh, wine or (any other) spirituous liquor, jaggery, sugarcane, vegetables, curd, roots and fruits, grass, wood, flowers, leaves, vessels of bell-metal, shoes, umbrella, bracelet, palanquin, soft seat, copper, lead, tin, bell-metal, or conch etc. that has come up from water, musical instrument like a flute, domestic utensils, (garments made of) wool, cotton or silken garments, objects belonging to the place of assembly or temples, or cotton or fine garments. He, who would snatch these and other objects, even in a small quantity, would quickly go to hell.

103b-114. There is no doubt that a man who snatches other's possession even of the measure of a mustard (i.e. even the smallest possession), goes to hell. There is no doubt that a man who takes away a small or a big object of another person, loved by the latter, goes to hell. Due to these and other sins, a man, immediately after his departure, would get (back) his former form or his body to be struck (by Yama's servants). The embodied ones go to Yama's world by the order of Yama. They are very much pained when they are being taken by the very fierce messengers of Yama. Dharmarāja (i.e. Yama) is said to be the punisher, due to various sorts of severe corporcal punishments meted out by him, to gods, lower animals and men who are governed by unrighteousness. A preceptor is the punisher through expiations (i.e. who makes them undergo expiations) of those who are endowed with decent behaviour but have soiled themselves through an error. Yama is not seen by them (i.e. their cases are not decided by Yama). A king is said to be the ruler of those who violate others' wives, who are thieves and who do their transactions unjustly; and Dharmarāja is the ruler of those who have hidden themselves. Therefore, one should undergo expiation for the sin that one has committed. There is no destruction of (the acts whose fruits) one has not enjoyed (or suffered) even after crores of kalpas. For him, who himself commits a sin, or causes (someone else) to commit it, or approves of it, by means of body, mind or speech, the fruit is going down (to hell). In this way, the three kinds of sin have been explained (by me) in brief. Different courses (followed by) men committing sins are narrated. O king, I have told you in minute detail, the fruit of righteousness. O best of men, tell me, what else I should explain to you. I have told you about the fruit of unrighteousness. I (shall) tell you about the fruit of righteousness also.

115. Thus Mātali spoke to the king loved by all. The magnanimous one thus spoke on the topic of righteousness.

CHAPTER SIXTYEIGHT

The Fruit of Righteous Deeds

Yayāti said :

1. O charioteer, O lord, I have heard everything about the fruit of unrighteousness. Tell me also about the fruit of righteousness. I have a curiosity to hear it.

Mātali said :

2-12. These four kinds of all the embodied ones, being helpless, go to Yama's world which causes fear and which is terrible, due to their sins. All beings, that remain in the womb, that are born, and children, young men, middle-aged men, old men, men, women and eunuchs have to go (to Yama's world). There the auspicious or inauspicious fruit (of the deeds) of human beings is decided by all like impartial and omniscient Citragupta and others. There are no beings (in the world) that do not go to Yama's abode. (The fruit of) the deed done (by a being) has to be enjoyed as decided by them. Those men, who do auspicious deeds, who have soft hearts, who are endowed with pity, go to Yama's abode along a pleasing path. A man who would give (i.e. who gives) shoes, wood or sandals to brāhmaṇas, happily goes to Yama's abode in a great aeroplane. By giving umbrellas (as gifts to brāhmaṇa) human beings go (to Yama's abode). By giving a palanquin (as a gift to a brāhmaṇa) one would happily go (to Yama's abode) along a path in the sky. Those who give garments (as gifts to brāhmaṇas), go, wearing divine garments (to Yama's abode). By giving a palanquin (as a gift to a brāhmaṇa) one would happily go (to Yama's abode) in an aeroplane. By giving a comfortable seat (to a brāhmaṇa) (human beings) happily go to Yama's abode. One who has constructed groves would go happily (enjoying) very cool shadows. Those who give gardens (with trees full of) flowers go to Yama's abode in the Puṣpaka aeroplane. He, who builds a temple, or a hermitage for ascetics, or pavilions for the helpless, playfully goes, due to (having constructed) best dwellings (to Yama's abode). So also he, who worships deities, fire, preceptors, brāhmaṇas, and his father and mother, (playfully goes to Yama's abode).

13-17. All that, even though little, which is given with faith to helpless, virtuous brāhmaṇas obtains (i.e. secures for him) all the desired objects. The saints say that in the world gifts (should be given) at a śrāddha. It should be realized that whatever—even of the measure of that which remains on the tip of a hair—is given with faith (gives good fruit); I always rely upon the four recipients (at a śrāddha). Therefore (if) one always has faith, the fruit of faith would be (obtained) by him. O king, he, who gives dwellings to the virtuous (but) helpless brāhmaṇas, goes to the abode of the grandsire, which satisfies all his desires. O king, he who has given with faith, (something even) of the size of a cowrie to a brāhmaṇa, would be a divine guest, enhancing the glory of gods. Therefore, those, who have faith, should give (i.e. human beings should give with faith). There is certainly (obtained) the fruit of that.

CHAPTER SIXTYNINE

Righteous Acts Enjoined by Śiva (Śivadharmas)

Mātali said :

1-4. Acts of righteousness have been told by Śiva (in) the excellent scriptures of the Śiva cult. Due to the difference in the manner of performance of acts they should be known to be many. The ancient acts as (told) by Śiva are free from blemishes like harming (others), are without suffering and exertion, are beneficial to all beings, are pure, involve little effort and give great fruit. They have many branches, but resort to (i.e. are supported by) the root (in the form) of Śiva. They have good flowers like knowledge and meditation. Since they sustain Śiva and are supported by the sayings of Śiva, they that help (human beings) to cross the ocean of the worldly existence, are known to be acts (liked) by Śiva.

5. Thus the ten, viz. harmlessness, forbearance, truth, sense of shame, faith, control of senses, charity, sacrifice, penance and gifts, are the means of (acquiring) righteousness.

6. The acts which are laid down by Śiva, and which have obtained identity with Śiva, when performed singly or collectively result in one course only.

7-11a. As the earth is said to be a common place for all beings, in the same way the city of Śiva is (said be a common place) for all the devotees of Śiva. As here (i.e. on the earth) enjoyments for all beings are said to be abundant, in the same way they are said to be many in Śiva's city, due to the preeminence of various (kinds) of religious merit. As even the good or bad fruit (of their acts) is enjoyed by all human beings, the fruit of the acts (enjoined) by Śiva is religious merit. One gets excellent, good enjoyments in Śiva's city, especially according to his faith, in accordance with his religious merit. He gets an (excellent) place, his undisturbed enjoyments are comparable to final beatitude.

11b-13. Therefore, to win great enjoyments one should do great meritorious acts. There would be (i.e. he would have) supremacy (i.e. control) over his own enjoyments, which alone is honoured by best gods as superior to everything. Some men engrossed in the pursuit of knowledge become free there only. Others intent on enjoying pleasures again come back to the mundane existence.

14. Therefore, he who desires salvation should give up attachment to enjoyments. He, being detached, and with his mind and heart tranquil, would obtain the knowledge of Śiva.

15-17a. To them also, who have set their heart on the lord (i.e. Śiva), and who perform sacrifices through devotion to him, the lord gives positions according to their nature. To them also who, with their sins destroyed, worship Rudra (even) once, the lord gives enjoyments in the worlds of goblins. All beings die (as a result of being) tormented by the burden of grief.

17b-22a. He who gives food is said to be the giver of religious merit, the giver of life and the giver of everything. Therefore, by giving food, one would get the fruit of giving everything. He who gives food (would obtain) all the gems, enjoyments, women and vehicles that there are in the three worlds, and would get the entire fruit (of giving food) here (i.e. in this world) and in the next world. There is no doubt that half of the collection of the (deeds of) religious merit which one who is nourished by the food and drink of a giver has, goes to the giver of the food, and half to the one (i.e. the receiver of the food and drink) doing the meritorious acts. The body is a great means of piety, material welfare and salvation. It is maintained by means of food and drink. Therefore it is the means of (obtaining) everything. Food is actually the creator, it is Viṣṇu himself, Śiva himself. Therefore, a gift like that of food was never there, nor will ever be there.

22b-24a. Water is said to be the life of all the three worlds. Water is purifying, divine, pure and is the elixir for all. Especially in the world of the departed spirits these eight gifts are commended: food, drink, horse, cow, garment, bed, thread and seat.

24b-26a. Since due to (these) special gifts a man happily goes to the city of Dharmarāja (i.e. Yama), therefore one should perform acts of charity. O prince, those again who do cruel deeds and are bereft of (i.e. have not given) gifts, experience terrible grief in hell.

26b-33a. Similarly the givers of gifts enjoy pleasures (in heaven). Happiness would be (coming) to them whose minds are engrossed in doing the deeds enjoined on them. That city is full of innumerable, excellent, divine aeroplanes, fulfilling all desires, and serving beings. That is called Rudra's heaven; it is bright like the lustre of a thousand moons, or lustrous like the sun. It is endowed with all excellences. The city is said to belong to all Śiva-devotees, and also to the mobile and the immobile who die in the place sacred to Rudra. Even he who worships Śiva even for a day, goes to Śiva's place. What to speak of him who worships him many times! The followers and devotees of Viṣṇu, intent on meditating on Viṣṇu, also go to Vaikuṇṭha in the vicinity of the god who holds the disc. He, the righteous-minded one, who talks about (i.e. praises) Brahmā, goes to Brahmā's world. The doer of acts of religious merit goes to a holy world.

33b-39. Therefore, one, who has knowledge and a devoted mind, should oneself create in one's heart devotion for the lord (i.e. Śiva) or for Viṣṇu, O great king. With full consideration and taking into account the weak point of (one's) disposition, one would, in this way, through the grace of Viṣṇu, and in accordance with one's deeds, obtain a position suitable to one's disposition. Thus is said to be the great and excellent city of Śiva; it is said to be returning the human beings, intent on performing their deeds, to the world. Above the city of Śiva excellent heaven of Viṣṇu should be known (to exist). All men intent upon meditating on Viṣṇu, go (to it). Brāhmaṇas, best men of excellent character go to Brahmā's heaven. All the sacrificers, knowing the first principle, go to that city. Similarly, kṣatriyas who fight, go to Indra's heaven; and others who perform acts of religious merit, go to meritorious worlds.

CHAPTER SEVENTY

Sinners in Hell

Mātali said :

1. I shall (now) tell (you) about the very poignant and very terrible torture caused by Yama (which) all the cruel, sinful killers of brāhmaṇas experience.

2-10. Sometimes the sinful ones are roasted with the fire of dry cow-dung; sometimes they are eaten up by fierce lions, wolves, tigers, gad-flies and worms. Sometimes (they are eaten up) by great leeches, or by huge cobras, and by terrible flies or sometimes by serpents with strong poison. (Sometimes they are eaten up) by great intoxicated and torturing herds of elephants, (or) by great bulls with sharp horns, scratching the path, and by buffaloes with big horns harming the bodies of the wicked, and by fierce female goblins and by terrible demons. Mounted on a great balance and being tormented by very terrible diseases and being burnt in a wild fire, they go (to Yama). They are very speedily shaken by very violent wind, and are shattered all round by the shower of great (slabs of) stone, and by the terrible falls of meteors having a sound like that of thunderbolt. Being struck by the shower of burning charcoal they go (to Yama). Being filled (i.e. covered) with a great shower of dust, they go to Yama. Men who are sinful experience terrible pain. Thus, the most sinful ones, who commit sins, experience, due to their particular sin, hell, full of many tortures.

11. I have thus explained to you all the difference between merit and demerit. What other excellent branch of religious knowledge shall I explain to you?

CHAPTER SEVENTYONE

Identity of Brahmā, Viṣṇu and Śiva

Yayāti said :

1-2. The faith of me, to whom you have excellently explained everything about merit and demerit, has been all the more stimulated by it. Tell me the number said to be that of the gods staying in the (various) worlds (i.e. tell me about their position in the various worlds), O Mātali, and also (tell me that) by whose contact with religious merit and by whom it (i.e. that position) is reached.

Mātali said :

3-9. I shall explain to you the position of gods' worlds endowed with (obtained by?) deep abstract meditation (*yoga-yuktam*), and attained by penance, and giving pleasures and enjoyments. I shall (also) separately explain to you the capacity of merit; and also (describe) in (proper) sequence the nature of the worlds above. There the earthly power of the goblins is eight times. Therefore the power of the men who have recently gone (to Yama's world) is said to be equal to that. That of the demons is sixteen-fold, and like that is that of the kings. Thus whatever is left of the lustre of the family is complete. Gandharvas have (power) from the wind; that of the Yakṣas is said to be full. That of Indra is (derived from) the five elements, and it is forty times great. That of Soma is mental and divine, and that of the lord of the universe is (derived from) the five elements. That of the lords of the created beings has the properties of the moon and has egoism as an additional quality. That of Brahmā is sixtyfour-fold and the power of knowledge is excellent. The pre-eminent ritual of Viṣṇu is the power of Brahmā's position.

10-18a. In the divine city of Śiva there is affluence capable of satisfying all desires. The infinite supremacy of Śiva is great and self-eminent. It is without beginning, middle or end; its true characteristic is pure; it illumines everything; it is subtle; it has no match; it is higher than the highest; it is quite full, has the garb of the world; it abandons the noose for the souls. A man enjoys the pleasure belonging to the place which he has reached; and due to the grace of the lord, the aeroplane would be in accordance with it; various forms of the stars are seen; there are crores of these; to the meritorious twentyeight become bright (i.e. manifest). Those, who at times salute the lord, through association, curiosity or greed obtain that aeroplane. He who, through recital of (the lord's) name occasionally salutes Śiva, does not perish. These are thus the ways of rites pertaining to Śiva. Even through internal act (i.e. mentally) men (may salute the lord) through devotion for him. Those men who occasionally remember Śiva, would get incomparable happiness; what to say of those who are intensely devoted to him?

18b-26. With their minds gone to (i.e. set upon) him

through meditation, men reflected on Viṣṇu. They go to the highest place. That is the highest position of Viṣṇu. O king, the form of Śiva and that of Viṣṇu are identical. There is no difference between the glorious two, who are of the same form. (One can) salute Śiva of the form of Viṣṇu, and Viṣṇu of the form of Śiva. Viṣṇu is the heart of Śiva, and Śiva is the heart of Viṣṇu. The three gods Brahmā, Viṣṇu and Śiva are (just) one form. There is no distinction among the three, only the qualitative differences are narrated. O king, you are a devotee of Śiva, so also you are a follower of Viṣṇu. Therefore the three gods Brahmā, Viṣṇu and Maheśvara are pleased with you. O you of a good vow, they—the givers of boons—are very much pleased with your deeds. O you, who remove the pride (of your enemies), I have come in your vicinity (i.e. to you) by the order of Indra. (First) go to the position of Indra, then to that of Brahmā, and then to that of Śiva. Go to Viṣṇu's position, free from tormentation and destruction. (Go to these places) in divine aeroplane, going everywhere. Being of a divine form, and getting into the Puṣpaka, moving comfortably, enjoy divine, charming pleasures.

Sukarman said :

27. Mātali, having thus spoken to king Yayāti, the son of Nahuṣa, who knew the essence of religion, O best brāhmaṇa, became silent.

CHAPTER SEVENTYTWO

Yayāti's Reluctance to Part with the Body

Pippala said :

1-2. O you highly intelligent one, tell me in detail, what the king, the son of Nahuṣa said on hearing the words of Mātali. O wise one, this is an all-meritorious story which destroys sins. I desire to hear it. I am not at all being satisfied.

Sukarman said :

3. Yayāti, the best king, the greatest among those who practised piety, said to the messenger Mātali, Indra's charioteer, who had come (to him):

Yayāti said :

4-7. O messenger, I shall not abandon my body. There is no doubt that I shall not go to heaven without (this) earthly body. Though you have thus narrated the great blemishes of the body, and though you have already described all its merits and demerits, yet I shall not abandon my body, and I shall not come to heaven. Going to Indra, the lord of gods, tell him like this: "O you very intelligent one, a man does not obtain perfection by means of the soul alone or with only the body. This is the mundane (existence).

8-14a. Body cannot remain without life (i.e. the soul), nor can the soul remain without the body. O Indra, they have friendship (i.e. they are mutual friends). I shall not destroy the body due to whose grace the soul obtains exclusive happiness and other pleasures according to his mind (i.e. as he desires)." O messenger of gods, knowing the enjoyments in heaven to be like this, I do not want them. O Mātali, due to blemishes painful and very sinful disease are(contracted). Old age is due to a defect. Observe my body endowed with religious merit and sixteen years old. Since my birth my body has gone to (i.e. lasted for) half a century. Still there is freshness of my body (still my body is fresh). (This) period (i.e. life) of me has passed excellently. As the body of a youth of sixteen years looks handsome, in the same way my body endowed with power and valour looks.

14b-16. I do not have fatigue, I do not have failure, I do not have exhaustion; nor do I have (i.e. suffer from) diseases or old age. O Mātali, my body also thrives with enthusiasm for piety; for, in olden days, the medicine—the divine, great medicine, the elixir, all full of nectar is prepared for the destruction of sins and diseases. My body is purified by that; (therefore)it is free from blemishes.

17-24. O messenger, I am always doing (i.e. taking) the elixir, viz. the meditation on Viṣṇu and the excellent utterance of his name. By that all my diseases and blemishes like sins have been destroyed, when, in this worldly existence, there is the great (i.e. effective) medicine like the name of Kṛṣṇa (i.e. Viṣṇu). Human beings suffering from sinful disease die (since) the very foolish ones do not drink the elixir of the name of Kṛṣṇa (i.e. Viṣṇu). O Mātali, my body is healthy due to that meditation, knowledge, worship, truthfulness, and religious merit caused by giving gifts. Diseases and sufferings torment him whose accomplishment is sins. There is no doubt that beings die here (i.e. in this world) due to sufferings. Therefore men, resorting to merit and truthfulness, should perform religious acts. The body is made of the five elements, and is worn out by the veins and joints. As an ornament is (fashioned) by a goldsmith with borax, so a human being is put together. In it always shine a great fire, a moving humour of the body, which is (made) of a hundred pieces. O brāhmaṇa, he who joins (these pieces) is intelligent.

25-30a. O Pippala, all these pieces (of the body) of the nature of the five elements and worn out by a hundred joints, are held together by the divine name of Viṣṇu and good fortune. The body is like a metal. The body becomes new by offering worship to Viṣṇu, meditation and restraint, truthfulness and charity. O Mātali, listen, the blemishes of the body—the diseases—perish. There is external and internal purity, and there is no foul smell. Then, O charioteer, due to the grace of the disc-holder (i.e. Viṣṇu), (the body) would be pure. I shall not go to heaven. I shall fashion heaven here (only). I shall make the earth of the nature of heaven by means of (my) penance, devotion, my own religious acts, and the grace of the disc-holder. Realising this, you (may please) go and tell Indra.

Sukarman said :

30b-32. Then, that charioteer, having heard the words of the king and having congratulated him with blessing, took the king's leave, and went (to heaven). He told everything to the noble Indra. Indra, having heard (the message) of the magnanimous Yayāti, thought as to how to bring Yayāti to heaven.

CHAPTER SEVENTYTHREE

The Efficacy of Viṣṇu's Name

Pippala said :

1. When that illustrious messenger had left (for heaven), what did that religious-minded Yayāti, the son of Nahuṣa, do?

Sukarman said :

2-7. When that messenger of the best god (i.e. Indra) had left, the son of king (Nahuṣa) thought (to himself). Having immediately called his excellent messengers, he instructed them with words of propriety: "The excellent messengers should go to an excellent city, to all regions and islands in the world. They should carry out my words (i.e. order) which is full of virtue. May people go along the good path of Viṣṇu, by means of devotional and very meritorious (acts), meditations resembling nectar, knowledge, sacrifices and austerities. Abandoning the worldly objects of sense, may they worship Viṣṇu alone with sacrifices and gifts. May they see only the enemy of the demons and of the nature of the soul everywhere—at dry places, wet and immobile places, in the clouds, on the earth, in mobile and immobile (objects) and even in their own bodies. With hospitality and rites in honour of their dead ancestors may they offer gifts dedicating them to that god. May they offer sacrifices to that best god Nārāyaṇa (i.e. Viṣṇu); you (i.e. they) will soon be free from blemishes. That shameless man who through greed or folly would not obey these words of me right now, would certainly be punished like a vile thief."

8. Having heard the words of the king, the messengers, with their minds delighted, (moved over) the entire earth, and made the order given by the king known among all the subjects.

9-16. "O mortals, brāhmaṇas and others, the king has brought on the earth the very meritorious nectar. Drink that meritorious (nectar) called Vaiṣṇava, free from blemishes and of a desirable effect. The king has already brought (to the earth) the nectar, removing blemishes, in the form of the name Śrī Keśava, which removes suffering, which is desirable, which is of the form of joy, and which itself is the highest truth. May people drink it. The good king has already brought (to the earth) the nectar, removing blemishes, in the form of the name of him, holding a sword in his hand, called Madhusūdana, the abode of Lakṣmī, and the meritorious lord of the gods. May people drink it. The good king has already brought (to the earth) nectar, removing blemishes, in the form of the name Śrī Padmanābha, of lotus-like eyes, the prop of the worlds, and the great lord. May the people drink it. The good king has already brought the nectar, removing blemishes, in the form of (Viṣṇu's) name, which destroys sins, which removes diseases, which gives joy, which destroys the dānavas and daityas (i.e. the demons). May people drink it. The good king has already brought the nectar, removing blemishes, in the form of the name Viṣṇu of the nature of sacrificial requisites, with a disc in his hand, the mine of religious merit, and of infinite happiness. May people drink it. The king has already brought the nectar, removing blemishes, in the form of the name of Viṣṇu, the abode of everything, pure, the end (of everything), named Rāma, the pleasing, and the enemy of Mura. May people drink it. The good king has already brought the nectar, removing blemishes, in the form of the name of (Viṣṇu), of the form of the sun, the destroyer of darkness, the destroyer of the bond of the lotuses in the form of minds. May people drink it.

17. He, the noble one, Viṣṇu's devotee, having restrained himself, studies (i.e. recites) this truthful, very meritorious nectar of (Viṣṇu's) name, goes to salvation. There is no (other) agent (than it)."

CHAPTER SEVENTYFOUR

Popularity of Viṣṇu Cult during Yayāti's Rule

Sukarman said :

1-2. All the messengers said (i.e. proclaimed) in the islands, regions and cities: "O people, listen to the command of the king. With all their glory may they worship Viṣṇu. May people with (devoted) minds desiring merit, reflect on Viṣṇu, by means of many gifts, sacrifices, austerities, and sacrificial rites." Such is the order of that king.

3-5. The people heard all these meritorious (words) thus well-proclaimed on the earth (by the messengers). Since then only the human beings sacrificed (in honour of) Viṣṇu, reflected on him, sang (in praise of) him, and muttered (prayers to him). All human beings, giving up the blemishes due to their bodies, minds and speech, by means of vows, fasts, restraints and gifts, and with their hearts gone to (i.e. set upon) him, worship that Śrī Keśava, Śrī Vāsudeva, the abode of Lakṣmī, and the habitation of the worlds, with well-recited, very meritorious and nectar-like hymns taught by the Vedas and with eulogies.

6-11. Thus prevails the order of that king on the globe. All those people are victorious due to their devotion to Viṣṇu. Those who are well-versed in knowledge, and who meditate and reflect on him and who are intent on worshipping him, adore Viṣṇu with (i.e. by reciting his) names and their deeds. As long as the globe lasts and the sun shines all human beings were (i.e. would continue to be) the followers of Bhagavān (Viṣṇu). Then the human beings, due to the power of meditation on Viṣṇu, due to his worship and (recital of) his eulogy and (his) names, became free from mental agonies and physical diseases. O brāhmaṇa, due to the grace of the disc-holder (i.e. Viṣṇu) all the devotees of Viṣṇu became free from grief, became meritorious and had penance as their wealth. They were free from diseases, were without blemishes or wrath; they were endowed with all (kinds of) splendour, and free from all maladies.

12-27. Due to the grace of that god, all men at that time became immortal, ageless and all were endowed with wealth and grains. The mortals were adorned with sons and grandsons by the favour of Viṣṇu. O you noble one, in the (regions near) the doors of their houses only there always were meritorious desire-yielding trees, which yielded the fruits of all their desires, and also all-desire-yielding cows, which satisfied all desires. By the favour of Viṣṇu only all men became immortal, were adorned with sons and grandsons and were free from all blemishes. They were endowed with good fortune and with merit and auspiciousness. They were very meritorious, were endowed with charity and were intent on knowledge and meditation. When that king Yayāti, who knew what was right, was ruling, there was no famine, no disease, and no premature death among human beings. All men were the devotees of Viṣṇu, all were intent upon (observing) the vow of (i.e. sacred to) Viṣṇu. They meditated on him, were devoted to him, and had their hearts set on him. O best brāhmaṇa, their divine and auspicious houses were furnished with white banners and with conches, and had their flags marked with maces and were marked with discs. The houses marked with lotuses and with the walls well-painted with good pictures resembled divine cars. O best ones, everywhere—near the doors of the houses and at holy places there were divine thickets of trees and auspicious grassy spots. O best brāhmaṇa, due to Tulasī and temples of Viṣṇu the auspicious and divine houses of (human) beings always shone. Everywhere meritorious devotion to Viṣṇu was seen to a great extent. O friend, O best brāhmaṇa, there on the earth the sounds of conches due to sounds (produced) by mutual crashing and destroying sin were heard. O best brāhmaṇa, through devotion for Viṣṇu women had drawn (the pictures of) conches, svastikas, lotuses on the doors of houses; and with music, songs, good words, regulated rise or fall of sounds through the musical scale people intent upon the meditation of Viṣṇu sing (in praise of) Viṣṇu.

28-29. They talk affectionately about Hari, Murāri, others about Keśava, Ajita, Mādhava,. They mutter the names of Viṣṇu, the refuge, (like) the lotus-eyed Govinda, the lord of Kamalā (i.e. Lakṣmī), Kṛṣṇa and Rāma, and worship with muttering (his names). Those great devotees of Viṣṇu, engaged in meditation on him salute him by fully prostrating themselves before him.

CHAPTER SEVENTYFIVE

Yayāti's Subjects became Deathless by the Grace of Viṣṇu

Sukarman said :

1-6. All men, children, old people, unmarried girls always uttered names (i.e. recited the various names of Viṣṇu like) Viṣṇu,

Kṛṣṇa, Hari, Rāma, Mukunda, Madhusūdana, Nārāyaṇa of the form of Viṣṇu, Narasiṁha, Acyuta, Keśava, Padmanābha, Vāsudeva, Vāmana, Varāha, Kamaṭha, Matsya, Hṛṣīkeśa, Surādhipa, Viśveśa, Viśvarūpa, Ananta, Anagha, Śuci, Puruṣa, Puṣkarākṣa, Śrīdhara, Śrīpati, Hari, Śrīnivāsa, Pītavāsa (i.e. clad in a yellow garment), Mādhava, Mokṣada (i.e. giver of salvation) and Prabhu. Women, engaged in domestic work always profusely sang (i.e. recited the names of) Hari, Mādhava, (so also when they were seated) on a seat, (when they were lying) in bed, (while they were going) in a vehicle and in meditation. Similarly children (while) playing saluted Govinda (i.e. Viṣṇu).

7-16. Day and night they uttered the very sweet name of Viṣṇu. O best brāhmaṇa, everywhere the utterance (of the name) of Viṣṇu was heard. Human beings lived on the earth (only) through the power of Viṣṇu. Discs (of Viṣṇu) shone as the (reflections of the) discs of the sun shine on the tops of the pitchers of palaces and temples. That condition which was seen in Vaikuṇṭha was seen on the earth. That noble king, Nahuṣa's son Yayāti, performed (acts of) merit, and made the earth resemble Viṣṇu's heaven. The appearance of both the worlds (being similar) the earth had become one (with Viṣṇu's heaven). No difference between the earth and Viṣṇu's heaven was noticed. As the devotees of Viṣṇu uttered the names of Viṣṇu in Vaikuṇṭha, like that (i.e. in the same way) men uttered Viṣṇu's names on the earth. O brāhmaṇa, identity between the two worlds was noticed. There was no fear from old age and diseases. People were free from death. On the earth greater grandeur of charity and enjoyment was seen. O best one, men happily enjoyed greater pleasure of (i.e. from) sons and grandsons. All the human beings—Viṣṇu's devotees—were always free from all diseases due to the gift of Viṣṇu's grace (which they received) and his instruction.

17-20a. The king brought about the grandeur of heaven on the earth. O best king, the years were of the extent of twentyfive (i.e. were very long). All men were free from diseases and were intent upon (getting) knowledge and meditation. All men were solely absorbed in (performing) sacrifices, and (giving) gifts, and all were kind. They were engaged in obliging (others);

those meritorious men, repositories of fame, were blessed. O brāhmaṇa, all men were solely devoted to religion and were solely absorbed in meditation. Instructed by that king, they became devoted to Viṣṇu on the earth.

Viṣṇu said :

20b-28a. O best king, listen to the account of that king. That son of Nahuṣa was always absorbed in all (deeds of) merit and a devotee of Viṣṇu. In this way he passed a lakh of years on the earth. His body endowed with maturity, appeared to be twenty-five years old by means of his (handsome) form. Those men (i.e. his subjects), having resorted to (i.e. living on) the earth, do not at all go to Yama. O king, all people free from attachment and hatred, bereft of the noose of suffering, happy on account of the merit (obtained) by (giving) gifts, and solely devoted to all religious deeds, always expanded (i.e. their number grew) with regard to progeny also. As the dūrvā (grass) and the bunyan trees spread on the earth, in the same way all those men expanded (i.e. grew in number) by means of sons and grandsons. Those men, free from the blemish of death, lived long. All (those) men with strong bodies, free from old age and diseases and (therefore) happy, were seen to be twentyfive years old (i.e. very young) on the earth. All were devoted to good conduct and absorbed in meditation on Viṣṇu.

28b-34a. Thus all mortals—all human beings—had become solely devoted to (giving) gifts and enjoyments, due to the grace of that disc-holder (i.e. Viṣṇu). O best man, no human being was heard to be dead. They did not see (i.e. meet with) grief, nor did they go to (i.e. have) blemish. O best of men, due to the favour of that disc-holder, the nature of the world had become just like that which was the nature of heaven. The messengers of Yama, beaten by Viṣṇu's messengers, disappeared. All of them, weeping with one another, went to Dharmarāja (i.e. Yama). The messengers told (Yama) all that the king (i.e. Yayāti) had done. (They said to Yama): "O Sun's son, due to (giving of) gifts and enjoyment the earth has become deathless. O god, Yayāti, the son of Nahuṣa, did it. That meritorious devotee of Viṣṇu, demonstrated the nature of heaven (on the earth)."

34b-35. At that time Dharmarāja heard all this. Then Dharmarāja, having heard in detail the activities of the king, considered the entire fact.

CHAPTER SEVENTYSIX

Dharmarāja Rendered Jobless

Sukarman said :

1-4a. The son of the Sun (i.e. Yama) went with all his messengers to heaven to see there Indra, surrounded by groups of gods. Then that king of gods (i.e. Indra) saw Dharmarāja in his assembly. Quickly getting up he presented excellent respectful offering to him, and asked him (the reason for) his arrival (saying:) "Tell me (why you have come)." Hearing the weighty words uttered by the king of gods, Dharmarāja narrated (to him) all the great account of Yayāti.

Dharmarāja said :

4b-11. O lord of gods, listen what for I have come. I will here only (i.e. just now) tell (you) why I have come. The noble son of Nahuṣa, the devotee of Viṣṇu, has made all human beings that live on the earth the devotees of Viṣṇu. He has made the nature of the mortal world like that of Vaikuṇṭha. Human beings have become immortal and free from old age and diseases. They just do not commit a sin, nor do they tell a lie. They are free from lust and wrath, and are without greed and delusion. The noble ones are given to charity and all of them are devoted to religion. With all good works they worship sound Nārāyaṇa. Due to (the practice of) that Vaiṣṇava religion all men on the earth are healthy, free from grief, and all have a steady youth. O god, as the Dūrvā (grass) and the bunyan trees spread on the earth, in the same way they have expanded (i.e. grown in number) due to their sons, grandsons and great-grandsons. With their sons and great-grandsons they have gone from one dynasty to another (i.e. have started various dynasties).

12-15a. Thus that son of Nahuṣa has made the entire mortal world the devotee of Viṣṇu and free from old age and death. Being free from (i.e. having no) function I have (as though) become deprived of my position. I have thus told you everything that puts an end to my job. Knowing thus, O thousand-eyed (Indra), do what is beneficial to this world. I have told you all this as I was asked by you. For this reason, O Indra, I have come into your proximity (i.e. to you).

Indra said :

15b-18a. O great Dharmarāja, formerly only I had sent my messenger (i.e. Mātali) for coming over of that noble one (i.e. to bring here that noble Yayāti). Even my messenger spoke to him. (But Yayāti said to him:) "I do not desire the pleasures in heaven. I shall not (at all) come to heaven. I shall make the entire globe of the nature of heaven." Thus the king told (my messenger). He is protecting his subjects. Due to the power of his righteousness I always remain imperiled.

Dharma said :

18b-19a. O illustrious lord of gods, if you desire what is dear to me, then bring that good king (to heaven) by any means.

19b-22a. O king, having heard these words of that Dharmarāja, the intelligent lord of gods considered everything from a factual point of view. God Indra of a noble mind, having called Cupid and Gandharvas, brought Cuckoo and Rati. (He told them:) "Do that by which the king will come (here). Ordered by me you should go to the earth. (There should be) no hesitation (about it)."

Kāma (i.e. Cupid) said :

22b-23a. There is no doubt that I shall do what is agreeable and favourable to you. See me and the king standing (opposite each other) in a battle.

23b-24. Saying, 'All right', all went there where that king, Nahuṣa's son, was. O brāhmaṇa, all of them, Kāma and others, in the form of actors (i.e. having disguised themselves) greeted the king with blessings and related their good drama (i.e. with good acting spoke to him).

25-33. Having heard those words of them, the intelligent lord of the earth, Yayāti, arranged a divine assembly, with very learned men. The king, proficient in sacred and profane knowledge, himself came (there). That king, the son of Nahuṣa, saw that drama. (He saw) the life of Vāmana, also his birth as a brāhmaṇa. At that time Jarā (i.e. old age), in the form of a woman matchless in beauty in the world, sang an excellent, melodious, song, O king. Due to the charm of her singing and due to her graceful laughter (i.e. smile), and on account of her sweet words, and due to the device, manner and divine behaviour of Cupid he was deluded. Cupid had a form as that of Bali, or of the row of Vindhya or of Vāmana, formerly. Cupid himself became the principal actor and the stage manager, and Spring was his assistant. That Rati, whose husband was delighted, put on the apparel of the chief actress. In that dance-performance she moved in the retiring room. The very intelligent Cuckoo excited the king. As the glorious king saw the excellent dance and listened to the excellent music he was deluded by (these) presented by the chief actress (i.e. Rati).

CHAPTER SEVENTYSEVEN

Yayāti Yields to Passion

Sukarman said :

1-5. The king of kings was allured by the charm of Cupid's music and his charming smile and his appearance as an actor, O Pippala. Having urinated and evacuated his bowels, the king, Nahuṣa's son, sat on his seat without having washed his feet. Having reached (i.e. seized) that opportunity, Jarā (i.e. old age) moved on to the king. Cupid also accomplished the act, beneficial to Indra, O best king. When the drama was over, and they had left, the religious-minded king was overcome with old age, had his mind attached to lust, was allured by the delusion (caused) by Cupid, was perturbed, had his organs weakened; the virtuous (king) was very much stupefied, and was driven away by objects of sense.

6-11a. Once the king eager for the vice of hunting (i.e. eager to go ahunting) went (to a forest). Being under the influence of infatuation and attachment, he sported in the forest. When the glorious king was sporting with interest a matchless deer with four horns came (there). O king, its entire body was beautiful, its hair was of golden appearance, its body was well spotted with gemlike brightness; it was beautiful and attractive. The archer (i.e. the king) with an arrow in his hand, ran (to it) with speed. The intelligent (king) thought that some demon had come (there). The deer too drew the king away. He went (after it) with the speed of a chariot, and suffered from exhaustion. While he was watching, the deer vanished.

11b-20. There he saw a wonderful forest, resembling Indra's garden; it was crowded with beautiful trees, and looked splendid with the five elements, with big sacred sandal trees and with charming groups of plantain trees, with (the trees like) Bakula, Aśoka, Punnāga, Nālikera (i.e. the cocoa-nut trees), Tinduka, Pūgiphala (betel-nut trees), date-trees, lotuses and Saptaparṇa trees, blossomed Karṇikāra (trees), and various trees that always had fruit, so also with Ketaka and Pāṭala. While seeing (these) the great king saw an excellent lake. It was full of holy water; it was extensive (spreading) over five yojanas; it was crowded with swans and ducks; it was resounding with aquatic birds; it was also delightful with lotuses; it looked charming with red lotuses, and was decorated with golden lotuses; it looked extremely charming due to white lotuses; it was everywhere resounding with intoxicated bees also. Thus he saw the lake endowed with all excellences. It was five yojanas broad and ten yojanas long. The lake was auspicious on all sides; and was adorned with divine objects. Fatigued by the speed of the chariot and tormented by weariness he sat in the shade of a mango tree on its bank.

21-26a. Having bathed in it, and having drunk (i.e. he drank) its cold water scented with fragrance of lotuses, resembling nectar, and removing all exhaustion. The king seated in the shade of the tree, somehow heard the sound of a song being sung (by someone). The sound was heard as (would be the sound of) the song which a divine woman would sing. The great king, who loved music, became extremely thoughtful. When the noble one was thus anxious and thought for a moment, a woman, with plump hips and breasts arrived in the forest, when the king was looking on. She, whose body looked beautiful with all ornaments, and having the wealth of good character and (auspicious) marks, came to the forest and stood before the king.

26b-32a. To her the king said: "Who are you? To whom do you belong? Why have you come here? Tell me the reason for it." O Pippala, that woman of an excellent face, when thus asked at that time by him, did not give either a good or a bad reply to the king. That woman, with the neck of the lute in her hand, laughed, and quickly went (away). The great king was then filled with great wonder: 'When talked to by me, she is not giving a reply.' Again that king Yayāti thought: '(This) four horns which I had seen. I think that is the truth. This must truly be a deceitful form of (i.e. taken up by) demons.' O brāhmaṇa, the king Yayāti, the son of Nahuṣa, thought (like this) for a moment.

32b-38a. When the king was thinking like this; the woman, laughing at the prince, vanished in the forest. In the meanwhile, he again heard the song, which was melodious, very divine, and accompanied with intonation and a regulated rise and fall of sounds through the musical scale. The king went to that place (from) where the great sound of the song was coming. In the water was an excellent lotus having a thousand petals. On it was an excellent woman, who was endowed with (good) character, beauty and virtues. She was possessing divine marks; she was adorned with divine ornaments; she shone with divine objects; her hand was engaged in holding the neck of a lute. She was singing a melodious song, accompanied with beating and measuring time and pause. With the power of that song she allured the mobile and the immobile, and also gods, groups of sages, all demons, Gandharvas and Kinnaras.

38b-42a. Seeing that (woman) of broad eyes and having beauty and lustre (he thought) in the mobile and the immobile world there is no other woman like her. Formerly, great Cupid, the actor, had got into the body of the king; he manifested himself at that time. As fire, having come in contact with ghee sends forth rays of light (i.e. is bright), so Cupid (i.e. passion) manifested himself, after having (i.e. after the king had) seen her. His mind was overpowered by Cupid (i.e. passion) on seeing that woman of charming eyes. (He thought:) 'I have never (before) seen such a young woman, alluring the world.'

42b-43. Thinking for a moment, the king had his mind attached to passion. Due to separation from her, the king, being burnt by the fire of passion and tormented by the fever of passion, longed for her.

44-46. (He thought:) 'How will she be mine? How will she have love (for me)? My life will be fruitful when this young girl having her face like a lotus and having lotus-like eyes embraces me, or if she is obtained by me.' Having thought like this that virtuous king Yayāti said to that beautiful woman: "O auspicious one, who are you? To whom do you belong?" That woman who was seen before is again seen (by me).

47-52a. The righteous one asked her: "Who is this (woman) by your side? O auspicious one, tell (me) everything. I am the son of Nahuṣa. O good one, I am born in the lunar dynasty and am the lord of the seven islands. O respectable lady, my name is Yayāti; I am well-known in the three worlds. My heart thus entertains a desire for union with you. O good lady, unite with me, do what is very dear (to me). O good lady, there is no doubt that I shall give you whatever you desire. O you of an excellent complexion, I am struck with invincible passion. Therefore, protect me, who am extremely helpless, and who have sought your shelter. For (i.e. in exchange for) the union with you I shall give my kingdom, the entire earth or even my body. All these three worlds are yours."

52b-55a. Having heard the words of that king, that woman with a lotus-like face said to her friend (named) Viśālā: "Tell the king that has come (here), my name, the place of my birth, (the names of) my father and mother, O you good lady. Also tell him about my love (for him)." Understanding her desire, Viśālā with sweet words then spoke to the king: "O prince, listen."

Viśālā said :

55b-71a. This Cupid was formerly burnt by Śambhu (i.e.

Śiva), the god of gods. That Rati, deprived of her husband, wept melodiously due to grief. O best king, at that time that Rati lived in this lake. O king of kings, then gods, having heard, like this, her melodious wailing attended by grief, had great compassion (on her). They spoke (these) words to Śaṅkara: "O great god, revive the mind-born (Cupid) again. O glorious one, of what nature will she be (i.e. what will be the plight of her) who is helpless, being deprived of her husband? Due to your affection for us (i.e. since you love us, please) make her united with Cupid." Hearing those words (Śiva) said: "I shall revive Cupid. This mind-born one (i.e. Cupid), having five arrows, even though without a body, will again be the friend of Spring. There is no doubt about it. He will live with a divine body; (and) not otherwise (i.e. not with any other body)." That fish-bannered god (i.e. Cupid), became alive due to the grace of the great god (i.e. Śiva). O best man, having thus approved of the desire of the respectable lady (i.e. Rati), with blessings (Śiva said:) "O Cupid, go and always thrive with your beloved." Thus (the god) of great lustre, the cause of the sustenance and destruction (of the world) said (to Cupid). Cupid again came to the lake where unhappy Rati remained. O king this is (that lake called) Kāmasaras (i.e. belonging to Cupid) where Rati is well-settled. She was overcome with grief when noble Cupid was burnt (by Śiva). From Rati's wrath sprang up a fire of a fearful form. He too, very much scorched Rati, who fainted. O best man, she, deprived of her husband, shed tears. From her eyes tears fell into the water. From them arose great grief destroying all happiness. O best king, after (that) Jarā (i.e. old age) came into being from the tears. From them the dull-headed destroyer, viz. Separation sprang up. Both the terrible Grief and Torture also then sprang up. From them was generated Delusion—terrible and destroying happiness. O great king, from Grief the Fever of Passion and Error originated. The distressed Wailing, Insanity and Death, destroying everything, arose from her tears.

71b-79. O great king, by Rati's side all assuming the body of torment and, all having the virtues of good feelings, originated incarnate. O king, then someone said: "This (is) Cupid (that) has come." Seeing Cupid that had come (there) she (i.e. Rati) was filled with great joy. Tears fell from her eyes . O great king, in the water beings quickly originated. O best man, at that time (a lady) named Love sprang up, so also Renown and Shame. O best king, from them (i.e. from the tears) rose great Joy and the other one, viz. Peace. Two auspicious daughters giving pleasures and enjoyments sprang up. O king, there was a great combination of diversion, sport and devotion of mind. O king, due to joy tears fell from Rati's left eye into water. From them sprang up a good lotus. O best man, from that good lotus came up this beautiful lady, the daughter of Rati, Aśrubindumatī by name. Through love for her, I, always pleased and virtuous, ever remain near her, giving her pleasure, due to my being her friend. My name is known as (i.e. I am known by the name) Viśālā. O king, I am Varuṇa's daughter.

80-81a. Being always affectionate to her, I remain near her through love for her. I have thus told you all her (account) and mine also. O lord of kings, this beautiful one, desiring a husband, practised penance.

The king said :

81b-83a. O auspicious one, I have understood everything that you have told me; listen, let this beautiful daughter of Rati choose me. I shall give this young lady all that she desires. O auspicious lady, do that by which she will be under my influence.

Viśālā said :

83b-88. I shall tell you her resolve. Listen to it, O king. She desires as her groom a man, who is endowed with youth; who is omniscient; who has the characteristics of a brave man; who resembles the lord of gods; who possesses righteous conduct; who is brilliant; very bright, a donor, and the best among sacrificers; who knows (i.e. appreciates) virtues and devotion to religion; who possesses righteousness and good conduct; who is like Indra in the world; who is intent on religious practices through (performing) great sacrifices; who is endowed with all grandeur; who is as it were another Viṣṇu; who is always very much liked by gods, and is very dear to brāhmaṇas; who is friendly to brāhmaṇas; who knows the truth of the Vedas; whose valour is known in the three worlds. She desires such a groom as is endowed with these qualities and is honoured in the three worlds, is very intelligent and very dear and handsome.

Yayāti said :

89. Know me, who have come here, to be endowed with these qualities. There is no doubt that the Creator has created (in me) a husband worthy of her.

Viśālā said :

90. O king, I know that in the three worlds you are rich with religious merit. The qualities which I have mentioned before exist in you.

91. Only due to one blemish she does not think highly of you. This doubt has arisen in me. (Otherwise) O king, you are full of Viṣṇu.

Yayāti said :

92. Tell me the great blemish which this one, beautiful in all limbs, does not really prize. Be well disposed to favour me.

Viśālā said :

93. O lord of the world why (i.e. how) do you not know your own blemish? Your body is covered with old age. Due to this (blemish) she does not prize you.

94. Hearing these great (important) and disagreeable words, the lord of the world, the king, overcome with great grief, again said:

95. "O auspicious lady, this blemish of old age in my body is not due to anybody's contact. I do not know (how) this old age has occurred to my body.

96. O auspicious one, whatever thing difficult to obtain in the world she desires, I am willing to give it to her. Choose the best boon."

Viśālā said :

97-100. When you would be free from old age, then she would be your very beloved (wife). This is certain, O king; I am telling (you) the truth (and) the truth (only). Youth would prevail over his body who passes on his old age to his son, (or) brother, (or) servant after taking youth from him and giving him his old age. Due to good taste a happy agreement takes place between the two. He, O king, has the same fruit as the merit of him who offers himself through pity. There is no doubt about it.

101-103. He would have great religious merit when the merit obtained through difficulty is given to someone else. The fruit of merit is (thus) obtained. Therefore, O king, give (your old age) to your son, and after having obtained (youth) from him, come back with (i.e. after having got) handsomeness. Do (so) then, O king, when you desire to enjoy (her).

Thus, speaking to the king, that Viśālā ceased (speaking).

Sukarman said :

104a. Having heard like this, the best king then spoke to Viśālā.

The king said :

104b-106. O noble one, let it be so; I shall do your words (i.e. do as you have told me).

That stupid lord of the earth, Yayāti, overcome with passion, having gone home, and having called his sons Turu, Pūru, Kuru and Yadu, loving the father, said (these) words (to them): "Upon my order, O sons, bring happiness (to me)."

The sons said :

107-108. The words (i.e. the order) of the father—whether good or bad—have (has) to be executed by the sons. O father, speak out quickly, and know that it (i.e. the order) is carried out. There is no doubt.

Having heard these words of the sons, the lord of the earth, with his mind overcome with joy, again spoke to them.

CHAPTER SEVENTYEIGHT

Pūru Gives His Youth to Yayāti

Yayāti said :

1-4. O my noble sons, the wise one among you should take this my old age which is giving me pain, and should give his own youth and excellent form (to me); (so that) I shall behave as I like. Today my very fickle mind is inflamed, and is attached to a woman. As fire whirls round the water in a pot, similarly, O (my) sons, my mind is very much shaken by the fire of passion. O (my) sons, one (of you) should take this my old age which is giving me pain, and should give (me) his youth; (so that) I shall behave according to my will.

5-6. He, the best son, who passes on his youth to me, will enjoy my kingdom, and will wield my bow (and carry on) my line. He will have happiness, ample wealth, riches and grains. He will have many children and glory and fame.

The sons said :

7. O king, you are a king who are devoted to religion. You are guarding your subjects truthfully. Due to what has this idea, naturally fickle, arisen in you?

The king said :

8-10. Formerly dancers, superior dancers, came to my city. Due to them such delusion has arisen in me, when Cupid had allured me. My body is covered with old age; and my mind was overcome with Cupid (i.e. passion). O best sons, I was smit and overcome by passion. I saw a beautiful maiden of a divine form. O sons, I spoke to her; but the good one did not say anything.

11-13. Her charming and clever friend is Viśālā by name. She spoke good words to me, giving me joy: "When you would be free from old age, the very dear one will be yours." I accepted (i.e. agreed to) these words spoken by her, and (then) came home. To get rid of my old age, I have thus told you that (she had told me). O good sons, realizing thus, you should do (what gives) me pleasure.

Turu said :

14-18. By the favour of the father and the mother, body is obtained by sons. O king, with the (help of the) body religious acts are done by a wise man. A son should especially serve his father. Yet, O king, this is not the time for me to give my youth (to you). O king, men should enjoy the pleasures of senses in youth. Now it is not properly the time for you (to enjoy these pleasures). (You say) O father, that pleasure would be enjoyed by you after you give your ripe old age to your sons; but (then) you would not have (that much) life (i.e. you would not live that long). Therefore, O great king, I shall not do your words (i.e. do as you say).

In this way the eldest son, Turu, spoke to him at that time.

19. Hearing those words of Turu, the king became angry. The pious one, with his eyes red with anger, cursed Turu.

20-26 "O you of a wicked heart, you have disobeyed this order of mine. Therefore, be a sinful person outcast by all religions. You will be without the lock of hair on the crown of the head; you will be deprived of the sacred texts; you will be without all manners. There is no doubt about this. You will be the killer of brāhmaṇas; you will be ruined by gods; you will be a drunkard; you will be without truthfulness; you will do fierce deeds; you will be the meanest man. You will be addicted to drinking; you will be hungry, sinful and a killer of cows. Your skin will be bad; you will have the hem of your lower garment untucked; you will hate brāhmaṇas; you will be deformed. You will be an adulterer; you will be very fierce; you will be very lustful; you will eat everything; you will always be wicked. You will have sexual intercourse with a woman of your own kin; you will destroy all religious practices; you will be without sacred knowledge; and you will suffer from leprosy. Your sons and grandsons also will destroy all holy objects, will be barbarians, and will be very much spoilt like this (i.e. in the same way)."

27. Having thus cursed Turu very badly, he spoke to (his other) son, Yadu: "Take on (my) old age now, and enjoy the kingdom free from any source of vexation."

28a. Joining the palms of his hands, Yadu said to the king:

Yadu said :

28b-30. O father, I am unable to bear the burden of (your) old age; (please) be kind to (i.e. excuse) me. There are five causes of old age: frigidity, journey, bad food, aged woman, and disinclination of the mind. O king, I am not able (to put up with) the misery in my youth (i.e. while I am young). Who is able to hold (up old age)? Now (please) excuse me.

31-32. O son of a brāhmaṇa, the angry great king cursed Yadu: "Your lineage shall never deserve a kingdom. It will be without power, lustre, forbearance, and will be deprived of the practices of kṣatriyas (since you have) turned (your) back upon my order. There is no uncertainty about it."

Yadu said :

33. O great king, I am faultless; why have you now cursed me? (Please) favour the poor one (i.e. me). Be pleased to favour me.

The king said :

34. O son, (when) the great god will take birth with his portion in your family, then your family will be purified.

Yadu said :

35. O great king, you have cursed me, your son, who am faultless; If you have compassion for me, (please) favour me.

The king said :

36. He who is the eldest son should remove the misery of the father. He well enjoys the inheritance of the kingdom, and he would bear the burden (of the kingdom).

37-38a. You have not done (your) duty, (therefore) you are certainly not fit to be talked to. You have destroyed (i.e. disobeyed) the order of me who (can) strike with a great (i.e. heavy) punishment. Therefore you cannot be favoured, do as you please.

Yadu said :

38b-42a. O king, since you have destroyed my kingdom, form and family, therefore, I, the chief of your family, will be wicked. In your family will be (born) kṣatriyas of various forms. There is no doubt that very fierce and very mighty (beings) will enjoy their villages, good regions, their women, and whatever gems they will have. From my family (will) be born Turuṣkas of the form of barbarians—those who were destroyed and who were cursed by you with very fierce curses.

O best king, the angry Yadu thus spoke to the king (Yayāti).

42b-45. Then the angry great king again cursed (Yadu) thus: "Listen, know all that will be born in your family will ruin my subjects. As long as the moon, the sun, the earth, the constellations and the stars (last) the mlecchas will be roasted in the Kumbhīpāka and the Raurava (hells)." Then seeing the young Kuru playing, and possessed of good marks, the king did not call that son (of him) a prince. Knowing Kuru to be a child, the king left him then.

46-47a. Then the lord of the world (i.e. Yayāti) called Pūru, the meritorious son of Śarmiṣṭhā, and said to him: "Take my old age and enjoy my extremely good kingdom, with the sources of nuisance eradicated, (and) given by me (to you)."

Pūru said :

47b-49a. The lord (if you) should enjoy the kingdom as was enjoyed by your father, I shall obey your order. O king, give me your old age in exchange for my youth. Today only appearing handsome, enjoy, with your mind attached to objects of sense, pleasures and good deeds.

49b-54a. O noble one, sport with her as long as you desire. O father, as long as I live I shall keep up old age.

Thus addressed by that Pūru, the lord of the world, with his heart full of great joy, said again to his son: "O child, since you did not disobey my order, (on the contrary) obeyed it, therefore I shall give you much happiness. O you very intelligent one, since you took my old age, and gave me your own youth, therefore you enjoy the kingdom given by me." O king, that good

Pūru, thus addressed by that king, gave him his youth and took old age from him.

54b-60a. When, O dear one, the exchange of the ages of the father and the son was effected, Pūru appeared to be older than the king in all his limbs. The king reached youth, (and looked like a man) sixteen years old, and possessing great charm (looked) as it were he was another Cupid. The great king gave that noble Pūru everything—(his) bow, kingdom, umbrella, fan, seat, and elephant, (so also) his entire treasure, country, army, chowrie and also the chariot. That Nahuṣa's righteous son, attached to passion, thinking of that maiden, went with quick steps, to that lake known as Kāma, and resembling an ocean, where Aśrubindumatī (stayed). Seeing that eminent maiden of large eyes and having beautiful and plump breasts, the great king, with his mind attracted by Cupid, said to Viśālā:

The king said :

60b-62a. O you noble and eminent one of charming eyes, I have, O auspicious one, given up my old age, and am (now) endowed with youth. Becoming a young man, I have come (here). Let her be mine now. There is no doubt that I shall give her whatever she desires.

Viśālā said :

62b-63a. When (now) you have come after having abandoned the wicked old age, (yet) you are still covered by one blemish. (Therefore) she does not prize you.

The king said :

63b-64. If you definitely know my blemish then tell it (to me). I shall certainly abandon that blemish of an inferior nature.

CHAPTER SEVENTYNINE

Youthful Yayāti Enjoys with Aśrubindumatī

Viśālā said:

1-2. There (i.e. in that king) only, whose wife is Śarmiṣṭhā and whose wife is beautiful Devayānī, good fortune is seen. This cannot be false, O king; then O glorious king, how are you fascinated by (the beauty of) this maiden's body* since you are known as a husband having two wives?

3-4a. Like sandal, O king, you are with serpents (around) you. O king, as a great sandal-tree is surrounded by serpents, so you are surrounded by serpents called co-wives.

4b-6a. It is better to enter fire, it is better to fall from (mountain) top, but not good to have the dear husband, possessing handsomeness and lustre, (but) with co-wives—with the poison in the form of co-wives. Therefore she does not prize you, an ocean of mertis, as her lover.

The king said:

6b-7a. O beautiful lady, I have nothing to do with Devayānī, nor with Śarmiṣṭhā; for this purpose see my treasure full of righteousness.

Aśrubindumatī said:

7b-9a. O king, I shall be the enjoyer of your kingdom and your body. O king you will certainly (have to) do whatever I shall tell you to do. For this purposes, O you who love piety, give me your hand endowed with many virtues and having auspicious marks.

The King said:

9b-11a. O you of an excellent complexion, I shall not have any other wife than you. O you beautiful lady, O you lady of charming body, enjoy my entire kingdom with its wealth, so

*The existing reading कार्यवशो does not give any sense. It should better be replaced by कायवशो which we have translated here. (Ed.)

also the whole earth and my body. (In proof of this) I have offered this my hand to you. O good lady, I (shall) do whatever you (will) tell (me).

Aśrubindumatī said:

11b. Just with this (promise), O noble one, I shall be your wife.

12-16a. Hearing this, Yayāti, the lord of the earth, the king of kings, with his eyes full of joy, married by the Gāndharva way that auspicious daughter of Cupid. The noble son of king (Nahuṣa) enjoyed with her, on sea-beaches, in forests and parks. The king, lord of kings, youthfully sported with her on mountains and in beautiful rivers. In this way, O best king, that noble king Yayāti passed twenty thousand (years) in sporting with her.

Viṣṇu said :

16b-17a. O very intelligent one, through the fraudulent act of Cupid, that great king Yayāti was thus allured by her for the benefit of Indra at that time.

Sukarman said:

17b-19. O Pippala, that lord of the earth, Yayāti, stupefied by Cupid's daughter by means of her alluring passion and charming union, was not aware of day or night. Once that daughter of Cupid of charming eyes said to that stupefied, submissive, obedient king Yayāti, who had bowed down:

Aśrubindumatī said :

20. O dear one, a desire is produced (in me); so satisfy (that) desire of me: perform the best sacrifice, viz. Aśvamedha, O lord of the earth.

The king said :

21-24a. O glorious one, let it be so; I shall do what you very much like.

He invited his eldest son, who had no desire to enjoy the kingdom. (The son), when called, came there with his neck (i.e. head) bent with devotion, and joining the palms of his hands, saluted (Yayāti) at that time. With his neck (i.e. head) bent, he also saluted her feet. "O King, give me an order since I, who was called, have come. O noble one, what should I do? I am your servant who has bowed to you."

The king said :

24b-29. O son, inviting brāhmaṇas, meritorious priests officiating at sacrifices, and kings, make preparations for a horse-sacrifice.

Thus addressed, that very lustrous and highly religious Pūru did everything in full as told by the glorious one. With the daughter of Cupid he took proper initiation (i.e. got himself consecrated for the sacrifice). Yayāti, the lord of the earth, gave various gifts to brāhmaṇas at the place of the sacrifice, so also endless, profuse gifts especially to the poor, O great king; and at the end of the sacrifice he said to that beautiful lady : "O young lady, tell me what else dear to you I should do. O beautiful lady, I shall do all that which is attainable and not attainable."

Sukarman said :

30-37. Thus addressed by the king, she spoke in reply "O king, a desire is produced in me; O innocent one, do (i.e. satisfy) it. O great king, I desire to see the very pleasing heaven of Indra, of Brahmā, so also of Śiva and of Viṣṇu. O noble one, show (these) to me, if I am very dear to you." Thus addressed by her, the king said to her who was very dear to him : "O you beautiful one, well, well, you are just saying pious things. O you beautiful lady, I think what you said due to feminine nature, fickleness and curiosity, is unattainable, O noble one. That is attainable by means of pious gifts, sacrifice, and austerities; what you told cannot be attained by any other means, O beautiful lady. You have just said something that is unattainable as it is mixed up (i.e. connected with) religious merit. I have not as yet seen or heard about a very meritorious man who has gone to heaven with his (human) body from the mortal world. Therefore, O you beautiful lady, what you said is unattainable for me. I shall do something else. O dear one tell me that."

The respectable lady said :

38-40. O king, it is certainly not attainable for other human beings; but it is attainable for you; I am telling the truth (and) truth only. O king, in the mortal world there is no other human being like you in (practising) penance, in fame, in doing valourous acts, (giving) gifts and (performing) sacrifices. Everything—the power of a kṣatriya, fire of energy—is established in you. Therefore, O son of Nahuṣa, this (thing) dear to me should be done (by you).

CHAPTER EIGHTY

Yadu Refuses to Kill His Mothers

Pippala said :

1-2. O best brāhmaṇa, when the king (Yayāti) married the daughter of Cupid, what did his two former, very auspicious, wives, viz. the noble Devayānī and Śarmiṣṭhā, the daughter of Vṛṣaparvan do? Tell me the entire account of the two.

Sukarman said :

3-9a. When that king took home Cupid's daughter, that high-minded Devayānī very much entered into rivalry (with her). "For her he, with his mind overcome with anger, cursed two of his sons (viz. Turu and Yadu)." The renowned one, having called Śarmiṣṭhā, said these words to her. Śarmiṣṭhā and Devayānī vied with her in beauty, lustre, charity, truthfulness and holy vows. Then Kāma's daughter knew their wickedness. Just then only she told everything to the king, O brāhmaṇa. Then the great king, getting angry, called Yadu and said to him : "Go and kill Śarmiṣṭhā and also (Devayānī) the daughter of Śukra. O son, if you care for felicity then do what is very dear to me." Having heard those words of his father, Yadu then replied to his father, the lord of kings :

9b-14. "O proud father, I shall not kill these two mothers, free from guilt. Those well-versed in the Vedas have declared a great sin in killing one's mother. Therefore, O great king, I shall not kill these two mothers. O great king, (even) if a mother or a sister or a daughter is stained with a hundred blemishes she should never be killed by sons or brothers. Knowing this, O great king, I shall never kill (these) two mothers." Hearing, at that time, the words of Yadu, the king became angry. Yayāti, the lord of the earth, then cursed his son: "Since you have disobeyed (my) order, you, resembling a sinner, polluted by my curse, enjoy a portion of your mother".

15-19. Speaking thus to his son Yadu, that lord of the earth, Yayāti, that great king of great glory, having cursed his son, and without being solely devoted to Viṣṇu, enjoyed pleasures with her. That Aśrubindumatī of charming eyes and beautiful in all limbs, enjoyed with him all lovely enjoyments as liked by her. Thus that noble Yayāti passed his time. All other subjects were without any loss or without old age; all people were solely devoted to the meditation of glorious Viṣṇu. O noble Pippala, all people were happy and served the good by means of penance, truthfulness and meditation on Viṣṇu.

CHAPTER EIGHTYONE

Destiny is Irresistible

Sukarman said :

1-3. This very intelligent Indra, always afraid of the noble Yayāti, seeing his valour and many meritorious acts like (giving) gifts, sent the celestial nymph Menakā to act as a messenger. (He said to her:) "O good and illustrious one, go and tell (i.e. convey) my order. Going from here tell Cupid's daughter the words (i.e. the order) of (me), the lord of gods: 'Bring the king here by any means (i.e. somehow).' "

4. Hearing this, that Menakā sent (by Indra) went there; and told her all that the lord of gods had said.

5-8. Having thus told her that Menakā, directed by her (i.e. Cupid's daughter) went (back to Indra). When Menakā had left, that high-minded, glorious daughter of Rati reminded the king of the lawful agreement: "O King, with a truthful speech, you formerly brought me (here); in the meantime you gave me your hand, and brought me to your residence. O king, you must do here (i.e. now) only what I tell you. O hero, you have not done what I told you; I shall abandon you and go (back) to my father's house."

The king said :

9. O good one, I shall certainly do what you have told me. O respectable lady, leaving (i.e. not telling) what is unattainable, tell me what is attainable.

Aśrubindumatī said :

10-19a. For this purpose, O lord of the earth, I choose you in marriage, knowing that you are having all (auspicious) marks and endowed with all virtues, and knowing that you would accomplish everything, support everything, practise all good usages and create (i.e. perform) religious rites, and would obtain all the three worlds, and knowing that you are matchless in the three worlds. I know you to be a devotee and the best among the followers of Viṣṇu. With this hope I formerly took you for my husband. He who has the grace of Viṣṇu would move everywhere. O lord of kings, here is nothing that cannot be accomplished (by you) in three worlds—mobile or immobile; for you of a good vow (everything) is (attainable) in all the worlds. Due to Viṣṇu's grace only you can freely move in the sky. Having come to the world of mortals, O lord of the earth, you have made people free from old age, grey hair and death. You yourself have devised many desire-yielding trees near all the doors of the houses of men, O king. To the houses of men you yourself have sent sages and have always firmly settled the desire-yielding cows in their houses, O king. You have made men happy by (satisfying) all their desires. In a house a thousand nobly born people are seen.

19b-26a. Thus you have increased the human race. In spite of Yama's opposition and that of Indra too, O king, you made the mortal world free from diseases and sins. O great king, by means of your prowess and self-respect you have shown the earth to have the form of heaven. There is no other king like you. No man is born or will be born like you. I know you to be the illuminator of the entire religion. Therefore I took you as my husband; giving up joke, O lord of kings, speak the truth before me. O king, if you have truth and piety then speak the truth. "I do not move in divine worlds, nor can I freely move in the sky". When, giving up truth, (you say like this), you will never go to heaven; your words will be certainly false; and all good things done formerly will be reduced to ashes.

The king said :

26b-29. O good lady, you spoke the truth, there is nothing like unattainable for me. Due to the good grace of the lord of the world everything is attainable for me. O respectable lady, listen to the reason for which I am not going to heaven. They will not allow deities to go to the mortal world; as a result all the human beings—my subjects—will be having death when abandoned by me; there is no doubt about this, O you beautiful lady. I do not desire to go to heaven; I have told you the truth, O you beautiful lady.

The respectable lady said :

30. O king, having seen the worlds, you will again come (back). Today fulfil my matchless strong desire.

The king said :

31-40. I shall certainly do all that you have said.

That very lustrous king Yayāti, the son of Nahuṣa, having (thus) observed and thus spoken to his beloved then thought : 'A fish though moving in the water, is bound (i.e. caught) in a net. A deer even having the speed like that of the wind is bound. A bird sees a prey even though it is at a distance of a thousand yojanas. Being deluded by destiny it does not see the noose sticking to its neck. Destiny brings about good and bad things. Destiny destroys honour. Destiny brings about humiliation by remaining wheresoever (it pleases). It makes a man a donor or a suitor. Destiny holds everything —all immobile and other beings (living) in heaven or on the earth. Destiny alone is this world. It is without origin and death and is the greatest cause of the world. Destiny ripens the worlds as the fruit laid on a tree. Hymns, penance, charity, friends or relatives are not able to protect a man oppressed by destiny. It is not possible to overcome the three nooses of destiny: marriage, birth and death—when and where one would have these, and with whom or through whom. As the clouds in the sky are moved by the wind, so the world is moved by destiny united with (the fruits of) the deeds (of beings).

Sukarman said :

41-67. But the destiny, which, united with Karman (the deeds), is adored by men, would (only) urge Karman (the fruits of the deeds), and does not create it. In the human (world), calamities, misfortunes, serpents and diseases, move (in accordance with) their being decided by (one's) deeds. All those that are the causes and means of happiness, being mixed with merit, are united with (the fruits of) deeds. They would not see (i.e. would not care for what is) auspicious and (what is) inauspicious. (Obscure!) relatives united with (the fruits of) deeds may exchange them*; but (the fruits of) deeds (alone) urge men on to happiness and unhappiness in this world. As gold or silver has its nature fixed, similarly a being is bound in accordance with his deeds. These five are produced (i.e. decided) when a man is just in (his mother's) womb: his life (i.e. longevity), deeds, wealth, learning and death. As an agent (potter) fashions from a lifeless lump whatever he wants to fashion, in the same way deeds performed before follow the doer. One becomes a god, or a man, or a beast, or a bird, or a lower animal, or an immobile object, according to one's deeds. He always enjoys in accordance with that only which is accomplished by himself—unhappiness results from one's own deeds; happiness results from one's own deeds. Obtaining the bed of womb, he enjoys the fruit of his deeds of the previous body (i.e. done in the previous existence). On the earth men never (i.e. can never) give up the fruits of their deeds. They

*कर्मदायदिवानोके is most probably a corrupt reading. (Ed.)

are not able to change them by means of their power or intelligence. They enjoy meritorious deeds, pains and pleasures. Reaching (i.e. due to) a cause, a man is always bound by the bonds of his deeds. As from among thousands of cows a calf finds out its mother, similarly the fruit of the auspicious or inauspicious deeds —which is not destroyed except by 'enjoyment (or suffering)— follows its agent. Who can change the fruit of a deed done in a former life? (The fruit of) the deed follows him also who runs very fast. The (fruit of) the deed of a former life, as it was done, sleeps with him who sleeps. It stands by him who stands, and follows him who goes. The (fruit of the) deed of him who acts, acts; it follows him like his shadow. As shade and light are always mutually connected, similarly a deed and its agent are well related. Planets, diseases, poisonous snakes, demonesses[1] and demons trouble a man who is first oppressed by his own deeds. He who is to enjoy happiness or (suffer) unhappiness at a place is bound there by a rope, is forcibly carried away by fate. In giving happiness or unhappiness, destiny alone is the master of beings. O wise one, a deed is conceived in one way by (a person) keeping awake or sleeping, and destiny destroys it (by giving it) another turn. It protects that which should be protected (i.e. which it wants to protect) from weapons, fire, poisons or difficulties. Truly that which cannot be protected, is protected by destiny in this way. That which is destroyed by destiny can never be protected. As seeds that are sown in earth and riches remain (dormant) and (then) grow (active), in the same way deeds remain (intact) in the soul and (then) become active. As due to the exhaustion of oil the flame goes out, so due to the exhaustion of (the fruits of) deeds a being goes to destruction (i.e. departs) from his body; since those who know the truth declare that death is due to the exhaustion (of the fruits) of (one's) deeds. Various beings and diseases are the cause of his death. 'Thus it is ripening of the deeds of my former existence. It is not otherwise. It has (now) certainly come (to me) in the form of this lady; there is no doubt about it. Actors, dancers and bards had to come to my house; due to their contact, old age

1. Sākini—a kind of female being, attendant on Durgā supposed to be a demoness or fairy.

has resorted to my body. I think everything is done by (i.e. due to) one's deeds (in a former existence), since it has (now) definitely sprung up.

68a. Therefore deeds are the main (factor); efforts are useless.

68b-74. Formerly the king of gods had sent the best messenger by name Mātali, for (taking) me (to heaven). I did not do his words (i.e. what he told me). I now see the ripening of those deeds.' He (Yayāti) was thus full of anxiety, and was overcome with great affliction. (He thought:) 'If with pleasure I do not do what she says, then both my truthfulness and piety would go (i.e. perish); there is no doubt about it. Whatever was decided in accordance with my deeds has come; (what is predestined) will certainly take place. Destiny is difficult to overcome.' Yayāti, the lord of the earth, was thus absorbed in thought. He sought the refuge of Kṛṣṇa, Hari, the remover of distress, by meditating upon him, saluting him, and praising him (as): 'O you to whom Lakṣmī is dear, protect me who have sought your refuge.'

CHAPTER EIGHTYTWO

Yayāti Takes Back His Old Age

Sukarman said :

1-8. When the king was thus absorbed in thinking, that beautiful daughter of Rati said : "O you very intelligent king, what do you think just now? There is no doubt that mostly women are fickle. I am not leading you away through fickleness. I am not making use of a fraudulent expedient today, O best king, (by speaking) as other greedy women speak, something that cannot be done, through greed and delusion. A strong desire to see all the worlds is produced in my heart. Seeing deities is meritorious, and is very difficult to be had even by good men. Say to me, O king, that you will cause (i.e. help) me to see the deities. Like another ordinary man, afraid of a great misery and fallen into the ditch of delusion, you are thinking if there would be a great sin due to my company now. Give up your anxiety; you should not go to heaven. I shall never do that which gives you pain."

9-11. The king, thus addressed (by her), said to that beautiful woman : "O respectable lady, now listen to what I have thought out. I see (here) insult, and not the (satisfying of) my mind. O beloved, when I go to the heaven, my subjects will be helpless. The wicked-minded Yama will trouble my subjects with diseases. O beautiful one, I shall go to heaven with you."

12-26. Having thus spoken to her and having called his best son Pūru, possessing old age and of a great intelligence (he said to him:) "Come on, O you who know all the customary observances, you certainly know your duty. O you religious-minded one, you have preserved piety by my order. O son, give me (my) old age back, and take back (your) youth. Protect this kingdom of mine along with the treasure, army and vehicles. Enjoy the earth full of gems, along with villages, forests and cities given (to you) by me. O sinless one, you should do the protection of the subjects which is meritorious; on the authority of the sacred texts you should always punish the wicked and protect the good. O glorious one, you should protect the brāhmaṇas by your deeds devoutly and according to the rules, since they are worthy of respect in the three worlds. Every fifth or seventh day inspect the treasure and meet the learned. You should always honour your army by favouring them and giving them wealth and food. Always use your spies as your eyes, and always be engaged in charity. Always be restrained in your consultation, since it is always to be guarded by very wise men. O son, always control yourself; do not go ahunting. Do not trust anybody—women, treasure or your great army. Always collect worthy persons and all arts. Worship Viṣṇu with sacrifices, and always be virtuous. Everyday crush the sources of nuisance among the subjects. Everyday give your subjects all that is desired by them. Give happiness to the subjects, support the subjects, O son. Have (sexual union with a woman) in your own family (only); do not have it with someone else's wife. Do not think ill about other's wealth; always follow your forefathers. Always ponder over the Vedas and the sacred texls; O child, be engaged in the study of (the science of handling) weapons. O child, always be contented, and be devoted to your own bed (i.e. wife). Always study elephants, horses and chariots."

27-28. Having thus instructed his son, having congratulated him with blessings, having put him (on the throne) with his own hand, he gave his weapon into his hand. Then Yayāti, the lord of the earth, having taken (back) from (Pūru) his old age, gave him (his youth) and desired to go to heaven.

CHAPTER EIGHTYTHREE

Yayāti Visits the Divine Worlds

Sukarman said :

1-5a. Having called all the subjects from all parts (of the world), the lord of the earth, full of great joy, said : "O best ones my subjects—brāhmaṇas, kṣatriyas, vaiśyas and śūdras, along with this lady I am going to Indra's heaven, Brahmā's heaven, Rudra's heaven and then to Viṣṇu's heaven, destroying all sins and causing salvation. There is no doubt about it. With (your) families (you) should stay happily on the earth. O people, I have appointed this glorious and wise Pūru as your guardian and king with the sceptre."

5b-13. Thus addressed, all those subjects said to the king : "O best king, in (i.e. from) all the Vedas and Purāṇas we hear about Dharma; but nobody has seen, as we saw, Dharma, like the one (i.e. you) born in Nahuṣa's great house, in the lunar dynasty, of ten constituents, loving truth, possessing hands, feet and face, propagating all (good) practices, endowed with spiritual and material knowledge, and a great treasure of religious merit, the mine of virtues and proficient in truth, O great king. Truthful and highly lustrous people practise great virtues. That Dharma we have seen in you, of a desirable form (or handsome like Cupid), satisfying (our) desires and so truth-speaking. Even with the three kinds of acts (i.e. of body, mind and speech) we are unable to abandon you. We shall happily and agreeably go wherever you go. There is no doubt that we shall be in hell where you will stay (i.e. if you live in a hell). O very great king, without you, what is the use of a wife, or enjoyments, or life? We have nothing to do with that (i.e. wife etc.). O lord of kings, we shall go with you only; this will not be otherwise."

14-26a. Hearing these words of the subjects, the lord of the earth, full of great joy said to the subjects : "O you all very meritorious people, come along with me." With Cupid's daughter the king got into the chariot. (That) Yayāti, Nahuṣa's son, shone like Indra, the lord of gods, with the chariot having the colour of swans and resembling the orb of the moon; he was free from distress (as he was) being fanned by chowries and fans; he also shone with that lucky, auspicious and great banner. He was praised by sages, bards and singers, so also by his subjects. Then all his subjects approached the lord of men in vehicles; and they proceeded to heaven with (i.e. having mounted on) elephants and horses (and having got into) chariots. They were brāhmaṇas, kṣatriyas, vaiśyas, śūdras and other common people. All they were followers of Viṣṇu and were absorbed in the meditation on Viṣṇu. Their banners were white and adorned with golden staffs. All were marked with conches and discs and were having staffs and flags. The banners urged by wind shone among the crowds of the subjects. All (the subjects) had put on divine garlands, and were adorned with Tulasī-leaves. Their bodies were smeared with divine sandal, and with (the paste of) divine black ale wood. They were adorned with divine garments and were decorated with divine ornaments. All those handsome people followed the king. All the subjects—the people numbering thousands, hundreds of lakhs and crores, and very large numbers like arva, kharva (i.e. 10,000,000,000) went (with the king). All of them, followers of Viṣṇu, doing meritorious acts, absorbed in the meditation of Viṣṇu, and in muttering (sacred names) and in charity (went) with the king.

Sukarman said :

26b-30a. Full of great joy all of them proceeded (with the king), O great king, having installed his son Pūru on his throne, that Yayāti, the lord of the earth, went to Viṣṇu's world. Due to his lustre, religious merit and piety all those people proceeded to the best heaven of Viṣṇu. Then along with the king of gods, gods with the Gandharvas, Kinnaras and bards came facing them (to greet them), honouring that very lord of kings, O best king.

Indra said :

30b. O great king, welcome to you. Enter my house.
31a. Enjoy here all divine pleasures as you like.

The king said :

31b-40a. O you thousand-eyed, very wise god, I am saluting your lotus-like couple of feet. I (shall) then go to Brahmā's heaven.

Being praised by the gods, he went to Brahmā's heaven. The very lustrous Brahmā along with excellent sages offered him hospitable reception with water for washing his feet and with respectful offering and excellent seats; (and) said to him : "By the power of your deeds go to Viṣṇu's heaven." Thus addressed by the Creator he went to Śiva's house. Śiva, along with Umā (i.e. Pārvatī) offered hospitable reception to that very king, and said these words to the king : "O lord of kings, you are the devotee of Kṛṣṇa, you are also very dear to me; therefore, O Yayāti, lord of kings, live in my house. Enjoy all pleasures difficult to be obtained by human beings. O lord of kings, there is certainly no difference between Viṣṇu and me. There is no doubt that he who has the form of Viṣṇu is Śiva, and O king, he who is Rudra (i.e. Śiva) is the ancient Viṣṇu. There is no difference between the two. Therefore only I speak (like this). I do give a place (in my abode) to a meritorious devotee of Viṣṇu. Therefore, O innocent great king, you should stay here."

40b-43a. Thus addressed by Śiva, Yayāti, dear to Viṣṇu, and with his neck (i.e. head) bent down in devotion, saluted Śiva, the lord of gods, (and said to him :) "O great god, whatever you have said is proper. There is no difference between you two. It is one form divided into two. I desire to go (to the heaven) of Viṣṇu; I salute your feet." "O great king, let it be so; go to the heaven of Viṣṇu."

43b-65a. (Thus) instructed by Śiva also, the lord of the earth, with Viṣṇu's very meritorious devotees, dear to Viṣṇu dancing before him—the king—, proceeded (towards Viṣṇu's heaven). He, accompanied by the conch-sounds destroying great sins, and very many roars of lions, many (other) sounds, being worshipped by good bards, (his praise) being sung in melodious tones by public readers skilled in scriptures, moved (on). Gandharvas, eagerly engaged in singing, sang before him. He was being praised by sages along with hosts of gods that had joined them. That son of Nahuṣa was being served by beautiful celestial damsels. That great king, being praised by meritorious and auspicious Gandharvas, Kinnaras, Siddhas, bards, Sādhyas, Vidyādharas, Maruts and Vasus, so also Rudra and groups of Ādityas, and by the Guardians and Lords of quarters, and by all the three worlds all around, saw the matchless and trouble-free heaven of Viṣṇu. O king, that excellent and best city shone with golden, heavenly cars, full of all beauty, with hundred-storied mansions shining with halls white like swans, the *kunda* (flowers) or the moon, and resembling the Meru and Mandāra mountains which with their tops touched the heaven and the sky, and with bright, golden pitchers (on their tops). It shone with the splendour of lustre like the sky with multitudes of stars; with flames of blazing lustre it, as it were, looked with eyes. O lord of kings, that Śiva's heaven, invited, with many jewels, as it were, with teeth showing while laughing, and under the pretext of the flag with tossing foliage, the meritorious devotees of Viṣṇu, dear to Viṣṇu. It was well adorned everywhere with charming tops of banners tossed by wind, and with golden staffs and bells. It shone with gates and watch-towers looking (bright) like the sun's lustre, with beautiful round windows, rows of lattices and windows with the lustres of the broad ways, and golden ramparts, with arches, good banners and many very auspicious sounds, with the tops of pitchers, mirror-like discs resembling in lustre the sun's orb, with great splendour, with hundreds of private chambers resembling water-less clouds, crowded with staffs and umbrellas and pitchers, with chambers like clouds in the rainy season, and the earth looked, with (so many) pitchers, like the sky with stars. The city of Viṣṇu looked beautiful with the mass of staffs and banners with lustre like the multitude of stars, of the form of crystal objects, looking like a conch or the moon, with crowds of golden palaces and (palaces) made of many metals, with divine cars numbering ten millions and thousands of hundreds of crores; and with all enjoyments. Those men, devotees of Viṣṇu, of righteous deeds and with all their sins washed away live, through his grace, in those houses, which are fully meritorious, divine and rich in all pleasures.

65b-75. The house of Viṣṇu was adorned with excellent (objects) like these. It was everywhere crowded with many kinds of trees, graced with sandal trees, having all desired fruits. It shone with wells, ponds and lakes beautified with cranes, so also with lakes, crowded with swans and ducks, beautified with white lotuses, (other) lotuses, big white lotuses, (other kinds of) lotuses and blue lotuses, and (others) having the colour of (i.e. resembling) golden lotuses. Vaikuṇṭha (i.e. Viṣṇu's heaven) was rich with all beauty, was adorned with divine parks, was full of divine charm and was graced by the devotees of Viṣṇu. The king saw (this) Vaikuṇṭha, the matchless place of salvation. Yayāti, Nahuṣa's son, entered that beautiful city, crowded with hosts of gods and free from any morbid heat. He saw that Viṣṇu, destroyer of all sufferings, free from any damage, shining with divine cars, resplendent with all ornaments, clad in a yellow garment, marked with Śrīvatsa, and very lustrous, mounted on Garuḍa accompanied by Śrī, higher than the highest, —the highest god, the refuge of all the worlds, (who) shone with perfect detachment of the form of the highest joy, and was being served by great, very meritorious devotees of Viṣṇu.

76-79. The lord of the earth, with his wife, saluted Nārāyaṇa (i.e. Viṣṇu) crowded with hosts of gods, waited upon by groups of Gandharvas and celestial nymphs , who was magnanimous and who removed all sufferings. All the men, devotees of Viṣṇu, who had gone with the king, saluted Viṣṇu, O you very intelligent one. O you highly intelligent one, they devoutly saluted his both feet. Viṣṇu said to the glorious king, who was blazing with lustre, and who was saluting him : "O you of a good vow, I am pleased with you. O lord of kings, ask for a boon which you have in your mind; I shall certainly grant it to you. You are my devotee, O you very intelligent one."

The king said :

80. O Madhusūdana, O lord of gods, if you are pleased, then, O lord of the worlds, always grant me your servitude (i.e. make me your servant).

Viṣṇu said :

81-83. O glorious one, let it be so; you are undoubtedly my devotee; O great king, with this lady you may stay in my heaven.

That great king Yayāti, the lord of the earth, thus addressed, lived, through the grace of that god, in the excellent heaven of Viṣṇu, which was decorated.

CHAPTER EIGHTYFOUR

Glorification of Devotion to Parents

Sukarman said :

1-10. I have narrated to you this entire account, which removes sins, which emancipates sons, which is divine, and which gives great religious merit. The well-known deeds of Yayāti are actually seen in the world. Pūru obtained the great kingdom as it was brought into existence, and Turu was reduced to a bad plight, due (respectively) to the father's favour and anger. It emancipates sons, gives glory and wealth and grains. Both Turu and Yadu were under the influence of a curse. There is no other giver of desirable fruits like the father or the mother. A father may call his son through love, and a mother (may call him saying:) 'O son, O son.' Listen to its meritorious fruit. When a son, who is called by his mother, goes to her with affection, he would get the fruit of having bathed in the Ganges. A very glorious son, who would wash the feet (of his parents) enjoys, through their grace, the fruit of (having visited) all the sacred places; and by shampooing their bodies he would obtain the fruit of a horse-sacrifice. In that son, who would nourish his father (and mother) with food, covering, and bath, merit equal to that obtained by the gift of the earth is produced. The Ganges is full of (the merit of) all sacred places. A mother is like that (only). There is no doubt about it. The ancient poets know that as the ocean is established as full of much merit, similarly is the father in this world.

Sukarman said :

11-19a. That son, who abandons or yells at his father or mother, undoubtedly goes to the hell called Raurava. That son, who, being a householder, does not support his old mother or father, goes to hell and would certainly meet with agony. For a wicked-minded and sinful son, who abuses his father (or mother), the ancient poets have never known any requital. O brāhmaṇa, knowing thus I am everyday worshipping devoutly and with my neck (i.e. head) bent my mother and father. My father, calling me, would tell me what ought and what ought not to be done. I do it with discrimination and according to my strength, O Pippala. Due to that I have obtained the highest knowledge giving me happiness. A man lives in the mundane existence due to the favour of these two (i.e. the parents). I know whatever men remaining on the earth do and when a householder proceeds to heaven. O Pippala, even while being here I know the movement of cruel persons. O best of the Vidyādharas, the three worlds have come under my sway. You should (please) worship Mādhava (i.e. Viṣṇu).

Viṣṇu said :

19b-21. Pippala, thus directed by him, having bowed down to the best brāhmaṇa, and also being ashamed, went to heaven in accordance with (the fruit of) his deeds. O king, that Sukarman of a religious mind, also served his father (and mother). I have thus told you everything pertaining to the holy place (in the form) of the father (and mother). O very intelligent Vena, tell me what else I should tell you.

CHAPTER EIGHTYFIVE

The Story of Cyavana : Kuñjal : Divyādevī

Vena said :

1-2. O venerable lord of gods, through your grace towards me, you have told me about the sacred place (in the form of) a wife, so also about the excellent holy place (in the form of) the father and (in the form) of the mother, giving great religious merit. Being gracious to me (now) tell me about the holy place (in the form) of the preceptor.

The Lord said :

3-10. O king, I shall tell you about the matchless holy place (in the form) of the preceptor, which is declared as the remover of all sins and the giver of happiness to the disciples, which being of the nature of ancient Dharma (i.e. religious merit) gives great virtue to the disciples, which is the highest sacred place, highest knowledge giving a visible fruit, (and) O lord of kings, by whose favour (the disciple) gets the fruit here (i.e. in this world) only; and O lord of kings, by the favour of the glorious preceptor he enjoys happiness and would obtain glory and fame in the next world. O prince, (by the preceptor's favour) the disciples actually see the three worlds along with the mobile and the immobile, so also the dealings and practices of the people. A disciple obtains wisdom and goes to salvation. As the sun illumines all the worlds, so the teacher enlightens his disciples and is the best refuge of them. O best king, the king Soma (i.e. the Moon) would shine at night only, and would keep a watch over the mobile and the immobile. O best king, a lamp would illumine a multitude (of objects) in the house, and would dispel the entire dense and impure darkness.

11-15a. O you very intelligent one, the preceptor, the light of the disciples, illumines a pupil, covered with the darkness of ignorance by means of the light of instruction. The sun shines by day, the moon at night, a lamp shines in the house, always dispelling darkness. The lamp shines at night in the house (and illumines it, but) the preceptor always enlightens the disciples. The preceptor would destroy all his darkness called ignorance.

Therefore, O lord of the earth, the preceptor is the highest holy place for the disciples. Realising this, a disciple should always worship the preceptor, full of merit, by means of three kinds of acts (i.e. bodily acts, mental acts and words).

15b-29. O brāhmaṇa, for this purpose (i.e. to illustrate this), an old account, removing all sins, is reported; it is told about the glorious Cyavana. The best sage Cyavana was born in the family of Bhārgava. O best king, once a thought arose in his (mind): 'When shall I be endowed with knowledge on the earth?' The best sage, longing for knowledge, would always think day and night. When he was thus reflecting, he had a thought: 'I shall go on a pilgrimage, giving the desired fruit.' Leaving his house and field and his wife, son and wealth, he roamed over the earth in course of a pilgrimage. O king, he went on a pilgrimage in the direction of the flow of the Ganges. Under the pretext of a pilgrimage (i.e. as a pilgrim), that lord of sages visited the holy places (on the banks) of Narmadā, Sarasvatī, and all (other) rivers like Godāvarī, and (on the shore) of the ocean and all other sacred places, so also places of deities and places having auspicious characteristics, O best king. The body of him, who was wandering over (i.e. visiting) best holy places, became pure (and lustrous) like the sun's lustre. Cyavana, with his mind purified by this act, shone with lustre. While wandering he (once) came to the best holy place on the right bank of Narmadā, called Amarakaṇṭaka. (There) he saw a great Phallus (of Śiva), giving happiness to all. Then he saluted, eulogised, and worshipped the great lord Siddhanātha, then he saw (i.e. visited) Jvāleśvara, then Amareśvara, Brahmeśa, Kapileśa and the best Mārkaṇḍeśa. Having thus finished his pilgrimage he then came to Oṃkāra. Having resorted to the cool shade of a bunyan tree, removing fatigue, the brāhmaṇa Cyavana, the son of Bhṛgu, remained there comfortably. There he then heard a note given out by a bird, which was full of divine speech and spiritual and worldly knowledge.

30-38. There was a parrot (on the tree) who lived there for a long time. His name was Kuñjala; he was religious-minded and had four sons and a wife. He had four sons who delighted their father (i.e. him). O lord of kings, I shall tell you their names: The eldest one was Ujjvala; the second was Samujjvala;

the third was Vijjvala, and the fourth was Kapiñjala. Thus, O very intelligent one, that meritorious parrot Kuñjala had four sons, who were very much devoted to their father and mother. Being disturbed and oppressed by hunger, they together roamed in the arbours of mountains and islands. O best king, they satiated the hunger in their bellies with agreeable fruits like nectar and with water sweet like nectar. The good sons gave a ripe juicy fruit to the couple (i.e. their parents), and carefully put (aside some) fruits (for them). Being contented, the glorious ones, full of devotion, procured food for their mother, (then) ate and recited. All of them engaged in sports, played and amused themselves there. Knowing (when it was) evening time they well (i.e. without fail) came to their father, after carefully having brought food for him (and their mother).

39-46a. When that noble brāhmaṇa Cyavana was watching all the (four) birds came to the very beautiful nest of their father. O you very intelligent one, they saluted both their father and mother. Having obtained food for the two (i.e. their parents), they stood by them. O king, all the best sons esteemed by their father and mother tenderly talked words full of love (to them). They also (fanned) with the cool wind from their wings their father and mother. O king, the two birds, having applauded with blessings, their good sons, nourished them. They too gave them very rich food resembling nectar. O best brāhmaṇa, the two just loved them (i.e. the sons) very much. The two, resorting to their own abode, with their minds pleased through happiness, drank pure water produced (i.e. procured) from crores of holy places, told a divine, very meritorious tale, destroying sins.

Viṣṇu said :

46b. The (eldest) son Ujjvala was (once) asked by his father Kuñjala:

47. "O my son, where had you gone today? What wonderful agreeable (event) did you see or hear there? Tell me that, my son."

48. Having heard the words of Kuñjala, his father, that Ujjvala, with his neck (i.e. head) bent down with devotion, replied:

49a. He saluted him with his head (bent down) and told him a pleasing story.

Ujjvala said :

49b-61. O you glorious one, O you very intelligent one, everyday I go to the Plakṣa island even with strenuous effort, for food. O great king, in the Plakṣa island there are many countries, mountains, rivers, parks, forests and lakes, so also villages and cities enjoyed by people. Those people are always contented, are endowed with charity, piety and muttering (of sacred hymns) and possess faith, and live happily. O great king, in the Plakṣa island lived Divodāsa, who was of a pious mind and was righteous. He had a matchless daughter, endowed with virtues and beauty, of a good character, charming and auspicious, known by the name Divyādevī and was incomparable in beauty on the earth. The father saw (i.e. noticed) her to be faring well with beauty and youth. She, the charming and auspicious one, was in the prime of youth. That Divodāsa, seeing his daughter Divyādevī, thought: 'To which noble, good groom should she be given?' (Then) the best king, having considered, thought of the king of Rūpadeśa, and the king invited him and the noble one gave his daughter to the intelligent Citrasena. O king, on the occasion of his marriage, when the right moment of the marriage came, Citrasena died due to fated time. The religious-minded king Divodāsa thought (to himself). The son of a king invited good brāhmaṇas and asked them: "At the time of her marriage Citrasena expired. Tell me what her fate will be."

The brāhmaṇas said :

62-66a. O king, the marriage of an unmarried daughter is seen to be performed according to the sacred injunctions. Her husband may die; if not, he will have union with her; (but) being stricken with great malady or physical disease he may abandon her and go; or he may become a recluse. This is what is seen in the religious works. Wise men get married their unmarried daughter(s). As long as she does not menstruate (i.e. does not attain puberty), another groom is enjoined for her. The father should certainly get her married according to the sacred injunctions. Thus, O king, the wise men have stated the sacred rules. Get her married.

Thus told the best brāhmaṇas.

Ujjvala said :

66b-70. Virtuous Divodāsa, the great king, prompted by the words of the brāhmaṇas, made preparations for the (his daughter's) marriage, O king. O best brāhmaṇa, he gave away Divyādevī (in marriage) to that virtuous and glorious king, Rūpasena. At the (time of) the marriage the lord of the earth (i.e. Rūpasena) died. Whenever Divyādavī (was married) her husband, a king, invariably died when the proper time for marriage had arrived. O father, twentyone husbands died (like this) time after time. Then the king (Divodāsa)of a well-known valour became very unhappy.

71-76. Having thought (this) over, the lord of the earth, called his ministers, and having held consultations with them, decided (to arrange) a self-choice marriage (for her). The glorious one invited the kings of Plakṣadvīpa. Those kings, who were greatly devoted to religion, who were invited to the self-choice marriage, being deluded by her beauty and prompted by death, foolishly fought (among themselves) and died on the battlefield. Thus O father, there was the destruction of the noble kṣatriyas. Divyādevī, being very much afflicted with grief, went to a cave in the forest. That virtuous young maiden Divyādevi wept piteously. O father, thus I witnessed (this) wonderful sight there. Then, O father, tell me its cause in detail.

CHAPTER EIGHTYSIX

Divyādevī As Citrā in Her Former Birth

Kuñjala said :

1. O boy, I (shall) tell you all the acts of that Divyādevī. Listen to all that she did in the former birth as I am telling you.

2-7a. There was an auspicious city named Vārāṇasī, the destroyer of sins. In it lived a very intelligent man named Suvīra, who was born in the Vaiśya caste and who possessed wealth and grains. O you very intelligent one, his wife was Citrā by name, who was well known. She, abandoning the family-practices, behaved improperly. She did not care for her husband, (and) behaved wantonly. Bereft of piety and merit she would act (i.e. she acted) sinfully only. She always reviled her husband, and always loved quarrelling. She always stayed in the house of another (person), and wandered from house to house. She would observe (i.e. she observed) the weak points of others, and was always wicked to beings. She was very much given to condemning the good, and always laughed.

7b-9a. Knowing her to be of an improper conduct and very sinful, Vīra reproached her. O you very intelligent one, that pious, highly intelligent (Vīra) of truthful and religious thoughts, abandoned her and married another Vaiśya's daughter; and stayed with her righteously.

9b-14. That bold Citrā, expelled by him, roamed over the earth. She became associated with wicked and sinful men. She of a wicked determination, worked as a go-between. The sinful one split the houses (i.e. families) of the good. She would call a chaste woman and would induce her with evil words. She violated customary observances. With convincing (but) evil words that Citrā would present the wife (the wives) of good men to someone else. Thus Citrā certainly split a hundred houses. The very wicked one created quarrels between husbands and sons. The sinful one would stir the minds of men for (i.e. make them sexually disposed to) women. She set up a quarrel making Yama thrive.

15-20. Thus having split a hundred houses (i.e. families), she then died. O good son, she was punished by king Yama with a heavy penalty. The Sun's son (i.e. Yama) threw her into many hells (like Raurava). Citrā was roasted in Raurava. Various afflictions were shown (i.e. imposed on her). As a deed is done so it (i.e. its fruit) is enjoyed. Due to a wicked resolve that Citrā split a hundred houses. O best brāhmaṇa, she experienced the fruit of the respective deeds. Since she split a hundred houses, therefore she is experiencing grief. When the time of (her) marriage came, her destiny had become ripe. When the proper time (for) her marriage came, her husband died. As she split a hundred houses, a hundred grooms died at the time of the self-choice marriage and twentyone (grooms died) at the time of (her proposed marriage).

21. As you asked me I have told you (the account) of, Divyādevī. I have told you all these—her former deeds.

Ujjvala said :

22. You first told me the former deeds of Divyādevī, so also the fierce sin called splitting the houses (that she committed).

23. Due to the prowess of which religious merit did that daughter of Divodāsa, the king of the Plakṣa island, obtain (a birth) in a great family?

24. This is my doubt, O father. Please tell it to me. How did the princess become (a woman) of such a sinful behaviour?

Kuñjala said :

25. I shall (now) tell you about all the pious acts of Citrā. O (my) son Ujjvala, listen to what Citrā did formerly.

26-30. A very wise Siddha (i.e. a man endowed with supernatural faculties), while wandering came to the door of Citrā's house. He wore tattered clothes, was without a (proper) garment, was a recluse, and had held a staff (in his hand). He had a small strip of cloth worn over his privities, had a pot in his hand and was (otherwise) naked. Having come to the door of Citrā's house, he remained there. He observed a vow of silence, was clean-shaved, had his mind and organs of sense conquered. He abstained from food, took a very small quantity, and knew the essence of everything. He was very much tired due to having been on a long journey, and his mind was distressed with heat; O good son, he was depressed with fatigue, and was overcome with thirst. Having come to the door of Citrā's house, he resorted to the shade (of a tree). The noble one, afflicted with fatigue, was seen by Citrā.

31-35. Citrā served that very noble one, by washing his feet and giving him an excellent seat. "Sir, be seated comfortably on a very soft seat. Eat excellent food to remove (i.e. satiate) your hunger. Being contented drink cold water as you like." Saying so, and doing like that (i.e. giving him food etc.), and worshipping him like a deity, she, O son, massaged his body and removed his fatigue. The noble Siddha, thus addressed by her, ate (food) and drank (water), O best brāhmaṇa. The Siddha, who knew the essence of everything, thus pleased by her, was gratified, and he, the soul of entire piety, remained steady for a while. That great meditating saint went (away) according to his will, as he had come.

36-44. When that noble and glorious Siddha had left, Citrā met with death, being under the sway of (i.e. according to) her deeds. She was punished by Dharmarāja (i.e. Yama) with very painful penalties. That Citrā reached hell causing a host of agonies. O great king, (there) she experienced misery for a thousand yugas. At the end of (i.e. after having) experienced (misery) she got the birth of (i.e. was born as) a human being. She had formerly worshipped the Siddha, the best among the meritorious. It is the ripening (i.e. the fruit) of her deeds that she came to (i.e. was born in) the house of Divodāsa, the great king, (and) in the family of meritorious Kṣatriyas. O best man, she got the name Divyādevī; and she had given good food and drink to the noble one. She enjoyed the meritorious consequence of the great righteous act of charity. She drank cold water, and ate dainty food. Enjoying divine pleasures, she lived in her father's house; and due to the power of this Siddha, she was born as a princess. O good son, due to the efficacy of her great sin of splitting the families, O king, that Divyādevī experienced widowhood.

45. I have thus told you all the deeds of Divyādevī. What else, which you ask me now, should I tell you?

Ujjvala said :

46-48. Tell me how she got free from grief and great affliction. What kind of young woman was she, who was afflicted with great grief? What kind of happiness did she have? What will be its consequence? O father, please remove this doubt of mine now. Tell me (about) the means by which she will obtain salvation. The noble one is all alone weeping in the great forest.

Viṣṇu said :

49-60. Having heard (those) great (i.e. important) words

of his son, and having thought for a moment, that very wise Kuñjala replied to his son: "O my noble son, listen; I am telling you the truth. Having reached (i.e. being born in) a sinful stock, due to my former deeds, and due to the contact with this tree, the knowledge of me, who was pious and noble, has now been lost in this existence of a lower animal, O son. I shall tell you about that instruction by which, and through the favour of Revā and grace of Viṣṇu, she has obtained knowledge and has reached salvation; being free from blemish, she will go to salvation, as gold becomes pure due to the contact with fire and gets (back) its own nature. O very intelligent one, due to the meditation on Hari (i.e. Viṣṇu) and due to the muttering (of prayers), sacrifices and vows the sin of the sinners perishes. As an elephant would always give up his intoxication due to the fear of a lion, so the sin goes away due to the recitation of the names of Viṣṇu. As the serpents become poisonless due to the lustre of (Garuḍa) the son of Vinatā, so all sins like the murder of a brāhmaṇa perish; and in no other way. They too go away due to the recitation of the names of Viṣṇu. When being steady, and free from lust and anger, she would mutter the hundred names, destroying heaps of sins, and when, having controlled all the organs of sense, would guard them through the knowledge of self, and when, having entered into his meditation, having become one with (i.e. having become sincerely devoted to) him, and being composed, she would mutter (the names of Viṣṇu) she would reach (i.e. obtain) highest knowledge and salvation. When she would be endowed with abstract meditation, and when she would set her heart upon him, she would be completely resting at his feet."

Ujjvala said :

61. O father, right now tell me about the great, highest knowledge; and after that the vow of meditation and the auspicious hundred names.

Kuñjala said :

62. I shall explain to you the highest knowledge, which nobody has perceived (i.e. acquired). O son, listen to (the description of) the perfect final emancipation, free from impurity.

Sūta said:

63-69a. O highly intelligent one, as a lamp in a place sheltered from wind, is steady (as it is) free from wind, burning brightly, (and) would destroy all darkness, in the same way the soul, free from blemishes, remains alone, free from desires, pure, and O son, he is never a friend or a foe. (He has) neither grief nor joy; (he has) neither greed nor jealousy. Being all alone, he is free from dejection, joy, happiness and unhappiness; so also free from all the objects of sense, (when) he would withdraw his organs of sense (from the objects). Then he has become absolute and salvation takes place (in his case). O lord of kings, a lamp, without any company (i.e. being solitary), and free from wind, would, through the contact of the movement of fire, dry up the oil due to the support of the wick. Then it emits soot, and on the top of the lamp a dark line of (i.e. due to) the oil is seen, O you very intelligent one. It itself draws oil and becomes spotless by means of the oil.

69b-72a. In the same way he (i.e. the soul) remains in the wick of the body and would draw the oil of the deeds; and would himself shine with lustre. Being free from anger etc. and winds called troubles, so also being desireless and steady he would glow with lustre. Remaining in his own place, he sees all the three worlds by means of his lustre.

72b-84. I have told (i.e. described to) you this (soul), of the nature of absolute knowledge. I shall (now) explain to you the meditation upon the disc-holder (i.e. Viṣṇu); he is seen with the eye of knowledge, of the nature of absolute knowledge. Whom (i.e. him) the noble ones, intent upon (obtaining) the highest object (i.e. salvation), and having abstract meditation, and being watchful, see. His penance (i.e. penance practised to reach him) manifests everything. Being without hands and feet, he moves everywhere. O son, he captures (i.e. pervades) all the three worlds—mobile and immobile. O son, (even being) without nose and mouth, he smells and eats. He, the witness (to everything), the lord of the world, (even though) without ears, hears everything. (Though) without a form he is connected with forms and is under the sway of the group of five (organs of sense). Who (i.e. he) is the life of the entire world, and is worshipped by the mobile and the immobile. O son, (though) tongue-less, he recites everything according to the Vedic texts. For him, who is without skin, touch of all objects is produced (i.e. he can touch everything). He is ever joyful, is detached, has one form (only), is independent, is without old age, without the feeling of mineness, just, possessing qualities, without the feeling of mineness, and pure. He is not under the control of anyone, (but) everything is under his control; he is the giver of everything and the best among the omniscient ones. He has no supporter; he, the eternal one, is full of everything. He who thus observes everything as full of meditation of the noble one, goes to the incorporeal, highest place, resembling nectar. I shall explain to you another meditation of this noble one. It is having a form, corporeal, formless and sound. O my son, he is called Vāsudeva since the entire matchless universe is occupied by him. His colour would be (i.e. is) that which is of the showering cloud. He, the lord of gods, resembles the sun's lustre and has four arms.

85-95. In his right hand shines a conch decorated with gold and jewels, and the disc resembling the sun's orb and a lotus are (held) in it. O boy, the mace Kaumodakī, destroying great demons, shines in the left hand of the illustrious one. A big lotus, rich with fragrance is (held) in his right hand. He, dear to Kamalā (i.e. Lakṣmī) always shines with weapons. (A man should meditate upon) Viṣṇu (whose) neck is like a conch, face is round, and eyes resemble lotus-leaves, who shines with teeth resembling jewels. His hair is (flowing) like treacle, and the lips have the form of a coral. O son, he having the eyes like lotuses, shines with a crown. Janārdana (i.e. Viṣṇu) shines with a glorious form and great lustre and is marked with the Kaustubha gem. Hari (i.e. Viṣṇu) shines with ear-rings resembling the sun's lustre and always shines with the auspicious mark of Śrīvatsa. Vijaya, the best among the victorious, shines with a body having armlets, bracelets, necklaces and pearls resembling stars. That Govinda also shines with a golden-coloured garment and with fingers with rings and gems. The creator of the worlds, the lord of the worlds (i.e. Viṣṇu), (shining with) all complete weapons and divine ornaments, is mounted upon Garuḍa. A man who thus meditates upon him with a concentrated mind is free from all sins, and goes to Viṣṇu's world.

96. I have thus told you everything about the meditation upon the lord of the world. I shall now tell you (about) the vow, destroying all sins.

CHAPTER EIGTHYSEVEN

'A Hundred Names of Viṣṇu'

Kuñjala said :

1-4. I shall explain to you the kinds of vows by which Hari (i.e. Viṣṇu) is propitiated. O good son, there are many kinds of Ekādaśī: Jayā, Vijayā, and Jayantī, Pāpanāśinī, Trispṛśā, Vañjulī; the next is Tiladagdhā, then the other one is Akhaṇḍā, Cārakanyā, and Manorathā. There is (the vow of) Aśūnya-śayana (i.e. not sleeping on a bed), and there is the great vow of Janmāṣṭamī. There is no doubt that the sin of beings goes away due to these very auspicious vows. I am telling you the truth (and) the truth (only).

Kuñjala said :

5-9. I shall tell you about his hymn, destroying a heap of sins, called 'Suputra-śata', and giving salvation to men. I shall now only tell you about the hymn of that god Kṛṣṇa, which is excellent and is called 'Śatanāma'. O best son, listen to it. I shall tell you the sage of (i.e. the composer of), and the metre of the hundred names of Viṣṇu. I shall also tell you about the deity, purifying all sins, O glorious one. Brahmā is said to be the sage (i.e. the author) of the hundred names of Viṣṇu. Oṃkāra is declared to be the deity, and anuṣṭubh is (said to be) the metre. It leads to the acquisition (i.e. fulfilment) of all desires and is employed in (obtaining) salvation. Of this hymn of the hundred names of Viṣṇu, Brahmā is the sage, Viṣṇu the deity, anuṣṭubh the metre. It is used for the fulfilment of all desires and for the destruction of all sins.

10-24. "I salute Hṛṣīkeśa, Keśava, Madhusūdana, the killer of all demons, sound Nārāyaṇa, Jayanta, Vijaya, Kṛṣṇa, Ananta,

Vāmana, Viṣṇu, the auspicious lord of the universe, the prop of the universe, worshipped by gods, sinless, destroyer of sins, Narasiṃha and dear to Śrī, lord of Lakṣmī, Śrīdhara (possessing glory of Lakṣmī), giver of wealth, Śrīnivāsa (i.e. abode of Lakṣmi), and very prosperous, Śrī Rāma, Mādhava, Mokṣa (i.e. Salvation), of the nature of forgiveness, Janārdana, omniscient, knowing and giving everything, the leader of all, Hari, Murāri, Govinda, Padmanābha, the lord of beings, giver of joy, endowed with knowledge, giver of knowledge, master of knowledge; Acyuta, possessing power, the moon, holding a disc in his hand, higher and lower, the support of the yugas, the source of the world, of the nature of Brahman, the great lord, Mukunda, good (i.e. great) Vaikuṇṭha (i.e. Viṣṇu), of one form, the lord of the world, glorious Vāsudeva, holy and dear to brāhmaṇas, loving and beneficial to the cows, sacrifice, constituent of the sacrifice, causing sacrifice to prosper, a good enjoyer of sacrifice, master of Vedas and Vedāṅgas; knower of the Vedas, of the form of the Vedas, abode of learning and lord of gods, the unmanifest one, a great Brahman, having a conch in his hand, the ancient man, lotus-eyed, (of the form of) Varāha (i.e. a boar), supporting the earth, Pradyumna, Kāmapāla, Vyāsa, Vyāla, and Maheśvara (i.e. the great lord), (full of) all pleasures (and) great pleasures, salvation and the highest lord, of the form of Yoga (i.e. abstract meditation), of great knowledge, giving salvation to the meditating saints and dear to them; the enemy of Mura, the protector of the world, the one having a lotus in his hand, and holding a mace, living in a cave, living everywhere, of an auspicious abode, and possessing large arms, lord of Vṛndā, of a huge body, purifier and destroyer of sins, lord of the gopīs (i.e. the cowherdesses), the friend of the cowherds, the protector of cows, the refuge of the herds of cattle, the highest soul, the highest lord, Kapila and having human activities, steady and eternal—I salute him with my mind, speech and bodily acts." He, doer of virtuous acts, who, even with (these) hundred names, praises, with a steady mind, Kṛṣṇa, (he) being purified by religious merit here (i.e. in this world), leaving (other) worlds, goes to Viṣṇu's heaven.

25-27. A man should mutter with a concentrated mind, the very meritorious hundred names, cleansing all sins, and should meditate upon them with abstract contemplation. Such a man would always obtain the fruit of having a bath in the Ganges with religious merit. Therefore a man should be very steady and mutter (these names) with a composed mind. A restrained man, being devoted, should mutter (these names) three times (a day). There is no doubt that for him there is (i.e. he gets) the fruit of (having performed) a hundred horse-sacrifices.

28-32a. I shall tell (you) about the religious merit of the man, who having fasted on the Ekādaśī day in front of Viṣṇu and (keeping) awake, would, mutter these names: The man obtains the fruit of Puṇḍarīka sacrifice (i.e. offered in honour of Viṣṇu). A man, who, remaining near Tulasī, would mentally mutter (these names) obtains the fruit of the Rājasūya sacrifice even after a year. One desiring happiness should mutter (these names) near the two (viz. at a place) where there is the Śālagrāma stone and the Dvārāvatī stone. A man (who does this) having enjoyed many pleasures and a hundred families would emancipate more than one along with him.

32b-39. He who would bathe (every morning) in Kārtika and would worship Viṣṇu, and also he, who, being purified, would recite the hymn (in honour of Viṣṇu) goes to (i.e. obtains) a superior position. The man, who bathes every morning in Māgha, having worshipped with devotion, Viṣṇu, the killer of (the demon) Madhu, and would meditate upon Hṛṣīkeśa (i.e. Viṣṇu), or would mutter (his names) or listens to them (being recited), and, giving up sinful (deeds) like drinking liquor, goes, without any difficulty, to Janārdana, O (my) son. The dead ancestors of the man, who at the time of a Śrāddha, would mutter the hymn (containing) the hundred names destroying sins, in front of the brāhmaṇas eating (food), become pleased, and being gratified obtain salvation. A brāhmaṇa who always mutters it, becomes learned in the Vedas; a kṣatriya, (who always mutters it) obtains (i.e. rules over) the earth; a vaiśya (who always mutters it) would enjoy wealth and prosperity; a śūdra (who always mutters it) enjoys happiness and obtains brāhmaṇahood after getting another (i.e. next) existence and obtains (mastery over) the Vedic lore. This hymn, giving happiness and salvation should always be muttered. There is no doubt that due to the grace of Viṣṇu a man would be equipped with everything.

CHAPTER EIGHTYEIGHT

Divyādevī Goes to Viṣṇu's Heaven

Kuñjala said :

1-4a. O good son, I have told you the vow, the hymn, the great knowledge and the meditation of Viṣṇu which destroy sins. When she (i.e. Divyādevī) would practise these auspicious four, she will go to Viṣṇu's world, difficult to be obtained even by gods. O child, going from here, teach the vow to Divyādevī. Tell (i.e. teach) her the king of vows called Aśūnya-śayana. Emanicipate the glorious princess from a great sin. You asked me (and therefore) I told (you about the vow) giving religious merit and destroying sins. O glorious one, go, (do) go.

Saying so, he ceased (to speak).

Śrī Viṣṇu said :

4b-10. That religious-minded and very intelligent Ujjvala, thus addressed by his father, having saluted the feet of his mother and father, quickly went to Plakṣadvīpa. He went to that mountain, auspicious on all sides, full of various minerals, and adorned with lofty peaks full of many kinds of jewels. O king, there were rivers with clean water flowing in many streams on that excellent mountain. O king, Kinnaras and Gandharvas sang there melodiously. It was crowded with the celestial nymphs; it was filled with hosts of gods; it was ringing with Siddhas and Cāraṇas; it was adorned with groups of sages. It was everywhere resounding with the notes of various birds.

11-13. The bright and quick-footed one thus reached that mountain. That woman also was weeping melodiously on that mountain. The wise one said (these) words to her who was again and again weeping. "O auspicious one, who are you? Why are you weeping now? Whom had you resorted to? Who has harmed you? Today only tell me the entire cause of your grief."

Divyādevī said :

14-18. O glorious one, it is properly the fruit of my deeds.

Being widowed I am staying here unhappily. O you illustrious one, who are you, afflicted by my grief?

O child, he, who had taken the form of a bird, having heard all that the princess had said, spoke enthusiastically, O child: "O glorious one, I am a bird, afflicted by your grief. I have taken the form of a bird, (but) I am neither a Siddha, nor a wise person. I saw you weeping here very loudly; therefore, O respectable lady, I am asking you. Tell me its cause, what happened in your father's house, and your own account."

19-24a. In brief and in proper order, she told everything that pained her. Having heard that, that large-hearted, great bird Ujjvala said to that Divyādevī who was very much pained: "At the time of your marriage your grooms died, the kṣatriyas also perished due to your self-choice marriage. O you lady of beautiful eyes, through compassion for you, my father told me the sinful deeds you had done in the other (i.e. former) existence. O you beautiful lady, strengthened by that blemish you are covered with that. Eat the fruit of the deeds you did in the previous birth. Be composed."

24b-27. That young humble lady, having heard those words of Ujjvala, replied to that magnanimous bird, who (thus) spoke (in human voice) in piteous words: "O bird, favour me. With (i.e. showing) grace, tell (me about) the atonement of that sin; also (tell me about) the expiation which will purify my sins, by which, being pure due to my sins washed, I shall go to a holy (place). Be gracious, and tell me about the expiation, O you glorious one."

Ujjvala said :

28-31. O you glorious one, for you only I asked my father. Then my father told (me) about the matchless expiation. O you illustrious one, you do that which would purify all your sins. Meditate upon Hṛṣīkeśa (i.e. Viṣṇu), mutter his hundred names. Be intent upon (obtaining) knowledge. Always practise the excellent, holy vow (called) 'Aśūnyaśayana' which destroys sins.

The religious-minded one explained to her knowledge, hymn, vow of and meditation upon the noble Viṣṇu, which reveals all knowledge.

Viṣṇu said :

32-35. Remaining in the solitary forest, she took it from him. She became free from all pairs of opposites and remained in penance. O great king, controlling her food, helpless and very much afflicted, free from lust and anger, and always controlling the group of the organs of sense and having abandoned great delusion, she practised the vow. When the fourth year came, the excellent lord Janārdana (i.e. Viṣṇu) who was very much pleased came there with a desire to grant her a boon. The lord, the giver of boons, manifested his form to her.

Sūta said :

36-42a. She, joining the palms of her hands, trembling and helpless, spoke in a faltering tone, after saluting Madhusūdana (i.e. Viṣṇu), the great lord, dark-green like a sapphire and a cloud, holding a conch, a disc and a mace, rich with charm due to all ornaments, having a lotus in his hand: "I am not at all able to stand your divine lustre. Be gracious and please tell me who you, of a divine form, are and what is the cause (of) your (coming over) here? With favour (i.e. favour me) and tell me everything, O highly intelligent one. Due to your lustre and gestures I know (i.e. I think) you are just a god. O lord of the world, I, who am ignorant, do not know your form and name. Are you Brahmā, or Viṣṇu or Śaṅkara himself?" Speaking like this, and bowing to him she fell (i.e. prostrated herself) on the ground like a staff. Viṣṇu spoke to that princess who had bent before him.

The lord said :

42b-46a. O you auspicious one, there is no difference among the three. O you beautiful lady, I am always worshipped by him who has worshipped Brahmā or Śaṅkara. No doubt should be raised about it. These two are not different from me. I always have these three forms. Those who worship me, worship well these two. I am god Viṣṇu, who has come here through pity for you and due to the hymn and this auspicious vow and your restraint. You have become free from blemishes. O you auspicious one, ask for a boon.

Divyādevi said :

46b-49a. O Viṣṇu, O Kṛṣṇa the remover of affliction, be victorious. I am saluting your couple of feet. O lord of gods, emancipate me. O you having the disc in your hand, you desire to grant me a boon. Be gracious to me. O you sinless one, give (i.e. create in) me devotion for the couple of your feet. O lord of the world, show (me) the sound path to salvation. If, O Janārdana, you are pleased, give me the status of your servant (i.e. make me your servant).

The Lord said :

49b-54. O you noble one, let it be so. Go, with your sins completely washed, to Viṣṇu's highest heaven, always difficult to be obtained (even) by meditating saints. Now, due to my grace, do go to the highest world.

When the magnanimous Viṣṇu uttered these words, Divyādevī became divine with her lustre resembling that of the sun. She, adorned with divine ornaments, with a divine garland, a divine necklace, went, when all the people were watching, to Viṣṇu's heaven, free from tormentation and destruction. The bird, full of joy, again came home. The best one told all that to his father.

CHAPTER EIGHTYNINE

The Miraculous Bath in the Water of Mānasa Lake

Viṣṇu said :

1-3a. Then Kuñjala said (these) words to his very bright son : "O son, tell me what you saw earlier. Tell me that. I am now very much pleased to listen to it." Thus ordering his son, that Kuñjala ceased speaking. The son, bending with modesty replied to the father:

Samujjvala said :

3b-14. O father, for your and my food, I go to Himālaya,

the best mountain, attended by hosts of gods. I saw a wonder there, not seen or heard of before. (I saw) a region crowded with groups of sages, adorned with celestial nymphs, rich in many beautiful things creating curiosity, auspicious, and endowed with auspicious things, attracting the mind with many curious things, full of many auspicious fruits. There, near the Mānasa (lake), O father, I saw a wonderful thing. A swan accompanied by many swans came there. In the same way, O glorious one, other black swans with white beaks and feet (also) came there. At other places their bodies were white (i.e. other parts of their bodies were white). They were black like that, and, O you very intelligent one, others were white. There were four females of formidable figures and fearful, fierce and cruel due to their fangs, with their hair erect and causing fear. Later they also came there to that Mānasa lake. O father, in front of me the black swans bathed in the Mānasa (lake). Others roamed around; they did not bathe there in the Mānasa (lake). Later the females also came there to that Mānasa (lake). O father, the women laughed loudly and fiercely. From that lake a swan of a huge body came out. Then three went out; they neglected the swan. Discussing with each other, they went along the aerial path. Those very fearful women wandered on all sides.

15-19a. All the birds, afflicted with great agonies, sat in the shades of trees on the auspicious peak of Vindhya. When they were well (i.e. minutely) watching there came a bhilla, holding a bow and with an arrow in his hand, after having harassed beasts. Resorting to a slab, he sat there happily. Then the female bhilla (the wife of that bhilla) came there carrying (i.e. with) food and water. She saw her husband endowed with superior marks of kings. Knowing (i.e. taking) her husband covered with lustre, full of divine lustre, like the sun remaining in the sky, to be someone else, she left him and went (i.e. started going).

The hunter said :

19b-22. O darling, come, come on, why do you not look at me? I, who am being tormented by hunger, am waiting for you.

Hearing his words, the female hunter came (there) quickly. Reaching the vicinity of her husband, she wondered : 'Who this lustrous god may be that is calling me?' Then the female hunter said to her husband of a blazing lustre : "O hero, what have you to do here? Who are you, having divine marks?'

Sūta said :

23. The hunter, thus addressed by the female hunter said to his wife : "O dear one, I am your husband, and you are my wife.

24. How do you not recognise me? Why is there a doubt (in your mind)? One who is oppressed by hunger expects water and food."

The female hunter said :

25-29. My husband is a barbarian, of a dark complexion and has put on a black dress. Such is my husband who causes fear to all beings. Who are you of a divine body, who would call (i.e. who addressed) me 'O dear one'? This is my doubt; tell me the truth.

For convincing his wife he told her (about) his family, his (native) village, his sports, his distinguishing mark, his son, his daughter. That female hunter, with her heart pleased said to her husband : "Due to what has your body become like this? Why have you put on a white dress? Tell me (about it). I am wondering." Hearing these words, the hunter, who was thus asked by his wife, full of respect (for him), replied to her:

Sūta said :

30-35a. "O you of a good vow, there is a confluence on the northern bank of Narmadā. O you very dear one, I, who was fatigued, quickly went to this (place of) confluence. I bathed (there), drank water, and have (now) come (here). Since then my body is covered with lustre like this. I became (fully) clad, and my garment turned white." By the marks, figure, family, place she recognised her husband, and having realised the possibility of religious merit, she then said to him : "Show me the (place of) confluence (first). I shall afterwards give you food with drink."

35b-42a. Thus addressed by his wife, the hunter quickly went (there); he subsequently showed her the confluence, the destroyer of sins. "O noble one, the birds of quick steps flew, and with her went to that excellent confluence of Revā. While birds and I were watching, she gave a bath to her husband, and she herself took a bath. Both turned (to be persons) possessing divine bodies and endowed with divine beauty, clad in divine garments, and (smeared) with (divine) unguents, having divine garlands, and smeared with divine sandal, O best of birds. Having got into Viṣṇu's vehicle, the two, worshipped by sages and Gandharvas, and honoured by Viṣṇu's devotees, went to Viṣṇu's heaven. I saw the noble couple being praised, and going along the heavenly path. Seeing the excellent best holy place, the birds also warbled with clear notes due to joy.

42b-50. The four black swans, having bathed at the confluence destroying sins, and with their hearts purified, again became bright. Having bathed and drunk water they again went out. All those black females died just due to that bath. O father, crying and moving, trembling with grief they went to Yama's world. I saw them then. Then the swans flew and went to their abode. O father, I actually saw this, and told it to you. O father, please tell me what those females with black sides and huge bodies will be (turned into). Tell me about the geese with black legs and bills, who went out of the Mānasa (lake). Tell it to me, O father, what they will be (i.e. turn into). How again, had the (white) swans become black? How did they become white again (just) at that moment only? O father, why did those females die? Such a doubt has arisen in my mind. Being favourable to me, you, who are clear-sighted, please remove, today only, the doubt of me who am always humble."

51. Speaking thus to his father, Samujjvala (or Ujjvala) ceased speaking. Then that parrot, named Kuñjala, started speaking.

CHAPTER NINETY

The Powers of the Holy Places

Sūta said :

1. Having heard all that Samujjvala said, that pious Kuñjala said in reply :

Kuñjala said :

2-7. O dear one, I shall explain it to you. Listen with a steady (i.e. attentive) mind to the account removing all doubts and destroying sins. In the assembly of that noble god Indra a debate, producing curiosity, was going on. (At that time) Nārada hurriedly came to see Indra. Indra, having seen him, with lustre like that of the sun, who had arrived, became glad and the very intelligent one, with his mind humble through devotion, offered him material of worship and water for washing his feet. Joining the palms of his hands, he saluted him. Seating the best brāhmaṇa on an auspicious, soft seat, and bowing down, he, full of great reverence, asked him : "Tell me now the reason for your arrival today."

8-10a. Thus addressed by the lord of gods, the great sage said : "Having bathed in holy regions and sacred places with great faith, having worshipped deities and dead ancestors, having seen many holy places, I have come, from the earth, to see you, O Indra. I have already told all this which you had formerly asked me."

The Lord of gods said :

10b-12a. O sage, you have seen auspicious, holy places and good regions. By visiting which sacred place, would a killer of a brāhmaṇa be free from (the sin of) murdering a brāhmaṇa, (or) a drunkard, or a killer of a cow, or one stealing gold, (would be free from the sin), (or) O illustrious one, how would one be free from plotting against one's master? (Or) how would the killer of a woman be happy?

Nārada said :

12b-23. O lord of gods, I do not know the speciality, regarding the destruction of sin, of such holy places as Gaṅgā etc. O Indra, I know that all great holy places are very auspicious and divine. But I do not know properly their special properties and lack of them. O god, ascertain the power of the holy places of giving salvation.

Having heard those words of that magnanimous Nārada, Indra called the Holy Places residing on the earth. By his order, all the Holy Places—divine ones—came there in embodied forms. O you of a good vow, the divine ones had joined the palms of their hands; they were adorned with good ornaments; their garments were divine, glossy and bright. They had especially taken up the form of women and men. They resembled gold and sandal, and had put on divine forms. O lord of men, they shone with the colour of pearls. Some of them had the complexion of heated gold and some were tawny. Some in the assembly were white and very yellow and bright. Some of the embodied ones resembled lotuses; still others resembled the sun's lustre, (or) the lustre (i.e. flash) of lightning; others shone in the assembly like fire. O lord of men, they shone with the richness of all ornaments, with necklaces, bracelets, armlets, garlands and good sandal. They, (with their bodies) smeared with divine sandal, fragrant and great, and with water-pots in their hands came into the assembly.

24-37. Gaṅgā, Narmadā, the holy Candrabhāgā, Sarasvatī, Devikā, Bimbikā, Kubjā, Kuñjalā, the well-known Mañjulā, Rambhā, the extremely holy Bhānumatī, Sughargharā, Śoṇā, Sindhu, Sauvirā, Kāverī, so also Kapilā, and Kumudā, the holy Vedanadī, the very holy Maheśvarī and the well-known Carmaṇvatī, Lopā and Sukauśikī, Suhaṃsī, Haṃsapādā, Haṃsavegā and Manorathā, Suruthā, Svārunā, Veṇā, Bhadraveṇā, Supadminī, Nāharī, Sumarī, the holy Pulindikā, Hemā, Manorathā, Divyā, Candrikā, Vedasaṃkramā, Jvālā, Hutāśanī, Svāhā, Kālā and Kampiñjalā, Svadhā and Sukalā, Liṅgā, Gambhīrā, Bhīmavāhinī, Devadrīcī, Vīravāhā, Lakṣahomā, Aghāpahā, Pārāśarī, Hemagarbhā, Subhadrā, Vasuputrikā—these very holy rivers, rich with the beauty of all ornaments, with pitchers in their hands, and well-honoured came there in embodied forms, O lord of men. Prayāga, Puṣkara, Arghadīrghā, Manorathā, the very holy Vārāṇasī, removing (the sin of) the murder of a brāhmaṇa, Dvārāvatī, Prabhāsa, and Avantī and Nimiṣa and Caṇḍaka, Mahāratna and Maheśvara and Kaleśvara, Kaliñjara, Brahmakṣetra, Māthura, Mānavāhaka, Māyā, Kāntī and other many very holy and divine places—sixty-eight in number—so also hundreds of crores of all rivers, led by Godāvarī came there by his (i.e. Indra's) order. All regions, very holy and great holy places, possessing bodies and marks came to Indra, the lord of gods; came there, obeying his order. With their heads bent down, they all saluted the lord of gods.

Sūta said :

38-47. The great Holy Places said to the victorious lord of gods : "O god of gods, tell us why you have called us. O lord of gods, tell us all the reason; salutation to you." Hearing these words of them, the lord of gods said : "Which holy place is able to remove (the sin of) the murder of a brāhmaṇa? Which holy place is able to destroy the great sin called the murder of a cow, or the matchless sin called the murder of a woman or the great sin due to plotting against one's master or the elders, or drinking liquor, or due to the terrible (sin of) causing abortion. (Which holy place is able to destroy) the great sin, giving great trouble, due to plotting against the king, (or) against (one's) friend, or any other sin of treachery, (or) changing the deity, (or) means of livelihood of brāhmaṇas, (or) destroying the pasture-ground of cows, or burning a dwelling or setting ablaze a house? These sixteen are major sins, so also illicit intercourse. Which best holy place would be able to destroy sins (like the sin) due to deserting one's master, or due to running away from the battle-field? From amongst you which one would certainly be able (to destroy a sin) without expiation? When all gods and Nārada are watching (i.e. in the presence of all gods and Nārada) may all of you speak after having properly decided."

48. When the magnanimous king of gods spoke like this, the Holy Places, after having consulted their lord, spoke to Indra, present in the assembly.

The Holy Places said :

49-54. Listen, we shall tell (it). O lord of gods, salutation to you. All holy places destroy sins; but, O Lord of gods, we are not able to destroy the very fearful and strong sins which you mentioned. Prayāga, Puṣkara, the matchless Aghatīrtha, and, O noble one, Vārāṇasī—(each one of these) is able to destroy sins. To destroy major sins these four are of unlimited power; so also they have unlimited power to destroy minor sins. O lord of gods, the very powerful Puṣkara and others have been created by the Creator.

Having heard these words of the Holy Places, the lord of gods, full of great joy, then praised them.